Handbook of
Human-Computer Interaction

Handbook of Human-Computer Interaction

Edited by
Samuel Wallace

www.willfordpress.com

Published by Willford Press,
118-35 Queens Blvd., Suite 400,
Forest Hills, NY 11375, USA

ISBN: 978-1-68285-760-1

Cataloging-in-Publication Data

Handbook of human-computer interaction / edited by Samuel Wallace.
    p. cm.
Includes bibliographical references and index.
ISBN 978-1-68285-760-1
1. Human-computer interaction. 2. Human computation. 3. User interfaces (Computer systems).
4. User-centered system design. I. Wallace, Samuel.
QA76.9.H85 H36 2020
004.019--dc23

For information on all Willford Press publications
visit our website at www.willfordpress.com

Contents

Preface

Human-computer interaction (HCI) is the study of human-computer interaction through interfaces. Such an interaction is analogous to human-to-human interaction. Graphical user interfaces and multi-modal interfaces enable humans to engage with embodied character agents. The techniques of operating systems, computer graphics, programming languages and developing environments are vital to this field. Human-machine interfaces, if poorly designed can lead to systems failure and accidents. Research in HCI is focused on the improvement in the usability of human-computer interfaces for improved interaction. Further, emphasis is placed on the development of design methodologies, prototyping of software and hardware systems, experimentation with devices, exploration of interaction paradigms, etc. The three areas of personal information management (PIM), computer-supported cooperative work (CSCW) and human interaction management (HIM) have significant overlap with HCI. While PIM studies the way people use and acquire personal information to complete tasks, CSCW focuses on the use of computing systems for collaborative work. HIM extends the scope of CSCW to the level of organizations. Human-computer interaction is an upcoming field of technology that has undergone rapid development over the past few decades. This book is a valuable compilation of topics, ranging from the basic to the most complex advancements in this field. It will help the readers in keeping pace with the rapid changes in this field.

The information contained in this book is the result of intensive hard work done by researchers in this field. All due efforts have been made to make this book serve as a complete guiding source for students and researchers. The topics in this book have been comprehensively explained to help readers understand the growing trends in the field.

I would like to thank the entire group of writers who made sincere efforts in this book and my family who supported me in my efforts of working on this book. I take this opportunity to thank all those who have been a guiding force throughout my life.

Editor

Heuristic Evaluation: Comparing Generic and Specific Usability Heuristics for Identification of Usability Problems in a Living Museum Mobile Guide App

Mohd Kamal Othman ⓘ**, Muhd Nur Shaful Sulaiman, and Shaziti Aman**

Faculty of Cognitive Sciences and Human Development, Universiti Malaysia Sarawak, Kota Samarahan, Sarawak, 94300, Malaysia

Correspondence should be addressed to Mohd Kamal Othman; omkamal@unimas.my

Academic Editor: Vesna Popovic

This paper reports on an empirical study that compares two sets of heuristics, Nielsen's heuristics and the SMART heuristics in the identification of usability problems in a mobile guide smartphone app for a living museum. Five experts used the severity rating scales to identify and determine the severity of the usability issues based on the two sets of usability heuristics. The study found that Nielsen's heuristics set is too general to detect usability problems in a mobile application compared to SMART heuristics which focuses on the smartphone application in the product development lifecycle instead of the generic Nielsen's heuristics which focuses on a wide range of interactive system. The study highlights the importance of utilizing domain specific usability heuristics in the evaluation process. This ensures that relevant usability issues were successfully identified which could then be given immediate attention to ensure optimal user experience.

1. Introduction

Cultural and heritage sites have a long history of adapting mobile technologies as visitor's guides. According to Tallon [1], mobile guide technology was first used at Stedelijk Museum in Amsterdam in 1952. Changes made throughout the years ranged from the digitization of the objects to the use of emerging technologies. The evolution of mobile guide technologies in cultural heritage sites has transformed the visitors' experiences at such venues. Kenteris and Gavalas & Economou [2] classified mobile guides used in museums into four different groups: (1) mobile guide applications, (2) web-to-mobile applications, (3) mobile phone navigational assistants, and (4) mobile web-based applications.

The use of smartphone technologies, particularly apps to replace other mobile guide technologies at cultural and heritage sites, could eliminate some issues faced by visitors. For example, it reduces the learning curve as visitors do not need to learn how to operate the technology and can focus on the content in the mobile guide. Jaěn, Mocholí, Esteve, and Bosch & Canós [3] highlighted this as an important criteria

in designing the multimedia content browsers on mobile guides. In addition, the use of different types of mobile guides in cultural heritage sites also enables the visits to become more visitor-oriented and not fully controlled by curator, particularly through the personalization of information in accordance to visitors' need [4–6]. A recent study by Pallud [7] on the use of interactive technologies in a French museum to engage the audience and promote positive learning experience suggested that the ease of use and interactivity features of the technologies provided could influence the emotional process (authenticity and cognitive engagement), which in turn could influence learning. A prior research by Othman et al. [8] also suggested that visitors who use multimedia guide during their visit to cultural heritage site are significantly more engaged in the experience as compared to those who do not use any multimedia guides.

Usability and user experience (UX) have always been the predominant concerns of software products [9]. Helyar [10] highlights that mobile apps suffered from usability issues such as inept content and interface design. This resulted in the lack of user acceptance and the applications being rejected within months of the launch [11]. Zhang and Adipat [12] discussed the challenges, methodologies, and issues in the usability testing of mobile application. For example, the unique features of mobile devices pose challenges in usability testing such as mobile context of use, connectivity which is usually related to the bandwidth or network, small screen size, different display resolutions, limited or different processing capabilities, and data entry methods.

Gomez et al. [13] suggested that usability evaluation technique can be carried out during the implementation of a particular system to make sure the system enables users to achieve their goals efficiently. For example, the usability aspects of interacting with the smartphone apps, presenting information on the screen, learning about the smartphone apps' functionality, and controlling the devices prior research have shown that inspection method such as heuristic evaluation (HE) is effective in detecting usability problems in an interface compared to other methods [14, 15]. The issues identified by experts during the heuristic evaluation will be rectified before conducting the usability testing with actual visitors.

Most of the time, specific heuristics will work better as it is completed by specific usability checklists. However, a previous study by Law and Hvannberg [16] also highlights that it is difficult to map the problem to the matching heuristic. Hvannberg, Law, and Lérusdóttir [17] suggested a framework to conduct heuristic evaluation by comparing two sets of heuristics and process, procedure, and support to conduct usability evaluation to ensure its' effectiveness. Joyce and Lilley [18] argued the effectiveness of the previously developed specific heuristic such as Inostroza' TMD heuristics due to the similarity of the heuristics with Nielsen's traditional heuristics. They further mentioned that experts may feel ambiguous as the heuristic title remain the same although the definitions are different. The SMASH heuristics also suffered from the same issues of having the same name with the traditional heuristics by Nielsen although only one heuristics modified and one new heuristics added. It is important to highlight that the issues of mapping the usability issues with the accurate heuristics could lead to confusion in construing the issues. This can be an obstacle to designing the best solution the problem. Thus, the objective of this study is to examine the importance of integrating domain specific heuristics evaluation in the design and development of the smartphone apps for a living museum.

1.1. Living Museum Mobile Guide Application at Sarawak Cultural Village (SCV). The smartphone app in this study was developed as a mobile guide for a living museum, namely, Sarawak Cultural Village (SCV). SCV is chosen for this study because it was set up to preserve and showcase the finest Sarawak cultural heritages for the past 25 years. SCV also serves as one of the remaining sources of Sarawak cultures and its' ethnics [19]. In addition, there are only a handful of living museums (living museum is best described by Anderson [20] as way of simulating life in another time, particularly the past that best presented as a living history filled with activities that could possibly have an impact on learning experiences.) in Malaysia and SCV is considered as

one of the best places to visit. Furthermore, SCV acts as a medium to preserved cultural heritages (i.e., architectures, artefacts, costumes, etc.) of major ethnics in Sarawak. Dellios [21] argued with the development of such themed museums and how these cultural villages could be considered as on par with the authentic traditional villages at the outskirts of civilization. She further acknowledged that this is possibly a solution to the various issues in cultural tourism in Sarawak. Although tourists are eager to visit the homes and experiencing the lives of different cultures, previous studies raised concerns associated with disturbing the real lives of the residents at traditional villages [19] and possibilities of endangerment or troubles during the visit [22, 23].

Hitchcock and Stanley & Siu [24] described living museum as a venue that combined tangible and intangible cultural heritage that influenced by the open-air folk museum in North America and Europe. They further discussed two types of living museum in South-east Asian such as China Folk Culture Village in China and Taman Mini museum in Indonesia, while Anderson [20] discussed the various types of living museum in Europe and North America.

Anderson [20] discussed three main reasons why living museums were built: to effectively interpret the tangible and intangible culture; a place for research to test archaeological thesis or ethnographic study; and a place for visitors to actively participate in the activities provided as part of learning experiences. Being a living museum, SCV has a different setting compared to a conventional museum and fulfilled 2 main reasons why living museums were built previously described by Anderson [20]. In SCV, groups of people (staffs) showcase the lives, daily activities, and artefacts of the various ethnic communities in Sarawak. The staff are the source of information to the visitors because minimal or no information is provided due to the natural setting of SCV. When there is a lack of available staffs such as during lunch breaks, this has a negative impact on the overall visitors' experience because visitors could not get the sufficient information when needed. Previous studies highlight the importance of different attributes particularly facilities and services provided to the visitors at SCV to improve their experiences [25, 26].

The introduction of a smartphone mobile guide app for SCV could possibly have a positive impact on visitors' experience because it offers information on the go to the visitors that can be accessed before, during, and after each visit. However, delivering a mobile guide app with unresolved usability issues will jeopardize this positive impact on the visitors' experience. It is important to address the usability issues in mobile guide applications before being deployed for use by visitors at the cultural and heritage sites.

1.2. Designing for User Experience (UX). Designing for user experience UX is not trivial, particularly mobile applications that require the users to seamlessly interact with the mobile applications and their environment. Charland & Leroux [27] discussed the importance of UX in both native and web mobile application development to ensure its adoption. They further added that mobile UX can be divided into two main categories: (1) the *context* in which the elements must be understood but not changeable such as hardware affordances

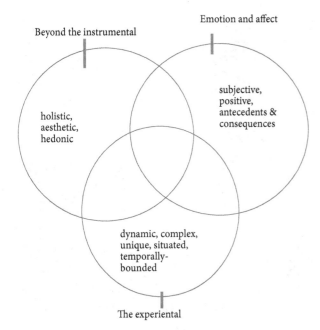

FIGURE 1: Facets of UX ([28], p 95).

and UI convention and (2) the *implementation* which refers to the elements that are changeable such as the design and features. Previous studies have shown that the focus of user experience (UX) studies has changed to the UX of technologies rather than the usability of devices thus making the user studies more complicated [28–32]. Hassenzahl & Tractinsky [28] stated that the UX comprises three different perspectives: emotion and affect and the experiential and beyond the instrumental as illustrated in the Figure 1.

The emotion and affect focus on users' emotion and how it is influenced by the affective computing concept. The experiential perspective focuses on the overall users' experience with the technology, whether it is *situated* or *temporally bounded*. The idea behind of experiential in UX is the duration of users' interaction with the product. This in turn will have impact on the UX, whether the short-term interaction between users and product only lasts for a short time or can be prolonged (e.g., [33–35]). The *temporally bounded* experience or temporality in UX have been discussed by the various researchers in the past (i.e., [33, 36–41]). The third perspective, which is beyond the instrumental, aims to create a more holistic computing system that takes human needs into consideration. For example, different technologies have been created to support different types of users. In the context of museums, Tate Modern Museum provides handheld devices that play videos with sign language for hearing impaired visitors. The British Sign Language (BSL) was used and first piloted in 2003. Evaluation on the guides showed that users were satisfied with the guide and it significantly improved their visit with 79% of visitors agreeing that they were highly satisfied with the BSL during their visit [42].

1.3. HE and Usability Evaluation of Smartphone Apps. Although Agarwal and Ventakesh [43] pointed out that

usability is not fundamentally objective but relative to evaluator' personal interaction during the evaluation, Yáñez Gómez, Caballero, and Sevillano [44] suggested that the evaluation can be designed to balance the personal interpretation. HE technique and usability testing are the mainstay of modern practice among usability professionals [45]. HE is a method for finding usability problems in a specific user interface design by taking a small set of evaluators to evaluate the interface and judge its compliance with recognized usability principles such as Nielsen's heuristics [46]. HE was originally developed as a usability engineering method for evaluators who had some knowledge of usability principles.

Heuristics is a well-established set of principles used to measure usability in an interface. There are mainly two alternatives which are to use either general heuristics or specific heuristics when performing a HE [47]. In the age of touchscreen-based mobile devices (e.g., mobile standard personal computer, mobile internet devices, handhelds, or PDAs and smartphone), researchers have proposed new sets of heuristics specific to such devices. In addition, previous studies have found that it is beneficial to have a specific set of heuristics for smartphone apps [48, 49].

Fung, Chiu, Ko, Ho, and Lo [50] conducted a heuristic usability evaluation on the University of Hong Kong Libraries website and its mobile version using Nielsen heuristic and discovered five (5) different usability issues with the mobile website. This poses the question as to whether usability heuristics sets are applicable across domains or whether usability heuristics sets should be domain specific for a more definite output of usability evaluations [48, 49].

Inostroza, Rusu, Roncagliolo, Jiminez, and Rusu [47] stated that heuristic evaluation is easy to apply but it is important to have a domain specific heuristic to ensure all usability issues are covered. Specific heuristics can detect usability problems related to the application domain, but it may be hard to understand and difficult to apply. On the other hand, general heuristics are easy to understand and apply; however, it is also easy to miss domain specific usability problems.

Indeed, there have been some studies in developing specific usability heuristics to fit application contexts. Mankoff et al. [51] conducted a study on the evaluation of ambient display using two different sets of usability heuristics, Nielsen's original heuristics and a modified version of the heuristics for ambient display. The application experts in the ambient heuristics group found significantly more usability issues than Nielsen's heuristics group, proving it to be more effective than Nielsen's heuristics.

Silva, Holden, and Jordan [52] described the use of specific usability heuristics for older adults. The work was based on several previous studies on older adults, such as Silva, Holden, and Nii [53]; Chisnell, Redish, and Lee [54] and Kurniawan and Zaphiris [55]. Diaz, Rusu, and Collazos [56] also held the view that using appropriate heuristics is highly relevant. They developed and validated usability heuristics set that is specific to ecommerce websites.

A specific set of heuristics which is known as Touchscreen Mobile Devices heuristics (TMD) was proposed by Inostroza et al. [47]. They found out that 40% usability problems were identified using TMD, while only 26% usability issues were identified using Nielsen's heuristics. Thus, indicate the effectiveness of specific heuristics as compared to Nielsen' heuristics. Recently, Inostroza et al. [57] validated their TMD and named it SMASH heuristics.

These studies support the use of domain specific usability heuristics as crucial in determining domain specific usability issues. Other than SMASH heuristics, various types of heuristics for smartphone apps have been made available for HE, for example, SMART heuristics [18]; mobile usability heuristics [58]; MATcH [59]; and many other heuristics as described by Inostroza et al. [57] and Salgado & Freire [60]. We have decided to use SMART and Nielsen heuristics in this study. Details of the heuristics used in this study can be found in Tables 1 and 2.

2. Methodology

2.1. Design and Development of Smartphone Apps. This project employed the Mobile Application Development Life Cycle (MADLC) that is specifically made for the development of smartphone apps. MADLC is commonly used in the design of Android mobile applications and was first introduced by Vithani and Kumar [62]. This system development lifecycle consists of seven stages: (1) identification, (2) design, (3) development, (4) prototyping, (5) testing, (6) deployment, and (7) maintenance.

In the identification stage, researchers analyzed existing mobile guide apps for museums and other cultural sites (i.e., [63–66]); this collected information was used as a point of references in designing the mobile guide app for SCV.

In addition, researchers made several visits to the SCV and conducted interviews with 10 staffs from different backgrounds, for example, general manager of SCV to gather insights into SCV and its future plans to ensure that the proposed mobile guide will be fully utilized. In addition, an interview with an assistant manager that oversees the operation of the SCV also took place to understand the operation of SCV and to ensure the proposed guide will not come in between the visitors and artefacts and its user experiences.

An open-ended interview with staff who were living at the SCV was conducted over a 2-weeks period to gather information and materials for the ethnic houses such as information and photographs of the architecture and the artefacts in the houses as illustrated in Figure 2. They were asked about the activities that they performed at SCV, information about various artefacts on display of different ethnicities, and their significance. For example, the information about the human skulls located above the fireplace in the *Baruk* (warrior house) as illustrated in Figure 3.

Furthermore, a short interview with five visitors was conducted during this stage to gather their insights and their overall experiences at SCV. It is important to get users' input from the beginning to ensure that the product will be acceptable. In addition, information searching was made by several visits to library and the ethnic foundations to gather related information about artefacts, lifestyles, culture, and architectures of the main ethnic in this study. Furthermore, online searching for related information was conducted too

FIGURE 2: Various artefacts and activities at one of the ethnic house.

FIGURE 3: Human skulls were place above the fireplace in the *Baruk* (warrior house).

because people are known to disseminate knowledge using online means. In the design stage, the information from the identification stage was transformed into an initial design of the mobile guide app. Storyboards were sketched out to visualize the flow and interaction within the mobile guide app. Figure 4 shows a sketch of an interface for the app.

In the development stage, the storyboard sketches from the identification stage were transformed into a functional system using Corona SDK software development kit simulator and Notepad++. A prototype, which is a fully functional system of the basic concepts of the application, was built. Prototypes are used for testing to examine any bugs or errors with the design of the system.

The testing stage is a critical aspect in system development. Usability testing is usually carried out during this stage

TABLE 1: Nielsen's Heuristics.

No	Nielsen's heuristics	Description
(1)	Visibility of system status	The system keeps users informed about the current situation through appropriate feedback within reasonable time.
(2)	Match between system and the real world	The system speaks users' language in which it uses words, phrases, and concepts that users are familiar with. It follows real world conventions, making information appear in a natural and logical manner.
(3)	User control and freedom	Provides clearly marked "emergency exit" for users to leave the unwanted state without go through an extended dialogue. System supports undo and redo.
(4)	Consistency and standards	Users not wondering whether different words, situations, or actions mean the same thing. Follows platform conventions.
(5)	Error prevention	The system either eliminates error-prone conditions or checks for them and presents users with a confirmation option before they commit to the action.
(6)	Recognition rather than recall	The system minimizes the users' memory load by making objects, actions, and options visible which indicated that users do not have to remember every detail. Instructions for use of the system.
(7)	Flexibility and efficiency of use	Speeds up the interaction for both inexperienced and experienced users. The system allows users to adapt frequent actions.
(8)	Aesthetic and minimalist design.	Elimination of information which is irrelevant.
(9)	Help users recognize, diagnose and recover from errors.	Error messages are expressed in plain language, concisely indicate the problems, and constructively suggest solution.
(10)	Help and documentation	Although it is better if the system can be used without documentation, it may be necessary to provide help and documentation for searching information easily and other purposes.

Note. Adopted from "Heuristic evaluation," by J. Nielsen, 1994 [61].

TABLE 2: Smartphone mobile application heuristics (SMART).

No	SMART	Description
(1)	Provide immediate notification of application status	Users are informed from the immediate application status.
(2)	Use a theme and consistent terms, as well as conventions and standards familiar to the user	Apply consistent themes for the screen of mobile application. Create a style guide and concepts that users are familiar with such as the same effects when gestures are used.
(3)	Prevent errors where possible; assist users should an error occur	Allows the mobile application to be error-proofed. If an error occurs, they let the users understand the error and offer advice to fix the error.
(4)	Display an overlay pointing out the main features when appropriate or requested	An overlay pointing out main features allows first-time users to get up-and-running quickly.
(5)	Each interface should focus on one task	To ensure that mobile interfaces are less cluttered and simple to the point.
(6)	Design a visually pleasing interface	Mobile interfaces that are attractive are more memorable and therefore used more often. Users are also more forgiving of attractive interfaces.
(7)	Intuitive interfaces make for easier user journeys	Mobile interfaces should be easy to learn in which next steps are obvious so that allows the users to complete their tasks easily.
(8)	Design a clear navigable path to task completion	Users are able to see the right way to interact with the application and navigate their way to task completion.
(9)	Allow configuration options and shortcuts	Depending on the target user, the mobile application might allow configuration options and shortcuts to the most important information and frequent tasks.
(10)	Cater for diverse mobile environments	Allow the users to change the interface brightness and sound settings.
(11)	Facilitate easier input	Ensure users can input content easily and accurately. For instance, displaying keyboards button as clear as possible.
(12)	Use the camera, microphone, and sensors when appropriate to lessen the users' workload	Consider the use of the camera, microphone, and sensors to reduce the users' workload.
(13)	Create an aesthetic and identifiable icon	The icon should be aesthetic and identifiable because icon is what a user first sees when searching for the application.

Note. Adapted from "Towards the Development of Usability Heuristics for Native Smartphone Mobile Applications," by G. Joyce and M. Lilley, 2014 [18].

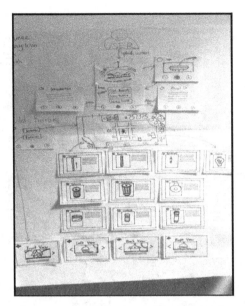

FIGURE 4: Mobile guide app interface sketch.

FIGURE 5: Mobile guide flash screen.

with actual users. However, this study employed the heuristic evaluation before user testing was conducted.

Prior to the evaluation stage, the researchers had successfully developed a mobile guide in the form of a smartphone app aimed to guide visitors at a living museum (Sarawak Cultural Village). This mobile guide is a native application that could be uploaded to the play store (Google Play, Apple App Store, etc.) whereby users can conveniently download it for free to their mobile devices.

2.2. Materials

2.2.1. SCV Smartphone App. When the users open the app, a splash screen (see Figure 5) will appear. Subsequently, users will be directed to the next screen, the map of the SCV, as illustrated in Figure 6.

When visitors tap on the "Bidayuh house" icon, they will be directed to the menu section as illustrated in Figure 7 that consists of the three different parts of the Bidayuh ethnic house; the *Barok, Panggah,* and *Longhouse.* Visitors will be provided with information about the house they selected from the menu as shown in Figure 8.

Subsequently, visitors will be directed to the floor plan of the house that shows the location of each artefacts available in each section of the house as illustrated in Figure 9. Information about each selected artefact will be provided in the next screen (for example, see Figure 10).

2.2.2. Heuristic Evaluation. To date, there are several types of heuristics available for HE that focused on smartphone. For example, touchscreen-based mobile device (TMD) heuristics [47]; SMASH heuristics [57]; SMART heuristics [18]; mobile usability heuristics [58]; mobile interface checklist [44]; MATcH [59]; and many other heuristics are described by Inostroza et al. [57] and Salgado & Freire [60].

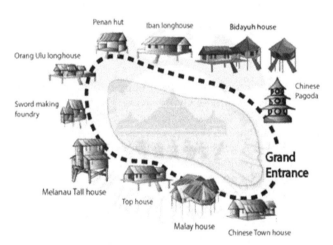

FIGURE 6: Map of SCV (location of each ethnic houses).

Two types of heuristic principles were used for comparison: Nielsen's heuristics [67] and SMART heuristics [18]. The set of heuristic principles by Nielsen is a well-established instrument that has been widely used for various types of interface design. The SMART heuristics, on the other hand, is a set of heuristics developed to particularly cover all aspects of a smartphone application interface. Though the mobile usability heuristics by Bertini and Gabrielli & Kimani [58] were considered, they were not selected due to the fact that the heuristics do not focus on the usability of the application icon.

During this stage, five (5) experts were recruited to evaluate the interface and the content of the application. They were instructed to identify the usability issues and determine

FIGURE 7: Main menu of the *Bidayuh* House.

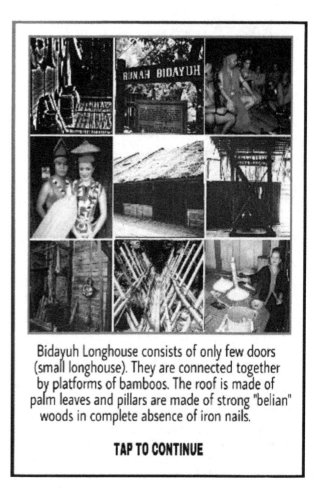

Bidayuh Longhouse consists of only few doors (small longhouse). They are connected together by platforms of bamboos. The roof is made of palm leaves and pillars are made of strong "belian" woods in complete absence of iron nails.

TAP TO CONTINUE

FIGURE 8: Information about the *Bidayuh* Longhouse.

their severity ratings using the severity rating scale [61] to rate the severity of usability problems. The severity ratings are as follows: 4—Catastrophic Problem—users will not be able to continue to their goal, must be fixed; 3—Major Problem—users will be frustrated/have difficulty continuing to their goal, could be fixed; 2—Minor Problem—users will be frustrated/have difficulty continuing to their goal, should be fixed; 1—Cosmetic Problem—user will be having minor problems that can be easily fixed; and 0 will have no usability issues at all. They were also instructed to map the usability issues to both Nielsen's Heuristics and SMART Heuristics.

2.3. Method. Below is the procedure of the study:

(1) **Briefing Session:** When the participants arrived, they were asked to take a seat. Participants were briefed on the purpose of the study by the researcher.

(2) **Interaction with the SCV mobile guide tour (smartphone apps):** Participants were handed a Samsung mini tablet with the SCV mobile guide tour app installed. They were briefed about the purpose of the app and how it will be used at Sarawak Cultural Village. This was to help the participants visualize how it will be used and critically analyze it for any issues they might encounter, regardless of minor or major issues.

(3) **Evaluation session:** Participants were asked to browse the mobile guide app screen by screen and

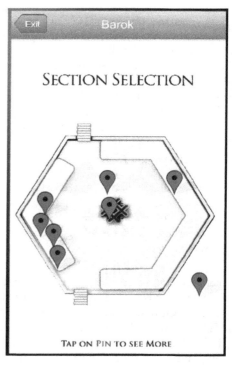

FIGURE 9: Floor plan.

FIGURE 10: The information about the selected artefact.

document any usability issues they found. Participants identified the usability issues and their severity ratings and mapped them to both Nielsen's Heuristics and SMART Heuristics.

(4) **Debriefing Session:** During the session, researchers thanked participants for their contributions and answered questions from the participants.

3. Results

The output of the heuristic evaluations was a list of usability problems with the severity scale provided in the Table 3. A total of 31 usability issues were identified. Out of the total, six issues were classified as catastrophic issues and needed immediate action while eight issues were categorized as major issues and needed to be rectified.

The usability issues listed in Table 3 were matched against the 10 Nielsen's Heuristic and SMART heuristic. Table 3 also summarized the mapping of each usability issues with Nielsen's and SMART heuristics. It is important to highlight that two (2) usability issues (issue 15 and 17) were not mapped to any Nielsen's heuristic because the issues were too specific to be mapped.

4. Discussion

Heuristic evaluation is an essential activity for securing highly usable smartphone apps and should not be disregarded in the mobile app development life cycle. This study presented an analysis of 31 usability issues. Six (6) issues (19.35%) were classified as catastrophic, while 8 issues (25.8%) were categorized

as major issues. The identification of these two categories of usability problems showed that a heuristic evaluation was needed so that usability issues could be addressed before the app reached the users. In addition, heuristic evaluations are low cost tools that could be easily executed to assess and improve the identified usability issues of the system during the development phase [68].

In this study, the aesthetic problems were identified more using the SMART heuristics. SMART heuristics have two principles dealing with aesthetics (#6 and #3) that describe the principle for overall interface aesthetics and specific icon aesthetics. However, though Nielsen's heuristics #4 mentions aesthetics, the description does not elaborate on aesthetics other than minimal design. There are two usability issues (issue 15 and 17 that are related to the icons) that are not easily matched against the Nielsen traditional heuristic because it is too general and researchers have decided to classify these issues under *aesthetic and minimalist design*. On the other hand, it is clear in the SMART heuristic that these two usability issues were categorized under *SMART13 (Create an aesthetic and identifiable icon)* although there is another category that is analogous to traditional heuristic, *aesthetic*, and *minimalist design* which is *SMART6: design a visually pleasing interface*. Aesthetics of the visual design component of a mobile guide interface design is crucial as it can enhance visitors' engagement [69]. SMART heuristics presents more detailed principles in evaluating aesthetics.

Usability issues in terms of consistency are the main problem found by the evaluators and this can be mapped to both Nielsen's heuristics (#4) and SMART principle (#2). However, it is interesting to note that although both heuristics are related to consistency and standard, the number of issues mapped to Nielsen's Heuristic and SMART principle is 8 and 11, respectively.

This study clearly showed the need to use domain specific heuristic evaluation as opposed to the general usability heuristics because there were difficulties in determining which heuristic was more appropriate for the issues identified especially when it came to the features that were only available for the smartphone. Joyce and Lilley [18] explained these difficulties because Nielsen heuristic is too general to detect usability problems because current systems are more interactive, complex, and diverse. In addition, a study by Alsumait and Al-Osaimi [70] concluded that Nielsen's heuristic is too general and not explained in details and is not suitable to be applied to domain specific application. A similar finding by Pinelle, Wong, and Stach [71] explained that more usability issues were found when using newly developed set heuristics due to the complexity of the application. Other previous studies also supported the need to use domain specific usability heuristics (e.g., [58, 68]). Furthermore, Petrie and Power [72] also highlight that it is inappropriate to compare problem faced by users in past decades and problems faced by users in 2010s. Hence, the categorization using the SMART principle is more apt because it is recently developed and has taken into consideration current technologies, i.e., smartphone and its applications. On the other hand, Nielsen's principles were developed before the advent of smartphone technologies; hence the categorizations were more general.

TABLE 3: Usability issues, average severity, and its mapping with Nielsen's Heuristic and SMART heuristics.

Problems/Usability Issues	Average Rating	Nielsen Heuristics	SMART heuristic
(1) Not consistent font	4	H4	SMART 2
(2) Not consistent image	3	H4	SMART 2
(3) Not consistent heading	2	H4	SMART 2
(4) About "plan layout"	3	H4	SMART 2
(5) No "back button" at description page	4	H3	SMART 8
(6) Grammatical error	2	H4	SMART 2
(7) The text is not justified	4	H8	SMART 6
(8) Lack information about Sarawak Cultural Village	2	H4	SMART 2
(9) No upview image more	1	H4	SMART 2
(10) Quality of the image	2	H8	SMART 6
(11) Unclear pin point	3	H4	SMART 2
(12) There is no "exit button"	4	H3	SMART 8
(13) Unattractive font colour for heading	1	H8	SMART 6
(14) Unclear about the Bidayuh's houses	2	H4	SMART 2
(15) Lack of icon use	3	n/a	SMART 13
(16) Redundancy word "welcome"	1	H4	SMART 2
(17) Not suitable icon for pin point	2	n/a	SMART 13
(18) Not appropriate link menu to exit	2	H3	SMART 8
(19) Missed coordinate the pin point	1	H3	SMART 8
(20) Texts are not aligned	4	H4	SMART 2
(21) Spacing between paragraph are not consistent	1	H8	SMART 6
(22) No "back button" to description page	4	H3	SMART 8
(23) Words have been distorted	2	H8	SMART 6
(24) Does not have the exact map	3	H2	SMART 1
(25) There are no artistic elements	1	H8	SMART 6
(26) Topic information	1	H6	SMART 6
(27) Indicator problem	1	H2	SMART 1
(28) Does not have the contrast colour	1	H8	SMART 6
(29) Floor map indicator problem	3	H2	SMART 1
(30) Does not have page name	3	H6	SMART 6
(31) Does not have labelling in type of the houses	3	H2	SMART 1
Total usability issues correctly mapped		29/31	31/31

5. Conclusions

This study compared two sets of heuristics, traditional and domain specific for mobile application for cultural heritage sites. It shows that domain specific measurement is more comprehensive for a more definite identification of usability issues. These issues then can be rectified so that the mobile guide application can evolve into a more usable application before the system is deployed to the target users. This will help to improve the acceptance of the application once deployed to the users at Sarawak Cultural Village through the development of a highly usable mobile guide application that enhance the user experience (UX) at these sites. Future works can focus on comparison of domain specific heuristics to define heuristics for mobile guide applications for cultural heritage sites.

Conflicts of Interest

The authors declare that there are no conflicts of interest regarding the publication of this paper.

Acknowledgments

The authors gratefully acknowledge the grant from Universiti Malaysia Sarawak (UNIMAS) (F04 (S148)/1128/2014(13)) and financial/nonfinancial support given by Sarawak Cultural Village (SCV).

References

[1] L. Tallon, "Introduction: Mobile, Digital and Personal," in *Walker, Digital Technologies and the Museum Experience: Handheld Guides and Other Media*, Altamira Press, 2008.

[2] M. Kenteris, D. Gavalas, and D. Economou, "Electronic mobile guides: A survey," *Personal and Ubiquitous Computing*, vol. 15, no. 1, pp. 97–111, 2011.

[3] J. Jaën, J. Mocholl, J. M. Esteve et al., "MoMo: Enabling social technology in hybrid museums," in *Proceedings of the International Workshop Rethinking technology in museum: towards a new understanding of people's experience in museums*, L. Ciolfi, M. Cooke, T. Hall, L. J. Bannon, and S. Olivia, Eds., pp. 245–251, University of Limerick, Limerick, Republic of Ireland, 2005.

[4] S. Filippini-Fantoni, "Personalization through IT in museums," in *Proceedings of the International Cultural Heritage Informatics Meeting (ICHIM 03)*, Museum Informatics Europe, Paris, France, 2003.

[5] S. Filippini-Fantoni, J. P. Bowen, and T. Numerico, "Personalization issues for science museum Web sites and E-learning," *E-Learning Methodologies and Computer Applications in Archaeology*, pp. 371–387, 2008.

[6] S. Filippini-Fantoni and J. P. Bowen, "Mobile multimedia: Reflections from ten years of practice," in *Digital Technologies and the Museum Experience: Handheld Guides and Other Media*, L. Tallon and K. Walker, Eds., AltaMira Press, Lanham, MD, USA, 2008.

[7] J. Pallud, "Impact of interactive technologies on stimulating learning experiences in a museum," *Information and Management*, vol. 54, no. 4, pp. 465–478, 2017.

[8] M. K. Othman, H. Petrie, and C. Power, "Engaging visitors in museums with technology: Scales for the measurement of visitor and multimedia guide experience," *Lecture Notes in Computer Science (including subseries Lecture Notes in Artificial Intelligence and Lecture Notes in Bioinformatics): Preface*, vol. 6949, no. 4, pp. 92–99, 2011.

[9] M. F. Mazlan, A. Sivaji, S. S. Tzuaan, and A. M. Lokman, "Enhancing the heuristic evaluation (HE) by development and validation of a collaborative design measurement system (CDMS)," in *In Proc Science Engineering Research (CHUSER*, pp. 473–478, Sabah, Kota Kinabalu, 2012.

[10] V. Helyar, *Usability issues and user perceptions of a 1st generation WAP service*, 2000, http://experiencelab.typepad.com/files/wap-paper-2.pdf.

[11] K. Wac, S. Ickin, J.-H. Hong, L. Janowski, M. Fiedler, and A. K. Dey, "Studying the experience of mobile applications used in different contexts of daily life," in *Proceedings of the 1st ACM SIGCOMM Workshop on Measurements Up the Stack, W-MUST'11, Co-located with SIGCOMM 2011*, pp. 7–12, Canada, August 2011.

[12] D. Zhang and B. Adipat, "Challenges, Methodologies, and Issues in the Usability Testing of Mobile Applications," in *Proceedings of the International Journal of Human–Computer Interaction*, vol. 18, pp. 293–308, 2005.

[13] Rosa Yáñez Gómez, Daniel Cascado Caballero, and José-Luis Sevillano, "Heuristic Evaluation on Mobile Interfaces: A New Checklist," *The Scientific World Journal*, vol. 2014, Article ID 434326, 19 pages, 2014.

[14] Z. Tang, T. R. Johnson, R. D. Tindall, and J. Zhang, "Applying heuristic evaluation to improve the usability of a telemedicine system," *Telemedicine and e-Health*, vol. 12, no. 1, pp. 24–34, 2006.

[15] F. Paz, F. A. Paz, D. Villanueva, and J. A. Pow-Sang, "Heuristic Evaluation as a Complement to Usability Testing: A Case Study in WEB Domain," in *Proceedings of the 12th International Conference on Information Technology: New Generations, ITNG 2015*, pp. 546–551, USA, April 2015.

[16] E. L. C. Law and E. T. Hvannberg, "Analysis of strategies for improving and estimating the effectiveness of heuristic evaluation," in *Proceedings of the third Nordic conference on Human-*

computer interaction, pp. 241–250, 2004.

[17] E. T. Hvannberg, E. L. C. Law, and M. K. Lérusdóttir, "Heuristic evaluation: Comparing ways of finding and reporting usability problems," *Interacting with Computers*, vol. 19, no. 2, pp. 225–240, 2006.

[18] G. Joyce and M. Lilley, "Towards the development of usability heuristics for native smartphone mobile applications," in *Design, User Experience, and Usability. Theories, Methods, and Tools for Designing the User Experience*, pp. 465–474, Springer International Publishing, Switzerland, 2014.

[19] H. Muzaini, "Informal heritage-making at the Sarawak Cultural Village, East Malaysia," *Tourism Geographies*, vol. 19, no. 2, pp. 244–264, 2017.

[20] J. Anderson, "Living History: Simulating Everyday Life in Living Museums," *American Quarterly*, vol. 34, no. 3, p. 290, 1982.

[21] P. Dellios, "The museumification of the village: cultural subversion in the 21st Century," *Culture Mandala: The Bulletin of the Centre for East-West Cultural and Economic Studies*, vol. 5, no. 1, 2002.

[22] S. C. Heilman and D. MacCannell, "The Tourist: A New Theory of the Leisure Class.," *Social Forces*, vol. 55, no. 4, p. 1104, 1977.

[23] C. Latrell, "Performance and Place-Making at Sarawak Cultural Village," *Journal of Ideas and Culture*, vol. 10, no. 3, pp. 127–142, 2006.

[24] M. Hitchcock, N. Stanley, and K. C. Siu, "The South-east Asian living museum' and its antecedents," in *Heritage, museums and galleries: An introductory reader*, vol. 291, 2005.

[25] J. Abi, "Visitors Evaluation on Facilities and Services Using Importance-Performance Analysis at Sarawak Cultural Village," in *Proceedings of the 2nd Regional Conference on Tourism Research*, p. 16, 2011.

[26] J. Abi, M. Mariapan, and A. Aziz, "Visitor's Evaluation on Facilities and Services using Importance Performance Analysis at Sarawak Cultural Village," *OSR Journal of Environmental Science, Technology and Food Technology*, vol. 9, no. 12, pp. 16–24, 2015, http://www.iosrjournals.org/iosr-jestft/papers/vol9-issue12/Version-1/D091211624.pdf.

[27] A. Charland and B. Leroux, "Mobile application development: web vs. native," *Communications of the ACM*, vol. 54, no. 5, pp. 49–53, 2011.

[28] M. Hassenzahl and N. Tractinsky, "User experience—a research agenda," *Behaviour & Information Technology*, vol. 25, no. 2, pp. 91–97, 2006.

[29] A. Civan, W. Jones, P. Klasnja, and H. Bruce, *Better to Organize Personal Information by Folders or by Tags? The Devil is in the Details*, vol. 45, American Society for Information Science and Technology, Silver Spring, Md, USA, 2009.

[30] H. L. O'Brien and E. G. Toms, "What is user engagement? A conceptual framework for defining user engagement with technology," *Journal of the Association for Information Science and Technology*, vol. 59, no. 6, pp. 938–955, 2008.

[31] M. Hassenzahl, "User experience (UX): towards an experiential perspective on product quality," in *Proceedings of the 20th Conference on l'Interaction Homme-Machine (IHM '08)*, pp. 11–15, ACM, Metz, France, September 2008.

[32] E. L.-C. Law, V. Roto, M. Hassenzahl, A. Vermeeren, P. O. S, and J. Kort, "Understanding, scoping and defining user experience: A survey approach," in *Proceedings of CHI09*, Boston, MA, USA, 2009.

[33] S. Kujala, V. Roto, K. Väänänen-Vainio-Mattila, E. Karapanos, and A. Sinnelä, "UX Curve: A method for evaluating long-term user experience," *Interacting with Computers*, vol. 23, no. 5, pp. 473–483, 2011.

[34] E. Karapanos, J. Zimmerman, J. Forlizzi, and JB. Marten, "User Experience over Time: An Initial Framework," in *Proceedings of the SIGCHI Conference on Human Factors in Computing Systems*, Boston, MA, USA, 2009.

[35] E. Karapanos, J.-B. Martens, and M. Hassenzahl, "Reconstructing experiences with iScale," *International Journal of Human-Computer Studies*, vol. 70, no. 11, pp. 849–865, 2012.

[36] I. Pattersson, *The Temporality of In-Vehicle User Experience: Exploring User Experiences from Past to Future*, Chalmers University of Technology, 2016.

[37] G. Joyce, M. Lilley, T. Barker, and A. Jefferies, "Evaluating the impact of changing contexts on mobile application usability within agile environments," in *Proceedings of the 2016 Future Technologies Conference, FTC 2016*, pp. 476–480, USA, December 2016.

[38] C. C. Huang, *Describing and Analyzing Interactive Experience Over Time [Ph.D. thesis]*, Indiana University, 2015.

[39] C. C. Huang and E. Stolterman, "Temporal Anchors in User Experience Research," in *Proceedings of the 2014 Conference on Designing Interactive Systems*, pp. 271–274, New York, NY, USA, 2014.

[40] S. Kujala and T. Miron-Shatz, "The Evolving Role of Expectations in Long-term User Experience," in *Proceedings of the 19th International Academic Mindtrek Conference on Academic-MindTrek*, vol. 15, pp. 167–174, New York, NY, USA, 2015.

[41] J. Varsaluoma and F. Sahar, "Usefulness of long-term user experience evaluation to product development: Practitioners' views from three case studies," in *Proceedings of the 8th Nordic Conference on Human-Computer Interaction, NordiCHI 2014*, pp. 79–88, Finland, October 2014.

[42] N. Proctor, "Providing deaf and hard-of-hearing visitors with on-demand independent access to museum information and interpretation through handheld computers," in *Museum and the Web*, J. Trant and D. Bearman, Eds., Archives & Museum Informatics, Toronto, Canada, 2004.

[43] R. Agarwal and V. Venkatesh, "Assessing a firm's web presence: a heuristic evaluation procedure for the measurement of usability," *Information Systems Research*, vol. 13, no. 2, pp. 168–186, 2002.

[44] R. Y. Gómez, D. C. Caballero, and J.-L. Sevillano, "Heuristic Evaluation on Mobile Interfaces: A New Checklist," *The Scientific World Journal*, vol. 2014, Article ID 434326, 2014.

[45] L. A. Lockwood and L. L. Constantine, "Usability by inspection: Collaborative techniques for software and web applications," in *Pro forUSE*, pp. 253–282, 2003.

[46] J. Nielsen, "Reliability of severity estimates for usability problems found by heuristic evaluation," in *Proceedings of the Posters and short talks of the 1992 SIGCHI conference*, p. 129, Monterey, California, May 1992.

[47] R. Inostroza, C. Rusu, S. Roncagliolo, and V. Rusu, "Usability heuristics for touchscreen-based mobile devices: Update," in *Proceedings of the 2013 Chilean Conference on Human - Computer Interaction, ChileCHI 2013*, pp. 24–29, Chile, November 2013.

[48] G. Joyce, M. Lilley, T. Barker, and A. Jefferies, "Smartphone app usability evaluation: The applicability of traditional heuristics," in *Proceedings of the International Conference, Design,*

[49] User Experience and Usability (DUXU 2015), pp. 541–550, Los Angeles, LA, USA, 2015.

[49] G. Reynaga, S. Chiasson, and P. C. Van Oorschot, "Heuristics for the evaluation of captchas on smartphones," in *Proceedings of the British HCI Conference, British HCI 2015*, pp. 126–135, UK, July 2015.

[50] R. H. Y. Fung, D. K. W. Chiu, E. H. T. Ko, K. K. W. Ho, and P. Lo, "Heuristic Usability Evaluation of University of Hong Kong Libraries' Mobile Website," *Journal of Academic Librarianship*, vol. 42, no. 5, pp. 581–594, 2016.

[51] J. Mankoff, A. K. Dey, G. Hsieh, J. Kientz, S. Lederer, and M. Ames, "Heuristic evaluation of ambient displays," in *Proceedings of the The CHI 2003 New Horizons Conference Proceedings: Conference on Human Factors in Computing Systems*, pp. 169–176, USA, April 2003.

[52] P. A. Silva, P. Jordan, and K. Holden, "Something Old, Something New, Something Borrowed: Gathering experts' feedback while performing heuristic evaluation with a list of heuristics targeted at older adults," in *Proceedings of the 11th Advances in Computer Entertainment Technology Conference, ACE 2014 Workshops*, Portugal, November 2014.

[53] P. A. Silva, K. Holden, and A. Nii, "Smartphones, smart seniors, but not-so-smart apps: A heuristic evaluation of fitness apps," in *Proceedings of the International Conference on Augmented Cognition*, pp. 347–358, Springer, Cham, Switzerland, 2014.

[54] D. E. Chisnell, J. C. Redish, and A. Lee, "New heuristics for understanding older adults as web users," *Technical Communication*, vol. 53, no. 1, pp. 39–59, 2006.

[55] S. Kurniawan and P. Zaphiris, "Research-derived web design guidelines for older people," in *Proceedings of the ASSETS 2005 - The Seventh International ACM SIGACCESS Conference on Computers and Accessibility*, pp. 129–135, USA, October 2005.

[56] J. Díaz, C. Rusu, and C. A. Collazos, "Experimental validation of a set of cultural-oriented usability heuristics: e-Commerce websites evaluation," *Computer Standards & Interfaces*, vol. 50, pp. 160–178, 2017.

[57] R. Inostroza, C. Rusu, S. Roncagliolo, V. Rusu, and C. A. Collazos, "Developing SMASH: A set of SMArtphone's uSability Heuristics," *Computer Standards & Interfaces*, vol. 43, pp. 40–52, 2016.

[58] E. Bertini, S. Gabrielli, and S. Kimani, "Appropriating and assessing heuristics for mobile computing," in *Proceedings of the working conference on Advanced visual interfaces*, pp. 119–126, 2006.

[59] L. H. Salazar, T. Lacerda, J. V. Nunes, and C. Gresse von Wangenheim, "A Systematic Literature Review on Usability Heuristics for Mobile Phones," *International Journal of Mobile Human Computer Interaction*, vol. 5, no. 2, pp. 50–61, 2013.

[60] A. Salgado and A. Freire, "Heuristic evaluation of mobile usability: a mapping study," in *Human Computer Interaction. Applications and services, Lecture Notes Computer Science*, vol. 8512, pp. 178–188, 2014.

[61] J. Nielsen and R. L. Mack, *Usability Inspection Methods*, John Wiley & Sons, New York, NY, USA, 1994.

[62] T. Vithani and A. Kumar, "Modeling the mobile application development lifecycle," in *Proceedings of the International Multi-Conference of Engineers and Computer Scientist*, Hong Kong, 2014.

[63] M. K. Othman, *Measuring Visitors Experiences with Mobile Guide Technology in Cultural [Phd thesis]*, University of York, 2012.

[64] S. Gray, C. Ross, A. Hudson-Smith, M. Terras, and C. Warwick, "Enhancing Museum Narratives with the QRator Project: a Tasmanian devil, a Platypus and a Dead Man in a Box," in *Proceedings of Museum and the Web*, Toronto, Archives, 2012.

[65] C. Bailey-Ross, S. Gray, J. Ashby, M. Terras, A. Hudson-Smith, and C. Warwick, "Engaging the Museum Space: Mobilizing visitor engagement with digital content creation," in *Digital Scholarship in the Humanities*, 2016.

[66] S. Boiano, J. P. Bowen, and G. Gaia, "Usability, design and content issues of mobile apps for cultural heritage promotion: The Malta culture guide experience," https://arxiv.org/abs/1207.3422.

[67] J. Nielsen, "Heuristic evaluation," in *Readings in Human–Computer Interaction*, vol. 17, Elsevier, 1994.

[68] L. Kuparinen, J. Silvennoinen, and H. Isomäki, "Introducing usability heuristics for mobile map applications," in *Proceedings of the 26th International Cartographic Conference (ICC, 2013)*, Dresden , Germany, 2013.

[69] M. K. Othman, K. I. Idris, S. Aman, and P. Talwar, "An Empirical Study of Visitors' Experience at Kuching Orchid Garden with Mobile Guide Application," *Advances in Human Computer Interaction*, vol. 2018, Article ID 5740520, 14 pages, 2018.

[70] A. Alsumait and A. Al-Osaimi, "Usability heuristics evaluation for child e-learning applications," *Journal of Software* , vol. 5, no. 6, pp. 654–661, 2010.

[71] D. Pinelle, N. Wong, and T. Stach, "Heuristic evaluation for games: usability principles for video game design," in *Proceedings of the SIGCHI Conference on Human Factors in Computing Systems (CHI '08)*, pp. 1453–1462, April 2008.

[72] H. Petrie and C. Power, "What do users really care about? A comparison of usability problems found by users and experts on highly interactive websites," in *Proceedings of the 30th ACM Conference on Human Factors in Computing Systems, CHI 2012*, pp. 2107–2116, USA, May 2012.

2

Student Evaluations of a (Rude) Spoken Dialogue System Insights from an Experimental Study

Regina Jucks ⓘ, Gesa A. Linnemann ⓘ, and Benjamin Brummernhenrich ⓘ

University of Muenster, Institute of Psychology for Education, Germany

Correspondence should be addressed to Regina Jucks; jucks@uni-muenster.de

Academic Editor: Thomas Mandl

Communicating with spoken dialogue systems (SDS) such as Apple's Siri® and Google's Now is becoming more and more common. We report a study that manipulates an SDS's word use with regard to politeness. In an experiment, 58 young adults evaluated the spoken messages of our self-developed SDS as it replied to typical questions posed by university freshmen. The answers were either formulated politely or rudely. Dependent measures were both holistic measures of how students perceived the SDS as well as detailed evaluations of each single answer. Results show that participants not only evaluated the content of rude answers as being less appropriate and less pleasant than the polite answers, but also evaluated the rude system as less accurate. Lack of politeness also impacted aspects of the perceived trustworthiness of the SDS. We conclude that users of SDS expect such systems to be polite, and we then discuss some practical implications for designing SDS.

1. Introduction

Advances in speech recognition move our interactions with spoken dialogue systems (SDS), such as Apple's Siri or Google Now, ever closer to human dialogue. Over and above the capability of conversing in natural language, one strain of development concerns genuinely social aspects of human communication, such as alignment, addressing by name, and politeness. This paper addresses how students evaluate the communication behavior of an SDS that employs the social strategies of politeness and rudeness. Their evaluations address variables such as acceptance, appropriateness, and competence, all of which are also relevant in evaluating human behavior. In the following, we briefly address the technological aspects of SDS. Then we outline politeness theory and introduce how speakers take their speech partners' autonomy and affiliation into account when formulating messages. Finally, we provide results of our empirical research on the perception of SDS, which offer insights about how to design them effectively.

1.1. Technology That Interacts: Insights into the Mechanisms and Usage of Spoken Dialogue Systems. More and more computers are now able to communicate with their users in natural language [1]. For example, spoken dialogue systems (SDS) serve as personal assistants and are implemented in smartphones (like Siri from Apple and Cortana® from Microsoft), cars [2], or special devices (such as Echo from Amazon: [3]). SDS are also used in educational contexts, e.g., in learning programs for children [4].

The first attempts at emulating human communication were simple chatbots such as Eliza which tried to emulate a psychotherapist in the Rogerian, person-centered tradition [5]. How chatbots can be made more human-like is still a very active field of development, for example, by evaluating the conditions of *uncanny valley* reactions in animated and text-based bots (e.g., [6]). Since 1990, the Loebner Prize has been held as an annual competition with an award given to the creator of the chatbot that most convincingly acts as a human interlocutor.

Whereas chatbots are usually text-based and often have entertainment purposes, SDS serve as an interface to a specific system and let computer systems and human users interact using spoken language; that is, the computer systems are capable of understanding and producing spoken language. This can reach from rather simple "command-and-control" interactions, which refer to short, single controlling functions (e.g., [4]), to systems that are able to handle complex input and to generate complex, natural language (e.g., [7, 8]).

SDS have become much better at mimicking human interactions. Incrementality allows the system to implement backchannels and barge-ins. These are associated with facilitated *grounding* [9] in human-human interaction, meaning that a user is more confident about whether the system shares the user's understanding off the topic of the conversation and the meaning of the words used in it [7]. Connecting and operating SDS via the Internet can help support the system and the user in a concrete situation, e.g., by searching the Internet for the answer the SDS does not "know" directly. Additionally, such searches can be analyzed and used to improve the SDS [1]. Due to their proactive behavior, SDS are no longer restricted to simple replies. They can now initiate conversations themselves and provide information without being asked [1]. Thus, concerning their language, SDS can possess a high degree of anthropomorphism [10–12].

Providing these characteristics, SDS can be employed as tutors, termed intelligent tutoring systems. Graesser and colleagues [13] recently introduced an intelligent tutoring system from a new, "mixed-initiative" generation. Their conversational agent is able to maintain interactions over multiple turns, presenting problems and questions to the learner. Thus, it promotes active knowledge construction and outperforms mere information-delivery systems. Besides its conversational capabilities, social aspects of SDS play an important role. Research on intelligent tutoring systems has recently turned its attention on agents that can act socially and respond to tutees' affective states (e.g., [14, 15]). When intelligent tutors and tutees are teammates, for instance, tutoring seems to be more effective [16]. Put differently, how intelligent tutors—and SDS in general—communicate plays an important role. Politeness has seemingly been neglected in conversational agents [17]. However, some computer tutors already exhibit different kinds of polite instruction [18]. In the next section, we will give an overview of politeness theory and its effects on communication.

1.2. Mitigating Face Threats: Insights into Politeness Theory. Communication involves more than just conveying information. It is a social activity that contributes to individuals' social needs and impacts their self-concepts. In their politeness theory, Brown and Levinson [19] argue that every person has a public self-perception, the so-called *face*, and that this face needs to be shaped positively. Individuals' needs for belonging and support affect the *positive face*, and the need for autonomy and freedom of action affect the *negative face*. Communication behavior that serves as support of a person's face is termed *face work*.

Actions that harm and affect someone's face are called *face-threatening acts* (FTAs). To what extent an FTA is perceived as serious depends on social distance, power relations, and the absolute imposition. During communication, every single contribution might include FTAs, be it through direct orders, which restrict autonomy and independence, or through corrections, which in a way serve as a rejection of the person. Politeness theory describes several strategies

for how to mitigate an FTA [20]. The first option is not to perform the FTA and, accordingly, the utterance (the topic/aspect is simply not addressed). Second, the FTA can be transmitted *off record*; that is, the speaker remains vague or ambiguous. Hence he/she cannot be sure if the intended meaning is conveyed. Third, negative politeness is used, which can reduce the direct imposition on the hearer (e.g., through apologizing, employing hedges, and being conventionally indirect). This includes formulating a request indirectly as a suggestion. Fourth, positive politeness aims to meet the hearer's need for belonging and at gratification. A message might be started with positive feedback on the communication partners' intelligence. Mitigating face threats whenever autonomy or affiliation is threatened is a natural communication behavior.

1.3. Human-Like Interaction? Empirical Research on the Perception of SDS. As SDS possess enormous capabilities, users are likely to consider them conversational partners. SDS are perceived with their human-like qualities even when users are aware that they are communicating with a computer [21]. Basic language capabilities, for example, giving simple responses such as "yes" and "no", seem to be enough to perceive the computer as a human-like being [22]. When users perceive the SDS as a competent partner, they also perceive it as a social actor [23]. In this way, an SDS with a female voice can, for example, potentially activate corresponding gender stereotypes [10]. Thus, it becomes relevant how users assess an SDS according to different aspects that humans are evaluated on. One aspect that also directly influences how the information conveyed by the SDS is processed is *trustworthiness*, which includes **a**bility, **b**enevolence, and integrity (see [24] and the ABI model; [25]).

If computers are perceived as social agents, this influences our interaction with them. For example, people prefer systems that communicate in a personal manner [21]. People also usually communicate politely with computers and avoid explicit face threats (e.g., [26]) but also sometimes lie or behave intentionally rudely toward them [27]. This could be caused by disinhibition but could also be a reflection of the prevalence of rudeness in human communication [28].

Given that people tend to treat computers as humans, are social behaviors such as politeness also expected from SDS [29]? In human communication, politeness improves social perceptions. Polite speakers appear more likable and recipient oriented [30, 31]. Some studies have also shown effects on attributes such as perceived integrity or competence [32]. Thus, if an SDS is perceived similarly to a human interlocutor, similar effects should be found.

Regarding trust, it can be argued that SDS can be conceptualized as receivers of trust, as trustees (see also [33]). McKnight [34] has stated that "trust in technology is built the same way as trust in people" (p. 330). In the vast majority of conceptualizations, trust incorporates the willingness to be vulnerable [35] and therefore the willingness to depend on somebody else (e.g., [36]).

Regarding politeness, users tend to communicate politely with computer systems (e.g., [26]). Pickard, Burgoon, and Derrick [37] have found that likeability, in turn, increases the tendency to align, e.g., using the same words and expressions to a conversational agent. Lexical alignment is perceived as polite [38, 39] and evokes positive feelings [38, 40]. Gupta, Swati, Walker, and Romano [41] developed a system which employs artificial spoken language and politeness principles in task-oriented dialogues. They found, for example, that the predictions of politeness theory are applicable to discourse with such systems: the strategies had an impact on the perception of politeness (see also [42]). However, we are unaware of any investigations into intentionally rude systems, with the exception of a rude intelligent tutoring system that has proven beneficial for some, but not all, of its students [43].

Nowadays, companies offer the possibility to personalize SDS (e.g., Siri can be taught the user's name and relationships; navigation systems' language style can be adjusted, e.g., restricted and elaborated language style: NIK-VWZ01 Navigation, n.d.). De Jong, Theune, and Hofs [44] developed an embodied conversational agent that is able to align to the politeness shown by its interlocutor. Some participants appreciated that the system aligned in terms of politeness, others preferred a version of the system that always displayed the same high degree of politeness, irrespective of whether the user showed no politeness.

2. Rationale

The above-reported literature strongly shows that communication with SDS is part of everyday life. Politeness theory has introduced the concept of face threats, e.g., affronts to a person's autonomy and/or needs of belonging. These face threats are mitigated via communicational behavior, such as hedges [45] and relativizing words.

Empirical studies indicate that SDS are evaluated on social dimensions comparably to humans. Those experimental studies have also shown that word usage impacts this evaluation.

The following study manipulates SDS word usage with regard to politeness. We conducted a 1x2 experimental design, where politeness was contrasted with rudeness. We define rudeness as a deliberate attack on the addressee's face that can be used both playfully and aggressively [46]. In this respect, rudeness is distinct from a mere lack of politeness when uttering a necessary face threat (i.e., a bald/on record strategy in the terms of politeness theory), as well as an unintentional face threat (e.g., an SDS asking a strongly religious user a question about a topic that is offensive to them) but consists of intentionally aggravating behavior. The interpretation often is dependent on the context (e.g., [47]).

We formulate three hypotheses that address participants' evaluation of both the social aspects of the SDS and its competence. Furthermore, by directly asking participants to suggest changes in SDS formulations, a direct measure on the word level was operationalized.

H1: A polite SDS will be judged as more likable and polite than will a rude SDS and its responses as more appropriate and pleasant than those from a rude SDS. A polite SDS will be more strongly perceived as a social interaction partner than a rude SDS.

H2: A polite SDS will be judged as more competent and trustworthy than a rude SDS.

H3: Rude responses will be perceived as more serious face threats than polite responses and will lead to more revisions than polite ones.

In the following, methods and materials are described.

3. Methods and Materials

In order to comply with the requirements of open science and to achieve transparency, we report how we determined our sample size, all (if any) data exclusions, all manipulations, and all measures in the study [48].

3.1. Participants. We recruited participants at an open house event that our university holds yearly for potential new students. We planned to recruit as many participants as possible, aiming for about 80. This would yield a power of about 80% in finding medium to large effects, as previous studies on similar phenomena have found.

In total, 58 persons participated in the study (35 females). The age of the participants ranged from 15 to 20 years old and the mean age was 16.91 ($SD = 1.08$) years old. All were native German speakers or spoke German since their early childhood. In Germany, students that aim for university entrance qualifications usually choose two intensive courses during the last two years of school. In our sample the most common choices were biology (36% of participants), English (33%), German (29%), and mathematics (21%). They reported to use a computer on average of 9.84 hours per week ($SD = 9.42$) and to use the Internet on average of 25.34 hours per week ($SD = 21.17$). Also, 86% of participants considered themselves to possess intermediate or advanced computer knowledge. Of all participants, 12% reported that they use SDS on a daily basis or several times a week, 8.6% reported to use SDS several times a month, and 77.6% reported that they rarely or never use SDS. Overall, 66% of participants indicated that they use SDS that are implemented in smartphones, like Siri and Google Now.

Experimental conditions did not differ for each of the above-reported descriptive variables, all Fs > 0.832, ps > .366. Hence, these variables were not considered further on. No data were removed from the analysis. Participants received no compensation.

3.2. Materials. The study was conducted at a German university; all materials were in German. Materials and stimuli are available at https://sites.google.com/site/sdspoliteness. The examples we present in this paper are translations of the original materials. The speech was created using a text-to-speech synthesis tool available on Apple Mac computers. It was a female voice.

We told participants that we built/designed and trained an SDS to provide answers to university freshmen's questions. We stated that we therefore wanted them to assess the SDS's answers. The participants were told that the SDS was part of a mobile app provided to new psychology students to help them find their way around the university and their courses. To this end, users could ostensibly ask the SDS questions about

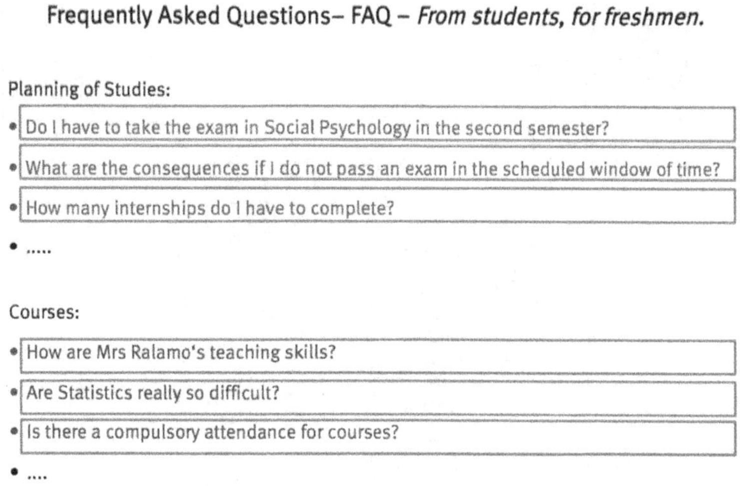

Frequently Asked Questions– FAQ – *From students, for freshmen.*

Planning of Studies:

- Do I have to take the exam in Social Psychology in the second semester?
- What are the consequences if I do not pass an exam in the scheduled window of time?
- How many internships do I have to complete?
- .....

Courses:

- How are Mrs Ralamo's teaching skills?
- Are Statistics really so difficult?
- Is there a compulsory attendance for courses?
- ....

FIGURE 1: Screenshot of the question list shown to participants.

different topics related to university life and the psychology program and receive informative answers. In reality, the app does not exist and participants were debriefed at the end of the experiment.

Participants listened to six answers presented by our own designed SDS, called ACURI. The answers addressed six typical questions of university freshmen. The questions were presented on a screen and after clicking on the respective question, the answer was presented as a sound file. The questions were the same in both experimental conditions, but the answers given by the SDS differed. In the *polite condition* the messages were phrased politely (e.g., "You can choose whether you want to..."). In the *rude condition* the face threats were strong(er), resulting in a rudely phrased message (e.g., "No, you have to do..."). Questions and answers as well as the original versions in German are shown in Table 1; see Table 2 for an example.

3.3. Procedure. Participants were tested in groups of five or six. Each member of the group was assigned the same experimental condition. A 1x2 between-subject design was realized, with $n = 29$ participants in each of the two conditions (polite versus rude). All participants were seated individually in front of a laptop computer and were provided with headphones. They received sheets containing information on the experimental procedure as well as a declaration of consent and data privacy. They also received a booklet with the questionnaire to be completed as part of the study. Our local ethics committee approved the study.

After reading the information and signing the form, the students' questions were presented on the computer screen. The participants were instructed to click on the questions to hear the SDS's responses. The responses were played as audio over the headphones. Participants were not free to choose which question to click; there was a fixed order in which the answers to the questions (sound files) were available (see Figure 1 for an example of a participants' screen).

After every response from the SDS, the participants were asked to turn a page of the booklet and respond to a number of questions concerning the response they just heard. After all responses had been heard, the participants were asked to rate the SDS per se and provide demographic information. After completing the questionnaire, the participants were debriefed. The session took about 30 minutes.

3.4. Dependent Measures. Participants were asked to rate every single response of ACURI on the perceived face threat as well as the holistic impression of ACURI at the end of the survey.

3.4.1. Evaluation of the Responses. The participants rated each of the six responses on the following.

Pleasantness and Appropriateness. Participants were asked to indicate on 7-point bipolar semantic differentials whether they found the response (1) pleasant–unpleasant and (2) appropriate–inappropriate.

Perceived Face Threat Scale (PFT; [49]). The scale was originally designed to rate utterances in workplace conversations and later complaints in interpersonal contexts, regarding how much they threatened positive and negative face aspects. The authors found that responses on the scale differed depending on the type of the complaint, such that complaints that had focused on the disposition of the receiver were judged as more face-threatening. This makes the scale adequate for our goals. We are unaware of any other measure for evaluating face threat.

Sample items are "My partner's actions showed disrespect toward me" for threatening positive face and "My partner's actions constrained my choices" for threatening negative face. Because we did not pose a hypothesis regarding the different face aspects, we averaged scores on all 14 items into a single value. For the current study, all items were translated into German and adapted to collect ratings on "ACURI" instead of "my partner". Participants responded on a 7-step Likert scale ranging from "not at all" to "very much". Scale reliability was good with Cronbach's $\alpha = .91$.

TABLE 1: Student's questions and polite and rude phrasings of face threats in ACURI's responses.

Student Question	Polite Phrasing in ACURI's Response	Rude Phrasing in ACURI's RESPONSE
Do I have to take the exam in Social Psychology in the second semester?	You can choose whether you want to do the exam in your second or third semester. You find this information on the website if you look for the link to syllabus and exam information.	No, you have to do the social psychology exam in the second or third semester. You find this information on the website if you look for the link to syllabus and exam information.
What are the consequences if I do not pass an exam in the scheduled window of time?	That can happen but it's regrettable. Other courses can only be taken once the exam is passed.	Well, hard luck! You have to pass the exam before you can take other courses.
How many internships do I have to complete?	For your Bachelor's degree this is around 12 weeks. The exact number of hours varies from Bachelor to Master degree. If you get a chance take a look at the syllabus. After completing your internships you will for sure have a good idea about the different fields Psychologists work in.	As many as you need in order to get an idea of the different fields Psychologists work in. The exact number of hours varies from Bachelor to Master degree. To find out you will have to look into the syllabus.
How are Mrs. Ralamo's teaching skills?	Students she perceives to be motivated to work will pass her class rather easily. So you will get a long with her well if you do the work in class.	Well it's going to be difficult for lazy ones. Make an effort and do the work in class and you won't have problems with her.
Are Statistics really that difficult?	If you make an effort you will do okay. In addition to that there is a statistics tutorial that you can enroll in.	People asking such a question will probably have problems. If you are already worried that you won't manage it'll probably turn out this way. Enroll in the statistics tutorial right away; the tutors regularly make miracles happen.
Is there a compulsory attendance for courses	For most lectures and classes attendance is not mandatory but you should try to go nonetheless because contents to be learned usually stick better this way then through self-study.	No, attendance is not mandatory for most lectures and classes. But how do you expect to learn if you don't go to class?

TABLE 2: Example of a student's question (SQ) and the polite and rude answers, respectively, of the spoken dialogue system named ACURI.

	Polite	Rude
SQ1	Do I need to take the social psychology exam in the second semester?	
ACURI	You can choose whether you want to do the exam in your second or third semester....	No, you have to do the social psychology exam in the second or third semester....

3.4.2. Evaluation of the SDS. The participants evaluated the SDS regarding several subjective appraisals, epistemic trust, and whether they perceived it as a social agent.

Subjective Assessment of Speech System Interfaces. The participants rated the SDS on the Subjective Assessment of Speech System Interfaces measure (SASSI, [50]). This instrument was developed as an extension of earlier measures to evaluate the usability of graphic interfaces and focuses on subjective aspects of SDS usability. It consists of six subscales: response accuracy (nine items, e.g., "the system makes few errors"), likability (nine items, e.g., "the system is pleasant"), cognitive demand (five items, e.g., "a high level of concentration is required when using the system"), annoyance (five items, e.g., "the interaction with the system is frustrating"), habitability (four items, e.g., "I was not always sure what the system was doing"), and speed (two items, e.g., "the interaction with the system is fast"). There are alternative measures focusing on SDS usability, most notably the CCIR-BT [51] with similar subscales. However, the SASSI measure has been more widely used in subsequent research (e.g., [52]).

In the current study, the participants indicated their agreement to the statements on 7-point Likert scales. Scale reliabilities for the response accuracy and likability subscales were good, with $\alpha = .84$ and .87, respectively. Reliabilities for the cognitive demand and annoyance subscales were acceptable with $\alpha = .68$ and .72, respectively. However, the subscale reliabilities for the habitability and speed subscales were inadequate with $\alpha = -.06$ and .12, respectively. This might be explained by the fact that the participants were not using the SDS themselves but merely judging the SDS's utterances. The two subscales were dropped from further analyses.

Hence, four measures, each one for a subscale of SASSI serves as subjective assessment of ACURI.

Perceiving the SDS as a Social Agent. The participants indicated how much they perceived the SDS as a social agent using a measure developed by Holtgraves, Ross, Weywadt, and Han [21]. This inventory was developed in order to assess whether users ascribe human-like qualities to chatbots. The measure consists of two subscales that measure perceptions of conversational skill (three items, e.g., "how engaging is the system?") and pleasantness (three items, e.g., "how thoughtful is the system?"). The participants responded on 7-point semantic differentials (e.g., "not at all thoughtful–very thoughtful"). In the original publication, chatbots using the user's first name were found to be evaluated more positively on these scales. In our study, subscale reliabilities were good to satisfactory with Cronbach's $\alpha = .67$ and .81, respectively.

Epistemic Trust. The participants rated how much they trusted the SDS as a source of knowledge using the Münster Epistemic Trustworthiness Inventory (METI; [53]). This measure is based upon the ABI model mentioned in the introduction [24] and consists of 5-point bipolar adjective pairs. The subscales measure goodwill (four items, e.g., "moral–immoral"), expertise (six items, e.g., "qualified–unqualified"), and integrity (five items, e.g., "honest–dishonest"). All subscales exhibited satisfactory consistencies with Cronbach's $\alpha = .73$, .81, and .60, respectively.

There are alternative measures that measure similar constructs, such as the Credibility scales by McCroskey and Teven [54]. However, the METI instrument differs from these in that it explicitly focuses on *epistemic* trust, that is, whether the target of the evaluations is a trustworthy source for the knowledge that the user seeks. This was desirable for our research question.

Suggestions for Rephrasing. Participants were given the opportunity to rephrase ACURIs answers and to mention things that, from their perspective, should be changed. They provided their answers in writing as response to this instruction: "Please listen to the answer of the question once again. You may now note potential suggestions for changing the answer."

For the analysis, we used a bottom-up, data-driven process to identify five categories of statements of what should be changed according to the participants: (1) apply strategies to mitigate FTAs (e.g., "use 'it is recommended that you...' instead of 'you have to...'"); (2) formulate the utterance in a more direct and neutral way, e.g., "should just answer the question and not make a proposal"; (3) change the prosody or pronunciation, e.g., "a brighter and less monotonous voice would be better"; (4) provide more precise information, e.g., "give information about where the tutorial takes place"; and (5) no changes are necessary, e.g., "the hint was helpful".

4. Results

We used the lme4 package [55] for the R statistical software and entered the six individual responses as a random effect and the politeness condition (polite/rude) as a fixed effect into linear mixed-effects models. For the ratings collected after the whole discourse, we calculated ANOVAs and MANOVAs, depending on the measure as reported below.

With **hypothesis 1**, we assumed that a polite SDS would be judged as more likable and polite responses as more appropriate and pleasant than a rude SDS. Furthermore, we expected a polite SDS to be more strongly perceived as a social interaction partner than a rude SDS. These expectations were partly confirmed: both ratings of pleasantness and appropriateness measures yielded the expected effects. Polite responses were perceived as more appropriate ($M = 6.53$, $SE = 0.28$) than rude responses ($M = 5.59$, $SE = 0.28$), $F(1,55)=13.59$, $p < .001$. Polite responses were also perceived as more pleasant ($M = 6.07$, $SE = 0.28$) than rude responses ($M = 4.97$, $SE = 0.29$), $F(1,55) = 10.43$, $p < .001$.

Contrary to our expectations, on the holistic level, the SASSI likability subscale did not show a significant effect for the politeness condition, $F(1,51) = 1.87$, $p =.177$. Both groups judged likability of ACURI as moderate (polite: $M = 4.62$, $SD = 1.07$; rude: $M = 4.18$, $SD = 1.19$).

Regarding how much participants perceived the SDS as a social agent with human-like properties, we used the measure by Holtgraves and colleagues [21]. The pleasantness subscale showed a significant effect of the politeness condition in the expected direction. As such, the polite SDS was also judged as more pleasant ($M = 5.67$, $SE = 0.23$) than the rude SDS ($M = 4.14$, $SE = 0.23$), $F(1,51) = 17.88$, $p < .001$. However, the polite SDS's conversational skill was not judged to be higher, $F(1,51) = 1.04$, $p = .31$.

With **hypothesis 2**, we assumed that a polite SDS would be judged as more competent and trustworthy than a rude SDS. This hypothesis was mostly confirmed. The polite SDS received higher ratings on the SASSI response accuracy subscale ($M = 4.65$, $SE = 0.13$) than the rude SDS ($M = 4.23$, $SE = 0.13$), $F(1,51) = 4.48$, $p =.039$. The MANOVA with the METI subscales showed a significant effect for the politeness condition, $F(3,49) = 4.15$, $p = .011$. The follow-up analyses showed that the polite SDS was judged as showing more goodwill (polite: $M = 3.63$, $SD = 0.72$; rude: $M = 2.90$, $SD = 0.78$) and integrity (polite: $M = 3.90$, $SD = 0.63$; rude: $M = 3.51$, $SD = 0.58$) but not more expertise (polite: $M = 3.70$, $SD = 0.71$; rude: $M = 3.54$, $SD = 0.73$) than the rude SDS.

With the **hypothesis 3**, we expected that rude responses would be perceived as more serious face threats than polite responses. H3 was confirmed. According to the PFT, rude responses were perceived as more face-threatening ($M = 3.22$, $SE = 0.14$) than polite responses ($M = 2.46$, $SE = 0.14$), $F(1,55) = 22.46$, $p < .001$.

The average amount of revision proposals regarding all respective answers was comparable in both conditions. On average, participants made suggestions on 2.48 ($SD = 2.13$) answers in the polite condition and on 2.62 answers in the rude condition ($SD = 1.97$; $F(1,56) = 0.07$, $p = .799$). However, the amount of suggestions regarding the categories differed depending on the respective response (see Table 3 for details). We calculated Fisher's exact tests for each response to test for differences between conditions. This is a statistical technique for the analysis of deviations from expectation in a contingency table [56] and is especially suited for smaller samples.

The condition had an influence on answers to SQ 2 ($\chi^2(4, N = 58) = 16.550$, $p < .001$), SQ4 ($\chi^2(4, N = 58) = 9.184$, $p = .029$), and SQ5 ($\chi^2(4, N = 58) = 12.025$, $p = .006$), but not on answers to SQ1 (SQ1: $\chi^2(4, N = 58) = 2.545$, $p = .725$, $ns.$), SQ3 ($\chi^2(5, N = 58) = 8.086$, $p = .110$, $ns.$), and SQ6 ($\chi^2(4, N = 58) = 5.463$, $p = .213$ $ns.$). In the rude condition, most changes were aimed at strategies to mitigate FTAs (29 % on

average). In the politeness condition, most suggestions were offered in categories 3 or 4. Participants referred to providing more precise information and on changing or enhancing the employed voice (both categories each around $M = 14\%$). These two categories were each chosen for 6% of the answers by participants of the rude condition.

5. Discussion

To sum up, the results of this study show that polite responses were perceived as more appropriate and pleasant than rude responses. Overall, the SDS was also perceived as more pleasant than the rude SDS. Both groups judged the likability of the SDS as moderate, with no differences between conditions. Also, conversational skill was not judged differently between conditions. The polite SDS was perceived as more accurate, showing more goodwill and integrity but not as having more expertise than the rude SDS. Rude responses were perceived as more face-threatening than polite responses. In the rude condition, most changes were aimed at strategies to mitigate FTAs (29 % on average), while, in the politeness condition, participants referred to providing more precise information and on changing or enhancing the employed voice.

Using a very clear and straightforward manipulation, we aimed to identify how the human principle of politeness is taken in consideration in SDS communication. In our setting, SDS answered to university freshmen's typical questions on student life. The only differences between our two experimental conditions were in the "how" part of the contribution, with rather rude or polite answers. The results mostly mirror those obtained with judgments of humans [12, 30]. These studies suggest that although both content and social information are transmitted with the same words, recipients seem to distinguish these two aspects; we routinely tease apart the "how" and "what" part of a contribution. In both previous studies and our present study, almost all social judgments, such as likability or the goodwill aspect of trustworthiness, were evaluated more positively in the polite condition. However, neither found evidence for differences in judgments of expertise, as a more content-related aspect of trustworthiness. However, in our study the accuracy of the system, which is also an arguably content-related aspect, was judged as higher for the polite system. Future research should ascertain whether this is a specific aspect of communication with an SDS or maybe a consequence of the specific realization of our conditions.

The results also indicate that advances on the technological side are expectations on the users' side. Politeness and adaptive communication require competent systems. Our between-subject design, which did not provide a direct comparison of rude and polite behavior, shows clearly that an SDS is judged relatively strictly according to its communication behavior. The users do not seem to be willing to be lenient simply because the system is not a human.

Our study has some limitations: one is that we had relatively young users assess the SDS. While those do represent typical users and the whole setting was ecologically valid for them, we cannot transfer the SDS evaluation results to other groups with less experience in technology (see the

TABLE 3: Change suggestions for each of the five categories from participants for each of the six SDS answers according to conditions (polite versus rude), reported in percentage.

	Answer 1		Answer 2		Answer 3		Answer 4		Answer 5		Answer 6		Total	
category	polite	rude	polite	rude	polite	rude	polite	rude	polite	rude	polite	rude	polite	rude
1 (mitigate FTA)	10	21	14	59	7	10	3	28	7	41	10	17	9	29
2 (direct)	3	0	3	0	3	0	0	0	3	0	10	10	4	2
3 (voice)	28	31	7	3	17	0	10	3	7	0	14	0	14	6
4 (precise)	7	3	21	0	21	21	14	3	21	7	3	0	15	6
5 (no change)	52	45	55	38	52	69	72	66	62	52	62	72	59	57

digital natives debate; [57]). Second, we simulated an indirect communication setting. Our participants did not interact with the SDS themselves; instead, they listened to responses of the SDS. There is evidence that a direct engagement with the SDS produces different results and absorbs some of the analytic abilities participants have shown in their evaluation of our ACURI [58].

One practical implication of this study might be drawn from our empirical evidence: regarding the first impression of an SDS and the evaluation of its acceptance and trustworthiness, the wording used by the SDS seems to have a considerable impact. Hence it might be worth engaging in creating more flexible and human-like technology. Communication principles such as politeness and alignment provide straightforward assumptions that might be embedded in technology and tested in experimental settings. Although the more attempts that are aimed at making assistants like ACURI become more human-like in their communication style, it is possible that such systems might also enhance miscommunication and misunderstanding. As an example, an SDS that is programmed to offer polite and indirect communication might produce responses that leave more room for interpretation and are thus less clear. In order to competently implement social communication factors in SDS, designers need to be aware how these principles come into play in different communication contexts. In this way, research into the social factors of human communication is highly relevant for the field of human-computer interaction.

Acknowledgments

This research was supported by a grant awarded to the second author within the German Research Foundation's (DFG) Research Training Group GRK 1712: *Trust and Communication in a Digitized World*.

References

[1] N. Mavridis, "A review of verbal and non-verbal human-robot interactive communication," *Robotics and Autonomous Systems*, vol. 63, no. 1, pp. 22–35, 2015.

[2] R. López-Cózar, Z. Callejas, D. Griol, and J. F. Quesada, "Review of spoken dialogue systems," *Loquens*, vol. 1, no. 2, Article ID e012, 2014.

[3] F. Manjoo, "The Echo from Amazon brims with ground-breaking promise," http://www.nytimes.com/2016/03/10/technology/the-echo-from-amazon-brims-with-groundbreaking-promise.html, 2016.

[4] M. F. McTear, *Spoken Dialogue Technology: toward The Conversational User Interface*, Springer Science & Business Media, 2004.

[5] J. Weizenbaum, "ELIZA—A computer program for the study of natural language communication between man and machine," *Communications of the ACM*, vol. 9, no. 1, pp. 36–45, 1966.

[6] L. Ciechanowski, A. Przegalinska, M. Magnuski, and P. Gloor, *In the Shades of the Uncanny Valley: An Experimental Study of Human–Chatbot Interaction*, Future Generation Computer Systems, 2018.

[7] N. Dethlefs, H. Hastie, H. Cuayáhuitl, Y. Yu, V. Rieser, and O. Lemon, "Information density and overlap in spoken dialogue," *Computer Speech Language*, vol. 37, pp. 82–97, 2016.

[8] O. Vinyals and Q. Le, "A neural conversational model," arXiv preprint, arXiv:1506.05869. ISO 690, 2015.

[9] G. A. Linnemann and R. Jucks, "As in the question, so in the answer? Language style of human and machine speakers affects interlocutors' convergence on wordings," *Journal of Language and Social Psychology*, vol. 35, no. 6, pp. 686–697, 2016.

[10] C. I. Nass and S. Brave, *Wired for Speech: How Voice Activates and Advances the Human-Computer Relationship*, MIT Press, Cambridge, UK, 2005.

[11] J. Edlund, J. Gustafson, M. Heldner, and A. Hjalmarsson, "Towards human-like dialogue systems," *Speech Communication*, vol. 50, no. 8, pp. 630–645, 2008.

[12] R. Jucks, G. A. Linnemann, F. M. Thon, and M. Zimmermann, "Trust the words: insights into the role of language in trust building in a digitalized world," in *Trust and Communication in a Digitized World*, B. Blöbaum, Ed., pp. 225–237, Springer International Publishing, 2016.

[13] A. C. Graesser, K. VanLehn, C. P. Rosé, P. W. Jordan, and D. Harter, "Intelligent tutoring systems with conversational dialogue," *AI Magazine*, vol. 22, no. 4, pp. 39–51, 2001.

[14] R. E. Mayer, W. L. Johnson, E. Shaw, and S. Sandhu, "Constructing computer-based tutors that are socially sensitive: politeness in educational software," *International Journal of Human-Computer Studies*, vol. 64, no. 1, pp. 36–42, 2006.

[15] K. Porayska-Pomsta, M. Mavrikis, and H. Pain, "Diagnosing and acting on student affect: the tutors perspective," *User Modeling and User-Adapted Interaction*, vol. 18, no. 1, pp. 125–173, 2008.

[16] M. Tai, I. Arroyo, and B. P. Woolf, "Teammate relationships improve help-seeking behavior in an intelligent tutoring system," in *Proceedings of the International Conference on Artificial Intelligence in Education*, pp. 239–248, Springer, Berlin, Heidelberg, 2013.

[17] B. Whitworth, "Politeness as a social software requirement," *International Journal of Virtual Communities and Social Networking*, vol. 1, no. 2, pp. 65–84, 2009.

[18] B. M. McLaren, K. E. DeLeeuw, and R. E. Mayer, "Polite web-based intelligent tutors: can they improve learning in classrooms?" *Computers & Education*, vol. 56, no. 3, pp. 574–584, 2011.

[19] P. Brown and S. C. Levinson, *Politeness, Some universals in language Usage*, Cambridge University Press, Cambridge, UK, 1987.

[20] B. Brummernhenrich and R. Jucks, "Managing face threats and instructions in online tutoring," *Journal of Educational Psychology*, vol. 105, no. 2, pp. 341–350, 2013.

[21] T. Holtgraves, S. Ross, C. Weywadt, and T. Han, "Perceiving artificial social agents," *Computers in Human Behavior*, vol. 23, no. 5, pp. 2163–2174, 2007.

[22] A. De Angeli, W. Gerbino, E. Nodari, and D. Petrelli, "From tools to friends: where is the borderline?" in *Proceedings of the UM99 Workshop on Attitude, Personality and Emotions in User-Adapted Interaction*, pp. 1–10, Springer, Berlin, Germany, 1999.

[23] C. Nass and K. M. Lee, "Does computer-synthesized speech manifest personality? experimental tests of recognition, similarity-attraction, and consistency-attraction," *Journal of Experimental Psychology: Applied*, vol. 7, no. 3, pp. 171–181, 2001.

[24] R. C. Mayer, J. H. Davis, and F. D. Shoorman, "An intergration model of organizational trust," *The Academy of Management Review*, vol. 20, no. 3, pp. 709–734, 1995.

[25] S. Tseng and B. J. Fogg, "Credibility and computing technology," *Communications of the ACM*, vol. 42, no. 5, pp. 39–44, 1999.

[26] L. Hoffmann, N. C. Krämer, A. Lam-chi, and S. Kopp, "Media equation revisited: do users show polite reactions towards an embodied agent?" in *Intelligent Virtual Agents*, Z. Ruttkay, M. Kipp, A. Nijholt, and H. H. Vilhjálmsson, Eds., pp. 159–165, Springer, Berlin, Germany, 2009.

[27] A. De Angeli and S. Brahnam, "I hate you! Disinhibition with virtual partners," *Interacting with Computers*, vol. 20, no. 3, pp. 302–310, 2008.

[28] J. Culpeper, "Towards an anatomy of impoliteness," *Journal of Pragmatics*, vol. 25, no. 3, pp. 349–367, 1996.

[29] C. Nass, "Etiquette equality: exhibitions and expectations of computer politeness," *Communications of the ACM*, vol. 47, no. 4, pp. 35–37, 2004.

[30] B. Brummernhenrich and R. Jucks, "'He shouldn't have put it that way!' How face threats and mitigation strategies affect person perception in online tutoring," *Communication Education*, 2015.

[31] R. Jucks, L. Päuler, and B. Brummernhenrich, "'I need to be explicit: you're wrong': impact of face threats on social evaluations in online instructional communication," *Interacting with Computers*, vol. 28, no. 1, pp. 73–84, 2016.

[32] S. L. Jessmer and D. Anderson, "The effect of politeness and grammar on user perceptions of electronic mail," *North American Journal of Psychology*, vol. 3, no. 2, pp. 331–346, 2001.

[33] L. Dybkjær and N. O. Bernsen, "Usability issues in spoken dialogue systems," *Natural Language Engineering*, vol. 6, pp. 243–271, 2000.

[34] D. H. McKnight, "Trust in information technology," in *The Blackwell Encyclopedia of Management*, B. G. Davis, Ed., vol. 7 of *Management Information Systems*, pp. 329–331, Blackwell, Malden, MA, USA, 2005.

[35] R. C. Mayer and J. H. Davis, "The effect of the performance appraisal system on trust for management: a field quasi-experiment," *Journal of Applied Psychology*, vol. 84, no. 1, pp. 123-10, 1999.

[36] D. H. McKnight and N. L. Chervany, "Trust and distrust definitions: one bite at a time," in *Trust in Cyber-Societies*, R. Falcone, M. Singh, and Y.-H. Tan, Eds., pp. 27–54, Springer, Berlin, Heidelberg, 2001.

[37] M. D. Pickard, J. K. Burgoon, and D. C. Derrick, "Toward an objective linguistic-based measure of perceived embodied conversational agent power and likeability," *International Journal of Human-Computer Interaction*, vol. 30, no. 6, pp. 495–516, 2014.

[38] H. P. Branigan, M. J. Pickering, J. Pearson, and J. F. McLean, "Linguistic alignment between people and computers," *Journal of Pragmatics*, vol. 42, no. 9, pp. 2355–2368, 2010.

[39] C. Torrey, A. Powers, M. Marge, S. R. Fussell, and S. Kiesler, "Effects of adaptive robot dialogue on information exchange and social relations," in *Proceedings of the HRI 2006: 2006 ACM Conference on Human-Robot Interaction*, pp. 126–133, USA, March 2006.

[40] J. J. Bradac, A. Mulac, and A. House, "Lexical diversity and magnitude of convergent versus divergent style shifting-: perceptual and evaluative consequences," *Language Communication*, vol. 8, no. 3, pp. 213–228, 1988.

[41] S. Gupta, M. Walker, and D. Romano, "How rude are you?: evaluating politeness and affect in interaction," *Affective Computing and Intelligent Interaction*, pp. 203–217, 2007.

[42] M. A. Walker, J. E. Cahn, and S. J. Whittaker, "Improvising linguistic style: social and affective bases for agent personality," in *Proceedings of the First International Conference on Autonomous Agents*, pp. 96–105, 1997.

[43] A. C. Graesser, "Learning, thinking, and emoting with discourse technologies," *American Psychologist*, vol. 66, no. 8, pp. 746–757, 2011.

[44] M. De Jong, M. Theune, and D. Hofs, "Politeness and alignment in dialogues with a virtual guide," in *Proceedings of the 7th International Joint Conference on Autonomous Agents and Multiagent Systems, AAMAS 2008*, pp. 206–213, Portugal, May 2008.

[45] M. Thiebach, E. Mayweg-Paus, and R. Jucks, ""Probably true" says the expert: how two types of lexical hedges influence students' evaluation of scientificness," *European Journal of Psychology of Education*, vol. 30, no. 3, pp. 369–384, 2015.

[46] D. Bousfield and J. Culpeper, "Impoliteness, eclecticism and diaspora," *Journal of Politeness Research*, vol. 4, no. 2, pp. 161–168, 2008.

[47] N. Vergis and M. Terkourafi, "The role of the speakers emotional state in im/politeness assessments," *Journal of Language and Social Psychology*, vol. 34, no. 3, pp. 316–342, 2015.

[48] J. P. Simmons, L. D. Nelson, and U. Simonsohn, "False-positive psychology: undisclosed flexibility in data collection and analysis allows presenting anything as significant," *Psychological Science*, vol. 22, no. 11, pp. 1359–1366, 2011.

[49] W. R. Cupach and C. L. Carson, "Characteristics and consequences of interpersonal complaints associated with perceived face threat," *Journal of Social and Personal Relationships*, vol. 19, no. 4, pp. 443–462, 2002.

[50] K. S. Hone and R. Graham, "Towards a tool for the subjective assessment of speech system interfaces (SASSI)," *Natural Language Engineering*, vol. 6, no. 3, pp. 287–303, 2000.

[51] L. B. Larsen, "Assessment of spoken dialogue system usability-what are we really measuring?" in *Proceedings of the Eighth European Conference on Speech Communication and Technology*, Geneva, Switzerland, 2003.

[52] S. Möller, P. Smeele, H. Boland, and J. Krebber, "Evaluating spoken dialogue systems according to de-facto standards: a case study," *Computer Speech & Language*, vol. 21, no. 1, pp. 26–53, 2007.

[53] F. Hendriks, D. Kienhues, and R. Bromme, "Measuring laypeoples trust in experts in a digital age the Muenster Epistemic Trustworthiness Inventory (METI)," *PLoS ONE*, vol. 10, no. 10, Article ID e0139309, 2015.

[54] J. C. McCroskey and J. J. Teven, "Goodwill, a reexamination of the construct and its measurement," *Communication Monographs*, vol. 66, no. 1, p. 90, 1999.

[55] D. Bates, M. Mächler, B. M. Bolker, and S. C. Walker, "Fitting linear mixed-effects models using lme4," *Journal of Statistical Software*, vol. 67, no. 1, 2015.

[56] A. Agresti, "A survey of exact inference for contingency tables," *Statistical Science*, vol. 7, no. 1, pp. 131–153, 1992.

[57] F. Salajan, D. Schonwetter, and B. Cleghorn, "Student and faculty inter-generational digital divide: fact or fiction?" *Computers and Education*, vol. 53, no. 3, pp. 1393–1403, 2010.

[58] G. A. Linnemann and R. Jucks, "Can I trust the spoken dialogue system because it uses the same words as i do?—influence of lexically aligned spoken dialogue systems on trustworthiness and unter satisfaction," *Interacting with Computers*, pp. 173–186, 2018.

3

A Method for Designing Physical User Interfaces for Intelligent Production Environments

Pierre Taner Kirisci⬥[1,2] **and Klaus-Dieter Thoben**⬥[1,2]

[1]*University of Bremen, Faculty of Production Engineering, Bagdasteiner Str. 1, 28359 Bremen, Germany*
[2]*Bremer Institut für Produktion und Logistik GmbH (BIBA), University of Bremen, Hochschulring 20, 28359 Bremen, Germany*

Correspondence should be addressed to Klaus-Dieter Thoben; tho@biba.uni-bremen.de

Academic Editor: Thomas Mandl

Physical user interfaces with enhanced interaction capabilities are emerging along with intelligent production environments. In this manner, we pose the question if contemporary design methods and tools are sufficient for the design of this new breed of user interfaces, or if there is rather a need for more efficient design methods and tools. The paper is initiated with a discussion about the need for more sophisticated physical user interfaces with enhanced capabilities for interacting in intelligent production environments. Based on this idea, we derive several functional and nonfunctional requirements for a suitable design method, supporting the conceptualisation of physical user interfaces in the early phases of product development. Hence, we suggest a model-based design method, which incorporates a comprehensive context model and modelling tool, applicable to intelligent production environments. In order to demonstrate the feasibility of the design method, we further conduct a validation and evaluation of the functional modelling tool, based on an industrial use case, in cooperation with design experts. In the final section of the paper, we critically discuss the key characteristics of the design method and thus identify potential issues for future improvement.

1. Introduction

There exists a need for design methods that support the conceptualisation phase of physical user interfaces. This particular early design phase requires techniques that are capable of ensuring that user context and requirements are adequately integrated into the entire design process from the very beginning [1]. The challenge is particularly evident when considering interaction within complex environments such as intelligent production environments, as this would require physical user interfaces with more sophisticated technical properties. These can include advanced input and output functionalities, wireless communication, and sensing techniques. The challenge of conceptualising physical user interfaces with suitable design methods becomes clearer when discussing intelligent production environments focussing on service processes as a case study in more detail, as outlined in Figure 1. In intelligent production environments, physical artefacts such as machinery, control devices, products, and vehicles increasingly possess enhanced technical capabilities.

These can extend from multimodal interaction possibilities to powerful processing capabilities. From a technical point of view, this is due to the integration of sensors, microcontrollers, and telemetric units as the enabling technologies. In this way physical artefacts such as control devices, tooling equipment, vehicles, and robotic systems are upgraded with enhanced technical properties, i.e., transforming from passive objects to interactive products with enhanced capabilities [2–4]. Humans interacting in these environments are therefore exposed to a variety of complex systems.

In combination with mobile interaction devices, humans are empowered with new interaction opportunities. New interaction opportunities include multimodal and situated interaction where an appropriate combination of specific interaction channels (e.g., acoustic, haptic, visual, and tactile) is activated according to the intermediate context of the user (see Figure 1).

Conclusively, there is a need for highly customised mobile interaction devices, which go beyond the capabilities of contemporary mobile devices. Thus, input, output, and

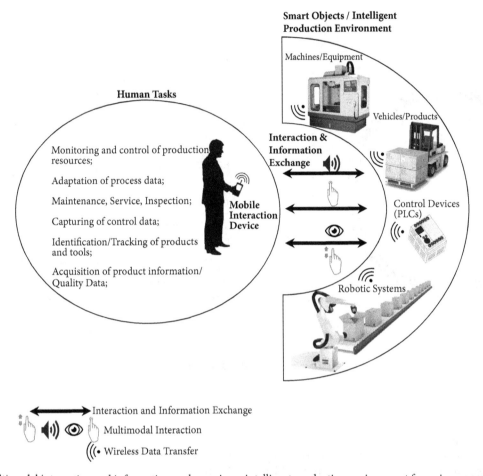

FIGURE 1: Multimodal interaction and information exchange in an intelligent production environment focussing on service processes.

communication devices have to fulfil a wide range of inter-action requirements. The reason lies not only in the fact that they are applied in different locations and situations but also because they have to be able to seamlessly integrate with the working context of the user. As such, devices must not only enable a seamless integration in the technical environment but also integrate with the activity of the user. As illustrated in Figure 1, mobile interaction devices are intermediary physical user interfaces acting as a means of interaction between the human and the environment [5]. The mobile interaction device supports the users accomplishing their primary tasks through explicit and implicit interaction. Typical tasks where a support through mobile interaction devices is possible are service processes. Service processes represent preventive or troubleshooting tasks which are performed in order to support the production process [6]. Apart from this, ser-vice processes are characterised through activities with an increased extent of mobility and thus often are performed in varying locations [7, 8].

Due to the need of enhanced capabilities of mobile inter-action devices, the design methods for mobile interaction devices will have to consider a wide spectrum of possible features as early as in the conceptualisation phase [9]. It becomes obvious from the industrial norm DIN EN ISO 9241-210:2011 (Human-centred design processes for inter-active systems/Ergonomics of human-system interaction) as illustrated in Figure 2 (left side) that the early phases of design processes during conceptualisation particularly include the first 2 phases of the user-centred design process. These formerly represent the task and user analysis, i.e., the analysis of user context and specification of requirements. Concurrently these represent the first 2 phases of the product development guideline VDI 2221 [10] as illustrated in Figure 2 (right side). The use of VDI 2221 as a sector-independent procedural guideline is recognised and recommended for development and engineering tasks of technical systems and products. Explicitly in these early design phases, there is a lack of methods and tools which allow a sufficient documentation, analysis, and communication of context of complex work situations [5]. In relation to intelligent production environ-ments, a major challenge for an appropriate design method is the sufficient incorporation of novel interaction concepts [11, 12] and user/usage requirements in the design process. Additionally, it has to be kept in mind that contemporary interaction devices such as control panels and operating device do not fully support potential interaction opportu-nities provided in intelligent environments (e.g., wireless and multimodal interfaces). Further on to guideline support,

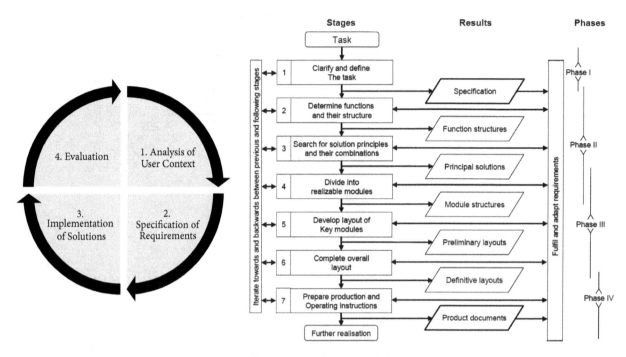

FIGURE 2: User-Centred Design Process according to DIN EN ISO 9241-210:2011 (left) and the product development process according to the guideline VDI 2221 (right).

existing guidelines and standards for user-centred design as various ISO guidelines such as the ISO 9241-210:2011 or the ISO TR 16982:2002 only provide a rough qualitative framework but do not consider the evolutionary steps of the product emergence [13, 14].

As a consequence, there is a need for appropriate methods and tools which not only support the efficient usage of the context in the conceptual design process but also facilitate the systematic description of the context in intelligent production environments [5]. Due to the high degree of complexity in intelligent production environments, it is not feasible for the designer to consider all contextual aspects of the working situation, without supportive methods and tools [15]. The specification of the contextual aspects can elementarily be described through models as suggested in model-based approaches for conceptual design of products and user interfaces [16–18, 18–20]. However, the essential and sufficient model elements that characterise an intelligent production environment are not adequately standardised. Further, if models were to include the different contextual elements necessary for describing intelligent production environments, it is still a contemporary issue to determine effective criteria and rules for mapping the model elements with one another [18]. Mapping of model elements refers to establishing descriptive or logical relations between the model elements as a basis for constructing rules how contextual elements are dependent upon each other. This is particularly relevant when the model is to be used as a data basis for a tool that supports the design process, as this would justify a connection between context and design information. Concurrently, the mapping of model

elements is crucial in the course of a tool for suggesting design recommendations for mobile interaction devices. Although the mapping of model elements has primarily been applied to challenges related to software user interface design (e.g., graphical user interfaces) it can be adopted to physical user interface design. This becomes obvious when logical relations between functionalities of user interfaces and the context of working situations are constructed. Under these circumstances, a relation to the "mapping problem" within the model-based design of software user interfaces can be established [21]. The mapping problem is described as the number of transformation rules which are required to transfer an abstract model to a concrete model [22]. While an abstract model can relate to the representation of user tasks, a concrete model represents the target platform where the user interface is to be implemented. The mapping problem itself originates from the modality theory and was described by Bernsen as "the general mapping problem" [23]: "For every information which is exchanged between the user and a system while performing a task, the input and output modalities are to be determined which offers the best solution for the representation and exchange of this information". When transferred to the context of physical user interfaces it can be interpreted that the technical functionalities of a mobile interaction device (concrete model) have to be in line with the context of the working situation (abstract model). In conjunction with our area, this means that the design recommendations of the functionalities of a mobile interaction device should be in line with the context of the working situation, the environment, and respective user group.

2. Materials and Methods

2.1. Related Work. When user requirements are to be integrated into the early design phases, often a mixture of qualitative and quantitative methods is common such as user studies, field and user trials, market studies, or interviews [24]. Since the early product development steps as promoted during the sketch phase where user context is analysed and specified are often characterised by loose creativity and innovation, software tools that provide a systematic design support in the sketch phase are rarely in use [25]. The reason is that loose creativity and innovation are more commonly supported by conceptual methods such as 635 Method, brainstorming, or storyboards than with specific software tools [26]. Moreover, information technology is limited to a more indirect role, such as providing structures for a quick idea exchange as in mind-maps or the preparation of sketches and initial drawings like in graphic design software such as Adobe Illustrator. On the other hand, for idea generation creative techniques like brainstorming or 635 Method are well known and used in product development; thus they still require a great deal of subjective interpretation to allow the practitioner to translate the results into tangible design features [27]. Regarding product development methods with a special focus on integrating customer requirements, it has been confirmed that methods which enable an active customer integration, in comparison to methods where customers, are integrated only passively and are more suitable for attaining customer knowledge within innovation development [28].

Having these aspects in mind, we discuss several design methods and tools in the following section. Notably, we have chosen methods and tools, which are in alignment with the criteria; they provide support in the early design phases and are fully or at least partially capable of integrating and considering user context. Thus, our intention was to uncover their strengths and limitations in accordance with the application to work situations and user interfaces in intelligent production environments.

2.1.1. Design Guidelines and Standards. Beside creative techniques, design guidelines and standards are well-established supportive tools for the early product development phases such as within the sketch phase and are nowadays in use in industry. As we have mentioned in the previous chapter, some of the most notorious guidelines are the ISO guidelines such as DIN EN ISO 9241-210:2011. This design standard is based on an iterative approach and runs through an unspecific number of design cycles until the final product is established. The decisions about which design techniques and tools are to be applied in the individual stages are among other aspects (e.g., company internal guidelines and checklists) dependent upon the preferences of the designer. The drawback of this kind of guidelines is however that they fail to consider all product variations and features [29]. Concerning mobile interaction devices, typical product features are represented through interaction features. This means that a guideline could be applicable to a mobile interaction device with conventional interaction possibilities. However, guidelines and standards are not sufficient in cases when more specific and advanced devices are required, such as devices supporting multimodal interaction. In this respect, ISO guidelines are usually much generalised and rarely of quantitative nature and thus are only sufficient for a concrete technology design up to a certain extent. Moreover, they are often described in descriptive texts and tables, which is not very much in line with preferences of product developers for the presentation or visualisation of design recommendations. Often these guidelines are complemented by company internal guidelines, such as user interface style guides and reference lists [30]. Due to the close conceptional relevance of some mobile interaction devices to mobile smart phones, design and user studies of modern smartphones and interaction concepts can be complementarily considered [31–35].

Complimentary to the abovementioned aspects and limitations, integrating the user context in the design process as early as possible is a primary aim in any respect in order to obtain mobile interaction devices which are fully in line with the aspects of the situation where the envisaged device is to be used.

2.1.2. Model-Based User Interface Development (MBUID) Tools. When regarding interaction design practices in human-computer interaction (HCI), the majority of approaches focus upon supporting the design process of software user interfaces [36, 37]. Thus, supporting the design process in this domain means to provide methods, tools, or frameworks, which support the user interface developer to implement software code on predefined platforms. Significant efforts are necessary to implement the user interface since the user interface must maintain compatibility to a variety of different platforms and support different modes of interaction. Having this in mind, the consideration of reusability, flexibility, and platform independence in user interface development has led to the proposal of model-based user interface development (MBUID) methods and tools [38]. These have been extensively discussed during the past 20 years for various individual aspects of software systems and for different application domains [39]. An established reference framework for model-based user interface development was developed in the European CAMELEON Project [40]. The reference framework is based on 4 layers, while the upper layers consist of the abstract and concrete models and the lower layer represents the software code of the user interface [41]. Another model-based development tool, focussing on the implementation of wearable user interfaces (WUI), called WUI-Toolkit, was proposed in [42]. Further well-known techniques and tools in the MBUID community were proposed by Puerta, Vanderdonckt, Luyten, Clerckx, and Calvary [38, 43–45]. However, in spite of the vast amount of research conducted in this area, only limited efforts have been spent so far in advancing model-based methods and tools for designing physical interaction components of industrial user interfaces [37]. Different from traditional mobile HCI where the physical platform or client often represented a GUI-based device such as a smartphone or tablet-PC, the physical platform can be any interactive physical object in the environment with processing capabilities and support different modes of interaction. This means that physical user interfaces supporting information exchange with the environment must be tailored to the specific interaction needs. A good example is represented by human-computer interaction scenarios, where the need for systematically conceptualising adequate technologies for interaction support becomes obvious.

2.1.3. Tools for Prototyping Physical Interaction. Prototyping of physical user interfaces is highly relevant to understanding physical interaction between the prototyping subject, i.e., the hardware component that can be any type of input/output device, embedded system or sensor/actuator, and the human. The design task itself is likely to be successful if the designer has sound technical understanding of the physical user interface and at the same time the required interaction procedures. For this purpose, a number of toolkits have emerged supporting different facets of physical prototyping of user interfaces [46–52]. Most well-known physical prototyping toolkits in the HCI domain include "Shared Phidgets" a toolkit for prototyping distributed physical user interfaces and "iStuff mobile" a rapid prototyping framework for exploring sensor-based interfaces with existing mobile phones [49]. Complimentarily there exist conceptual frameworks such as for tangible user interfaces, a paradigm of providing physical form to digital information, thus making bits directly manipulable [46]. Independent of the embedded characteristics of these toolkits and frameworks, prototyping physical interaction is specifically dominated by challenges such as programming interactions among physical and digital user interfaces, implementing functionality for different platforms and programming languages, and building customised electronic objects [52]. While the abovementioned toolkits are more or less subject to these challenges, more recent efforts such as the "ECCE Toolkit" successfully address these issues by substantially lowering the complexity of prototyping small-scale sensor-based physical interfaces [52]. In spite of these approaches, it must be noted that these tools usually support prototyping of a specific type or category of physical user interfaces (e.g., sensors). More important is the fact that these tools do not sufficiently consider processes and task descriptions and their concurrent interrelations to appropriate user interface functionalities.

2.1.4. Inclusive Design Toolkits. An approach to support the design process of physical interaction devices (e.g., keyboards, displays) was developed by the Engineering Design Centre of the University of Cambridge [29, 46]. The approach is based on a web-based toolkit called "Inclusive Design Toolkit," which can be considered as an online repository of design knowledge and interactive resources, leading to a proposal of inclusive design procedures and further more specific inclusive design tools, which designers may consult to accompany them through their product development process. In accordance with the definition of the British Standards Institution from 2005, inclusive design as such can be considered as a general design approach for products, services, and environments that include the needs of the

widest number of people in a wide variety of situations and to the greatest extent possible [53, 54]. Generally, inclusive design approaches are currently present in the consumer product sector. Although these approaches are more commonly applied to special user groups, from a technical point of view there exist no limits regarding its application to industrial products such as physical user interfaces. In this respect, inclusive design can be seen as progressive, goal-oriented process, an aspect of business strategy and design practice [46]. However, an application to industrial use cases is not feasible as the focus is upon fulfilling only the requirements of users but less upon the entire context of the application. Apart from this shortcoming, offered tools for inclusive design rely on the designers' assumptions; thus assumptions have a risk of not being accurate, which can drive to incorrect assessments [29]. For supporting the early design phase of user interfaces the University of Bremen developed a set of design tools which support designers of physical user interfaces from the sketch to the evaluation phase with a virtual user model [55]. The results of the related EU project VICON (http://www.vicon-project.eu) can be obtained from the open source platform Sourceforge and from the project website. Although the focus was primarily set upon users with special accessibility needs, the approach extends inclusive design principles by considering not only the user requirements but also complementarily other contextual aspects such as environmental context. Additionally, the approach implies model-based options for an adaptation upon other context domains beyond the consumer product sector.

2.1.5. Design Patterns. Another design approach which can be applied to physical user interfaces is the design pattern approach as described by [56]. The theoretical background of design patterns was proposed as early as in the 1960s by Christopher Alexander [57]. In the 1970s Alexander developed a pattern language for an architectural design where 253 design patterns were proposed with universal character [58]. These allow a catalogue style description of patterns based on their properties. In later years the design pattern theory was adopted to the area of software development [59, 60] as well as extended to other subdomains of computer science such as ubiquitous computing and interaction design [61]. More recently design pattern approaches have been applied to the context of adaptive user interfaces [56, 62], although up until now there exist no complete collection of design patterns regarding the reusability of physical interaction components.

Through the analysis of the abovementioned design methods, approaches, and tools, we have unveiled a number of limitations and insufficiencies regarding their application to designing physical user interfaces for intelligent production environments. These are summarised in Table 1.

In Figure 3 the functional requirements are summarised in relation to the limitations identified in Table 1.

Although the definition of an appropriate context model will be discussed in a later section, it is reasonable to consider the role of emotional awareness in designing physical user interfaces. Integrating emotions in context for developing emotional aware systems have been particularly investigated in several research papers [63–68]. In [63] an approach is

TABLE 1: User interface design methods and the limitations.

User Interface Design Methods	Limitations
Design Guidelines and Standards	(i) Descriptive and qualitative nature, not sufficient for detailed technology design (ii) Fail to consider all product variations and features (iii) Not in line with preferences of product developers for the presentation or visualisation of production processes design recommendations
Model-Based User Interface Development Tools	(i) Main focus upon software user interfaces (ii) Physical platform is predefined
Tools for Prototyping Physical Interaction	(i) No support in defining, configuring and integrating user context in the prototyping process (ii) Support of only certain categories of physical user interfaces and components
Inclusive Design Toolkits	(i) Considers only user context (ii) Major focus on consumer products Strong reliance on the designers' assumptions
Design Patterns	(i) No complete collection of design patterns regarding the reusability of physical interaction components

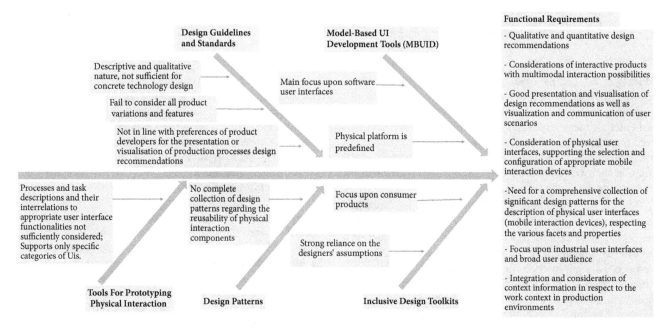

FIGURE 3: Limitations of user interface design methods and resulting functional requirements of an appropriate design method.

introduced for building shared digital spaces where emotional interaction occurs and is expressed according to the WYSIWIF (what you see is what I feel) paradigm. The concept focusses upon interpersonal communication use cases and, as such, ways of affective communication have been demonstrated through TUIs and component Phidgets as a means of a physical emotional communication device. In spite of the general notion that emotional awareness is more relevant to applications for consumers, it is complimentarily recognised that emotional aware techniques can also provide value for collaborative work scenarios, e.g., as a means of improving interaction among group members. A comprehensive survey of mobile affective sensing systems has been conducted in [64]. A major focus was on breaking down and understanding the interrelation of the elements of sensing, analysis and application when designing affective sensing

systems. For this purpose, a component model for affective sensing has been proposed, expressing that the most crucial challenges still rely on understanding the link between people's emotions and behaviour in different contexts yielding in the need of more sophisticated emotional models. From a more practical point of view, the aggregation of emotional data across places over time, privacy, and energy awareness is seen as the most significant challenges for implementing affective sensing systems. When viewing contemporary technologies, facial recognition, voice analytics, eye tracking, VR and AR technology, biosensors, and sentiment analysis are considered as key enabling technologies for realising emotional awareness in physical user interfaces [64, 65]. Furthermore, these technologies are necessary for making emotions machine-readable and interpretable. The most recent research efforts from 2015 until today see the greatest

TABLE 2: Dependence between functional and nonfunctional requirements.

Functional Requirements (FR)	Non-Functional Requirements	Non-Functional Requirements for software ISO/IEC 9126-1
FR1-Qualitative and quantitative design recommendations on a more comprehensive level or quantitative design recommendations	Applicability, Inferability, and Universality	Functionality
FR2-Considerations of interactive products with multimodal interaction possibilities; Consideration of physical user interfaces, supporting the selection and configuration of appropriate mobile interaction devices	Inferability and Analysability	Functionality, Maintainability
FR3-Good presentation and visualisation of design recommendations as well as visualisation and communication of user scenarios	Applicability and Analysability	Reliability, Maintainability
FR4-Need for a comprehensive collection of significant design patterns for the description of physical user interfaces (mobile interaction devices), respecting the various facets and properties	Reusability and Extensibility	Usability, Maintainability
FR5-Integration and consideration of context information in respect to the work context in intelligent production environments	Adaptability	Portability
FR6-Focus upon industrial user interfaces and a broad audience of users in mobile working situations	Applicability	Reliability, Usability

benefits of integrating emotional context through affective sensing systems in consumer-based applications such as marketing and consumer applications, health and wellbeing, and entertainment. This tendency unveils that there exists a need for more comprehensive research efforts regarding the value and implications of emotional awareness in professional domains such as in service processes in intelligent production environments.

Finally, the limitations in Table 1 served as an essential basis for us in order to define requirements for a design method appropriate for conceptualising mobile interaction devices in intelligent production environments. As the envisaged design method should not only be declarative but also provide mechanisms, which fulfil certain functions with qualitative criteria, it is reasonable to distinguish between functional requirements and nonfunctional requirements. Likewise, the differentiation between functional and nonfunctional requirements is well-established practice in requirements engineering [26]. In this manner, the identified limitations in Table 1 provided us with a basis for deriving functional and nonfunctional requirements for a respective design method.

2.2. Design Method Requirements. In accordance with the limitations defined in Table 1, it was possible for us to relate a number of functional requirements for an appropriate design method. Concurrently, the identified limitations represent functional limitations of existing design approaches with respect to designing physical user interfaces for intelligent production environments. The functional requirements are therefore directly derived from the respective functional limitation and can be considered as requirements for specific functionalities that an appropriate design method has to fulfil in order to provide a sufficient support for conceptualising mobile interaction devices.

Nonfunctional requirements, on the other hand, can be seen as quality criteria for a set of functional requirements, which can be applied to infer concrete procedures of the design method. When adopting a model-based character for the design method, generally valid requirements for reference models such as reusability, universality, adaptability, and recommending ability can serve as an orientation for defining nonfunctional requirements [57, 58]. Likewise, a set of nonfunctional requirements, which at the same time correspond to the general properties of reference models, can be derived from the above-defined functional requirements. These are illustrated and interrelated in Table 2. Concurrently the identified nonfunctional requirements additionally can be related to some of the major qualities of a software according to ISO/IEC 9126-1 (norm for product quality in software engineering). These are specifically functionality, reliability, usability, maintainability, and portability, which are mapped to the nonfunctional requirements for and functional requirements (FR) of the envisaged design method. Emphasizing the relation of functional and nonfunctional requirements of the design method to quality attributes for evaluating software makes sense as it enables a standardised validation process through well-defined and recognised validation criteria.

Under these circumstances, the nonfunctional requirements in Table 2 illustrate that there exists a connection between the qualitative characteristics of the envisaged design method and the general properties of reference models (middle column). This aspect underpins that the design method should incorporate a model-based character. In other words, the basis for designing mobile interaction devices for intelligent production environments should be represented by a model, which describes and interrelates the context of intelligent production environments. Concurrently, the model can be used in order to infer design recommendations and present these in a comprehensive way. In the next

TABLE 3: Procedural guidelines for the design method.

Non-Functional Requirements	Procedural Guideline	Functional Requirements
Universality	Identification of necessary partial models and their description in the style of working situations within a reference concept	FR5-Integration and consideration of context information in respect to the work context in intelligent production environments
Applicability, Inferability, Universality	Inclusion of a partial model, which incorporates potential design recommendations and interrelates these to remaining contextual elements	FR1-Qualitative and quantitative design recommendations on a more comprehensive level or quantitative design recommendations
Applicability and Analysability	Easy set-up and handling of partial models as well as their visual presentation	FR5-Integration and consideration of context information in respect to the work context in intelligent production environments FR3-Good presentation and visualisation of design recommendations as well as visualisation and communication of user scenarios
Inferability and Adaptability	Integration of a mechanism for the configuration of context elements supported by a modelling tool	FR5-Integration and consideration of context information in respect to the work context in intelligent production environments
Analysability and Inferability	Realisation of a well-defined rule framework between partial models as well as the selection and implementation of an appropriate analytical technique for validating the consistency of logical rules	FR6-Focus upon physically unimpaired users in mobile working situations FR2-Considerations of interactive products with multimodal interaction possibilities; Consideration of physical user interfaces, supporting the selection and configuration of appropriate mobile interaction devices FR3-Good presentation and visualisation of design recommendations as well as visualisation and communication of user scenarios
Inferability	Description of the context model in a semantic language in order to infer new knowledge based on existing knowledge (open world assumption). The interpretation and assessment of rules have to be ensured in order to infer new knowledge.	FR2-Considerations of interactive products with multimodal interaction possibilities; Consideration of physical user interfaces, supporting the selection and configuration of appropriate mobile interaction devices

section of the paper, the identified requirements will be consulted in order to develop concrete procedures and define a conceptional framework in alignment to the design method.

2.3. Conceptual Design Framework. In the preceding chapter, we pointed out that a key property of the design method is model-based, which results in the need for a model-based design method. In respect to the identified functional requirements (FR1-FR6), it is constructive that we consider models or modelling principles as one of the major means for attaining the functional requirements. Modelling principles likewise imply techniques and tools for establishing and combining information. In this case, the information is represented in context elements, which is particularly relevant for working situations in intelligent production environments. Through the qualitative analysis of the functional and nonfunctional requirements, it is possible for us to elaborate several tangible procedures, which can be directly incorporated into procedural guidelines of the design method. These are described in Table 3.

The compilation of the procedures in the table provides further insight regarding scope and structure of necessary context elements. As such, we propose that the sufficient

description of the context which, e.g., includes the working situation, the environment, and potential design recommendations can be described with specific partial models.

The aim at this point is described as identifying the scope and type of partial models that are sufficient for describing a context in intelligent production environments. The identification of relevant context elements is based upon a qualitative analysis regarding the categorisation of context for intelligent production environments. In this analysis, we identified necessary context elements and extended these into a context model for intelligent production environments. The foundation of the model is loosely related to Schmidt's model for context-aware computing [69]. The model of Schmidt proposes a context feature space for context-aware mobile computing that incorporates human and physical environment factors. On a high level, these factors can be interrelated to the functional requirement FR5—integration and consideration of context information in respect to the work context in intelligent production environments. Having this in mind, Schmidt's model was considered as a rudimentary basis for specifying the context in intelligent production environments. Figure 4 illustrates an extended context model for intelligent production environments, where Schmidt's

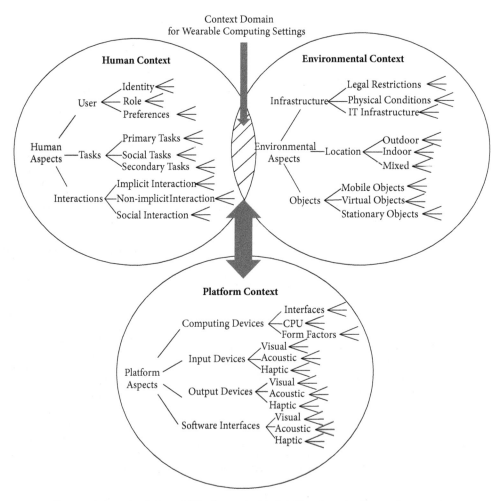

FIGURE 4: An extended model for the context in intelligent production environments.

model was used as a basis [8]. The extended context model focusses towards supporting the design of wearable computing systems in intelligent production environments. Likewise, wearable computing systems consist of configurable input and output devices and offer advanced interaction opportunities to the user. Accordingly, they represent mobile interaction devices in the broader sense. Pertaining to the model of Schmidt, we have maintained the differentiation between human and environmental context. These context elements are concurrently connected to the functionalities and properties of a potential mobile interaction device. In this scheme, human context is directly related to the role of the users, tasks, and interactions with the environment. All situations that can be captured with human senses are relevant here. The environmental context is defined through a type of context that may result from human context and that can be captured with the help of an intermediary system [70]. Thus, an intermediary system can be represented by a technical device that is capable of capturing environment data for instance through sensors. As such, the environmental context is a dynamic context like physical conditions of a working environment (e.g., light conditions, infrastructure,

and temperature), as well as the technical properties and artefacts of the environment.

The underlying idea of the extended model is based on the assumption that human and environmental context directly affects the type of interaction resource and interaction modality of the envisaged interaction device. Therefore a partial model describing the characteristics of potential interaction devices is necessary which is referred to as "platform context" in the extended context model in Figure 4. Notably, the area where human context and environmental context is connected over different instances can be regarded as the context domain of a mobile interaction device. The reason is that it represents the area where both human and environmental contexts are directly connected to the platform context. As an example, considering solely very bright light conditions in the working environment may lead to the design recommendation of a light adaptive display. However, when also considering the human context, e.g., that the primary task of the user requires full visual attention, the resulting design recommendation would be further constrained and consequently lead to an alternative design recommendation for the related platform. This

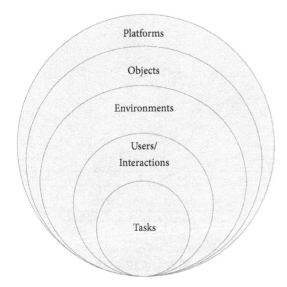

FIGURE 5: The context elements for an appropriate context model.

example shows that considering only human context is not sufficient to acquire a valid recommendation for the most appropriate platform. Moreover, we think it is necessary to consider all relevant contextual aspects and their mutual impacts in order to attain a valid design recommendation for the most appropriate mobile platform. Accordingly, we have consulted the extended context model in Figure 4 for identifying the most significant context elements for setting up an appropriate context model. For this purpose, it is constructive to cluster the context elements of the extended context model according to their correlation. Elements that have a high correlation can be united to a single context element. As a result, six context elements were abstracted which concurrently implies all context main and subelements of the extended context model, as highlighted in Figure 5. With the identified context elements, it is possible to specify the context model more comprehensively. Six context elements can be transferred into six individual partial models. From this perspective, the different context elements provide insight into the scope and type of possible partial models for the design method. However, when considering that an implementation of the context model is foreseen, the complexity of the model should be held as low as possible while maintaining functional requirements. This means that the fulfilment of the requirement universality of the context model yields in describing context elements in a higher level of abstraction. This prevents the consideration of interactions as a means of refinement/detailing of work tasks. Moreover, we propose to rather consider interaction constraints, interaction preferences, and exemplary interactions since these are likely to have a direct impact on the type of interaction resources. When the user interactions are reduced to interaction constraints of the user, the interaction model can be merged into the user model that results to one partial model. In detail, this means that six context elements are the basis for five partial models, namely, task model, user model, environment model, object model, and platform model.

In spite the fact that the six context elements in Figure 5 are sufficient for describing the context in an intelligent production environment, the model does not yet incorporate design recommendations that are necessary in order to gain qualitative design recommendations as a main function of the design method. In alignment with the model-based character, we find it reasonable that the context model should, therefore, include design recommendations as an additional context element resulting to an additional partial model. This additional partial model provides the necessary data basis for inferring design recommendations, which implies that there must be data relations between the design recommendations and all other remaining context elements. Strictly speaking, the recommendation model possesses data relations to all other partial models such as task model, user model, environment model, object model, and platform model. In this way, the extended context model can be leveraged to include seven context elements that are the basis for six partial models. The partial models as highlighted in the upper right side in Figure 6 include task model, user model, environment model, object model, platform model, and recommendation model. The first four partial models, namely, task model, user model, environment model, object model, and platform model, provide context information for potential aspects of a working situation in an intelligent production environment. When these are interlinked with the recommendation model, the initial basis is finally prepared for an overall, functional context model.

Structure and contents of the context model represent a formal collection of terminologies or in other words a terminological reference framework for a specific application domain. This view is in line with the notion of an ontology. Accordingly, it is legitimate to describe the partial models of the context model as an ontology. In this way, the model data is applied as a representation of the context. One of the main advantages of describing partial models in a semantic language like OWL (Web Ontology Language) is that already existing information is not negated when subjoining new information (Open World Assumption). Concurrently this is the necessary condition in order to be able to infer new knowledge. As a consequence, the six partial models can be realised on the basis of ontology classes.

Figure 7 highlights the data interrelations described in the data properties between the recommendation model and the task model of the overall context model. The example describes an inspection process (class) where testing (instance) is required. The description of the inspection task within the ontology implies the description of the required component and functionality of the interaction device as a data property. Thus, the functionality is described as input, output, and communication functionality, while the relevant component is described as input, output, and a communication unit. On this level, data relations to the recommendation model are established through the matching terms included in the descriptions of the data properties. Considering the recommendation class "implicit_interaction_identification_techniques", the data relation to the task model that means the description of the required functionality and components for the corresponding recommendation are defined. The data

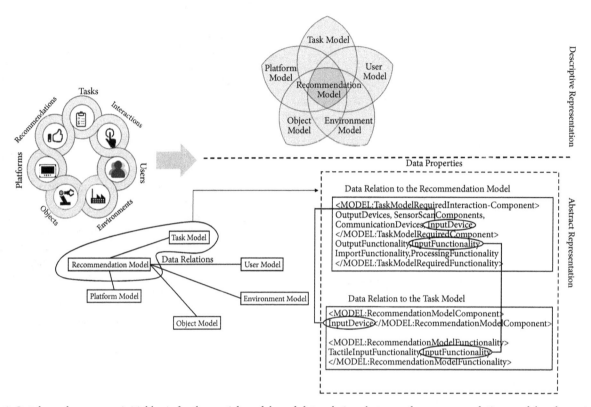

FIGURE 6: Ontology classes as an initial basis for the partial models and data relations between the recommendation model and remaining partial models.

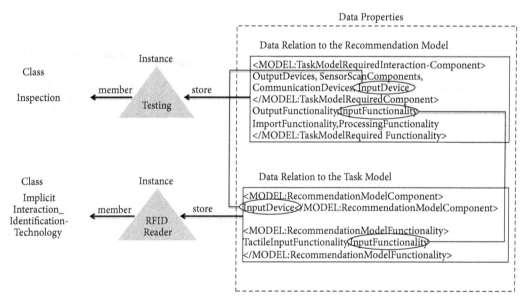

FIGURE 7: Example of data relations between the recommendation model and task model.

interrelation represents the basis for specifying logical rules with the support of a reasoning engine while a reasoner is able to identify data properties between the partial models that correspond to one another and infer a logical rule. As a result, an input device as a communication device, which supports implicit interaction (RFID reader), is recommended. The

relations of the remaining ontology classes such as user, environment, object, and platform also include descriptions of the data relations to the recommendation model. Vice versa, the recommendation model is defined by data relations to the remaining partial models. As such, these are handled in the same manner as described with the task model. As

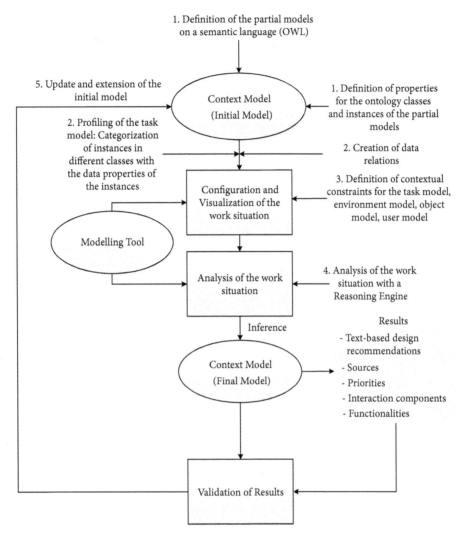

1. Definition of the partial models
on a semantic language (OWL)

5. Update and extension of the
initial model

Context Model
(Initial Model)

1. Definition of properties
for the ontology classes
and instances of the partial
models

2. Profiling of the task
model: Categorization
of instances in
different classes with
the data properties of
the instances

2. Creation of data
relations

3. Definition of contextual
constraints for the task model,
environment model, object
model, user model

Configuration and
Visualization of the
work situation

Modelling Tool

Analysis of the work
situation

4. Analysis of the work
situation with a
Reasoning Engine

Inference

Results
- Text-based design
recommendations
- Sources
- Priorities
- Interaction components
- Functionalities

Context Model
(Final Model)

Validation of Results

FIGURE 8: Procedural model for the design method.

a consequence, each recommendation (E1...En) is defined through data properties of the instances of the ontology classes.

2.4. Procedural Model for the Design Method. According to the procedural guidelines identified in the preceding section, we propose the corresponding procedure model in Figure 8. The procedure model is initiated by the procedure of constructing six partial models, yielding to a basic context model that combines all six partial models into an initial model. The requirement for setting up the initial model is described stepwise as follows:

(1) Definition of partial models in a semantic language and definition of data properties (i.e., name, real value, and category) for all six ontology classes and instances. This implies manually defining the properties of the ontology classes and partial models.

(2) Profiling of the task model and creation of data relations.

The task model should follow the predefined task definitions, which are configured to match mobile working situations in production environments. For this purpose, we have chosen a generic and standardised task description based upon the task catalogue for maintenance according to the DIN 31051 (German industrial standard for the fundamentals of maintenance). In this respect, profiling is a necessary step in order to pursue a task and activity selection. To achieve this, the instances (activities) are grouped into different classes (tasks) according to their data properties. At the same time, data relations between the instances and ontology classes are defined as a foundation for the generation of rules. Through completing these two steps, the requirement for the configuration of the working situation is prepared and the manual configuration of a working situation is conducted, which leads to the third step in the procedural model.

(3) The configuration of the working situation. This step takes place manually with the support of a modelling tool.

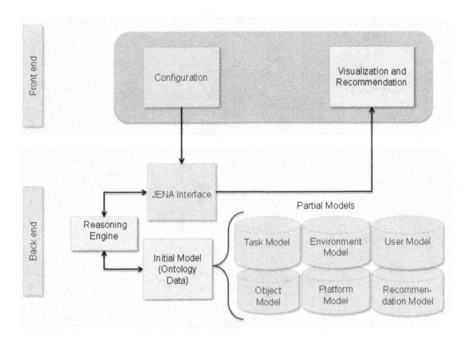

FIGURE 9: System architecture of the modelling tool.

For this purpose, the task of the user is specified with the task model by selecting predefined tasks and activities in accordance with the work situation. As such, the basis for the modelling of the work situation is the database of the initial model. In order to enable and visualise the configuration process, we propose to apply a modelling tool, which shall be described in a later section. After the tasks of the working situation are selected, a number of text-based design recommendations are presented. Subsequently, further contextual constraints such as environmental aspects, interaction and user constraints, user preferences, and object aspects are defined with the modelling tool.

(4) Analysis of the work situation with a reasoning engine as an integral part of the modelling tool.

This is carried out automatically through the principle of inference. Through this approach new knowledge is inferred from existing knowledge (within the initial model), which finally is incorporated in the final model. Practically this implies that the amount of context information is reduced to the specific context-dependent information. The result is a list of text-based design recommendations in accordance with platform components, functionalities, and variations, which refer to a specific production context of an intelligent production environment.

(5) Validation of the results.

In this final manual step, potential contradictions and inconsistencies are uncovered, which might lead to an adaptation of the initial model such as the introduction of new data interrelations. Thus, an adaptation or extension of partial models is required in order to add new expert knowledge and can be practically performed through an ontology.

2.5. Implementation of the Modelling Tool. The implementation of the modelling tool as seen in Figure 9 is technically regarded as an implementation of the system architecture of the required modelling tool. At the same time it is important to note that the implementation of the modelling tool can be considered as a major part of formalizing the design method. This is because the modelling tool incorporates and connects the context models on the basis of an ontology as discussed in the preceding sections. Based on the requirements and guidelines elaborated in the last sections, Figure 9 presents the system architecture of a prototypical modelling tool that is composed of a front end (user interface) and backend (reasoning engine and ontology model). As illustrated in the third and fourth step of the procedural model in Figure 8, the modelling tool should allow the configuration, visualisation, and analysis of the work situation, as well as the output of design recommendations. In order to fulfil these requirements, the configuration of the work situation is accomplished with the ontology data of the partial model (initial model) in the backend sphere. Thus, to process the ontology data, we have applied the Apache Jena Framework. Jena as such provides a collection of tools and Java libraries to develop Java applications. As a rule-based inference system, Jena includes a reasoning engine. The reasoning engine is responsible for analysing the consistency of ontology data and assessing the rule framework. Due to this inference process, the final model is created. Finally, the created ontology data of the partial models are imported and exported through the Jena interface.

Figure 10 provides an overview of the initial model, which is represented by the ontology data of the six partial models.

A more comprehensive overview of the database of the partial models is made visible by applying the prototypical

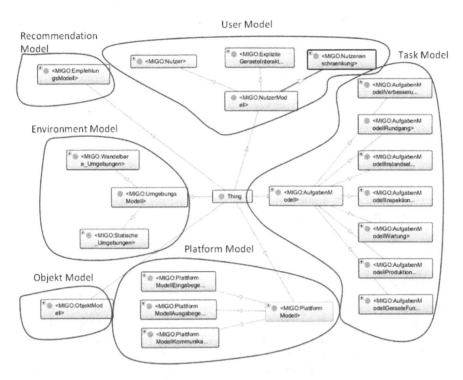

FIGURE 10: Visualisation of the initial model as an ontology.

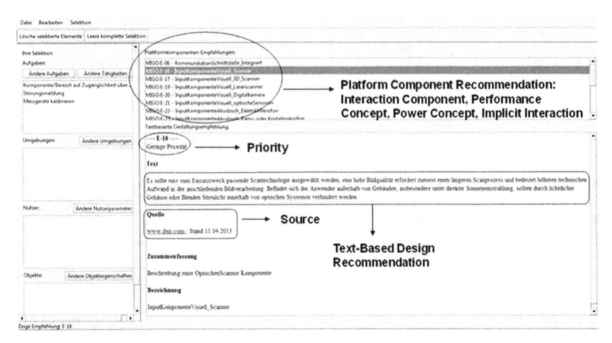

FIGURE 11: The graphical user interface of the prototypical modelling tool.

modelling tool. The focus of the modelling tool is restricted to the data basis of the partial models, and as such to the sequential configuration of a mobile work situation within a production scenario in order to acquire appropriate physical platform components and design recommendations for conceptualising mobile interaction devices. These are to be in line with the predefined context of a mobile work situation.

The necessary steps that lead to a design recommendation are dependent upon 4 modelling steps by configuring tasks, environment, user, and objects. Figure 11 shows the original version of the graphical user interface (front end) of the prototypical modelling tool. We have programmed the modelling tool in Java with the support of the Java Development Kit (JDK) and the Java Runtime Environment (JRE). The

TABLE 4: Validation results of the modelling tool according to nonfunctional qualities of software systems.

Non-Functional Qualities according to ISO/IEC 9126-1	Low Fulfilment	Medium Fulfilment	High Fulfilment
Functionality			X
Reliability		X	
Usability	X		
Maintainability	X		
Portability		X	

layout of the user interface and the arrangement of the functional icons follow a classical programming structure.

Figure 11 was at the same time the basis for a technical validation and an evaluation with end users.

3. Results and Discussion

3.1. Validation and Evaluation of the Modelling Tool. We have conducted the validation of the modelling tool through the configuration of a representative working situation and comparison to the internal data relations of the model [5]. As such, the validation provides the evidence that the modelling tool and finally the design method is capable of continuously generating the appropriate design recommendations for mobile interaction devices, which are in line with a specified work situation. As a typical work situation, we have chosen a maintenance process in a production environment where troubleshooting and calibration represent the tasks that are performed. In the work situation, the user is interacting with tools, wearing protective gloves and prefers visual data acquisition. We have further conducted the verification of the design recommendations on basis of the ontology data of the initial model. For every stepwise configuration of the work situation (task, environment, user, and object), the data relation of the design recommendation has been manually read out of the data model and documented. Afterwards, we have compared these results to the results provided by the modelling tool when successively configuring the described work situation. The results confirm that the manually determined recommendations are fully in line with the results determined by the modelling tool. This means the manually determined design recommendations from the initial model are identical to the automatically determined design recommendation by the reasoning engine. The identification of inconsistencies would have been an evidence that there is a bug in the data relations, which might lead to different or inappropriate recommendations.

Afterwards, we have performed the evaluation of the design method in cooperation with design experts from several companies. Among the participants were user interface designers, mobile technology developers, and technical consultants. The purpose was to test the method in practice in order to gather feedback from designers regarding the applicability and usability of the method. The evaluation involved the usage of the modelling tool while configuring a given mobile service process. Subsequently, the designers answered an online questionnaire in LimeSurvey, an open

source online survey tool. As a use case, we have selected an inspection process in a factory plant as this represents a typical process where large amounts of data have to be collected by interacting with the environment with the help of physical user interfaces. To support the participants, we have described the inspection process as a comprehensive text, while highlighting certain keywords (process steps and tasks), which can be easily identified in the modelling tool. A time slot of seven days with three days follow-up was predetermined for the participants. The whole evaluation process, which involved installing the modelling tool, configuring the use case, and answering the online questionnaire, took averagely 45-60 minutes per participant. Although 22 companies confirmed their participation, only the representatives of 11 companies practically conducted the whole evaluation. The results of the evaluation were significantly constructive for the refinement of the modelling tool, which is described in the next chapter.

During the configuration of the use case, the majority of the participants had difficulties to distinguish clearly between the context elements user tasks and user interactions as according to the proposed context model, tasks, and interactions were integrated into one single submodel. While configuring the process some participants expressed the requirement to be able to add individually and more detailed defined context elements, which go beyond the data basis of the initial model. Regarding the quality of the design recommendations, the majority of the participants considered these as comprehensive. Besides, the participants perceived the design recommendations as beneficial since they still left enough space for implementing creative efforts of the designers. However, the participants had a consensus that the visual presentation of the design recommendations should be improved since the modelling tool claims to provide a significant benefit in the early design process. In this respect, the use of examples with images such as illustrations of the platform components was proposed.

Table 4 provides an overview up to what qualitative extent the modelling tool fulfils the nonfunctional qualities of a software according to ISO/IEC 9126-1. Classifications between low, medium, and high fulfilment are based on the feedback of the evaluation results.

Usability and maintainability were considered as being fulfilled to a low extent since; e.g., the presentation and visualisation of design recommendations as well as the limitation regarding extension were unsatisfactory to the majority of the participants. In addition, the user interface

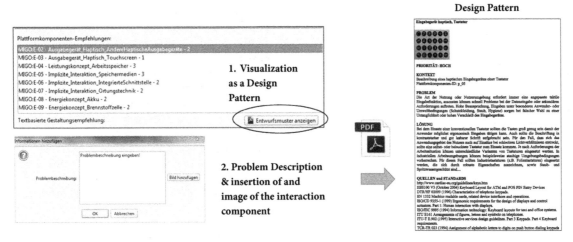

FIGURE 12: Extension of the modelling tool with a functionality for an automatic generation of design patterns.

for configuring the work situations was not implemented in a self-explaining manner and thus still has room for further improvement. On the other hand, functionality in the sense of general applicability and inferability, namely, obtaining design recommendations from context, was perceived very well be the participants.

3.2. Refinement of the Modelling Tool.

The refinement of the modelling tool focussed upon two major aspects identified during the evaluation: the extension of the context model and the improvement of the visual representation of the design recommendations.

For this purpose, we suggested incorporating a technique that improves the visual presentation of design recommendations and at the same time ensures capturing and integration of expert knowledge in a straightforward way. When considering design pattern techniques as described by [56, 61], it appears reasonable to apply this approach in the design method. The advantages of this form of information presentation lie particularly in the standardised structuring and processing of design information. Concurrently, this may lead to a simplification of design information exchange and reuse between design teams. Besides, a better visualisation and communication of design recommendations can be achieved by applying a mechanism that compiles text-based design information to a PDF file, which follows the structure of a design pattern. The objective from a designer perspective would be to have a tool that automatically generates design patterns from acquired design recommendations, which originate from the data of the initial model. This means that instead of relying on a collection of existing design patterns and matching these to a given context, the approach here pursues to create the design patterns from the obtained platform components and design recommendations.

In this manner, we decided to extend the modelling tool with a functionality that enables the automatic generation of physical design patterns as highlighted in Figure 12. In order to demonstrate the feasibility of this approach, we found it reasonable to realise twenty exemplary design patterns, consisting of input, output, and communication devices.

Subsequently, we have implemented an automatic mechanism in the modelling tool that enables an automatic generation of design patterns based on the design recommendations of the tool. The design patterns can then further be grouped according to their affiliation to ontology subclasses and instances with the aim of validating the consistency of design patterns for a certain working situation. This means design patterns belonging to the same ontology subclasses and instances can be grouped by a certain category, while design patterns with overlapping ontology subclasses and instances can be considered interrelated. For example, two design patterns describing a keyboard and a flexible display, although mainly possessing different ontology subclasses and instances, could both belong to the task instance "maintenance" and therefore be regarded as interrelated to one another. Subsequently, for a configured work situation, although design patterns belonging to different subclasses and instances are suggested, it can nevertheless be assumed that there exists a relation between these individual design patterns. Finally, related design patterns are more likely to be appropriate for a certain work situation than design patterns, which are not related in any sense. Thus, the property of relations between design patterns represents one of the main requirements of a design pattern language, which is a good basis for an extension of this work.

The solution space of the platform component consists of a text-based recommendation, a description of the functionality, of the platform component, the variations, and the sources as illustrated exemplarily in Figure 13.

In alignment with the introduction of design patterns, we believe it is a reasonable path to facilitate the creation of additional design patterns based on the expertise of the designers. The creation of additional design patterns would fulfil the requirement of ensuring a continuous update of the design recommendations and platform components. Vice versa, extending design patterns by the users of the modelling tool indirectly leads to an extension of the context model as suggested during the evaluation process. This becomes obvious when the considering that the data from the additional design patterns can be seamlessly integrated into the

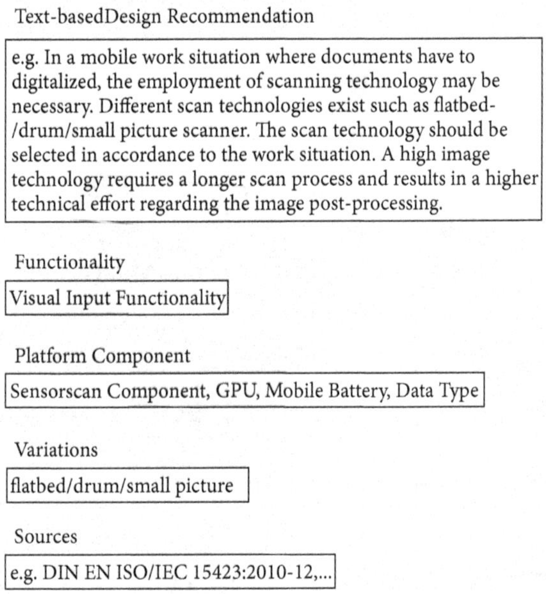

Text-basedDesign Recommendation

e.g. In a mobile work situation where documents have to
digitalized, the employment of scanning technology may be
necessary. Different scan technologies exist such as flatbed-
/drum/small picture scanner. The scan technology should be
selected in accordance to the work situation. A high image
technology requires a longer scan process and results in a higher
technical effort regarding the image post-processing.

Functionality

Visual Input Functionality

Platform Component

Sensorscan Component, GPU, Mobile Battery, Data Type

Variations

flatbed/drum/small picture

Sources

e.g. DIN EN ISO/IEC 15423:2010-12,...

FIGURE 13: Solution space for the design recommendation.

platform and recommendation models. At the same time,
this approach would grant dynamic properties to the context
model.

Under the premise that these approaches are integrated
into the procedural model in Figure 8, the model is refined
and extended with respect to the procedural steps. Figure 14
illustrates the procedural model of the design method, which
is extended by the feature of visualising and generating design
patterns. The lower part of the model shows the extended
procedural steps of the design method. From a practical
point of view, the functionality of creating design recommendations is employed in the modelling tool by a designated
functionality that automatically retrieves the design pattern,
which corresponds to the particular design recommendation.
As mentioned, the design pattern follows the composition
of HCI design patterns, which incorporates a description of
the context, problem, solution, and an image of the platform
component. However, the design recommendation and the
platform component information do not per default include
a description of the problem and an image of the mobile
interaction device.

Therefore, it is necessary to complement this information
a priori to the design pattern generation in order to bring the
design pattern in line with the HCI design pattern structure.
Finally, the emerged design patterns are crosschecked and
validated by an expert and subsequently incorporated in the
initial model. In this manner, it is ensured that the data of
the initial model is continuously updated and thus upgraded
from a nonfunctional perspective with dynamical properties.

3.3. Potentials of the Modelling Tool. In the first version of the
modelling tool as described in Section 2.5, the design recommendations are prioritised regarding their relevance, based
upon the approval of the applied user interface technologies

in practice. However, the prioritisation is limited by a fixed
predefinition in the initial model (high, medium, and low),
which does not provide a mechanism to further distinguish
between same priority levels of design recommendations.
Practically, this means that two or more design recommendations having the same priority levels and belonging to
the same type of interaction component are not further
distinguished. This leads to the fact that the designer has to
decide which design recommendation is most suitable for the
work context. Through dynamically assigning priority levels
to the design recommendations, it would be possible to differ,
e.g., between relevant and optional design recommendations.
This could be achieved by employing an intelligent algorithm,
which may keep track of how often a design recommendation
has been proposed and employed for a certain work context.

A further aspect was the implication of the design
recommendations upon the overall user interface concept
when concurrently implementing multiple design recommendations. Likely, the implementation of a quantitative
design recommendation may have a negative implication
(undesired effect) on other interaction components; i.e.,
design recommendations may affect each other when these
are all implemented. As an example, a recommendation of a
discrete distance between the keys of a keyboard may lead
to the situation that the arrangement and form factor of
nearby interaction components are affected accordingly. In
order to minimise this effect, it is necessary to investigate the
contextual relations between design recommendations more
thoroughly. A major step could be to define dependencies
between design patterns, which may result in developing
a pattern language. Conclusively, we believe that the conception of a design pattern language for mobile interaction
devices in intelligent production environments should lead
to a significant contribution to the advancement of design
pattern languages. However, at this point, the necessity for
the development of a design pattern language is less an
issue for qualitative design patterns because of the broader
design space and a higher freedom of design. As qualitative
recommendations are more suitable for the realisation of
new user interface concepts, quantitative recommendations
are more efficient for the refinement and adaptation of
existing user interface concepts. For this reason, we advise
considering a balance between qualitative and quantitative
design recommendations.

4. Conclusions

In this paper, we dealt with the realisation of a design method
for conceptualising physical user interfaces, namely, mobile
interaction devices for intelligent production environments.
The analysis of the state of the art had the aim of identifying
the shortcomings of existing design methods, tools, and
techniques. This enabled us to derive a series of functional
and nonfunctional requirements. These were interrelated to
one another while construing (at this point loosely defined)
procedural guidelines for a suitable design method, which
yielded in a comprehensive procedural model. In alignment
with the procedural model, we proposed a model-based
conceptual framework, which considers the scope, structure,

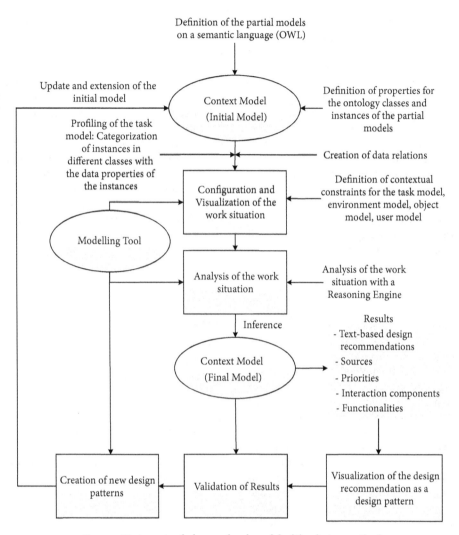

FIGURE 14: An extended procedural model of the design method.

and modelling techniques for describing the features of mobile interaction devices. Thus, in line with the notion of a model-based framework, we further proposed an ontology-based context model, which consists of six interrelated partial models that provide the means for describing intelligent production contexts. Correspondingly, we suggested the need for a modelling tool, which enables not only the configuration of work situations but also the inference of design recommendations through the utilisation of a reasoning technique. This allows the elaboration of text-based design recommendations in relation to platform components and their priority level for mobile interaction devices.

The implementation of a modelling tool as a part of the design method was achieved through the implementation of a system architecture, which includes all modules required for the applying of the design method. Within the prototypical version of the modelling tool, we managed to demonstrate that a series of design recommendations are inferred, including also those recommendations that are not explicitly excluded. Due to this fact, the design recommendations were categorised context-dependently according to "high," "medium," and "low" priority.

We have then enhanced the prototypical modelling tool with the additional functional requirement of considering an improvement of the visualisation of design recommendations and an extension of the context model. In this respect, we have introduced a mechanism that enables the automatic generation of design patterns from the context-dependent design recommendations and platform components. In close correlation to this feature, we have recognised that there is a need for a feature that ensures that the underlying context model is continuously held up to date. For this purpose, we have employed a feature that enables an on-demand creation of additional design patterns while integrated into the initial model. In summary, this led to a revised procedural model for the design method.

We note that the challenges incorporated with the early design phases in user interface conceptualisation are not yet entirely exploited. The fact that intelligent production environments are characterised by cyberphysical systems will increase the need for specialised mobile interaction devices, which support the interaction with distributed information in the cyberphysical work environment. As a consequence, methods and tools, which consider and efficiently utilise the context within the product development process, will play a significant role. Moreover, it will eventually be recognised that emotional awareness is an equally important context element, which cannot be neglected in the early design phases. Examples include maintenance processes and collaborative working in intelligent production environments where emotions as fear, inconvenience, fatigue, boredom, and distraction can have a severe impact on safety conditions and quality of work of the human.

Conclusively, in economic terms, within the design organizations and divisions, we consider that supporting methods and tools should be able to seamlessly integrate into already existing development processes. Particularly, methods and tools which are least-disruptive regarding existing and well-established design processes will possess the potential to be accepted by product-developing companies in the long run.

5. Outlook and Future Work

In this paper, we have set the focus on the early design phase (sketch phase) of mobile interaction devices, particularly suitable for work situations concerning intelligent production environments. Beyond the sketch phase, the proposed context model definitely possesses the potential to be integrated and utilised in the CAx design phase. Hence, the advantage of this possibility lies in the realisation of (data) annotations to priority existing 3D conceptional designs of product data models. Accordingly, in the EU research project VICON (http://www.vicon-project.eu) first approaches were developed for realising annotations between product data models and design recommendations from the sketch phase. This approach and the underlying techniques were demonstrated with quantitative design recommendations for user interfaces of mobile phones and washing machines. It is conceivable that these results may be used effectively for leveraging the introduced design method to be integrated into the CAx design phase. Next to the integration in the CAx design phase, we definitely see a great potential for integrating our modelling approach with prototyping tools for physical interaction such as for tangible user interfaces and phidget components. In this respect, the formal presentation of design recommendations of our modelling tool can be construed as XML-defined design patterns in order to achieve an interoperability with physical UI prototyping tools such as the ECCE toolkit and vice versa [52]. In this way, process and tasks configurations for work situations and their interrelation to design recommendations can be seamlessly integrated on an abstract level, complementing the contemporary features of physical UI prototyping tools.

Apart from the challenges related to the subsequent design phases, we expect that software user interfaces will converge with physical user interfaces. An appropriate example which highlights this paradigm is to consider touch screens, as hardware and software elements are directly entangled with one another. Thus, design methods in this area should be capable of considering both development strands. Additionally, due to the continuous advancement of mobile interaction devices including wearable technology, we anticipate that adaptive hardware concepts will play an increasingly

vital role in cyberphysical production environments. Further, we believe that it is likely that adaptive physical user interfaces are capable of coping with a wide range of situations, as it is currently possible with discrete mobile interaction devices. Thereby, new requirements and possibilities will emerge within user interface design. It will be less the case to uncover relations between interaction concepts and work situations. Moreover, the point will be to describe the spectrum of configuration possibilities of adaptive interaction devices in relation to different work situations. When we consider the continuous emergence of the fourth industrial revolution, it is reasonable to predict that adaptive hardware concepts will be a well-established interaction concept in the future. This tendency will concurrently foster new paradigms in product development, which possess the potential of dissolving the limitations between the design process and the designed artefact.

References

[1] C. Courage and K. Baxter, *Understanding Your Users: A Practical Guide to User Requirements Methods*, Morgan Kaufmann, 2005.

[2] B. Buxton, *Sketching User Experiences: Getting the Design Right and the Right Design*, Morgan Kaufmann, 2010.

[3] M. E. Porter and J. E. Heppelmann, "How Smart, Connected Products Are Transforming Companies," *Harvard Business Review*, vol. 93, no. 10, pp. 96–114, 2015.

[4] R. Schmidt, M. Möhring, R.-C. Härting, C. Reichstein, P. Neumaier, and P. Jozinovic, "Industry 4.0-potentials for creating smart products: empirical research results," in *Proceedings of the International Conference on Business Information Systems*, pp. 16–27, 2015.

[5] P. T. Kirisci, *Gestaltung mobiler Interaktionsgeräte: Modellierung für intelligente Produktionsumgebungen [Design of mobile interaction devices: Modelling for intelligent production environments]*, 1 Auflage. Springer Vieweg, 2016.

[6] S. Biege, G. Lay, and D. Buschak, "Mapping service processes in manufacturing companies: Industrial service blueprinting," *International Journal of Operations and Production Management*, vol. 32, no. 8, pp. 932–957, 2012.

[7] T. W. Zängler, *Mikroanalyse des Mobilitätsverhaltens in Alltag und Freizeit*, Springer, Berlin, Germany, 2000.

[8] P. Kirisci, E. Morales-Kluge, E. Angelescu, and K.-D. Thoben, "Design of Wearable Computing Systems for Future Industrial Environments," in *Handbook of Research on Mobility and Computing: Evolving Technologies and Ubiquitous Impacts and Computing*, pp. 1226–1246, IGI Global, 2011.

[9] D. Holman, A. Girouard, H. Benko, and R. Vertegaal, "The design of organic user interfaces: Shape, sketching and hypercontext," *Interacting with Computers*, vol. 25, no. 2, pp. 133–142, 2013.

[10] J. Jänsch and H. Birkhofer, "The development of the guideline VDI 2221 - The change of direction," in *Proceedings of the 9th International Design Conference, DESIGN 2006*, pp. 45–52, Croatia, May 2006.

[11] K. Luyten, C. Vandervelpen, and K. Coninx, "Task modeling for ambient intelligent environments: Design support for situated

task executions," in *Proceedings of the 4th International Workshop on Task Models and Diagrams, TAMODIA '05*, pp. 87–94, Gdansk, Poland, September 2005.

[12] E. Riedenklau, *Development of Actuated Tangible User Interfaces: New Interaction Concepts and Evaluation Methods*, Bielefeld University, 2016.

[13] N. Bevan, J. Carter, and S. Harker, "Iso 9241-11 revised: What have we learnt about usability since 1998?" *Lecture Notes in Computer Science (including subseries Lecture Notes in Artificial Intelligence and Lecture Notes in Bioinformatics): Preface*, vol. 9169, pp. 143–151, 2015.

[14] N. Bevan, "International standards for HCI and usability," *International Journal of Human-Computer Studies*, vol. 55, no. 4, pp. 533–552, 2001.

[15] P. T. Kirisci and K.-D. Thoben, "The role of context for specifying Wearable computers," in *Proceedings of the 3rd IASTED International Conference on Human-Computer Interaction, HCI 2008*, pp. 248–253, Austria, March 2008.

[16] M. M. Andreasen, "Modelling—The Language of the Designer," *Journal of Engineering Design*, vol. 5, no. 2, pp. 103–115, 1994.

[17] G. Maarten Bonnema and F. J. A. M. van Houten, "Use of models in conceptual design," *Journal of Engineering Design*, vol. 17, no. 6, pp. 549–562, 2006.

[18] M. Modzelewski, M. Lawo, P. Kirisci et al., "Creative Design for Inclusion Using Virtual User Models," in *Computers Helping People with Special Needs*, vol. 7382 of *Lecture Notes in Computer Science*, pp. 288–294, Springer Berlin Heidelberg, Berlin, Germany, 2012.

[19] P. Biswas, P. Robinson, and P. Langdon, "Designing inclusive interfaces through user modeling and simulation," *International Journal of Human-Computer Interaction*, vol. 28, no. 1, pp. 1–33, 2012.

[20] E. Castillejo, A. Almeida, and D. López-de-Ipiña, "Ontology-Based Model for Supporting Dynamic and Adaptive User Interfaces," *International Journal of Human-Computer Interaction*, vol. 30, no. 10, pp. 771–786, 2014.

[21] T. Clerckx, K. Luyten, and K. Coninx, "The mapping problem back and forth: Customizing dynamic models while preserving consistency," in *Proceedings of the 3rd Annual Conference on Task Models and Diagrams, TAMODIA '04*, pp. 33–42, Czech Republic, November 2004.

[22] A. Puerta and J. Eisenstein, "Towards a General Computational Framework for Model-Based Interface Development Systems," in *Proceedings of the Intelligent User Interfaces, IUI 99*, pp. 171–178, 1999.

[23] N. O. Bernsen, "Modality theory in support of multimodal interface design," in *Proceedings of the Spring Symposium on Intelligent Multi -Media Multi-Modal Systems*, pp. 37–44, 1994.

[24] P. Kirisci, K.-D. Thoben, P. Klein, and M. Modzelewski, "Supporting Inclusive Design of Mobile Devices with a Context Model," *Advances and Applications in Mobile Computing*, pp. 65–88, 2012.

[25] P. Kirisci, K.-D. Thoben, P. Klein, and M. Modzelewski, "Supporting inclusive product design with virtual user models at the early stages of product development," in *Proceedings of the 18th International Conference on Engineering Design (ICED 11), Impacting Society through Engineering Design*, vol. 9, pp. 80–90, 2011.

[26] C. Ebert, *Systematisches Requirements Engineering*, Heidelberg: dpunkt.verlag, 4th edition, 2012.

[27] C. Barnes and S. P. Lillford, "Decision support for the design of affective products," *Journal of Engineering Design*, vol. 20, no. 5, pp. 477–492, 2009.

[28] S. Zogaj and U. Bretschneider, "Customer Integration in New Product Development: a Literature Review Concerning the Appropriateness of Different Customer Integration Methods to Attain customer Knowledge," in *Proceedings of the ECIS 2012: The 20th European Conference on Information Systems (ECIS'12)*, vol. 2, pp. 1–14, 2012.

[29] E. Zitkus, P. Langdon, and J. Clarkson, "Accessibility Evaluation:Assistive Tools for Design Activity," in *Proceedings of the 1st International Conference Sustainable Intelligent Manufacturing*, pp. 659–670, IST Press, Leiria, Portugal, 2011.

[30] M. Schickler, *Entwicklung mobiler Apps im Business und E-Health Bereich*, 2015.

[31] J. Agar, *Constant touch: A global history of the mobile phone*, Icon Books Limited, 2013.

[32] M. S. Al-Razgan, H. S. Al-Khalifa, M. D. Al-Shahrani, and H. H. AlAjmi, "Touch-Based Mobile Phone Interface Guidelines and Design Recommendations for Elderly People: A Survey of the Literature," in *Neural Information Processing*, vol. 7666 of *Lecture Notes in Computer Science*, pp. 568–574, Springer, Berlin, Germany, 2012.

[33] P. Beigl, F. Schneider, and S. Salhofer, "Takeback systems for mobile phones: review and recommendations," *Proceedings of the Institution of Civil Engineers - Waste and Resource Management*, vol. 165, no. 1, pp. 25–35, 2012.

[34] N. Gedik, A. Hanci-Karademirci, E. Kursun, and K. Cagiltay, "Key instructional design issues in a cellular phone-based mobile learning project," *Computers & Education*, vol. 58, no. 4, pp. 1149–1159, 2012.

[35] Y. S. Park and S. H. Han, "Touch key design for one-handed thumb interaction with a mobile phone: effects of touch key size and touch key location," *International Journal of Industrial Ergonomics*, vol. 40, no. 1, pp. 68–76, 2010.

[36] E. Goodman, E. Stolterman, and R. Wakkary, "Understanding interaction design practices," in *Proceedings of the the 2011 annual conference*, p. 1061, Vancouver, BC, Canada, May 2011.

[37] P. T. Kirisci and K. Thoben, "Vergleich von Methoden für die Gestaltung Mobiler Endgeräte [Comparison of methods for the design of mobile devices]," *icom - Zeitschrift für interaktive und Koop. Medien*, vol. 8, no. 1, pp. 52–59, 2009.

[38] A. Puerta, "A model-based interface development environment," *IEEE Software*, vol. 14, no. 4, pp. 40–47, 1997.

[39] E. Yigitbas, H. Fischer, and S. Sauer, "Model-Based User Interface Development for Adaptive Self-Service Systems," in *Design, User Experience, and Usability. Theories, Methods, and Tools for Designing the User Experience*, vol. 8517 of *Lecture Notes in Computer Science*, pp. 206–213, Springer International Publishing, Cham, 2014.

[40] G. Calvary, J. Coutaz, D. Thevenin, Q. Limbourg, L. Bouillon, and J. Vanderdonckt, "A unifying reference framework for multi-target user interfaces," *Interacting with Computers*, vol. 15, no. 3, pp. 289–308, 2003.

[41] G. Meixner, "Modellbasierte Entwicklung von Benutzungsschnittstellen," *Informatik-Spektrum*, vol. 34, no. 4, pp. 400–404, 2011.

[42] H. Witt, T. Nicolai, and H. Kenn, "The WUI-Toolkit: A Model-Driven UI Development Framework for Wearable User Interfaces," in *Proceedings of the 27th International Conference on Distributed Computing Systems Workshops (ICDCSW'07)*, pp. 43-43, Toronto, ON, Canada, June 2007.

[43] J. Vanderdonckt and M. Florins, "Model-based design of mobile user interfaces," in *Proceedings of the Mobile HCI2001: Third International Workshop on Human Computer Interaction with Mobile Devices*, 2001.

[44] T. Clerckx, F. Winters, and K. Coninx, "Tool support for designing context-sensitive user interfaces using a model-based approach," in *Proceedings of the 4th international workshop on Task models and diagrams*, ACM International Conference Proceedings Series, pp. 11–17, Gdansk, Poland, September 2005.

[45] G. Calvary, J. Coutaz, and D. Thevenin, "A Unifying Reference Framework for the Development of Plastic User Interfaces," in *Engineering for Human-Computer Interaction*, vol. 2254 of *Lecture Notes in Computer Science*, pp. 173–192, Springer Berlin Heidelberg, Berlin, Germany, 2001.

[46] B. Ullmer and H. Ishii, "Emerging frameworks for tangible user interfaces," *IBM Systems Journal*, vol. 39, no. 3-4, pp. 915–930, 2000.

[47] S. Greenberg and C. Fitchett, "Phidgets: Easy development of physical interfaces through physical widgets," in *Proceedings of the 14th Annual ACM Symposium on User Interface Software and Technology (UIST'01)*, pp. 209–218, USA, November 2001.

[48] H. Gellersen, G. Kortuem, A. Schmidt, and M. Beigl, "Physical prototyping with smart-its," *IEEE Pervasive Computing*, vol. 3, no. 3, pp. 74–82, 2004.

[49] R. Ballagas and F. Memon, "iStuff mobile: rapidly prototyping new mobile phone interfaces for ubiquitous computing," in *Proceedings of the SIGCHI Conference on Human Factors in Computing Systems*, pp. 1107–1116, 2007.

[50] S. Houben and N. Marquardt, "WATCH connect: A toolkit for prototyping smartwatch-centric cross-device applications," in *Proceedings of the 33rd Annual CHI Conference on Human Factors in Computing Systems, CHI 2015*, pp. 1247–1256, Republic of Korea, April 2015.

[51] B. Hartmann, S. R. Klemmer, M. Bernstein et al., "Reflective physical prototyping through integrated design, test, and analysis," in *Proceedings of the 19th Annual ACM Symposium on User Interface Software and Technology 2006, UIST'06*, pp. 299–308, Switzerland, October 2006.

[52] A. Bellucci, I. Aedo, and P. Díaz, "ECCE toolkit: Prototyping sensor-based interaction," *Sensors*, vol. 17, no. 3, 2017.

[53] R. Herriott, "Are inclusive designers designing inclusively? An analysis of 66 design cases," *The Design Journal*, vol. 16, no. 2, pp. 138–158, 2013.

[54] P. John Clarkson and R. Coleman, "History of inclusive design in the UK," *Applied Ergonomics*, vol. 46, pp. 235–247, 2015.

[55] S. Matiouk, M. Modzelewski, Y. Mohamad et al., "Prototype of a Virtual User Modeling Software Framework for Inclusive Design of Consumer Products and User Interfaces," in *Universal Access in Human-Computer Interaction. Design Methods, Tools, and Interaction Techniques for eInclusion*, vol. 8009 of *Lecture Notes in Computer Science*, pp. 59–66, Springer Berlin Heidelberg, Berlin, Germany, 2013.

[56] J. O. Borchers, "A pattern approach to interaction design," *AI & Society*, vol. 15, no. 4, pp. 359–376, 2001.

[57] C. Alexander, *Notes on the Synthesis of Form*, Harvard University Press, Cambridge, Mass, USA, 1964.

[58] C. Alexander, *A Pattern Language: Towns, Buildings, Construction*, Oxford University Press, 1977.

[59] D. C. Schmidt, "Using Design Patterns to Develop Reusable Object- Oriented Communication Software," *Communications of the ACM*, vol. 38, no. 10, pp. 65–74, 1995.

[60] D. Riehle and H. Züllighoven, "Understanding and using patterns in software development," *TAPOS*, vol. 2, no. 1, pp. 3–13, 1996.

[61] J. A. Landay and G. Borriello, "Design patterns for ubiquitous computing," *The Computer Journal*, vol. 36, no. 8, pp. 93–95, 2003.

[62] S. Imtiaz, "User Centered Design Patterns and Related Issues A Review," *International Journal of Human–Computer Interaction*, vol. 4, no. 1, pp. 19–24, 2013.

[63] A. Neyem, C. Aracena, C. A. Collazos, and R. Alarcón, "Designing emotional awareness devices: what one sees is what one feels," *Ingeniare. Revista chilena de ingeniería*, vol. 15, no. 3, pp. 227–235, 2007.

[64] E. Kanjo, L. Al-Husain, and A. Chamberlain, "Emotions in context: examining pervasive affective sensing systems, applications, and analyses," *Personal and Ubiquitous Computing*, vol. 19, no. 7, pp. 1197–1212, 2015.

[65] A. Mcstay, *Empathic Media: The Rise of Emotional AI*, SAGE Publications Ltd, 1st edition, 2018.

[66] D. Cernea and A. Kerren, "A survey of technologies on the rise for emotion-enhanced interaction," *Journal of Visual Languages and Computing*, vol. 31, pp. 70–86, 2015.

[67] D. Lottridge, M. Chignell, and A. Jovicic, "Affective interaction: understanding, evaluating, and designing for human emotion," *Reviews of Human Factors and Ergonomics*, vol. 7, no. 1, pp. 197–217, 2011.

[68] A. Alibage, A. Jetter, and A. Alibage, *PDXScholar Drivers of Consumers' Emotional Engagement with Everyday Products: An Intensive Review of the Literature and an Attempt to Conceptualize the Consumer-Product Interactions Within the Emotional Design Process Engineering and Technology Management*, 2017.

[69] A. Schmidt, M. Beigl, and H.-W. Gellersen, "There is more to context than location," *Computers & Graphics*, vol. 23, no. 6, pp. 893–901, 1999.

[70] E. Reponen and K. Mihalic, "Model of primary and secondary context," in *Proceedings of the the international workshop in conjunciton with AVI 2006*, pp. 37-38, Venice, Italy, May 2006.

4

An Integrated Support to Collaborative Semantic Annotation

**Annamaria Goy, Diego Magro, Giovanna Petrone, Claudia Picardi,
Marco Rovera, and Marino Segnan**

Dipartimento di Informatica, Università di Torino, C. Svizzera 185, 10149 Torino, Italy

Correspondence should be addressed to Annamaria Goy; annamaria.goy@unito.it

Academic Editor: Thomas Mandl

Everybody experiences every day the need to manage a huge amount of heterogeneous shared resources, causing information overload and fragmentation problems. Collaborative annotation tools are the most common way to address these issues, but collaboratively tagging resources is usually perceived as a boring and time consuming activity and a possible source of conflicts. To face this challenge, collaborative systems should effectively support users in the resource annotation activity and in the definition of a shared view. The main contribution of this paper is the presentation and the evaluation of a set of mechanisms (personal annotations over shared resources and tag suggestions) that provide users with the mentioned support. The goal of the evaluation was to (1) assess the improvement with respect to the situation without support; (2) evaluate the satisfaction of the users, with respect to both the final choice of annotations and possible conflicts; (3) evaluate the usefulness of the support mechanisms in terms of actual usage and user perception. The experiment consisted in a simulated collaborative work scenario, where small groups of users annotated a few resources and then answered a questionnaire. The evaluation results demonstrate that the proposed support mechanisms can reduce both overload and possible disagreement.

1. Introduction

Everybody, even less technologically skilled people, experiences every day the need to manage a huge amount of heterogeneous digital resources (documents, web pages, images, posts, emails, etc.): almost every kind of activity and service, in fact, has evolved from being based on a collection of paper documents, phone calls, and physical interactions to being fully digital. Public Administration services, stores, entertainment events, business interactions, reservations and payments, personal communications, and so on rely on web-based applications, accessible from desktop computers, tablets, smartphone, or other devices.

This trend poses a great challenge to individual users, who are often victims of both *information overload* and *information fragmentation* [1–3]: overload, since too many digital items (services, applications, contents, and resources) are available; fragmentation, because digital items are typically stored in different places, handled by different applications, encoded in different data formats, and accessed through different accounts. As a consequence, users have to manage an increasing number of storages and folders, usually with similar names and related contents but handled by different applications [4].

Besides the challenge for individual users, another issue has emerged from the synergy between the cloud paradigm and the Social Web: knowledge sharing and web-based user collaboration. In many cases, in fact, the problem is not simply managing huge amounts of heterogeneous resources but doing it collaboratively, within shared virtual spaces, like social networks, collaboration tools, and shared workspaces. Collaborating in small groups or participating in large communities, people usually have different needs, goals, and perspectives, strongly influencing the way they organize information.

As we will try to show in detail in Sections 2 and 3, the idea of annotating information items, with tags and comments, is probably the most used way to address these issues: tags and comments, in fact, are the basic mechanism exploited by almost all web-based tools to support collaborative work, and in particular collaborative organization of shared resources.

However, the annotation activity is usually considered a heavy and time-consuming task. As a consequence, users are not encouraged to do it, or fail to do it properly, with the result that organization, and thus retrieval, of shared resources becomes even harder than without additional annotations.

To face this challenge, collaborative systems should become smart, in order to be able to effectively support users both in the individual activity of resource annotation and in the collaborative task of defining a shared, meaningful, and useful view over them.

The main contribution of this paper is the presentation and the evaluation of a set of mechanisms providing users with the mentioned support to the collaborative annotation of resources.

In the following, Section 2 will present the background related work; Section 3 will discuss the motivations and the overall goal of our approach; moreover, it will sketch the ontology exploited by our system (described in a previous work [5]). Section 4 will describe in detail the different mechanisms we propose to support collaborative semantic annotation of shared resources: a Tag Recommender (representing a novel contribution of this paper) and a Personal View Manager (whose implementation is described in a previous work [6]); Section 5 will present the user evaluation of the prototype implementing the proposed functionalities and represents the major contribution of this paper. Finally, Section 6 will conclude the paper.

2. Related Work

As already sketched in Section 1, the availability of an increasing number of heterogeneous digital resources and services led to an overload and fragmentation problem. The main aspects that must be taken into account by new interaction models that try to face these challenges emerge from the analysis of the limits of the *desktop metaphor*, conducted by Kaptelinin and Czerwinski [7], and can be summarized in (a) user *collaboration*; (b) organization of resources and people around an *activity*; (c) *uniform* management of *heterogeneous* objects and, in particular, uniform *annotations*. These aspects are partially supported by a number of approaches, with different emphasis on different features.

On a slightly different track, an interesting approach is represented by TellTable [8], a web-based framework for synchronous work in a virtual collaborative office; the work of Adler and colleagues is particularly interesting since it emphasizes the importance of providing users with the possibility of keeping a private section within the shared workspace (e.g., private notes).

As far as the organization around activities is concerned, several works can be mentioned. For example, Haystack [9] is built around the concept of customizable workspaces; the approaches based on the Activity-Based Computing paradigm [10] claim that thematic contexts should be built around user activities, and a similar principle is used in the Kimura system [11]; co-Activity Manager, built on top of Windows 7, is a more recent approach in the same direction, providing a cloud-based ubiquitous access [12].

A number of works explicitly face the issue of collaborative resource annotation: an interesting approach is represented by the work of Rau and colleagues [13], who present a hypertext annotation system in an e-learning perspective. Pearson and colleagues [14] describe a digital environment for collaborative reading, enabling note-taking in a way that mimics paper-based annotation which the users are used to. Jan and colleagues [15] present a web-based collaborative annotation system in which two types of filters are used in order to reduce the number of annotations on the basis of their quality; the authors show how annotation filtering can improve reading comprehension.

Not all of these approaches rely on semantic annotation and, even when they enable it, they lack an effective support for the annotation of resources. The integration of desktop-based user interfaces and semantic technologies is the goal of the *Semantic Desktop* initiative [16], mainly developed within the NEPOMUK project (http://nepomuk.semanticdesktop .org/). This approach aims at supporting the collaboration among knowledge workers, thanks to an open-source framework enabling the implementation of semantic desktops that integrate different applications and ontologies. A further development toward the integration of Web of Data sources can be found in [17].

The use of semantic knowledge to support users in the collaborative management of shared resources underlies many other approaches. For example, Koning and colleagues [18] describe the ontology used in the CineGrid Exchange network to support media data management. Uflacker and Zeier [19] present TCN (Team Collaboration Networks), a system for the analysis of patterns in collaboration activities within multidisciplinary design teams, based on an ontology that provides the vocabulary for describing interactions between people and/or information elements.

Strategies used to organize digital resources have been largely studied within the Personal Information Management field [20, 21]. The most popular approach to overcome the rigidity of traditional classification systems (e.g., folder hierarchies) is represented by tagging systems and folksonomies [22, 23]. Our approach is more structured than simple tagging systems, it does not aim at aggregating tags into a folksonomy, and it cannot be considered an actual crowdsourcing system, since it targets relatively small groups of people knowing each other and focusing on a specific collaborative activity. However, these systems provide interesting ideas and thus deserve some further discussion.

Folksonomies represent a user-centered view of the resource space, since they enable multifacets classifications by associating items with metadata representing different aspects (*facets*) of the shared resources [24]. Although very popular, also tagging systems and folksonomies have some limitations, as demonstrated by studies that compare the two models [25].

Interesting enhancements have been proposed by endowing tagging systems with semantic technologies [26, 27]. For example, FLOR [28] enriches folksonomies with online available semantic knowledge; GroupMe! [22] enables users to group content items related to a given topic; MOAT (*Meaning Of A Tag*) [29] allows the definition of shared machine-readable meanings of tags, linked to Linked Open Data sets; SemKey [30] exploits Wikipedia and WordNet to provide semantic features to a collaborative tagging systems.

One of the main drawbacks of tagging systems is the fact that tags usually refer to different aspects of the tagged resource, often related to user goals; for example, tags can be used to define the resource type ("letter"), to describe the resource content ("seasonal diseases"), to provide an opinion ("good presentation"), and to link the resource to a task ("to read") [31]. In order to account, in a systematic way, for this heterogeneity, a more structured semantic representation of resources is needed. A research field where such a structure is usually provided is Natural Language Processing (NLP). In tools used in the NLP community, in fact, annotations usually rely on a predefined schema that supports the association of tags with phrases within documents. The annotation schema and the vocabulary are usually provided by ontologies [32–34], which can define the metadata structure (e.g., Dublin Core: http://www.dublincore.org/) or provide domain-dependent vocabularies (e.g., the Getty Thesaurus of Geographic Names: https://www.getty.edu/research/tools/vocabularies/tgn, for the geographic domain). Interestingly, there are also collaborative versions of some NLP-oriented annotation tools [35, 36]. Useful surveys of (ontology-based) annotation frameworks can be found in [37, 38].

We conclude this section by mentioning a quite different concept of annotation, that is, the one implemented in tools explicitly aimed at supporting collaborative work by enabling users to add comments to digital documents (web pages, pdf documents, etc.) and share them; in these tools, the annotation is typically free text, with no semantic schema. The most popular example is Google Docs (https://docs.google.com); other examples are A.nnotate (https://www.a.nnotate.com), HyLighter (http://www.hylighter.com/), and Marqueed (https://www.marqueed.com) for images.

3. Semantic Annotation in Collaborative Workspaces

As already stated, shared workspaces used by groups of people to collaboratively carry on different types of activities, belonging both to business and personal spheres, pose new challenges: the huge number of resources, formats, storages, applications, services, and accounts produces a significant overload problem, coupled with an information fragmentation issue [1–3]. The result is usually twofold: the user is lost in the information space and the management of resources turns into a largely inefficient activity.

The sharing opportunities supported by cloud infrastructures, social software, and tagging systems, although representing a great advantage, can—meanwhile—cause new problems.

In particular, tagging within collaborative resource management systems raises some major problems:

(a) Tags are typically used to express very heterogeneous aspects of a resource (e.g., its type, its content, an opinion about it, or its use) [31].

(b) Resource tagging is typically perceived as burdensome (boring and uninteresting) by users.

(c) Different users, even though belonging to the same group (team or community), often have different perspectives over shared resources and thus tend to disagree about the proper tags that should describe resources.

In order to face issue (a), the resource management system should provide a more structured, machine-readable, semantic representation of resources, in line with ontology-driven approaches to resource annotation [38]. To this purpose, we defined an ontology, representing resources as *information objects* characterized by a set of properties: an information object can thus have an *encoding format* (e.g., *pdf*), an *author* (e.g., *Paris Municipality*), a *language* (e.g., *written French*), a *content*, represented by a main *topic* (e.g., *Paris*), and a number of *objects of discourse* (i.e., entities the resource "is about"; e.g., *Montmartre, Louvre*, and *Jardin du Luxembourg*). Moreover, an information object can have *parts*: for example, a web page typically has links to other pages or includes multimedia contents (images, videos, etc.).

The proposed ontology is based on existing models, namely, DOLCE [39], its extension OIO [40], and the Knowledge Module of O-CREAM-v2 [41]. It enables us to provide a structured and uniform representation of heterogeneous resources (documents, web pages, multimedia items, emails, etc.): for instance, thanks to the structure provided by the ontology, the tag describing the author of a document becomes the value of the *author* property, while tags describing the content become values for the *topic* and *object of discourse* properties.

A simplified example of the semantic representation of a web page (*wp*), according to the ontology, is shown in "*Simplified Example of a Semantic Representation of a Web Page.*" The predicates include a time parameter (*t*) that has been omitted in the OWL (http://www.w3.org/TR/owl-features) version of the ontology exploited in our prototype (see Section 4).

Simplified Example of a Semantic Representation of a Web Page

```
specifiedIn(wp, written_French, t)

hasEncodingSpecifiedIn(wp, pdf, t)

hasTopic(wp, Paris, t)

hasObjectOfDiscourse(wp, Montmartre, t)

hasObjectOfDiscourse(wp, Louvre, t)

hasObjectOfDiscourse(wp,
Jardin_du_Luxembourg, t)

hasAuthor(wp, Paris_Municipality, t)

hasURL(wp, http://www.myparis.org, t)

DOLCE:part(wp, image_JLux01, t)

DOLCE:part(wp, hyperlink_LouvreWebSite,
t)
```

The collaborative building the semantic representation of a resource can thus be seen as a "semantic annotation" activity, where annotations are represented by assertions (e.g., *hasTopic*(*wp*, *Paris*, *t*)), based on the underlying ontology, in which the specific value (e.g., *Paris*) can be seen as a "tag."

It is worth noting that the ontology provides the *structure* for the annotation by distinguishing different properties (topic, objects of discourse, author, format, etc.), but the values (and in particular the values of the *topic* and *object of discourse* properties) are free texts.

This solution enables users to organize resources on the basis of a highly structured information that provides a flexible access, based on the combination of different criteria (e.g., I can select all resources written in French by the Paris Municipality and talking about Montmartre).

The mentioned ontology has been implemented within our collaborative resource management system, SemT++ [42], and is described in detail in [5], where the reader can also find an evaluation of its benefits in performing resource selection.

An initial step toward the solution to issue (b) was provided by the identification of values for some of the mentioned properties, based on the automatic analysis of the resources. For example, by analyzing the HTML code of a web page, it is usually possible to understand its format (e.g., UTF-8/HTML) and sometimes its language (e.g., English); see [5] for details. However, the most challenging properties, with respect to user-burdening (issue (b)), but also interuser disagreement (issue (c)), are those referring to the *content* of the resource, that is, *topic* and *object of discourse*, which typically require to be manually provided by users.

In order to analyze the collaboration process and devise a strategy to support users in this task, and thus providing solutions to issues (b) and (c), we conducted a first preliminary user study—reported in [43]—where we asked users to collaboratively tag resources by focusing on the description of their content, with the goal of reaching a shared annotation, and without any specific support mechanism. Users were asked to write their annotations in a shared document (in particular, we used a Google Docs shared file) where everyone could freely edit others' annotations, possibly deleting them. We monitored their process, without intervening. The aim of the study was to evaluate, among other things, the attitude people held toward the experience (users were asked to assess how interesting/engaging/easy/useful it was), as well as the degree of collaboration and/or disagreement perceived. Users tested different policies for deciding the final set of annotations (consensual, supervised by an external supervisor, or supervised by an internal owner of the resource). At the end of the collaborative process, users had to fill in a questionnaire where they evaluated the overall experience as well as their degree of satisfaction both with respect to the final result and with respect to the decision policy.

The study confirmed that users found the task not-so-engaging and only moderately interesting, in particular because of the initial difficulty in coming up with adequate tags and because of the difficulty in giving up one's own view over the annotations in favor of someone else's one. Also, the study showed that, while having the resource owner making the final decision is perceived as the most adequate policy, it does not lead to a great level of satisfaction in the resulting annotations.

We built on the guidelines derived from such study by designing and implementing, within a proof-of-concept prototype, a set of mechanisms for effectively supporting users during the collaborative semantic annotation of shared resources (described in Section 4). We then performed an evaluation with users (reported in Section 5) in order to assess the degree of improvement with respect to the initial situation and to collect the users' opinion about the support mechanisms.

4. An Integrated Support to Collaborative Semantic Annotation

In order to prototype and test our support mechanisms for collaborative annotation, we implemented them within our collaborative resource management environment, SemT++ [5, 42], in which shared workspaces are seen as *round tables*, devoted to specific activities (e.g., the organization of a holiday) and hosting resources of different types (documents, web pages, emails, images, etc.). Users "sitting" around a table (*table participants*) can collaboratively organize, retrieve, and use resources present on the table. These tasks are supported by the availability of semantic representations of resources themselves, based on the underlying ontology (see Section 3 and "*Simplified Example of a Semantic Representation of a Web Page*"), and in particular by the automatic identification of some resource properties, such as resource *parts* (basically, hyperlinks and multimedia objects), and all format-related properties. Moreover, the system tries to identify the language used and the authors, and, if it finds possible values (e.g., *written French* and *Paris Municipality*), it asks users for a confirmation. As we will see in Section 5, when describing the evaluation scenario, SemT++ uses the extracted parts to suggest new resources (e.g., linked pages) to table participants, who can select the most interesting ones and add them to the table.

However, as already mentioned, the most challenging properties, which require a significant user contribution, are those describing the content of the resource, that is, the main *topic* and the *objects of discourse* (entities the document is about). In order to support table participants in this annotation activity (i.e., in providing values for the *topic* and *object of discourse* properties), we designed and implemented two features, aimed at

(i) reducing the overload in defining semantic tags (i.e., values for the mentioned properties)—that is, providing a partial solution to issue (b), as introduced in Section 3;

(ii) handling possible disagreement among users—that is, providing a solution to issue (c), as introduced in Section 3.

These features are tag suggestion and personal views, and will be described in the following.

4.1. Suggestions. Our first hypothesis was that the most effective way to reduce the overload imposed by semantic annotation of resources is providing users with suggestions of content tags (i.e., values for *topic* and *object of discourse* properties). We thus built an integrated *Tag Recommender*, with the role of proposing semantic tags: when annotating a resource, users can accept a suggestion, by selecting the proposed value, or refuse it and add a new value.

The Tag Recommender has three components:

(1) The *Resource Analyzer* extracts suggestions from the syntactic analysis of the resource itself. The current prototype only analyzes web pages and extracts the value of the *content* attribute of the *keywords* metatag of the HTML code.

(2) The *Named Entity Extractor* provides suggestions on the basis of Named Entity Recognition (NER). In particular, in the current implementation, the Named Entity Extractor relies on Text Razor (https://www.textrazor.com), an NLP tool that includes a NER service offering a RESTful API for remote access. Text Razor analyzes the resource and extracts all Named Entities (e.g., *Paris, Tour Eiffel, Sorbonne*, etc.), each one associated with two attributes (among others): the estimated relevance of the entity within the document (a measure of "how on-topic or important that entity is to the document") and a confidence score ("a measure of the engine's confidence that the entity is a valid entity given the document context"); see Text Razor online documentation (https://www.textrazor.com/docs/rest). In the version of the prototype used for the evaluation presented in Section 5, we considered extracted entities with relevance > 0.5 (relevance range is $[0\cdots 1]$) and confidence > 5 (confidence range is $[0.5\cdots 10]$); such thresholds can be configured with different values, if needed.

(3) The *Semantic Knowledge Manager* leverages the underlying ontology to infer candidate tags, by exploiting the reasoning module (currently, Facts++: http://owl.cs.manchester.ac.uk/tools/fact/). In particular, in the current version, it uses the *DOLCE: part(x, z, t)* property, thanks to a set of axioms enabling it to infer tags for a resource from tags used for its parts (e.g., hyperlinks included in it) and vice versa. For example, the following axiom states that if a resource *x* contains a part *z*, which has *y* as an object of discourse, then *y* is a candidate object of discourse for *x*.

$$InformationElement\,(x) \wedge DOLCE : part\,(x, z, t)$$

$$\wedge\; hasObjectOfDiscourse\,(z, y, t) \tag{1}$$

$$\longrightarrow hasCandidateObjectOfDiscourse\,(x, y, t)$$

As an example, the suggestions provided by the system for the *object of discourse* property belonging to the semantic representation of a web page about tourism in Ireland (http://www.cliffsofmoher.ie/about-the-cliffs/obriens-tower) are shown in the bottom part of Figure 1.

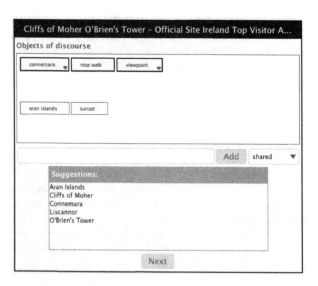

FIGURE 1: The property window of a table resource.

4.2. Personal Views. Our second hypothesis was that the availability of *personal views* over semantic annotations of shared resources can reduce possible conflicts deriving from disagreement about tags among collaborating users. Following this hypothesis, we designed and implemented Personal View Manager, that is, a mechanism enabling table participants to keep personal annotations over shared resources. A detailed description of the model and its implementation within SemT++ can be found in [6]; in the following we briefly summarize the most significant aspects, from the user viewpoint.

When a user decides to add a semantic annotation (e.g., an object of discourse, describing the content of a resource), they can decide to add it to the *shared view*, or to their *personal view*: in the first case, the tag will be visible to all table participants; in the second case, it will be only visible to themselves. Tags added to the personal view can be shared later on. Moreover, when looking at the tags added by somebody else in the shared view, the user can decide to mark them as "I like," in order to include them also in their personal view; the main consequence is that if deleted from the shared view, such tags will remain available in their personal view.

Figure 1 shows the property window of a web page (http://www.cliffsofmoher.ie/about-the-cliffs/obriens-tower), in which the values for the *object of discourse* property are shown: bold face boxes represent shared annotations, the small heart is the marker meaning that the current user "likes" the annotation, and thin-face boxes identify "private" annotations that are visible only to the current user.

The personal view of an individual user over a shared resource thus includes "private" tags (thin-face boxes) and shared tags marked as "I like" (boldface boxes with small heart); in fact these last ones will be automatically turned into "private" tags if another participant deletes them from the shared view. The shared view of a table resource, from the perspective of each individual user, includes all shared tags, being marked as "I like" or not (i.e., all boldface boxes, with and without the small heart).

These functionalities are available for all property values that can be edited by users; values automatically set by the system (e.g., encoding formats) are by default assigned to the shared view and to all personal views (i.e., represented as bold face boxes with the small heart) and cannot be deleted. Finally, by right-clicking on a tag, table participants can see the author of an annotation.

5. User Evaluation

The goal of the user evaluation was the assessment of the support mechanisms described in Section 4 in relation to the problems of user-burdening (task perceived as boring, time-consuming, and often uninteresting)—issue (b) in Section 3—and interuser disagreement (conflict on annotations and no satisfaction in the results)—issue (c) in Section 3. More precisely our goal was to

(1) evaluate the *attitude* users held *toward the experience* and assess the improvement with respect to the situation where users had no-support mechanisms [43];

(2) evaluate the *satisfaction* of the users at the end of the process, both with respect to the final choice of annotations and with respect to possible conflicts in the group, again assessing the improvement with respect to the absence of support mechanisms;

(3) evaluate the *usefulness of the support mechanisms* both in terms of actual usage and in terms of user perception.

Our hypothesis was that providing users with suggestions for the tags describing resource content (i.e., values of the *object of discourse* property) could make the task less burdening, while the availability of personal views could alleviate disagreements, allowing each participant to keep their own version of the annotations.

In order to test our hypothesis, we simulated a collaborative work situation where small groups of users had to annotate, by means of our tool, a few resources, focusing in particular on the *object of discourse* property, for which multiple values can be selected. In each group the resource "owner" (i.e., the user who added the resource to the table) had the final say on the annotations—as this had been perceived as the most adequate policy in the preliminary user study; see [43]. Each group had half an hour to an hour to perform the task, at the end of which each participant had to answer a questionnaire.

One of us was physically present with each test participant to record possible verbal comments and to help with the application user interface, which was novel to them. Moreover, their actions within the application were recorded.

5.1. Methodology. We recruited 15 participants among our colleagues, in order to have technology-acquainted people, familiar with collaborative tools, thus representing potential users of a collaborative environment like SemT++ (according to several authors (e.g., [44]) 15 is within the acceptable sample size range, albeit, admittedly, on the lower-bound side,

for qualitative evaluations, especially when the evaluation involves an in-depth analysis of a reasonably homogeneous group [45]; since our main goal was not a quantitative, statistically relevant evaluation, but rather a qualitative feedback from potential real users, we did not explicitly take into account the sample statistical representativeness).

We built 3 groups of 5 people each. All groups were asked to participate in the same scenario that was presented to the participants, in order to set the context, as follows: you are the organizers of a scientific workshop that will take place in Galway (Ireland). In order to carry on the organization activity, you set up a SemT++ table, on which you are currently discussing the destination of the social trip. You already informally talked about Cliffs of Moher and Aran Islands as possible destinations, but the decision is still open.

For each group, we identified a "leader" who had the task of selecting the resource to be added to the table and to be tagged during the test. In order to make the selection easier and less time-consuming, we preidentified a small group of web pages concerning interesting places in Ireland, not far from Galway. When the leader had selected the preferred resource and added it to the table, the system started the analysis and (among other things) extracted its *parts* (see Section 4), which—in the current version—correspond to images contained in the selected web page and hyperlinks referring to related resources. The extracted parts (images and related pages) were then suggested to the user, who could add the most interesting ones to the table (see Figure 2). In the test scenario, we asked each group leader to select 2 or 3 resources from this list.

At this point, the table was populated with 3 or 4 resources that could be tagged by table participants. Each user was asked to edit the values for the *object of discourse* property, which means adding/removing/sharing/liking tags describing the content of the resource, bearing in mind the overall goal (organizing the social trip for the Galway workshop). We also briefly showed them the features offered by the system, that is, the possibility of selecting values from the list of system suggestions, the possibility of maintaining a personal view, and the Like feature.

The tagging activity ended when the leader (i.e., the "owner" of the tagged resources) decided that they were satisfied with the tags, that is, with the semantic description of the resources.

After the tagging activity was completed, each participant was asked to fill in a questionnaire. The results of the user evaluation thus consist in the questionnaire answers, together with a log of the action performed by users while interacting with the application.

5.2. Results. The questionnaire consisted of four sections:

(1) User profiling.

(2) Overall quality of the experience.

(3) User satisfaction.

(4) Evaluation of support mechanisms.

In the *user profiling* section, we asked subjects to self-assess their familiarity with web tools and with collaborative tools,

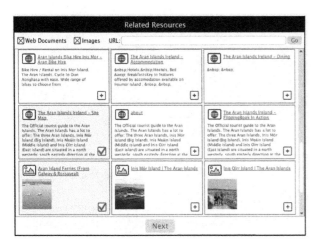

FIGURE 2: Selection of related resources suggested by the system.

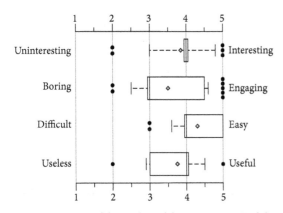

FIGURE 3: Assessment of the quality of the experience. Each boxplot shows the I, II, and III quartiles (box), the standard deviation (whiskers), outliers (black dots), and mean value (diamond).

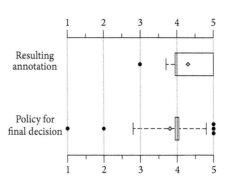

FIGURE 4: User satisfaction with respect to resulting annotations and decision policy.

on a 5-point scale. Most people declared a high or very high familiarity with web tools (4 people answered "4" and 11 people answered "5"; no one answered "1" to "3"); they were slightly less familiar with collaborative tools (9 people answered "3"; 5 people answered "4"; only one person answered "2").

Concerning the *overall quality of the experience* (the second section in the questionnaire) we asked them to express on a 5-point scale four different quality indicators (the same used in the preliminary user study [43] in order to be able to fit them to the same grid): Uninteresting/Interesting, Boring/Engaging, Difficult/Easy, and Useless/Useful. Figure 3 shows a boxplot of the subjects' answers.

The experience was considered *interesting* by most people (only 2 people gave a score lower than "4") and, on the overall, more *engaging* than boring. The task was also perceived as very *easy* and reasonably *useful*.

Section 3 of the survey inquired on *user satisfaction* with respect to the final result and with respect to the decision policy (i.e., having the resource owner choose). Figure 4 shows the answers, again by means of boxplots. It can be seen that people were well satisfied with the chosen annotations

(and also reasonably satisfied with the decision policy). We also explicitly asked if they had perceived conflicts within their group. Only 1 person out of 15 said she did.

Section 4 focused on the *evaluation of support mechanisms*. We asked users if they had used and/or found useful each of the following features:

(i) The suggestions.

(ii) The possibility of having personal tags invisible to others.

(iii) The possibility of "liking" a tag.

Notice that the last two features both concur in creating the *personal view*; however, from the point of view of the interaction with our application, they could be accessed separately, and were, as a matter of fact, perceived as two different—albeit related—tools.

According to our test subjects, only one-third of them (5 people) explicitly interacted with the "private" annotations area (by adding, removing, or sharing a tag). Conversely, most of them said they used the Like feature (12 people). The action log confirms that only 5 people explicitly inserted a "private" tag, while another 4 actually interacted with the "private" area after a "private" tag had been generated due to the removal of a liked tag in the shared area. On the overall, 12.1% of the actions performed by our users concerned directly the personal annotations. However, 23.8% of the actions were either a "like" or "unlike," and they were performed by 12 users out of 15, confirming the questionnaire answers.

Concerning system suggestions, we did not ask the subjects if they had "used" them because there were different ways of using the suggestions, for example, as a simple source of inspiration. Our action log, however, tells us that out of 106 tags added during the test, 19.8% were taken from those suggested by the system. Table 1 summarizes information on application usage.

The subjects' answers on the usefulness of the different mechanisms are shown in Figure 5.

The last section of the survey focused more specifically on the suggestions provided by the system, asking subjects to assess their quality in terms of number, precision, and adherence to the resource topic, on a 3-point scale. Figure 6 shows the answers we obtained, represented as histograms.

TABLE 1: Summary of data on application usage logged during the evaluation.

(a)		
Total number of tag actions (add, remove, like, unlike, and share)	"Private" tag actions (add/remove from personal area, share a personal tag)	Like/unlike actions
206	25 (12.1%)	49 (23.8%)

(b)	
Total numbers of tags added	Tags added based on system suggestion
106	21 (19,8%)

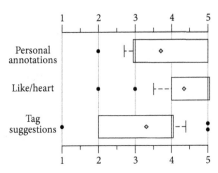

FIGURE 5: Users' assessment of the usefulness of each support mechanism.

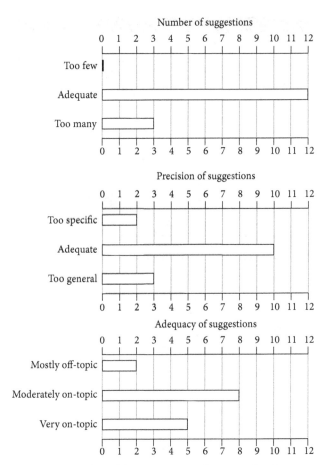

FIGURE 6: Quality of suggestions according to study subjects.

Most people saw the suggestions as adequate in number (12) and in precision (10). No one thought the suggestions were too few, while 3 people thought they were too many. Among the 5 users not satisfied about the precision of suggestions, 2 found them too specific and 3 found them too general. While only 2 users found the suggestions off-topic, only 5 of them found them truly on-topic. Most users (8) saw them as moderately on-topic.

In the following section we discuss these results with respect to the initial goals of our investigation.

5.3. Analysis and Discussion. As discussed in the introduction of Section 5, our first goal was to "evaluate the attitude users held toward the experience and assess the improvement with respect to the situation where users had no-support mechanisms."

In order to analyze this point, let us compare the users' answers on the quality of the experience in the two cases, namely, with or without support mechanisms. Figure 7 shows, for each quality indicator, the users' assessment in both situations.

It can be immediately noticed that there has been a significant improvement with respect to the Boring/Engaging indicator and a noticeable improvement also with respect to the Uninteresting/Interesting indicator. The other two indicators, Difficult/Easy and Useless/Useful, received a similar assessment in both questionnaires.

Although these answers do not specifically concern the support mechanisms, we can observe that including such

mechanisms in the prototype had a positive impact on the quality of the experience, in particular making it more engaging and interesting. It is worth noting that, in the user evaluation (II), the low outlier answers were given by the same people. In other words, while almost everyone found the experience at least not too difficult (no scores below 3 in the Difficult/Easy indicator), there were 2 people who were generally unsatisfied with the experience. Their free-text remarks lead us to think that they did not feel motivated or did not "see the practical utility" of the task they had been asked to perform. We can argue that the usefulness (or uselessness) of a task is somewhat subjective and does not depend on the tool used to perform it. The fact that the task was also seen by these people as somewhat boring and not so interesting can be seen as a consequence of this lack of motivation.

On the other hand, the fact that our application did not make things easier (referring to the Difficult/Easy indicator) for the participants can be ascribed to the intrinsic simplicity of the task itself. The task was indeed perceived as easy even in the preliminary study, where users had no specific tool to aid them.

Our second goal was to "evaluate the satisfaction of the users at the end of the process, both with respect to the final choice of annotations and with respect to possible conflicts

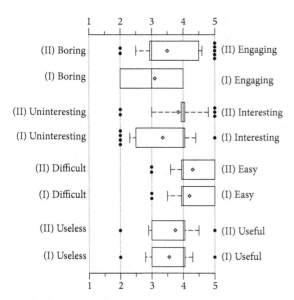

FIGURE 7: Comparison between questionnaire answers on experience assessment *with* (II) and *without* support mechanisms (I).

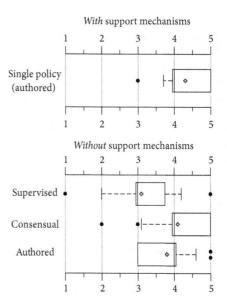

FIGURE 8: Comparison of satisfaction with resulting annotations between the evaluations *with* and *without support mechanisms*.

in the group, again assessing the improvement with respect to the absence of support mechanisms."

In the evaluation presented in this paper we adopted an *authored* policy, which means that the resource owner (the person who initially chose it) had the final say on the annotations. In the preliminary study without support mechanisms we had in fact experimented with three different policies (authored, *consensual*, a decision was considered definitive only when everyone agreed upon it, and *supervised*, where an external supervisor, not participating in the annotation, had the final say).

In that case, the *authored* policy had been deemed the most adequate, but not the most satisfactory in terms of final annotation. Figure 8 compares the degree of satisfaction obtained in the user evaluation *with support mechanisms* to the score obtained by the three different policies in the case *without support mechanisms*.

The degree of satisfaction is similar (indeed, slightly higher) to the one obtained by the *consensual* policy without support mechanisms, definitely improving on the previous score for the *authored* policy. From the free-text comments of the subjects, we understand that the possibility of saving one's own work in the personal view, rather than losing it if the resource owner decides to remove someone else's tags, definitely contributes to this improvement in satisfaction.

Our third and last goal was to "evaluate the usefulness of the support mechanisms both in terms of actual usage and in terms of user perception." The support mechanisms under investigation were the personal view and tag suggestions.

The personal view could be accessed by our users in two ways: by explicitly adding or removing private tags or by "liking" a shared tag, which had the effect of inserting it in the personal view too. Questionnaire answers reported in Figure 5, together with usage data in Table 1, show that users found the Like feature more useful and actually preferred to use it, rather than directly adding tags in the personal view.

The free-text comments generally express the idea that the availability of a "private" annotation area is mostly considered useful for "saving" the preferred tags when they get removed by some other user. Interacting directly with it is, on the other hand, perceived by one-third of the users as redundant and unnecessary. Many participants pointed out that they saw "private" annotations as a sort of memo or back-up, and they should not be given in the user interface the same relevance as the shared ones (presently, the only difference is that shared tags are shown with a thick border, private ones with a thin one). A few users asked what was the point of adding personal annotations when the purpose was collaboration— they understood the idea of preserving removed tags, but beyond that they saw no use for the feature.

When asked explicitly about the Like/Unlike feature, most users noted that it allowed them to feel relaxed about the intervention of the other participants and in particular about the final choice of the resource owner. More than two-thirds of the participants (11 out of 15) said that they would have preferred the "likes" to be public (while no one was interested in others seeing their "private" tags), as a way of capturing the trend of the group. Some observed that, even in absence of an explicit voting mechanism, being able to see other people's "likes" could help the resource owner to make the final choice, and in general help the group to understand what other people were at with their tags.

Concerning tag suggestions, we can see from Table 1 that about one-fifth of the tags were added following a hint from the system. The usefulness of the suggestion feature is however perceived as lower than the others. Some users (6 people) found the idea of receiving suggestions interesting but did not find that the suggestions themselves were adequate either in number, level of detail, or topic; 3 people reported that the problem was that suggestions focused on the content of the resource, while their tagging was goal-oriented; in other words, they were interested in expressing the relationship between the content of the document and the purpose of their joint work. This type of tags could be more easily derived—in a real situation, where the table contained more resources—from tags associated with other resources, rather than from the textual content of the resource under analysis.

Finally, when asked if they found suggested tags with an unknown meaning, almost half of the participants (7 out of 15) answered positively, suggesting the need for an explanation tool, providing information about the suggested tags.

Overall, the feedback we received on the improvement with respect to a no-support situation was positive, and the support mechanisms we devised were perceived as valuable by the participants. In particular, the overall tagging experience was perceived as more engaging and more interesting, the availability of "private" tags was considered useful in order to reach a satisfactory final annotation, and system suggestions were (moderately) used. However, the evaluation results also show that improvements are required in order for such mechanisms to be more effective. They include the following.

(i) The Like/Unlike feature should be empowered. In particular (i) other participants' "likes" should be made immediately visible; (ii) information on how much a tag is "liked" should also be conveyed by the user interface.

(ii) The management of "private" tags should be slightly revised taking into account the following points: (i) the possibility of saving the tags one "likes" in case they get removed by someone else should be kept; (ii) "private" tags should be available but visualized in a different way, less prominent with respect to shared ones.

(iii) The suggestion functionality should be empowered in two directions: (i) the system should provide suggestions more closely related to the resource topic and also tags related to the goal of the collaboration (e.g., the very same resource could be differently tagged if used in a workspace devoted to the organization of a holiday in Ireland or to writing a scientific paper about Irish geology); this improvement could be obtained by taking into account the workspace context, mainly represented by the activity the workspace itself is devoted too and by the specific collaboration goals; the information about context and goals could be derived either from previously tagged resources or from some general workspace knowledge provided by users themselves as they develop their joint work; (ii) the system should be endowed with an explanation mechanism, providing users with information about the suggested tags; a preliminary work in this direction can be found in [46].

6. Conclusions

In this paper we described the design and a prototype implementation of a set of integrated mechanisms aimed at supporting users in the collaborative semantic annotation of shared resources. The proposed approach includes the availability of *personal views*—that is, the possibility of keeping personal tags along with shared ones—and the suggestion of tags, based on both a syntactic and semantic analysis of the resource to be annotated.

We also presented a user evaluation, aimed at assessing such support mechanisms, in particular with respect to the problems highlighted by a previous user study, namely, the burden caused by the annotation activity and the possible disagreement among users about annotations. The evaluation showed that the devised support mechanisms actually improve the user experience and reduce both overload and possible disagreement. However, the evaluation results also provided us with interesting directions for our future work. In particular, besides revising the user interface according to the evaluation results, we plan to investigate the most effective way to enhance system suggestions by taking into account the workspace *context*, that is, a machine-readable representation of the activities the shared workspace is devoted to, and in particular of the *goals* they are aimed at.

Competing Interests

The authors declare that there is no conflict of interests regarding the publication of this paper.

References

[1] Indratmo and J. Vassileva, "A review of organizational structures of personal information management," *Journal of Digital Information*, vol. 9, no. 26, pp. 1–19, 2008.

[2] W. Jones, *Keeping Found Things Found*, Elsevier, Amsterdam, The Netherlands, 2007.

[3] P. Ravasio and V. Tscherter, "Users' theories of the desktop metaphor, or why we should seek metaphor-free interfaces," in *Beyond the Desktop Metaphor*, V. Kaptelinin and M. Czerwinski, Eds., pp. 265–294, MIT Press, Cambridge, Mass, USA, 2007.

[4] R. Boardman, R. Spence, and M. A. Sasse, "Too many hierarchies? The daily struggle for control of the workspace," in *Human-Computer Interaction: Theory and Practice*, J. A. Jacko and C. Stephanidis, Eds., pp. 616–620, Erlbaum Associates, Mahwah, NJ, USA, 2003.

[5] A. Goy, D. Magro, G. Petrone, and M. Segnan, "Semantic representation of information objects for digital resources management," *Intelligenza Artificiale*, vol. 8, no. 2, pp. 145–161, 2014.

[6] A. Goy, D. Magro, G. Petrone, C. Picardi, and M. Segnan, "Shared and personal views on collaborative semantic tables," in *Semantic Web Collaborative Spaces*, P. Molli, J. Breslin, and M. E. Vidal, Eds., vol. 9507 of *Lecture Notes in Computer Science*, pp. 13–32, Springer, Heidelberg, Germany, 2016.

[7] V. Kaptelinin and M. Czerwinski, Eds., *Beyond the Desktop Metaphor*, MIT Press, Cambridge, Mass, USA, 2007.

[8] A. Adler, J. C. Nash, and S. Noël, "Evaluating and implementing a collaborative office document system," *Interacting with Computers*, vol. 18, no. 4, pp. 665–682, 2006.

[9] D. R. Karger, "Haystack: per-user information environments based on semistructured data," in *Beyond the Desktop Metaphor*,

V. Kaptelinin and M. Czerwinski, Eds., pp. 49–100, MIT Press, Cambridge, Mass, USA, 2007.

[10] J. E. Bardram, "Activity-based computing: support for mobility and collaboration in ubiquitous computing," *Personal and Ubiquitous Computing*, vol. 9, no. 5, pp. 312–322, 2005.

[11] S. Voida, E. D. Mynatt, and B. Macintyre, "Supporting activity in desktop and ubiquitous computing," in *Beyond the Desktop Metaphor*, V. Kaptelinin and M. Czerwinski, Eds., pp. 195–222, MIT Press, Cambridge, Mass, USA, 2007.

[12] S. Houben, J. Vermeulen, K. Luyten, and K. Coninx, "Co-activity manager: integrating activity-based collaboration into the desktop interface," in *Proceedings of the International Working Conference on Advanced Visual Interfaces (AVI '12)*, pp. 398–401, ACM, Capri Island, Italy, May 2012.

[13] P.-L. P. Rau, S.-H. Chen, and Y.-T. Chin, "Developing web annotation tools for learners and instructors," *Interacting with Computers*, vol. 16, no. 2, pp. 163–181, 2004.

[14] J. Pearson, G. Buchanan, H. Thimbleby, and M. Jones, "The digital reading desk: a lightweight approach to digital note-taking," *Interacting with Computers*, vol. 24, no. 5, pp. 327–338, 2012.

[15] J.-C. Jan, C.-M. Chen, and P.-H. Huang, "Enhancement of digital reading performance by using a novel web-based collaborative reading annotation system with two quality annotation filtering mechanisms," *International Journal of Human Computer Studies*, vol. 86, pp. 81–93, 2016.

[16] L. Sauermann, A. Bernardi, and A. Dengel, "Overview and outlook on the semantic desktop," in *Proceedings of the Workshop on the Semantic Desktop at ISWC 2005*, vol. 175, CEUR-WS, 2005.

[17] L. Drăgan, R. Delbru, T. Groza, S. Handschuh, and S. Decker, "Linking semantic desktop data to the web of data," in *The Semantic Web—ISWC 2011*, L. Aroyo, C. Welty, H. Alani et al., Eds., vol. 7032 of *Lecture Notes in Computer Science*, pp. 33–48, Springer, Heidelberg, Germany, 2011.

[18] R. Koning, P. Grosso, and C. de Laat, "Using ontologies for resource description in the CineGrid Exchange," *Future Generation Computer Systems*, vol. 27, no. 7, pp. 960–965, 2011.

[19] M. Uflacker and A. Zeier, "A semantic network approach to analyzing virtual team interactions in the early stages of conceptual design," *Future Generation Computer Systems*, vol. 27, no. 1, pp. 88–99, 2011.

[20] D. K. Barreau and B. Nardi, "Finding and reminding: file organization from the desktop," *ACM SIGCHI Bulletin*, vol. 27, no. 3, pp. 39–43, 1995.

[21] J. Teevan, C. Alvarado, M. S. Ackerman, and D. R. Karger, "The perfect search engine is not enough: a study of orienteering behavior in directed search," in *Proceedings of the Conference on Human Factors in Computing Systems—Proceedings (CHI '04)*, pp. 415–422, Vienna, Austria, April 2004.

[22] F. Abel, N. Henze, D. Krause, and M. Kriesell, "Semantic enhancement of social tagging systems," in *Web 2.0 & Semantic Web*, V. Devedžić and D. Gašević, Eds., vol. 6 of *Annals of Information Systems*, pp. 25–54, Springer, Boston, Mass, USA, 2009.

[23] R. Pak, S. Pautz, and R. Iden, "Information organization and retrieval: an assessment of taxonomical and tagging systems," *Cognitive Technology*, vol. 12, no. 1, pp. 31–44, 2007.

[24] P. Dourish, W. K. Edwards, A. LaMarca et al., "Extending document management systems with user-specific active properties," *ACM Transactions on Information Systems*, vol. 18, no. 2, pp. 140–170, 2000.

[25] A. Civan, W. Jones, P. Klasnja, and H. Bruce, *Better to Organize Personal Information by Folders or by Tags? The Devil is in the Details*, vol. 45, American Society for Information Science and Technology, Silver Spring, Md, USA, 2009.

[26] H. L. Kim, S. Scerri, J. G. Breslin, S. Decker, and H. G. Kim, "The state of the art in tag ontologies: a semantic model for tagging and folksonomies," in *Proceedings of the 8th Annual International Conference on Dublin Core and Metadata Applications (DC '08)*, pp. 128–137, Berlin, Germany, September 2008.

[27] S. Lohmann, P. Díaz, and I. Aedo, "MUTO: the modular unified tagging ontology," in *Proceedings of the 7th International Conference on Semantic Systems (I-SEMANTICS '11)*, pp. 95–104, Graz, Austria, September 2011.

[28] S. Angeletou, "Semantic enrichment of folksonomy tagspaces," in *The Semantic Web—ISWC 2008*, A. Sheth, S. Staab, M. Dean et al., Eds., vol. 5318 of *Lecture Notes in Computer Science*, pp. 889–894, Springer, Heidelberg, Germany, 2008.

[29] A. Passant and P. Laublet, "Meaning of a tag: a collaborative approach to bridge the gap between tagging and linked data," in *Proceedings of the WWW 2008 Workshop Linked Data on the Web (LDOW '08)*, C. Bizer, T. Heath, K. Idehen, and T. Berners-Lee, Eds., vol. 369, CEUR-WS, Beijing, China, April 2008.

[30] A. Marchetti, M. Tesconi, F. Ronzano, M. Rosella, and S. Minutoli, "SemKey: a semantic collaborative tagging system," in *Proceedings of the Workshop on Tagging and Metadata for Social Information Organization at WWW2007*, pp. 8–12, 2007.

[31] S. A. Golder and B. A. Huberman, "Usage patterns of collaborative tagging systems," *Journal of Information Science*, vol. 32, no. 2, pp. 198–208, 2006.

[32] H. Cunningham, D. Maynard, K. Bontcheva et al., *Text Processing with GATE (Version 6)*, 2011, https://gate.ac.uk/.

[33] M. Erdmann, A. Maedche, H. P. Schnurr, and S. Staab, "From manual to semi-automatic semantic annotation: about ontology-based text annotation tools," in *Proceedings of the Workshop on Semantic Annotation and Intelligent Content (COLING '00)*, pp. 79–85, ACL Press, Stroudsburg, Pa, USA, 2000.

[34] P. Fragkou, G. Petasis, A. Theodorakos, V. Karkaletsis, and C. Spyropoulos, "Boemie ontology-based text annotation tool," in *Proceedings of the International Conference on Language Resources and Evaluation (LREC '08)*, N. Calzolari, K. Choukri, B. Maegaard et al., Eds., pp. 1273–1279, ELRA, 2008.

[35] K. Bontcheva, H. Cunningham, I. Roberts et al., "GATE Teamware: a web-based, collaborative text annotation framework," *Language Resources & Evaluation*, vol. 47, no. 4, pp. 1007–1029, 2013.

[36] G. Petasis, "The SYNC3 collaborative annotation tool," in *Proceedings of the International Conference on Language Resources and Evaluation (LREC '12)*, pp. 363–370, ELRA, 2012.

[37] V. Uren, P. Cimiano, J. Iria et al., "Semantic annotation for knowledge management: requirements and a survey of the state of the art," *Web Semantics: Science, Services and Agents on the World Wide Web*, vol. 4, no. 1, pp. 14–28, 2006.

[38] O. Corcho, "Ontology based document annotation: trends and open research problems," *International Journal of Metadata, Semantics and Ontologies*, vol. 1, no. 1, pp. 47–57, 2006.

[39] S. Borgo and C. Masolo, "Foundational choices in DOLCE," in *Handbook on Ontologies*, S. Staab and R. Studer, Eds., pp. 361–381, Springer, Heidelberg, Germany, 2nd edition, 2009.

[40] A. Gangemi, S. Borgo, C. Catenacci, and J. Lehmann, *Task Taxonomies for Knowledge Content*, Metokis Deliverable D07, 2005.

[41] D. Magro and A. Goy, "A core reference ontology for the customer relationship domain," *Applied Ontology*, vol. 7, no. 1, pp. 1–48, 2012.

[42] A. Goy, G. Petrone, and M. Segnan, "A cloud-based environment for collaborative resources management," *International Journal of Cloud Applications and Computing*, vol. 4, no. 4, pp. 7–31, 2014.

[43] A. Goy, D. Magro, G. Petrone, C. Picardi, and M. Segnan, "Ontology-driven collaborative annotation in shared workspaces," *Future Generation Computer Systems*, vol. 54, pp. 435–449, 2016.

[44] G. Guest, A. Bunce, and L. Johnson, "How many interviews are enough? An experiment with data saturation and variability," *Field Methods*, vol. 18, no. 1, p. 24, 2006.

[45] M. Crouch and H. McKenzie, "The logic of small samples in interview-based qualitative research," *Social Science Information*, vol. 45, no. 4, pp. 483–499, 2006.

[46] A. Goy, D. Magro, G. Petrone, M. Rovera, and M. Segnan, "A semantic framework to enrich collaborative tables with domain knowledge," in *Proceedings of the International Joint Conference on Knowledge Discovery, Knowledge Engineering and Knowledge Management Vol. 3: KMIS*, pp. 371–381, SciTePress, Setúbal, Portugal, 2015.

5

User Experiences from L2 Children Using a Speech Learning Application: Implications for Developing Speech Training Applications for Children

Maria Uther ⓘ,[1,2] **Anna-Riikka Smolander,**[3] **Katja Junttila,**[3] **Mikko Kurimo,**[4] **Reima Karhila,**[4] **Seppo Enarvi,**[4] **and Sari Ylinen**[3,5]

[1]*Department of Psychology, University of Winchester, Sparkford Rd., Winchester SO22 4NR, UK*
[2]*Department of Psychology, University of Wolverhampton, Faculty of Education, Health and Wellbeing, MC Building (Room MC305), University of Wolverhampton, Wolverhampton WV1 1LY, UK*
[3]*Cognitive Brain Research Unit, Department of Psychology and Logopedics, Faculty of Medicine, University of Helsinki, P.O. Box 9, 00014 Helsinki, Finland*
[4]*Department of Signal Processing and Acoustics, School of Electrical Engineering, Aalto University, P.O. Box 13000, 00076 AALTO Espoo, Finland*
[5]*Cicero Learning, Faculty of Educational Sciences, P.O. Box 9, 00014 Helsinki, Finland*

Correspondence should be addressed to Maria Uther; m.uther@wlv.ac.uk

Guest Editor: Rafal Rzepka

We investigated user experiences from 117 Finnish children aged between 8 and 12 years in a trial of an English language learning programme that used automatic speech recognition (ASR). We used measures that encompassed both affective reactions and questions tapping into the children' sense of pedagogical utility. We also tested their perception of sound quality and compared reactions of game and nongame-based versions of the application. Results showed that children expressed higher affective ratings for the game compared to nongame version of the application. Children also expressed a preference to play with a friend compared to playing alone or playing within a group. They found that assessment of their speech is useful although they did not necessarily enjoy hearing their own voices. The results are discussed in terms of the implications for user interface (UI) design in speech learning applications for children.

1. Introduction

This study investigated child user experiences from a game-based language learning application that used automatic speech recognition (ASR) technology. The application, called 'Say it again, kid!' (SIAK) [1, 2], is designed to assist foreign language learning (vocabulary and production) in children. The technology behind the application is designed for both computers and tablets and uses ASR components for the assessment of children's speech produced while learning new words in a new, nonnative language. Thus far, the use of ASR engines in language learning has primarily been aimed at assisting language learning in native context (e.g., reading tutors such as listen [3], tball [4], space [5], and flora [6]).

In itself, the use of automatic speech recognition engines in children is challenging [7, 8], but the use of ASR to aid foreign language learning is a venture that poses even further challenges and is still a field that is underdeveloped [7–11].

Nonetheless, the SIAK project sought to address this research gap by developing and implementing a foreign language learning application. The application uses a Hidden Markov Model (HMM) segmenter to find phoneme boundaries in players' utterances. Phoneme segments are individually evaluated by a Recurrent Neural Network (RNN) bilingual phoneme classifier. The classifier results are then fed into a Support Vector Machine (SVM) scoring regressor which outputs a 0-100 score, which is further mapped into a rejection or a 1-5 star score. The latency for scoring an utterance is 2-3 seconds. The scoring mechanism is trained with in-game second-language (L2) utterances that were collected in previous experiments and scored by a human expert. The game is designed to produce a score computed using speech recognition technology after each utterance. We designed the trial of the game such that we compared performance and user reactions to a nongamified pronunciation learning environment. We used gamification since it has been suggested that this lends itself to more situated learning and a more immersive, engaging experience, which can be helpful within the language learning context (see [12–14] for a review).

The goal of the SIAK project was broadly to develop and test a novel, automatic speech recognition application to assist children in learning a new language. We have already published details of the algorithms and implementation itself [1]. In this paper, the research questions were as follows:

(i) What are the child's affective reactions to the SIAK?

(ii) What are their perceptions of pedagogical utility of gamified applications?

(iii) Where there any user aspects relating to the use of audio and interaction with speech in such applications that were problematic? This final point is crucial since the implementation of spoken language learning applications necessarily requires audio input and output.

Answering these research questions with a robust data set on user experience from actual child language learners is clearly needed in this underresearched and underdeveloped area.

As we were measuring child user experience in our application, we followed the framework for steps in usability testing according to Markopoulous & Bekker [15], namely, (1) develop assessment criteria (goals); (2) develop usability testing measurements (contexts, tasks); and (3) consider child characteristics that may constrain the design of the measurements/tasks (e.g., knowledge, age, and language ability). To this end, we focused on three areas in terms of assessment: (1) affective reactions and user engagement, (2) the perceived pedagogical value, and (3) audio interaction issues. As SIAK was an application which necessarily involved audio, we were interested in the users' perceptions of sound quality, which may then in turn affect their learning experience [16]. We were also interested in the use of speech production scoring. It should be emphasized that our goal here was not to present the actual learning outcomes (these will be presented in due course separately), but rather to report on the user experience feedback that would in turn inform the design of any future iterations of this application (and indeed speech training applications for children in general).

To measure the areas we wished to assess, we included questions regarding basic affective reactions (e.g., 'did you like this game?') as well as questions related to the elements which were pertinent to using speech-based applications (e.g., 'how clear was the sound?' and 'did you like hearing your own pronunciation during the game?'. For these questions, we used the smiley-o-meter method from the 'fun toolkit' techniques (see [17] for a review) with reference to

Likert-scale answers to agree to the statement with 5 points ('not at all' to 'very much' at the extremes). There were also items from an 'again again' table (also from the 'fun toolkit'), where the player was asked questions comparing game and nongame versions of the application. The 'again again' method was chosen for comparison of the game and nongame version as it allowed freedom for the children to express a preference (or dislike) for both versions simultaneously. The 'again again' items included questions on (a) Would you like this game for yourself (yes/no or maybe)? or (b) Would your teacher like this (yes/no/maybe)? The latter question (on the teacher's presumed preferences) was selected as it has been shown to tap into the child's sense of pedagogical utility more easily than a direct question of education value. Within other studies [18], it has been shown that the perception of whether a teacher chooses an application is related to the child's perception of how good it was for learning.

In line with our research questions, we hypothesized that

(a) The user experience (in particular, affective reactions) to our new SIAK software in the target audience of 8 to 12 year olds would be positive and especially so for the game-based version of the software.

(b) Although gamification of the application would presumably add positively to the user experience, the perceived pedagogical value may be rated less positively. In addition, there may be further desire for collaborative learning as games are often enjoyed as social endeavours.

(c) Participants rating of sound quality may be affected by application or device type [16] and although not studied explicitly before to our knowledge, we also wished to explore the children's reaction to their voice being scored by computers, which may cause self-consciousness for example.

2. Materials and Methods

2.1. Participants. We recruited 117 children (59 females and 58 males) aged between 8 and 12 years (mean=9.5; SD=1.2) from the Helsinki area. The children were recruited via local schools in Helsinki, with the consent of schools to recruit and consent of the children and parents to participate. There were also some children that were recruited directly via social and community networks.

2.2. Materials. The speech learning application (SIAK) is implemented as a computer board game that runs on an Android tablet or a Windows PC (laptop) and a headset [1]. Following the testing period, the children also were given a questionnaire that modeled itself on the 'fun toolkit'—namely using the 'smiley-o-meter' scale and the 'Again again table' [17]—where they were asked to respond to a question such as 'Would you like to use this game again' responding with either 'yes', 'no', or 'maybe'. The again again items were especially used to compare game and nongame versions. There were 15 questions in total (7 smiley-o-meter items, 7 again again items and one qualitative open-ended question asking whether they

 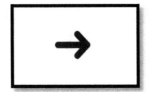

FIGURE 1: Screen shot of game and nongame versions of SIAK. Left panel shows example game 'world' that the learners explore. Right panel shows a nongame simple interface.

would like any particular item more (e.g., certain characters, sounds, etc.). All questionnaire items were given to the children in Finnish, which was their native language (any reference to questions in this paper are a translation into English of the original Finnish).

2.3. Procedure. The children were given the SIAK application which functioned to improve their pronunciation and broaden their vocabulary in English by introducing new English single words. As the children progressed in the game, they then encountered sentences which contained the new words. Children heard the word in Finnish and in English (produced by different native English speakers) and saw a related picture. The child was required to repeat the pronunciation of the word aloud. The children then received feedback on their pronunciation as a numerical score. The child's own and native English speaker's utterances were played again for comparison, and they received a one to five star rating based on the utterance score.

While testing, there were elements of the program that were not implemented as a game (instead of an immersive experience, they were shown a simple white background, forced order of stimulus presentation, no feedback) although the stimulation and the speech production task were the same as the game version which is described in [19]. Figure 1 shows the comparison of the screen between game and nongame version. A video of child participants playing SIAK is also available at: https://www.youtube.com/watch?v=-cgyJFV8-58&feature=youtu.be

All children evaluated the game and asked to compare game and nongame versions using the 'again again' question items (note that for 21 participants in the light user group, they did not evaluate the nongame version). The sample was divided into two groups: light users and experienced users. This was done as because we wanted a large sample of game players to give feedback on the application for user acceptance testing (UAT) and user experience (UX) reasons. For UAT/UX testing, we did not need the participants to test for many weeks at a time, but a minimum of one week – hence a 'light usage' group. On the other hand, to judge *efficacy* of the intervention, we also tested a set of 'experienced' users who have been using the application for at least 4 weeks. For this latter sample, we tested educational outcomes and brain measures as a result of training (those data will be reported separately), as training effects are typically seen over a minimum 1 month period. But it was not necessary for all

TABLE 1: Affective reactions from the SIAK application using the smiley-o-meter rating scale (NB: some items had lower N due to participants not filling in every question).

Question item	N	Range of scores	Mean rating	SD
How much do you like the application? (1=not at all; 5=very much)	116	1-5	4.07	.85
How easy did you find the application? (1= very difficult; 5= very easy)	116	2-5	3.86	.78
Did you have any problems with the game? (1=very much; 5=no problems)	114	1-5	3.62	.94

participants to be tested over such a long period, which is why we had two groups. Nonetheless, the experienced user group's user experience was also tested to determine whether length of time of use might have had an impact on the user ratings.

For the light users, the children played approximately 10-15 min per day, 3-4 days a week. The testing period was either 1-3 weeks for light users (n=50) or 4-5 weeks for experienced users (n=67). Out of these participants, 52 used Windows laptops and 65 used Android tablets. Following the testing period, they were given the questionnaire of 15 items in their native Finnish language, which covered the breadth of three key areas: overall affective reactions; value and interest in game/nongame versions and perceived pedagogical value (indexed by question on whether their teacher would like the game for the students) and finally a set of questions relating to audio and speech interaction (e.g., perceived sound quality, utility and affective reactions to having their speech samples tested).

3. Results

3.1. Affective Reactions. From Table 1, it can be seen that the children had a generally positive reaction to the software (mean scores around 4 on a scale of 1-5, with 5 being a positive rating). There were no differences between light users and extensive users on any of these measures.

Children were also asked about affective reactions in relation to the game and nongame versions of the program using the 'Again again table'—i.e., "Would you like to use this program again?"—and they could say either 'Yes', 'No' or 'Maybe'. Data from this method was analyzed for counts in each category using chi-squared analysis and showed that there was a significant difference between the game and nongame version ($\chi2=11.89$, p<0.05, df=4). For the game version, children were less ambivalent and generally more positive (63 out of 101 said yes to the question, 32 said maybe and only 6 said no). By contrast, for the nongame version, children were less positive and more ambivalent (only 28 out of 101 said yes, 36 said maybe and 37 said no).

TABLE 2: Assessment of whether teacher or self would like the game version.

	yes	maybe	no
Like game for self	59	40	13
Teacher would like the game[1]	38	72	2

[1]NB: this question was worded slightly differently in the first 50 participants but had wording changed later to ensure that the children would not misunderstand this question, from (a translation from Finnish) 'Would my teacher like this?' to 'Do you think your English teacher would like pupils to use this game'? We analysed the results from both wording versions and there was no statistically significant difference.

TABLE 3: Assessment of whether teacher or self would like the nongame version.

	yes	maybe	no
Like program for self	23	35	37
Teacher would like the program	22	59	14

TABLE 4: Rating of whether the player would prefer to play alone, with a friend or in a group.

	yes	maybe	no
Like to play alone	41	44	48
Like to play with friend	57	40	16
Like to play in a group	35	44	35

3.2. Perceived Pedagogical Utility and Collaboration Preferences for Game and Nongame Versions. The children were asked specifically about the perceived pedagogical utility by asking their views on whether their teacher would like the game versus whether they would like the game for themselves.

There was a tendency for the children to rate themselves as certainly liking the game for themselves (more 'yes' judgements) and a more ambivalent rating (more 'maybe' judgements) for the teacher ($\chi2=22.21$, p<0.01), see Table 2.

For the nongame version, the children appeared to rate the self and teacher liking the game differently ($\chi2=32.22$, p<0.01). In particular, they felt proportionally less ambivalent (when considering their yes/no responses) compared to the ratings the teachers who they felt would be more ambivalent and proportionally less negative, see Table 3.

Finally, when the children were asked separate questions as to whether they preferred to play alone, with a friend or with a group (results in Table 4).

It appears that in general the children appear to prefer playing with a friend more than they preferred to play alone or in a group. The differences between playing with a friend versus group might be due to the fact that 'group' may mean a group of people not known to the children and therefore they may be more ambivalent. Nonetheless, the finding that a greater proportion of positives and fewer negatives for playing with friends (compared to playing alone) would suggest that this age group tend towards preferring to play with known peers.

TABLE 5: Reactions from the SIAK application relating to speech and audio elements using the smiley-o-meter rating scale (NB: some items had lower N due to participants not filling in every question).

Question item	N	Range of scores	Mean rating	SD
How clear was the sound for the Finnish words? (1=not at all clear; 5=very clear)	116	2-5	4.13	0.97
How clear was the sound for the English words? (1=not at all clear; 5=very clear)	116	1-5	3.71	1.00
Did you like hearing your own pronunciation? (1=not at all; 5=very much)	114	1-5	3.83	1.21
Did you like getting feedback regarding your pronunciation? (1=not at all; 5=very much)	114	1-5	4.16	0.96

3.3. Reactions to Elements Related to Speech Training Software. In this category, there were two sets of questions posed to the children that are useful to consider when designing speech training software. The first set was in relation to the rating of speech quality. Here, the children were asked two separate questions: 'How clear was the sound for the Finnish-speaking words?' and 'How clear was the sound for the English-speaking words?'. The second set of questions related to the use of speech pronunciation feedback. As the program involved not only getting scoring as feedback, but also a replay in comparison to the native speech, they were asked two questions: 'Did you like getting feedback regarding your own pronunciation?' and 'Did you like hearing your own pronunciation during the game?'

Interestingly, the children rated the Finnish samples as having better sound quality than the native English samples ($F_{1,112}=7.703$, p<0.01), see Table 5. Although the sampling rate, microphone frequency responses were the same, they were not collected in identical labs and hence there may have been subtle differences. However, it appears that experience with the samples may have also played a part in the rating. The more experienced users rated samples better compared to the less experienced users of the application ($F_{1,112}=4.739$, p<0.05). This would suggest that the tendency to rate English sounds as worse quality than the Finnish ones might be due to exposure to that particular language.

With respect to the other questions regarding pronunciation, we looked at the aspects of perceived helpfulness of pronunciation training versus the actual experience of hearing their own voice. As one might have predicted, the children liked getting feedback more than the process of actually hearing their own voice. This is probably due to the children feeling self-conscious about their voices, but yet seeing the value of feedback.

4. Discussion

The results from our extensive user trial show that children in general had a positive user experience from the speech training SIAK game, answering our first question regarding the affective responses of children in this age group to the application. There was evidence that they in general were positive about the application (scoring over 4 out of 5 on a scale of 1-5) and they had found the application fun and helpful. They also did not report major difficulties with the application and found it easy to use. This is encouraging as it is helpful to have a tool that is perceived to be easy to use and elicits positive user feedback in this group.

With respect to our second research objective, the game version was perceived more positively in this age group compared to the nongame version. Interestingly though, the children ranked the perceived pedagogical value (marked by the question of whether the teacher liked the game) as being more definitely more negative to the nongame version than the game version. This contradicts our initial hypothesis that the game-based version may be perceived as having less 'educational value' and therefore be perceived by the children as being less favourably rated by their teachers. On the other hand, this was coupled with the finding that the children rated their teachers as more ambivalent towards the game (and nongame) versions than the children, suggesting that children may not necessarily be clear as to what their teachers would think. When interpreting these results, we need to be mindful that the children thought the question was meant to ask whether the teachers would choose the application for themselves, whereas instead, the intended focus was to ask whether the teachers would choose the application for the child. As [20] states, usability testing in children can often lead to unexpected results and raise more issues in testing than originally envisaged. However, this explanation is unlikely given that an elaboration of the wording was made in a later stage of data collection to clarify understanding, which did not change the results. Of course, further research is needed to definitively tell whether the children understood the question in the way intended. For example, one possibility could be that 'theory of mind' might not be fully operational in the children at the lower end of the age range of the sample [21]. However, we did not see any age differences in the way these questions were answered either.

With respect to the issue of collaboration, it appeared that this age group slightly preferred interaction with friends. Although more data would be needed to confirm this, the trend seen in these data accord with the results of other studies (e.g., Heikkinen et al.'s JamMo implementation [22]) which showed that children of this age group report liking working in pairs or very small groups, particularly on mobile devices.

With respect to the third research question, we also sought to investigate whether there were any auditory interaction issues (perceptions of sound quality, experience of pronunciation feedback) that may impact on the user learning experience or learning outcomes. With respect to the listening experience: it appears that there were some perceptions of difference in sound quality between native and nonnative speech. Although at the time of writing, detailed acoustical analysis on the speech was not available to know whether the perceived differences were the result of actual real subtle differences, the effect seemed to be moderated by experience (in other words, the heavy users of the program rated the nonnative speech better in sound quality than the more naïve users of the program). That is, the perception of sound quality may be affected by the difficulty to map speech input into existing mental representations. Further research is needed to determine whether sound quality is being affected by language experience.

With respect to pronunciation feedback, it was clear that this age group found feedback useful, but was less positive about hearing their own voice. These less positive ratings could be potentially mitigated by including assurances for the learners about confidentiality and the value of receiving a replay of their own voice. It is unclear whether this might reflect performance anxiety which may in turn see effects on performance. Further analysis on actual learning outcomes could explore whether there is a relationship as has been seen in other contexts [23].

In summary, future research will need to focus on the following areas:

(1) Whether user perceptions of voice clarity occur in native versus nonnative language in other samples and differ as a function of nonnative language experience (as we found here). We would also be interested in investigating whether such biases in perceived clarity impacts negatively on learning outcomes in foreign language learning contexts.

(2) Whether children in general are self-conscious of automated recognition as we found here and it would be useful to know whether such effects are modulated by age.

(3) Whether the positive affect ratings for gaming result in improved language learning outcomes compared to nongamified versions of the implementation. Such data would be helpful to determine whether the value of gaming in other domains also transfers to automatic speech recognition.

(4) Finally, we would be also interested in exploring whether children in general prefer to work with their friends in all learning contexts – or are there some situations where they may prefer to work alone (e.g., when they are being assessed and could be self-conscious).

5. Conclusions

In conclusion, these data serve a starting point of observations around speech training elements that are useful and well received for this 8-12-age group. Further work around the perception of speech quality in nonnative language and preference for collaboration is needed. What is clearly confirmed from the data is that the gaming aspect of the application is well-received and serves well as a positive tool to deliver speech training in this group. Children also interestingly appear to rate their teachers as being more ambivalent but also less negative for the game version. This may suggest that they do not necessarily perceive the game aspect to have less pedagogical value than the nongame version, although further research is needed to clarify.

Acknowledgments

The authors gratefully acknowledge funding from Academy of Finland (Grant no. 1274058) and the funding from Visiting Professor Grant awarded to Professor Uther by Nokia Foundation to complete the work on this evaluation while on a visit hosted by Cicero Learning.

References

[1] K. Reima et al., "SIAK - A Game for Foreign Language Pronunciation Learning," *Interspeech*, vol. 2017, 2017.

[2] A. Rouhe, R. Karhila, K. Heini, and M. Kurimo, "A pipeline for automatic assessment of foreign language pronunciation," *ISCA Workshop on Speech and Language Technology in Education (SLaTE)*, vol. 2017, 2017.

[3] J. Mostow, S. F. Roth, A. G. Hauptmann, and M. Kane, "Prototype reading coach that listens," in *Proceedings of the 12th National Conference on Artificial Intelligence. Part 1 (of 2)*, pp. 785–792, August 1994.

[4] M. Black, J. Tepperman, S. Lee, P. Price, and S. Narayanan, "Automatic detection and classification of disfluent reading miscues in young children's speech for the purpose of assessment," in *Proceedings of the 8th Annual Conference of the International Speech Communication Association, Interspeech 2007*, pp. 941–944, Belgium, August 2007.

[5] J. Duchateau, Y. O. Kong, L. Cleuren et al., "Developing a reading tutor: Design and evaluation of dedicated speech recognition and synthesis modules," *Speech Communication*, vol. 51, no. 10, pp. 985–994, 2009.

[6] D. Bolan-Os, R. A. Cole, W. Ward, E. Borts, and E. Svirsky, "FLORA: Fluent oral reading assessment of children's speech," *ACM Transactions on Speech and Language Processing*, vol. 7, no. 4, 2011.

[7] M. Gerosa, D. Giuliani, S. Narayanan, and A. Potamianos, "A review of ASR technologies for children's speech," in *Proceedings of the 2nd Workshop on Child, Computer and Interaction, WOCCI '09*, USA, November 2009.

[8] J. Proença et al., "Mispronunciation Detection in Childrens Reading of Sentences," *IEEE/ACM Trans. AUDIO*, vol. 26, no. 7, pp. 1203–1215, 2018.

[9] E. M. Golonka, A. R. Bowles, V. M. Frank, D. L. Richardson, and S. Freynik, "Technologies for foreign language learning: A review of technology types and their effectiveness," *Computer Assisted Language Learning*, vol. 27, no. 1, pp. 70–105, 2014.

[10] T. Cincarek, R. Gruhn, C. Hacker, E. Nöth, and S. Nakamura, "Automatic pronunciation scoring of words and sentences independent from the non-native's first language," *Computer Speech and Language*, vol. 23, no. 1, pp. 65–88, 2009.

[11] S. M. Abdou, S. E. Hamid, M. Rashwan et al., "Computer aided pronunciation learning system using speech recognition techniques," in *Proceedings of the INTERSPEECH 2006 and 9th International Conference on Spoken Language Processing, INTERSPEECH 2006 - ICSLP*, pp. 849–852, USA, September 2006.

[12] F. Cornillie, S. L. Thorne, and P. Desmet, "ReCALL special issue: Digital games for language learning: Challenges and opportunities," *ReCALL*, vol. 24, no. 3, pp. 243–256, 2012.

[13] T. M. Connolly, E. A. Boyle, E. MacArthur, T. Hainey, and J. M. Boyle, "A systematic literature review of empirical evidence on computer games and serious games," *Computers & Education*, vol. 59, no. 2, pp. 661–686, 2012.

[14] B. DaCosta and S. Seok, "Developing a Clearer Understanding of Genre and Mobile Gameplay," in *Handbook of Research on Immersive Digital Games in Educational Environments*, Advances in Educational Technologies and Instructional Design, pp. 201–231, IGI Global, 2019.

[15] P. Markopoulos and M. Bekker, "On the assessment of usability testing methods for children," *Interacting with Computers*, vol. 15, no. 2, pp. 227–243, 2003.

[16] M. Uther and A. P. Banks, "The influence of affordances on user preferences for multimedia language learning applications," *Behaviour & Information Technology*, vol. 35, no. 4, pp. 277–289, 2016.

[17] G. Sim and M. Horton, "Investigating children's opinions of games," in *Proceedings of the the 11th International Conference*, p. 70, Bremen, Germany, June 2012.

[18] G. Sim, S. MacFarlane, and J. Read, "All work and no play: Measuring fun, usability, and learning in software for children," *Computers & Education*, vol. 46, no. 3, pp. 235–248, 2006.

[19] R. Karhila, "SIAK - A game for foreign language pronunciation learning," in *Proceedings of the Annual Conference of the International Speech Communication Association, INTERSPEECH*, vol. 2017, p. 2017, 2017.

[20] G. Sim, J. Read, and M. Horton, "Practical and ethical concerns in usability testing with children," in *Games User Research: Study Approach, Case*, A. Peters, Ed., pp. 1–33, CRC Press, 2016.

[21] C. I. Calero, A. Salles, M. Semelman, and M. Sigman, "Age and gender dependent development of theory of mind in 6- to 8-years old children," *Frontiers in Human Neuroscience*, no. MAY, 2013.

[22] K. Heikkinen, J. Porras, J. Read, and G. F. Welch, "Designing Mobile Applications for children," in *User Requirements for Wireless, No. September*, L. T. Sorensen and and K. E. Skouby, Eds., pp. 501–512, River publishers, Aalborg, Denmark, 2015.

[23] D. E. Callan and N. Schweighofer, "Positive and negative modulation of word learning by reward anticipation," *Human Brain Mapping*, vol. 29, no. 2, pp. 237–249, 2008.

6

An Empirical Study of Visitors' Experience at Kuching Orchid Garden with Mobile Guide Application

Mohd Kamal Othman (ID), **Khairul Izham Idris, Shaziti Aman, and Prashanth Talwar**

Faculty of Cognitive Sciences and Human Development, Universiti Malaysia Sarawak, Kota Samarahan, 94300 Sarawak, Malaysia

Correspondence should be addressed to Mohd Kamal Othman; omkamal@unimas.my

Academic Editor: Francesco Bellotti

This empirical study was conducted to measure visitors' experiences with a mobile guide application at Kuching Orchid Garden (KOG). A between-group experimental design with 114 participants was conducted to test three groups; (1) a group using the mobile guide application as an information aid, (2) a control group (with no information aid), and (3) a group using pamphlets to explore the KOG. The Museum Experience Scale (MES) was used to evaluate visitors' experience for all participants, whilst the Multimedia Guide Scale (MMGS) was used to evaluate the visitors' experience with the mobile guide group. The most notable result from the Museum Experience Scale (MES) showed an impact on the visitors in terms of knowledge and learning when using the mobile guide application. However, the study found that enhancing visitors experience goes beyond simply providing interactive technologies in public settings to aid with information delivery. A limitation was providing relevant information in a timely and seamless manner due to inaccuracies of mapping between physical and digital environments. Future works should consider beacons and other Bluetooth low energy (BLE) technology to address the issues with location based devices. It is also important to highlight that the use of one's own device had a significant impact on learnability and control of the device, thus suggesting that the BYOD concept should be widely used in informal educational settings implementing mobile guide applications. The use of MES and MMGS informs future researches with an understanding of the different dimensions of visitors' experiences with mobile guide technology in public spaces to inform mobile application development that may further boost visitors' engagement, emotional connection, and meaningful experience.

1. Introduction

"Dewey's two aspects of the quality experience can be restated as follows: (1) the visitor interacts with the exhibit and has an experience, and (2) the visitor assimilates the experience so that later experiences are affected" [1, p. 36]. Mobile guide applications in public spaces offer visitors a different approach of engagement and experience [2–4]. The Ansbacher notion on visitors' experiences motivated this study to look at the impact of mobile guide technology on visitors' experience at Kuching Orchid Garden (KOG).

This current research aims to design, develop, and evaluate a mobile guide application by comparing visitors' experience at Kuching Orchid Garden (KOG) with and without the aid of the mobile guide application. The mobile guide application for Kuching Orchid Garden (KOG) uses

the *free-choice* learning approach in which visitors have the freedom to choose the content they want to learn, thus emulating the real visiting experience at Kuching Orchid Garden (KOG). This study also employed the Bring-Your-Own-Device (BYOD) model to eliminate familiarizing users with the technical workings of a new device as they would use their own devices, thus easing the users' interaction with the mobile guide application.

Kuching Orchid Garden (KOG) is a 15.4-acre property housing a wide collection of orchids in Borneo. This orchid garden houses a total of 75,000 plants comprising 85 genera. KOG is divided into two sections, a nursery, and a display area and it is open to visitors every day except Monday. Admission to the KOG is free. Currently, KOG does not provide enough support to the visitors. Despite having vast resources about orchids, many visitors had difficulties in learning about the genera on display at KOG due to the lack of information delivery. Hence visitors can be seen going through the orchids with no particular purpose. This could be explained by a study conducted by Templeton [5] who found that many visitors were not engaged or were disconnected when there were lingering unanswered queries as they went through the entire museum exhibition. The use of an interactive mobile guide application can possibly alleviate the issue by providing real-time information to the visitors.

Visitors' experience with the mobile guide application was evaluated using Multimedia Guide Scale (MMGS) and Museum Experience Scale (MES) developed by Othman et al. [6]. Petrie et al. [7] successfully conducted a few studies to measure visitors' experiences at historical churches with mobile guides and this has contributed to the understanding of different types of visitors' experiences. They also noted that visitors to public spaces varied and expected different things when they visited the places, be it with friends, companions, family members or even with school trips. Hence, this study was conducted to measure the impact of using a mobile technology (mobile guide) at a public space particularly at Kuching Orchid Garden (KOG).

The following were the key hypotheses investigated as part of this study:

(1) The level of knowledge and learning improves with the use of mobile guide at Kuching Orchid Garden (KOG).

(2) The visitors' engagement improves with the use of mobile guide at Kuching Orchid Garden (KOG).

(3) The visitors' emotional connection improves with the use of mobile guide at Kuching Orchid Garden (KOG).

(4) The visitors' emotional experience improves with the use of mobile guide at Kuching Orchid Garden (KOG).

It is important to highlight that the mobile guide application developed for this study is only suitable for android platform users as 81% of smartphone users in Malaysia are android users. In addition, other features such as RFID, Bluetooth, GPS, and other related features on the mobile guide were not utilized and discussed. This research article only focuses on users' experiences with the mobile guide application as an information aid at Kuching orchid Garden as opposed to the paper-based pamphlet and no guide users.

1.1. Technologies for Informal Educational Settings. The evolution of technologies has enabled the use of a variety of technologies in informal educational settings to enhance visitor experience such as 3D visualizations, wall projection displays, tablets, and mobile devices. It cannot be denied that these various technologies have a significant impact on their visitors, but it is important to understand how technologies can be used to improve the visitor experience at such places. Recently, Zimmerman and Land [8] addressed the use of mobile devices for informal science education at public spaces and provided four suggestions: (1) support social interaction within informal settings; (2) enhance the visitors'

experiences through the use of games, scientific narrative, and disciplinary-relevant aspects; (3) integrate activities to avoid visitors becoming passive learners; (4) provide after-visit support to bridge the learning using social media or other relevant media. Previous studies have highlighted the use of mobile guide technologies at various informal educational settings such as museums [3, 9–16] botanic gardens [2, 17]; zoos [18]; and aquariums [10, 19–21].

Though public space institutions are keen to adopt the newest available technology to attract more visitors, several studies showed that, in the early years of the adoption of mobile technologies in public space, it has failed to improve visitors' experience [22, 23]. Pekarik [24] highlighted that the visitors' experiences at public spaces, particularly cultural heritage sites, were extremely diverse, and providing the technology might not be the optimal solution. It is important to know about the visitors' engagement with the exhibits on displays or if they spent too much time understanding the technologies used. For example, the Personal Digital Assistant (PDA) was adopted to enhance the learning experience of museum visitors. However, visitors stumbled into situations that required them to troubleshoot the device because they were unfamiliar with it and this might affect the learning experience [9]. In addition, it was also found that the device put visitors in a passive "curator mode" because they had no freedom to explore the museum at their own will. This in turn resulted in low scores of visitors' experience, as they were not fully engaged with the museum artefacts.

The reason why previous use of mobile technologies in public spaces was not very successful was in part due to the lack of an understanding of visitor needs and experiences. This was highlighted by Sharples et al. (2010) who pointed out that "the main barriers to developing new modes of mobile learning are not just technical but social" (Sharples et al., 2010; p. 4). Brown [25] shared a similar view and stated that the most important aspect of mobile learning was that learners were constantly on the move whilst accessing information. It differs significantly from traditional instructional design in that it is more of a learner-controlled environment. Burston [26] highlighted that one of the main reasons the failure in the adoption of mobile technology in learning is the pedagogical innovation in which it did not fully utilize the mobile device affordance. Therefore, the design of the mobile guide application should follow the "free learning concept" in which the visitors can choose which content they would like to view. This allows visitors to actively construct their experience in more meaningful ways in accordance with their needs.

A major benefit of the use of technology is that it can deliver text, images, audio, video, multimedia, and other types of information visualization to the users. This helps users to gather more information on what they are learning in formal and informal educational settings. However, it is also important to highlight issues with the amount of information provided particularly on the mobile devices. In the context of informal educational settings, too much information could possibly lead to "cognitive overload" and users can become "lost in hyperspace" [27]. Therefore, personalization of users' learning experiences to suit different user needs is important.

A study by Walker [17] highlighted the importance of accommodating different user needs in informal learning settings such as historical sites, botanic gardens, and museums.

In addition, the question as to whether visitors at such places (informal educational settings) should use their own devices whilst viewing the information about the exhibition and its' artefacts surfaced due to the time spent by visitors to understand the technologies provided on site. This begets the concept of Bring Your Own Device (BYOD) where individuals are to bring their own Internet-enabled device to aid them with their work and learning. The BYOD model has been widely used (i.e., [28–32]). BYOD would make the visitors spend less time familiarizing themselves with the workings of the device as they are using their own devices.

1.2. Personalization Concepts and Bring Your Own Device (BYOD). Personalization has been around before the advent of Internet technologies and was mainly focused on the personalization of computer interfaces. Currently, the personalization concept is widely used for different purposes, for example, e-commerce applications, tourism, education, finance, culture, health, and many other related areas [33–35]. Informal educational settings such as museums have started to adopt this concept for their virtual museums as well as their guides at the exhibition galleries to improve the information delivery to their visitors. Personalization could ease the users' visit [36] by filtering information according to their needs, facilitating navigation and information access [34].

In the context of mobile guide for informal educational settings, the personalization concept should not be limited to the contents of the guides but can also include personalization of devices. For example, visitors may bring their own mobile devices (BYOD) which allows them to personalize the interface to access the information, such as viewing it on a bigger screen with a tablet or phablet or even changing the font or colour combination of the text. BYOD also helps to save cost for museums and other informal educational settings and their visitors because the institutions do not have to buy any devices or systems and the visitors do not need to pay extra rental of the devices [37]. The organizations also do not have to pay for manning or maintenance of the devices and systems.

1.3. User Experience (UX). Garrett [38] defined UX as the experience created by a product for the person who uses it (user) whilst Hassenzahl and Tractinsky [39] believed that the phenomenon of UX consists of several key elements which are emotion and effect, the experiential and beyond the instrumental. Experience is a concept that consists of meaning and history to an individual [39–41], whilst according to Bell et al. [10], Falk and Dierking [42], and Falk [20] it is the result of individuals who are engaged in the process of meaning-making. Therefore, UX is often related to the concept of engagement.

The engagement concept was highlighted as one of the qualities of UX with mobile device [4, 6], whilst Schaeffer and Polgreen [43] valued engagement as the interaction between visitors or users and the content provided in the mobile application. O'Brien and Toms [44] discussed how the UX

could be evaluated using the user engagement components. They further explained that the quality of user experience was based on a positive interaction with the computer which involved the relationship between the user engagement and the UX based on various experiential attributes such as aesthetics, novelty, involvement, perceived usability, and endurability. Recently, Pallud [45] discussed the use of interactive technologies in a French museum to engage their audience and promote a positive learning experience. Results indicated that ease of use and interactivity could influence the emotional process (authenticity and cognitive engagement) which in turn could influence learning.

Several studies have looked into measuring engagement and visitor experience. For example, Lykke and Jantzen [46] developed 10 dimensions of experience and evaluated them at the Center for Art and Media (ZKM), Karlsruhe (Germany). The ten dimensions of experience were as follows: (1) involving, (2) spontaneous, (3) interesting, (4) relevant, (5) learning, (6) unique, (7) interactive, (8) fun, (9) close, and (10) authentic. They found that experiences such as interesting, interactive, relevance, and involving were more frequently expressed. Other studies (for example, [3, 6]) used three components in measuring engagement with mobile guide technologies at informal learning settings particularly museum and historic churches: (1) general usability, (2) quality of interaction, and (3) learnability and control. Although learnability was usually associated with general usability, a previous study by Othman et. al. [3, 6] showed that it formed a different component with mobile guide technology. Quality of interaction is an important measure in evaluating engagement as it was posited that visitors have more meaningful learning or experience [47–50] without the trouble of learning to manage a technology, device, or an application. Learnability and control is a component that takes into consideration the visitors' capabilities to learn and control the application without any prior knowledge. The familiarity of users with their own device cancelled out the factors of learning to manage new devices [2, 51]. Thus, these components are essential in evaluating and improving visitors' engagement in public space.

2. Methodology

This experimental design study was conducted *in the wild* at Kuching Orchid Garden (KOG), a 15.4-acre property housing 75,000 plants comprising nearly 82 genera of orchids in Borneo. Participants were randomly assigned into three groups: control group (no aids/guide), paper-based pamphlet, and mobile guide. The research was performed with the aid of pamphlet and mobile guide application and designed and developed by the researchers with the information provided by the KOG management. The mobile guide application, which was developed, followed the *free-choice* version which enabled visitors to select points of interest during their visit. Although there were 82 genera of orchids at KOG, only 35 genera were available for visitors during the period of this study.

TABLE 1: Participants distribution.

Group	Number of Participants
Control group	42
Paper based pamphlets	34
	38
Mobile guide application	Native English speakers (17)
	Non-native English speakers (21)

3. Participants

As the research was conducted *in the wild*, which meant that the research was done in situ, participants were recruited from the available pool of visitors to KOG. A total of 114 participants of which 60 were males and 54 were females took part in this study over a one-month period. Convenience sampling technique was used in recruiting the participants. Participants were randomly assigned to groups. The participants varied from local tourists to tourists from various parts of the world such as France, Germany, Russia, and Switzerland. Among the participants, 53 were native speakers of English.

The participants were divided into three groups: control group (no aids/guide), paper-based pamphlet, and mobile guide as illustrated in Table 1.

Participants who used the mobile application were further categorized into two groups, which included native and nonnative speakers of the English language. It is important to highlight this aspect because the mobile application guide is in English and English is not the first language for the local participants. Hence, it might affect the overall experience, especially the knowledge and learning components.

4. Materials and Equipment

4.1. Mobile Guide Application. The mobile guide application was developed by implementing the mobile application development life cycle (MADL) that included requirement analysis, designing the application, implementation (development), testing, deployment, and maintenance [52]. During a visit to KOG, it was obvious that there was no information provided about the orchids, thus making it difficult for visitors to get more information about the orchids. As most visitors had their mobile devices with them, this presented an opportunity for the use of a mobile guide application to be designed to deliver information about the orchids.

In the requirement stage, it was determined based on visitors' behavior that the design of the mobile guide application should follow the free learning concept. Visitors preferred to choose which orchids they would like to view as they moved randomly in the garden instead of following a set path. This allowed visitors to actively construct their experience in a more meaningful way according to their needs. Information was to be made available corresponding to the location of the orchids within the KOG.

The design process started with different interfaces sketches to form a storyboard. This process continued with the development of low fidelity prototypes before it was coded

FIGURE 1: Main screen.

FIGURE 2: Main menu.

into a software application builder (Corona SDK) using LUA script. The application was tested using emulators followed by the actual device. The mobile guide application was further evaluated with the real users at KOG to gain more insights. The final product of the mobile guide application can be seen in Figures 1–5.

Figure 1 depicts the first page of the mobile guide when a visitor accesses the mobile guide application. Then, the visitor will be directed to the main menu as illustrated in Figure 2 and subsequently to the map of the KOG which contains point of interest markers (in red colours) on which users can tap as shown in Figure 3. These points of interest markers then lead to screens that have photographs of the orchids on the left and a genera name on the right, as illustrated in Figure 4.

Figure 5 portrays the screen for the orchid genera, with the beginning of the associated text visible.

4.2. Paper-Based Pamphlet Design. Paper-based pamphlets for KOG were designed using Microsoft Publisher. Figure 6 shows the information provided on the front page of the pamphlet, whilst Figure 7 shows the information on the back page. Care was taken to make sure that information and

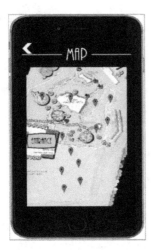

FIGURE 3: Kuching Orchid Garden with points of interest markers.

FIGURE 5: Information of the orchid based on genera.

FIGURE 4: Information associated with points of interest markers.

FIGURE 6: Information about orchid (front page).

FIGURE 7: Information about orchid (back page).

graphics in the pamphlet are the same as the mobile guide application to avoid any biases between the two information presentation modes.

4.3. Instruments. Participants who visited the Kuching Orchids Garden were requested to complete two questionnaires. The Museum Experience Scale (MES) consists of 37 items with a 5-point Likert scale rating. The scale was developed by Othman et al. [6] and comprises four factors for measuring visitors' experiences at museum and other cultural spaces. The factors of the MES are as follows:

(i) *Engagement (MES-Engagement)*, which refers to the engagement with the exhibitions and exhibits

(ii) *Knowledge/Learning (MES-Knowledge and Learning)*, which refers to the knowledge gained and understanding from the information provided

(iii) *Emotional Connection (MES-Emotional Connection)*, which refers to the emotional attachment with the contents and context of the exhibits/exhibitions

(iv) *Meaningful Experience (MES-Meaningful Experience)*, which refers to the quality of interaction with other visitors and the exhibits/exhibitions.

Visitors were also asked to complete a Multimedia Guide Scale (MMGS) also developed by Othman et al. [6] which contains 20 items with a 5-point Likert scale rating to evaluate the usability of the mobile application. The factors of MMGS are as a follows:

(i) *General Usability,* which refers to the usability of the mobile guide application, whether its functionality is appropriate

(ii) *Learnability and Control,* which refers to the ease of use of the guide

(iii) *Quality of Interaction,* which refers to the usability of the guide. Although it is often associated with usability component, a separate component was formed within the mobile guide for cultural heritage sites and museum.

4.4. Instruments Selection. It is important to highlight that the rationale of using MMGS and MES in this study is because Orchid Garden is considered as an informal learning setting like museums and other cultural heritage sites. The evolving definition of museums by the International Councils of Museum (ICOM) includes botanic gardens, zoos, aquariums, and science centres. Moreover, previous studies (i.e., [17, 53, 54]) have also discussed their studies within similar contexts.

The instruments have been used to measure visitors' experiences in different museums and historical churches in UK [3, 6, 7], Korea [55], Malaysia [56], China [57], and Austria [58, 59]. In addition, previous studies such as Baker et al. [60]; Kabassi [61]; Konstantakis et al. [62]; Moesgaard et al. [63] also highlighted the instruments development to measure visitors' experiences. The current study is part of study conducted by Idris [64]. Furthermore, one of the authors was involved in the development of the instruments used in this study. The Cronbach alpha for both instruments MES and MMGS was 0.94 which is considered highly reliable [4]. Details of the instruments items are illustrated in Tables 2 and 3.

4.5. Procedure. The present study involved three groups of participants; (i) visitors equipped with the mobile guide; (ii) visitors without any guide; and (iii) visitors with paper-based pamphlets as information guide. The research procedure was as follows:

(1) Visitors to the KOG were approached during a one-month duration in April 2016, (during operating hours) and asked if they would like to participate in this study.

(2) They were given a brief description of the study relating to visitors' experiences at KOG, with and without the mobile guide technology.

(3) Visitors who agreed to participate were informed about their right to withdraw from the study at any time without prejudice.

(4) Subsequently, they were asked to read and sign the consent form and were provided with the research instruction.

(5) Visitors were randomly assigned to the three groups.

(6) Visitors in the mobile guide group were requested to install the KOG mobile guide application on their mobile phones.

(7) Visitors then commenced their journey through KOG.

(8) All visitors were asked to complete the questionnaire (MES) after their visit.

(9) Visitors in the mobile group were asked to complete another set of questionnaire (MMGS) after they completed the MES.

(10) After a short debriefing session, the researchers answered any queries by the visitors.

5. Results

5.1. Museum Experience Scale (MES-Engagement). As illustrated in Table 4, statistically significant differences were noted between the groups as determined by one-way ANOVA $F(2, 111) = 9.082$, $p < 0.05$, $\eta^2 = 0.141$, thus, rejecting our hypothesis.

A small effect size of .14 was observed between the groups. In addition, a post hoc Tukey test was also carried out to have a better understanding on whether there were any statistical significant differences between the groups (modes of visit). The Tukey post hoc test revealed that the mean score for the mobile guide group (M = 3.721, SD = 0.587) was not statistically significant different compared to the no guide group (M = 3.943, SD = 0.647). On the other hand, there were statistically significant differences between mobile guide and paper-based pamphlet group (M = 3.400, SD = 0.348). Statistically significant difference was also noted between paper-based pamphlet and no guide group. In conclusion, although the no guide group showed a higher mean ranking compared to the mobile guide group, the differences were not statistically significant on the visitors' engagement.

5.2. Museum Experience Scale (MES-Knowledge and Learning). The result of the one-way ANOVA showed that there was a significant difference between the modes of visit $F(2, 111) = 6.833$, $p < 0.05$, $\eta^2 = 0.110$ for the *Knowledge/Learning* component, thus, rejecting our hypothesis. A small effect size of .11 was observed between the groups. In other words, the magnitude of effect accounted for 11%. In addition, a post hoc Tukey test was also carried out to have a better understanding on whether there were any statistical significant differences between the groups (modes of visit). Results indicated that there was no statistically significant difference between mobile guide (M = 3.805, SD = 0.508) and paper-based pamphlet groups (M = 3.706, SD = 0.335). On the other hand, there was a statistically significant difference between the mobile guide and no guide groups (M = 3.409, SD = 0.593), as well as between the no guide and paper-based pamphlet groups (M = 3.147, SD = 0.342). Hence, it showed that the use of mobile guide and paper-based pamphlet had a greater impact on the visitors' learning process at KOG.

5.3. Museum Experience Scale (MES-Emotional Connection). The result from the one-way ANOVA indicated that there was a statistical significant difference between the modes of visit on *Emotional Connection* $F(2, 111) = 16.744$, $p < 0.05$, $\eta^2 = 0.232$, thus, rejecting our hypothesis.

TABLE 2: MES instruments' items [4].

Engagement
I enjoyed visiting the exhibition
I felt engaged with the exhibition
My visit to the exhibition was very interesting
I felt I was experiencing the exhibition, rather than just visiting it
I was completely immersed in the exhibition
I felt focused on the exhibition
My visit to the exhibition was inspiring
The exhibition held my attention
I was interested in seeing how the exhibition would unfold as my visit progressed
I felt emotionally involved with the exhibition
While at the exhibition, I became unaware of what was happening around me

Meaningful Experience
During my visit, I was able to reflect on the significance of the exhibits and their meaning
During my visit, I put a lot of effort into thinking about the exhibition
Seeing rare exhibits gave me a sense of wonder about the exhibition
After visiting the exhibition, I was still interested to know more about the topic of the exhibition
Seeing real exhibits of importance was the most satisfying aspect of my visit to the exhibition

Knowledge/Learning
The information provided about the exhibits was clear
I could make sense of most of the things which I saw and did at the exhibition
I liked graphics associated with the exhibition
My visit enriched my knowledge and understanding about specific exhibits
Visiting the exhibition was fun
I like graphic-based information as supporting material at museum exhibitions
I discovered new information from the exhibits
I gained knowledge that I can use or have used as a result of my visit

Emotional Connection
The exhibition enabled me to reminisce about my past
My sense of being in the exhibition was stronger than my sense of being in the real world *(reversed relationship)*
I was overwhelmed with the aesthetic/beauty aspect of the exhibits
I wanted to own exhibits like those that I saw in the exhibition
I felt connected with the exhibits
I like text-based information as supporting material at exhibitions *(reversed relationship)*

TABLE 3: MMGS instruments' items [4].

General Usability	Learnability and Control	Quality of Interaction with the Guide
I will use mobile guide again when I visit an exhibition (*reversed relationship*)	I felt I was in control of the mobile guide	The mobile guide clearly provided feedback about my actions
Using the mobile guide enhanced my exhibition visit (*reversed relationship*)	I found it difficult to read the text on the screen of the audio/mm guide (*reversed relationship*)	It was clear to me when the mobile guide was taking the initiative to offer me information and when I needed to ask it for information
The information given by the mobile guide was too lengthy	Using the mobile guide did not require much training	I became unaware that I was even using any controls on the mobile guide
It was difficult to determine where I was in the exhibition with the mobile guide	The controls of the mobile guide were difficult to understand (*reversed relationship*)	
The mobile guide helped me to navigate around the exhibition (*reversed relationship*)	The mobile guide presented information in an understandable manner	
The mobile guide was a distraction	Learning to operate the mobile guide was easy	
The mobile guide was complicated to use It was difficult to select the option I wanted with the mobile guide		

TABLE 4: Statistical significance of one-way ANOVA (engagement).

			Tests of Between-Subjects Effects Engagement			
Source	Type III Sum of Squares	df	Mean Square	F	Sig.	Partial Eta Squared
Corrected Model	5.548[a]	2	2.774	9.082	.000	.141
Intercept	1539.032	1	1539.032	5038.414	.000	.978
Modes of visit	5.548	2	2.774	9.082	.000	.141
Error	33.906	111	.305			
Total	1606.040	114				
Corrected Total	39.454	113				

[a]R squared = .141 (adjusted R squared = .125).

A medium effect size of .23 was observed between the groups. Variance explained was 23% for the modes of visit. In addition, a post hoc Tukey test was also carried out to have a better understanding on whether there were any statistical significant differences between the groups (modes of visit) and the result revealed that there was no statistically significant difference between mobile guide (M = 3.531, SD = 0.583) and no guide groups (M = 3.575, SD = 0.411). However, there was a statistically significant difference between paper-based pamphlet (M = 3.147, SD = 0.342) and mobile guide groups. In addition, it was also identified that there was a statistically significant difference between paper-based pamphlet and no guide groups. In conclusion, although the no guide group had the highest mean score, the difference was not significant enough to be considered as an apparent outcome.

5.4. Museum Experience Scale (MES-Meaningful Experience). Further analysis of the meaningful experiences showed that there was a statistically significant difference between groups as determined by one-way ANOVA $F(2, 111) = 15.552$, $p < 0.05$, $\eta^2 = 0.219$, thus, rejecting our hypothesis. Eta revealed a medium effect size of 0.22 for the two groups which also stipulated a 22% variance. In addition, a post hoc Tukey test was also carried out to have a better understanding on whether there were any significant statistical differences between the groups (modes of visit). The result indicated that there was a significant difference between mobile guide (M = 3.563, SD = 0.338) and paper-based pamphlet groups (M = 3.159, SD = 0.377) and also that there was a significant difference between paper-based pamphlet and no guide groups (M = 3.657, SD = 0.474). However, there was no statistically significant difference between mobile guide and no guide groups.

5.5. Multimedia Guide Scale (MMGS). Figure 8 shows that there were differences in the mean scores of the components in MMGS (*General Usability, Quality of Interaction,* and *Learnability and Control*). Figure 8 also indicates that native speakers of English language had a higher mean score on all three components compared to nonnative speakers of English language. The component of *General Usability* had a mean score (M = 2.86, SD = 0.253), *Quality of Interaction* (M = 3.35, SD = 0.385), and *Learnability and Control* (M = 3.49, SD = 0.181). To investigate whether the differences were

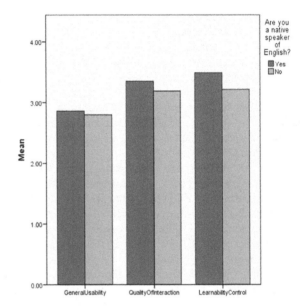

FIGURE 8: Mean scores of components in MMGS for native and nonnative speaker.

significant, further analysis was conducted using one-way ANOVA.

The result from the one-way ANOVA showed that there were statistically no significant differences in the mean score between the native and nonnative English speaker in the component of *General Usability* $F(1, 36) = 0.400$, $p = 0.531$ and *Quality of Interaction* $F(1, 36) = 1.171$, $p = 0.286$. On the other hand, there was a statistically significant difference between the native and nonnative English speaker $F(1, 36) = 6.296$, $p = 0.017$ in the component of *Learnability and Control*.

6. Discussions

All hypotheses were validated using the MES and MMGS instruments. The four components of the MES were used to compare the visitors' engagement among three different groups (no guide, paper-based pamphlet, and mobile guide application). The results showed that there was a significant difference between modes of visit at KOG as indicated by each of the MES components in the previous section.

Schaeffer and Polgreen [43] defined engagement as the visitors' interaction with the contents. Though this aim of the mobile guide was to enhance visitors' engagement at KOGS, the result (MES-Engagement) showed the opposite whereby the highest mean score for engagement was for visitors with no guide. This could be due to engagement being the direct interaction between the visitors and the orchids (content) at the garden. However, comparison between the mobile guide application and paper-based pamphlet showed that the use of mobile application had a higher mean score on visitors' engagement. This could be due to the interactive component of mobile guide content as stated by Hart et al. [65] which found that higher effect (engagement) ratings were extracted from the more interactive contents compared to textual content (menu-link navigation). This is further supported by Wakkary et al. [16] who found that using media (e.g., audio, video, or image) would spawn the visitors' engagement that resulted in the interest of the visitors towards the artefacts. A more recent study concretized the notion that the use of technology influenced the emotional process (authenticity and cognitive engagement) due to the ease-of-use and interactivity factors, which subsequently positively influence learning [45].

The result from the *Knowledge/Learning* component (MES-Knowledge and Learning) clearly justifies the need for providing information about the orchid displays at KOG. The group that did not use any guide scored the lowest mean whilst the mobile application group ranked the highest in *Knowledge/Learning*. This is obviously due to the lack of information about the orchids displayed at the garden. The mobile guide provided information that enabled visitors to acquire knowledge about the orchid displays, thus enhancing the *Knowledge/Learning* component. However, the mode of information delivery played a significant role as the paper-based pamphlet group had a lower mean score on the *Knowledge/Learning* component than the mobile application group though the stimuli (text and graphics) presented in the paper-based pamphlet were the same as in the mobile guide application. This could be due to the way the information was presented to the visitors. The interactivity of information delivery may affect the knowledge/learning experience of the visitors. A study by Findlay [2] found that mobile application gave visitors more opportunity when learning about the content and this was influenced by their needs. This is further supported by Pallud [45] who stated that ease-of-use and interactivity factors positively influenced learning [45]. Hence, informal educational institutions need to find solutions to deliver the information to visitors using the appropriate medium that will benefit both visitors and the informal educational institution.

Like the *Engagement* component (MES-*Engagement*), the highest rank in the *Emotional Connection* component (MES-*Emotional Connection*) is the group that did not use any guides during their exploration at the garden. This relates back to the *Engagement* component of the MES (MES-*Engagement*) that is directly proportional to the *Emotional Connection* component. Findings by Schaeffer and Polgreen [43] as well as [45] stated that visitors were likely to be engaged when they were emotionally attached. Therefore,

the group that did not use any guides scored the highest on both components. This could be due to a few factors as presented by previous studies. A research by Falk and Gillespie [66] found that the external factor such as the layout design might affect emotion, which contributes to the visitors' engagement at science centres. It could be said that the external environment was more appealing than the interface design of the digital environment in the mobile guide. This could be due to lack of aesthetics resulting in low emotional arousal with regard to the mobile guide environment as compared to the actual surrounding area. Emotional connection is crucial as it can enhance visitors' engagement, which would then supply the basics for visitors to construct their knowledge on the subject matter of the public space [67]. Therefore, future work must pay attention to the aesthetics of the visual design component of the mobile guide interface design.

One of the aims for visiting informal education institutions and public spaces such as museums, historical sites, and botanical gardens is to achieve a *Meaningful Experience* A study by Falk et al. [19] showed that 7 percent of zoo or aquarium (public space) visitors were experience seekers. Therefore, this suggested that a meaningful experience might indicate an impactful experience that was beyond information acquisition [68]. The result from this study (MES-*Meaningful Experience*) shows that the group that used the mobile application came second to the group that did not use any guide in terms of having a meaningful experience. However, the differences were not statistically significant between the two (2) groups. Hence, both groups of visitors had an impactful episode during their visit to KOG. This result echoes Chiodo and Rupp [67] who stated that an exhibit should be more than just knowledge that individuals could acquire in order to have an impact on the visitors [67]. It is important that the design best suits the subject matter and the visitor needs [41, 67]. This may imply that the current design of the mobile guide application is not the best design for the subject matter and visitor needs. Therefore, it is proposed that participatory design be used for future works on the mobile guide application where users are included as cocreators to delve deeper into the design the suits the visitor needs.

The three components of MMGS, *General Usability, Quality of Interaction,* and *Learnability and Control,* were used to evaluate the use of the mobile application in this study. The result shows that native English speakers had a higher mean score on the *General Usability* compared to nonnative speakers. This could be due to the mobile guide application being in English, which could pose comprehension issues for some nonnative speakers that was perceived as a usability issue. However, the difference between the two (2) groups was not statistically significant. The overall result of *General Usability* shows that the total mean score is on the middle of the verdict. In short, the *General Usability* of the developed mobile application can still be enhanced to improve the score. Usability is one of the most essential aspects of a mobile application as users need usable products [38]. According to Hart et al. [65] the general usability is also affected by the interface design. In the case of the mobile guide application, the interface for points of interests may not match up exactly with the location of each orchid in the physical environment because it is not a GPS-based application. This localization issue could pose as a usability issue. It is proposed that future design utilized GPS or RFID tags to enable a more accurate mapping between physical and digital environments.

Recently, many informal educational settings have focused on the use of beacons and other Bluetooth low energy (BLE) technology to address the issues with location based devices. Visitors at such places are expecting to receive relevant information about the artefacts in a timely and seamless manner. The use of beacons technology can possibly eliminate the boundary between the physical and digital user experiences whilst visiting such informal educational settings thus improves their meaningful experiences and engagement. In addition, the mobile guide developed in this study can be used as an indicator to address the amount of information required for the exhibition, thus affecting their knowledge and learning. The findings from this study could benefit future researchers who want to implement beacons technology in such settings

The *Quality of Interaction* between the visitors and the mobile application as an information aid is one of the important measures of user experience (UX) [4]. The MMGS result indicates a good response from the visitors who used the mobile application. However, it also shows that there are still some room for improvements for the application. This relates to the component of *Meaningful Experience* in the MES. The group that used the mobile application had a relatively high score that was higher than the paper-based pamphlet group but lower in comparison to the group without any guide. Therefore, though Othman [4] stated that visitors would have a more meaningful experience if the technologies were interactive, the *Quality of Interaction* goes beyond simply providing technologies.

The *Learnability and Control* component shows the most positive outcome out of the other MMGS's components. The results show a significant difference between the native and nonnative English speaker whereby native speakers of English found it easier to understand and use. As mentioned before, the level of English proficiency may impede comprehension thus affecting, users' ability to understand and use the mobile guide application. However, the result from native speakers is a positive indicator that the developed mobile guide application is easy to understand and use. Learnability is an important aspect of user experience as it also affects the quality of interaction [69]. Therefore, a remediation could be to provide dual language selection for visitors using the mobile guide application at KOG.

Othman [4] stated that technology should not be a barrier between visitors and the content of the public space. Research conducted by Bartneck et al. [9] found that visitors who were unfamiliar with mobile guides had a negative experience during their visit. Thus, this research used the concept of Bring Your Own Device (BYOD). This allowed the visitors to install the application on their own device; thus there was no need to familiarize themselves with new devices. Therefore, the user has prior understanding of the control of the device, consequently reducing or eliminating the learning curve.

This contributed to the high mean score for both native and nonnative groups.

7. Conclusions

The advancement of today's technologies such as smartphones, tablets, and phablets has enabled the use of a variety of technologies in informal educational settings to enhance visitor experience, particularly mobile guide applications. Mobile guide applications in public spaces offer visitors a different approach of engagement and experience [2–4]; however it cannot be assumed that the deployment of such technologies will automatically enhance the visitor engagement and overall experience as evidenced by the results of this study.

The most notable result from the Museum Experience Scale (MES) used to investigate the overall visitors' experience showed an impact on the visitors in terms of knowledge and learning when using the mobile guide application. The MES result shows that the visitors' engagement with the use of the mobile guide application has a higher mean score and a significant difference in terms of knowledge or learning compared to those who have either used the paper-based pamphlet or did not use any guide. However, the study found that enhancing visitors experience goes beyond simply providing interactive technologies in public settings to aid with information delivery. This is evidenced by the results in the other three (3) components of MES (engagement, emotional connection, and meaningful experience) where though the mean score is higher than the paper-based pamphlet, it is lower than the group using no guide at all. This may imply that the mobile guide design did not best suit the subject matter and the visitors' needs. This was also reflected in the mean score for the General Usability and Quality Interaction component of the Multimedia Guide Scale (MMGS).

Future works should focus on improving the mobile guide design on a few issues notably on the aesthetics of the visual design component of the mobile guide interface design to evoke emotional arousal similar to the actual surrounding area and utilizing GPS or RFID tags to enable a more accurate mapping between physical and digital environments. It is also important to highlight that the study found that the use of own device has a significant impact on the ease of use as it eliminates issues with learnability and control of the device. Therefore, the BYOD concept should be widely used in informal education institutions implementing mobile guide applications.

In conclusion, the use of MES and MMGS helped us understand the different dimensions of visitors' experiences with mobile guide technology in public spaces particularly at KOG. Future researches may also explore and improve the developed mobile application that may further boost the visitors' engagement, emotional connection, and meaningful experience.

References

[1] T. Ansbacher, "John Dewey's experience and education: Lessons for museums," *Curator: The Museum Journal*, vol. 41, no. 1, pp. 36–50, 1998.

[2] K. Findlay, *Visitor Use of Mobile Devices: The Botanic Garden & Otari-Wilton's Bush*, 2015, https://pdfs.semanticscholar.org/e8f1/5f3118fb33183ec4c0a1b35181feb0c79851.pdf.

[3] M. K. Othman, H. Petrie, and C. Power, "Visitors' emotions, touristic or spiritual experiences in historic churches: the development of church experience scale (CES)," in *Proceedings of the 9th International Conference on Cognitive Science*, Procedia - Social and Behavioral Sciences, Elsevier, 2013.

[4] M. K. Othman, *Measuring Visitors' Experiences with Mobile Guide Technology in Cultural Spaces [Ph.D. thesis]*, University of York, 2012.

[5] C. A. Templeton, *Museum Visitor Engagement Through Resonant, Rich and Interactive Experiences [M.S. thesis]*, Carnegie Mellon University, 2011, http://repository.cmu.edu/cgi/viewcontent.cgi?article=1024&context=theses.

[6] M. K. Othman, H. Petrie, and C. Power, "Engaging visitors in museums with technology: Scales for the measurement of visitor and multimedia guide experience," *Lecture Notes in Computer Science (including subseries Lecture Notes in Artificial Intelligence and Lecture Notes in Bioinformatics): Preface*, vol. 6949, no. 4, pp. 92–99, 2011.

[7] H. Petrie, M. K. Othman, and C. Power, "Smartphone guide technology on cultural spaces: measuring visitors' experience with an iphone multimedia guide in shakespeare's church," *International Journal of Human Computer Interaction*, 2017, http://dx.doi.org/10.1080/10447318.2017.

[8] H. T. Zimmerman and S. M. Land, "Integrating Mobile Computers into Informal Science Education," in *Proceedings of the Preparing Informal Science Educators*, pp. 169–183, Springer International Publishing, 2017.

[9] C. Bartneck, A. Masuoka, T. Takahashi, and T. Fukaya, "The learning experience with electronic museum guides," *Psychology of Aesthetics, Creativity, and the Arts*, vol. 1, no. 1, pp. 18–25, 2006.

[10] P. Bell, B. Lewenstein, W. A. Shouse, and M. A. Feder, *Learning Science in Informal Environments-People, Places and Pursuits*, 2009, http://doi.org/10.1080/00958964.2011.623734.

[11] A. Feix, S. Göbel, and R. Zumack, "DinoHunter: Platform for mobile edutainment applications in museums," in *Technologies for Interactive Digital Storytelling and Entertainment (TIDSE 2004)*, pp. 3105-2004, Springer-Verlag, Berlin, Germany, 2004.

[12] E. Klopfer, J. Perry, K. Squire, M.-F. Jan, and C. Steinkuehler, "Mystery at the museum - A collaborative game for museum education," in *Proceedings of the Computer Supported Cooperative Learning (CSCL)*, International Society of the Learning Sciences, Taipei, Taiwan, 2005.

[13] N. Proctor and C. Tellis, "The state of the art in museum handhelds in 2003," in *Museum and the Web*, Archives and Museums Informatics, Charlotte, NC, USA, 2003.

[14] F. Sparacino, "The museum wearable?: real-time sensor-driven understanding of visitors interests for personalized visually-augmented museum experiences," in *Proceedings of the Museums and the Web*, J. Trant and D. Bearman, Eds., Archives & Museum Informatics, Toronto, Canda, 2002.

[15] B. Turan and H. Keser, "Museum Guide Mobile App: The Case of the Near," in *Procedia - Social and Behavioral Sciences*, vol. 131, pp. 278–285, 2014.

[16] R. Wakkary, K. Newby, M. Hatala, D. Evernden, and M. Droumeva, "Interactive audio content?: an approach to audio content for a dynamic museum experience through augmented audio reality and adaptive information retrieval," in *Proceedings of the Museums and the Web Conference*, 2004.

[17] K. Walker, "Visitor constructed personalized learning trails," in *Museums and the Web*, D. A. Bearman and J. Trant, Eds., Archives Museum Informatics, Toronto, Canada, 2007.

[18] B. Wagoner and E. Jensen, "Science learning at the zoo?: evaluating childrens developing understanding of animals and their habitats," *Psychology Society*, vol. 3, no. 1, pp. 65–76, 2010, http://wrap.warwick.ac.uk/46484/Retrieved from.

[19] J. H. Falk, E. M. Reinhard, C. L. Vernon, K. Bronnenkant, J. E. Heimlich, and N. L. Deans, "Why zoos & aquariums matter: assessing the impact of a visit to a zoo or aquarium," *Association of Zoos Aquariums*, vol. 24, Article ID 0205843, pp. 1–24, 2007.

[20] J. Falk and M. Storksdieck, "Using the contextual model of learning to understand visitor learning from a science center exhibition," *Science Education*, vol. 89, no. 5, 2005, http://doi.org/10.1002/sce.20078.744778.

[21] R. Malamud, L. Marino, N. Nobis, R. Broglio, and S. O. Lilienfeld, "Do zoos and aquariums promote attitude change in visitors? a critical evaluation of the american zoo and aquarium study," *Society & Animals*, vol. 18, no. 2, Article ID 156853010, pp. 126–138, 2010, http://doi.org/10.1163/.

[22] M. Fleck, M. Frid, T. Kindberg, E. O'Brien-Strain, R. Rajani, and M. Spasojevic, "From informing to remembering: Ubiquitous systems in interactive museums," *IEEE Pervasive Computing*, vol. 1, no. 2, pp. 13–21, 2002.

[23] N. Proctor and J. Burton, *Tate Modern Multimedia Tour Pilots 2002-2003. Mlearn2003: Learning with Mobile Devices*, Research and Development, Learning and Skills Development Agency, 2003.

[24] A. J. Pekarik, "The long horizon: The shared values of museum," *Curator: The Museum Journal*, vol. 54, no. 1, pp. 75–78, 2011.

[25] E. J. Brown, *Education in The Wild: Contextual And Location-Based Mobile Learning in Action. A Report from The STELLAR Alpine Rendezvous Workshop Series*, E. Brown, Ed., University of Nottingham, Learning Sciences Research Institute, Nottingham, UK, 2010, http://oro.open.ac.uk/29882/1/ARV_Education_in_the_wild.pdf.

[26] J. Burston, "Twenty years of MALL project implementation: A meta-analysis of learning outcomes," *ReCALL*, vol. 27, no. 1, pp. 4–20, 2015.

[27] M. Otter and H. Johnson, "Lost in hyperspace: metrics and mental models," *Interacting with Computers*, vol. 13, no. 1, pp. 1–40, 2000.

[28] Project Tomorrow, Learning in the 21st century: Mobile devices + social media=personalized learning. Reports from Speak Up, 2012, Retrieved May 16, 2013 from http://www.tomorrow.org/speakup/speakup_reports.html.

[29] Alberta Education, *Bring Your Own Device: A Guide for Schools*, 2012, http://education.alberta.ca/admin/technology/research.aspx.

[30] D. Rinehart, *Students Using Mobile Phones in The Classroom: Can The Phones Increase Content Learning (Proquest Digital Dissertations)*, 2012, http://gradworks.umi.com/15/17/1517773.html.

[31] Y. Song, "Bring Your Own Device (BYOD)" for seamless science inquiry in a primary school," *Computers & Education*, vol. 74, pp. 50–60, 2014.

[32] Y. Song and S. C. Kong, "Affordances and constraints of BYOD (Bring Your Own Device) for learning and teaching in higher education: Teachers perspectives," *The Internet and Higher Education*, vol. 32, pp. 39–46, 2017.

[33] J. P. Bowen and S. Filippini-Fantoni, "Personalization and The Web from A Museum Perspective," in *Museums and the Web*, D. Bearman and J. Trant, Eds., Archives & Museum Informatics, Toronto, Canada, 2004.

[34] S. Filippini-Fantoni, J. P. Bowen, and T. Numerico, "Personalization issues for science museum," in *E-learning and Virtual Science Centers*, W. H. Leo and S. R. Tan, Eds., Idea Group Publishing, Pennsylvania, PA, USA, 2005.

[35] S. Filippini-Fantoni, "Personalization through IT in museums," in *Proceedings of the International Cultural Heritage Informatics Meeting (ICHIM '03)*, Archives & Museum Informatics Europe, Paris, France, 2003.

[36] A. C. Bertoletti, M. C. Moraes, and A. C. da Rocha Costa, "Providing Personal Assistance in the SAGRES Virtual Museum," in *Museums and the Web*, Archives & Museum Informatics, Toronto, Canda, 2001.

[37] R. V. D. M. Gartner, *Gartner Says Tablets Are the Sweet Spot of BYOD Programs*, 2014, https://www.gartner.com/newsroom/id/290921.

[38] J. J. Garrett, *The Elements of User Experience*, Pearson Education, California, Calif, USA, 2nd edition, 2011.

[39] M. Hassenzahl and N. Tractinsky, "User experience research agenda," *Behaviour & Information Technology*, vol. 25, no. 2, Article ID 01449290500330331, pp. 91–97, 2006, http://doi.org/10.1080/01449290500330331.

[40] M. Hassenzahl, "User experience (UX): towards an experiential perspective on product quality," in *Proceedings of the 20th Conference on l'Interaction Homme-Machine (IHM '08)*, pp. 11–15, ACM, Metz, France, September 2008.

[41] M. Hassenzahl, K. Eckoldt, S. Diefenbach, M. Laschke, E. Lenz, and J. Kim, "Designing moments of meaning and pleasure. Experience design and happiness," *International Journal of Design*, vol. 7, no. 3, pp. 21–31, 2013.

[42] J. H. Falk and L. D. Dierking, "The 95 percent solution," *American Scientist*, vol. 98, no. 6, pp. 486–493, 2010, http://doi.org/10.1511/2010.87.486.

[43] J. Schaeffer and E. Polgreen, *Engaging Audiences: Measuring Interactions, Engagement and Conversions*, New Mexico, NM, USA, 2012, http://www.j-lab.org/publications/engaging-audiences.

[44] H. L. O'Brien and E. G. Toms, "Examining the generalizability of the User Engagement Scale (UES) in exploratory search," *Information Processing & Management*, vol. 49, no. 5, pp. 1092–1107, 2013.

[45] J. Pallud, "Impact of interactive technologies on stimulating learning experiences in a museum," *Information and Management*, vol. 54, no. 4, pp. 465–478, 2017.

[46] M. Lykke and C. Jantzen, "User experience dimensions: A systematic approach to experiential qualities for evaluating information interaction in museums," in *Proceedings of the ACM Conference on Human Information Interaction and Retrieval, CHIIR 2016*, pp. 81–90, Association for Computing Machinery, New York, NY, USA, March 2016.

[47] L. D. Dierking, J. J. Luke, K. A. Foat, and L. Adelman, "The family and free-choice learning," *Museum News-Washington*, vol. 80, no. 6, pp. 38–43, 2001.

[48] J. H. Falk, "Free-choice environmental learning: framing the discussion," *Environmental Education Research*, vol. 11, no. 3, Article ID 13504620500081129, pp. 265–280, 2005, http://doi.org/10.1080/13504620500081129.

[49] C. W. Glenn, "Cognitive free will learning theory," *Procedia - Social and Behavioral Sciences*, vol. 97, pp. 292–298, 2013.

[50] A. K. Houseal, C. M. Bourque, K. M. Welsh, and M. Wenger, "Free-Choice Family Learning?: A Literature Review for the National Park Service," *Journal of Interpretation Research*, vol. 19, no. 1, pp. 7–29, 2014.

[51] M. C. Cheh and T. Weng, "Research and development of application of mobile barcode to mobile sightseeing guide on mobile phone," *WSEAS Transactions on Information Science and Applications*, vol. 7, no. 1, pp. 16–25, 2010.

[52] A. Kumar and T. Vithani, "A Comprehensive Mobile Application Development and Testing Lifecycle," in *Proceedings of the IT Professional Conference*, pp. 1–27, 2014, http://doi.org/10.1109/ITPRO.2014.7029289.

[53] L. Naismith and P. Smith, "Context-sensitive information delivery to visitors in a botanic garden," in *Proceedings of the ED-MEDIA World Conference on Educational Multimedia, Hypermedia and Telecommunications*, Lugano, Switzerland, 2004.

[54] L. Naismith, M. Sharples, and J. Ting, "Evaluation of CAERUS: a Context Aware Mobile Guide," in *Proceedings of Mlearn 2005 - Mobile Technology: The Future of Learning in Your Hands*, pp. 112–115, Cape Town, South Africa, 2005.

[55] J. Jeon, G. Chae, and W. S. Yeo, "Developing a location-aware mobile guide system for GLAMs based on TAPIR sound tag: A case study of the Lee Ungno museum," in *International Conference on Human-Computer Interaction*, pp. 425–433, Springer, Cham, Switzerland, 2014.

[56] M. K. Othman, N. E. Young, and S. Aman, "Viewing islamic art museum exhibits on the smartphone: re-examining visitors experiences," *Journal of Cognitive Sciences Human Development*, vol. 1, no. 1, pp. 102–118, 2015.

[57] G. Chen, Y. Zhang, N. S. Chen, and Z. Fan, "Context-aware ubiquitous learning in science museum with ibeacon technology," in *Learning, Design, and Technology*, pp. 1–24, Springer International Publishing, 2016.

[58] L. Neuburger and R. Egger, "An Afternoon at the Museum: Through the Lens of Augmented Reality," in *Information and Communication Technologies in Tourism*, R. Schegg and B. Stangl, Eds., Springer, Cham, Switzerland, 2017.

[59] L. Neuburger and R. Egger, "Augmented reality: providing a different dimension for museum visitors," in *Augmented Reality and Virtual Reality*, T. Jung and M. Tom Dieck, Eds., Springer, Cham, Switzerland, 2018.

[60] E. J. Baker, J. A. A. Bakar, and A. N. Zulkifli, "Elements of museum mobile augmented reality for engaging hearing impaired visitors," in *Proceedings of the 2nd International Conference on Applied Science and Technology, (ICAST '17)*, vol. 1891, pp. 20–33, AIP Publishing, April 2017.

[61] K. Kabassi, "Evaluating websites of museums: State of the art," *Journal of Cultural Heritage*, vol. 24, pp. 184–196, 2017.

[62] M. Konstantakis, K. Michalakis, J. Aliprantis, E. Kalatha, and G. Caridakis, "Formalising and evaluating Cultural User Experience," in *Proceedings of the 12th International Workshop on Semantic and Social Media Adaptation and Personalization (SMAP '17)*, pp. 90–94, IEEE, July 2017.

[63] T. G. Moesgaard, M. Witt, J. Fiss et al., "Implicit and explicit information mediation in a virtual reality museum installation

and its effects on retention and learning outcomes," in *Proceedings of the 9th European Conference on Games-Based Learning: ECGBL 2015*, R. Munkvold and L. Kolås, Eds., pp. 387–394, Academic Conferences and Publishing International, UK, 2015.

[64] K. I. Idris, *Enhancing Visitors' Engagement Using Mobile Guide Application at Kuching Orchid Garden (KOG)*, Universiti Malaysia, Malaysia, 2016, https://www.researchgate.net/publication/304657297_ENHANCING_VISITORS%27_ENGAGEMENT_USING_MOBILE_GUIDE_APPLICATION_AT_KUCHING_ORCHID_GARDEN_KO.

[65] J. Hart, A. G. Sutcliffe, and A. Angeli, *Evaluating User Engagement Theory*, CHI, 2012.

[66] J. H. Falk and K. L. Gillespie, "Investigating the role of emotion in science center visitor learning," *Visitor Studies*, vol. 12, no. 2, pp. 112–132, 2009.

[67] J. Chiodo and A. Rupp, "Setting the Stage for Meaningful Exhibits," in *Exhibitionist*, The Portico Group, 1999.

[68] D. G. Oblinger, *Learning Spaces*, EDUCAUSE, 2006.

[69] N. Bevan, "Measuring usability as quality of use," *Software Quality Journal*, vol. 4, no. 2, pp. 115–130, 1995.

7

Organizational and Technological Aspects of a Platform for Collective Food Awareness

Antonio P. Volpentesta, Alberto M. Felicetti ⓘ, and Nicola Frega

Department of Mechanical Energy and Management Engineering, University of Calabria, Arcavacata di Rende (CS), 87036, Italy

Correspondence should be addressed to Alberto M. Felicetti; alberto.felicetti@unical.it

Guest Editor: Kashif Zia

Can Internet-of-food technologies foster collective food awareness within a food consumer community? The paper contributes to answer this question in a fourfold aspect. Firstly, we model a cooperative process for generating and sharing reliable food information that is derived from food instrumental measurements performed by consumers via smart food things. Secondly, we outline the functional architecture of a platform capable to support such a process and to let a consumer community share reliable food information. Thirdly, we identify main entities and their attributes necessary to model the contextualized interaction between a consumer and the platform. Lastly, we review articles reviewing technologies capable of acquiring and quantifying food characteristics for food performances assessment. The purpose is to give an insight into current research directions on technologies employable in a platform for collective food awareness.

1. Introduction

Modern food consumers are ever more engaged in open discussions, comments, and feedback on characteristics, quality, and safety of food that has become a very trending topic (to give an idea, think of the many food pictures and messages that are daily posted on online social media). Also, among them, food consumers communicate and interact with food suppliers and third parties in loose, open, effective, and flexible ways in a continuous search for food information transparency and more visibility of food supply chains.

On the other hand, new technological advances, especially in food sensor miniaturization, have made possible the development of lab-on-smartphone platforms for mobile food diagnostics that allow a rapid and on-site food analysis for preliminary and meaningful food information extraction. These lab-on-smartphone platforms use hand-held and low-cost devices (e.g. food scanners or food sniffers) to capture and communicate food data (e.g., data from measures of physical, chemical, biological, and microbiological food properties) or food-related entities data (e.g., data from label, package, container, and environment) with some specialized

smartphone/tablet apps. These devices are easy to use and incorporate an analytical precision and resolution almost equivalent to bench-top instruments.

These trends let envisage future scenarios where consumers and other stakeholders of the food supply chain, using their own capabilities integrated with ICT and food diagnostics technologies, could collaboratively constitute a large-scale socio-technical superorganism capable to foster collective food awareness. Here, we refer to collective food awareness (shortly, CFA) as food beliefs, knowledge and information, shared within a consumer community, that drive food consumption patterns of community members in terms of culinary preferences, and food habits and needs.

The need of sharing food information and knowledge is due to the fact that quality and safety issues about food are difficult to identify and, in the majority of cases, recognizable only after their consumption. In fact, depending on the type of attribute, food is an experience (some food attributes can be determined just after purchasing and consumption) or credence good (some food attributes that cannot be determined by consumer even after consumption). In food markets, this intrinsic nature of food facilitates the occurrence of information asymmetries that deeply affect consumers' decisions and behaviour. Main consequences of asymmetric information are moral hazard (a food producer takes more risks, e.g., false labelling or food adulteration, because consumers bear the burden of those risks) and adverse selection (producers hide some food information in a transaction, leading consumers to poor decisions making).

A broad CFA contributes to make many "problems" linked up with information asymmetries vanish and beyond that could drive consumers to greater consciousness about health, and environmental choices compatible with social goals. It can be fostered by a sociotechnical infrastructure based on a platform that empowers consumers by collectively managing (generating, verifying/validating, and distributing) information on safety and quality of food products and processes, as well as on issues around environmental, social, and ethical aspects.

In line with other works on collective awareness platforms [1–3], we view a CFA platform as an ICT system leveraging for gathering and making use of open food data, by combining social media, distributed knowledge creation and IoF (IoF (Internet of Food) is an offshoot of the Internet of things. It can be viewed as a network of smart food things, i.e., food-related objects and devices that are augmented with sensing, computing, and communication capabilities in order to provide advanced services. Smart food things include sensor-equipped information artifacts (e.g., food labels with RFID or NFC tags), time-temperature indicators, and other sensors on packages to detect spoiled foods, sensor devices that spots bacterial infection in food and water, kitchen devices that generate a record of compliance with food safety protocols, wearables to count bites and estimate calories, and so on [4]) technologies, in order to support the creation of CFA within a food consumer community.

A general research question that is crucial for sociotechnical infrastructures aimed to create a CFA is the following:

How can a CFA platform empower food consumers to have control over their own food and be responsive to their expectations of reliable food information?

In this paper, we focus on four implied questions flowing from this general question and reflecting different point of views:

(1) How can a consumer community share reliable food information derived from food properties instrumental measurements performed by consumers?

(2) What is the functional architecture of a CFA platform that supports such a process and lets a consumer community share reliable food information?

(3) What are the entities with their relevant properties characterizing the CFA platform interaction context?

(4) Which technologies can allow a CFA platform to generate food information based on scientific instrumental measurements of food properties?

The rest of the paper includes a short background discussion on the superorganism paradigm and four sections devoted to answer these questions.

2. Backgrounds

As people are increasingly becoming connected and active participants in smart environments, the convergence of "Internet of Things" and "Social Networks" worlds is gaining momentum in many researches [5], paving the way to a new generation of "user-in-the-loop" context aware systems [6]. The challenge is to harness the collaborative power of ICT networks (networks of people, of knowledge, and of sensors) to create collective and individual awareness [7].

A single "individual" is characterized by heterogeneity and limited reasoning capabilities, acting in an autonomous way within a smart environment. However, when many individuals join together they can self-organize into large-scale cooperative collectives, based on the assumption that a large number of individuals tied in a social network can provide far more accurate answers to complex problems than a single individual or a small group [8]. According to this perspective, the very large number of interconnected objects or people can be exploited to create what several researches define "superorganism" [9] or "swarm intelligence" [10], since they exhibit properties of a living organism (e.g., "collective intelligence") on their own. In fact, such approach is inspired by self-organizational behaviour of complex systems in nature [11], with particular reference to ant colonies. While a single ant has very limited sensing and actuating capabilities and little or no cognitive abilities, by and large, ants can indirectly coordinate their movements and activities, via spreading and sensing of pheromones in the environment, exhibiting, as a colony, a very powerful collective behaviour [12].

Collective intelligence and nature-inspired computing represent an extremely interesting phenomenon that has been addressed in several application fields, e.g., smart cities [13], manufacturing [14], healthcare [15], energy [16], and finance [17].

The food sector is another promising application area. The increasing demand on safe, high-quality, and healthy food, the recent food safety incidents and scandals, and the availability of new smart food technologies have led substantial changes in both food consumer's behaviour and food information user's behaviour [4, 18]. Today's consumers may have access to a wealth of mobile app-based services that provide them with food information (food traceability, nutrition advices, recipes, and purchasing support). At the same time, new digital businesses can collect and process big amount of food data through data analytics and intelligence tools for better understanding food consumers and increasing food processes effectiveness.

Moreover, the coupling of smart food technologies with social networking technologies is disclosing a world where consumers can interact, communicate, and collaborate with each other in loose, open, effective, and flexible ways for enhancing the transparency and visibility of food supply chains through collective wisdom and intelligence [19].

In a similar way we see that individual ants behave as if they were a single superorganism; we can envisage a near future where food consumers are engaged in large-scale coordinated activities for the good of everyone. In our opinion, it is advisable that some of these activities should address the creation of CFA. Although the superorganism paradigm has been employed for building collective awareness in many fields, prior research has not been explicitly focused on organizational and technological aspects in creating CFA within a consumers' community.

3. Collectively Generating and Sharing Reliable Food Information

As a first attempt to answer question 1, described in the introduction section, we introduce a process that allows a consumer community to share reliable information on food performances of some food items belonging to a same food class. In our process model, we assume that the reliability of a food performance is determined by a collective interpretation of food items' characteristics that are derived from instrumental measurements performed by some consumer community members. According to Peri [9], we refer to food characteristics as physical, chemical, biological, and microbiological food properties that are objectively attributable to food and do not change by changing the consumer (food shape, weight, size, structure, and composition, in terms of chemical or bioactive compounds). We refer to food performances as functional and subjective food properties; i.e., they relate to the consumer and do not exist except in the interaction between food products and consumers. They include sensory, nutritional, safety, and aesthetic properties.

In what follows we describe the process under a perspective that addresses its structure in terms of components and roles, and we include a process scenario.

3.1. Process Actors and Roles. Main roles, actors, and interrelationships are the following:

(i) *Recipient (R)*: he/she is a consumer community member who needs reliable information about a food item performance. He/she makes a request $r(i, p)$ to a Food Information Broker, where i refers to some identity property values of a food item (e.g., a product batch number, production date and place, etc.) and p is the identifier of a performance he/she wants to know the value. In order to provide these data, he/she possibly interacts with a technological CFA platform through his/her own handheld device and Food Information Artifact (FIA) (according to [20], a FIA is a physical entity expressly created to bear food information (e.g., labels, tables, RFID chips, and NFC tags)) located in the surrounding spatial environment.

(ii) *Contributor (C)*: he/she is a consumer community member that contributes to the process by providing a Food Information Broker with some food item data. In particular:

(a) he/she implicitly or explicitly acquires food item data through smart food things, i.e., sensor devices that capture implicit or explicit signals from a food item (e.g., food near-infrared emission, food volatile compounds) or the consumer

body (e.g., blood glucose level, chewing sound, and skin temperature);

(b) he/she explicitly acquires other descriptive identity data of a food item (e.g., batch number, production date, and provenance) from a FIA;

(c) he/she uses his/her own handheld device to communicate acquired food item data to the Food Information Broker.

(iii) *Food Information Broker (FIB)* is an intermediate agent that plays a threefold role. Firstly, it receives a request $r(i, p)$ coming from R, and controls if it has been already satisfied. Otherwise, it submits a new challenge question to a Collective Challenge Solver (CCS). A challenge consists in knowing to what extent food items with same values i share the same value of p, and, possibly, in finding this value. Secondly, it possibly receives challenge answers from the CCS, and makes them understandable (human-readable) to R. Thirdly, It receives and controls both data acquired by C and other interaction context data captured by environmental sensors, and passes them to a Food Analysis Manager;

(iv) *Food Analysis Manager (FAM)* is a food data analyst that is able to perform a food item diagnosis. It receives food item data and other interaction context data from FIB, and applies some intelligent methods to determine food item characteristics. Generally, these methods analyse food item data versus food characteristics specific knowledge through machine learning techniques and/or statistical analysis (such as principal components analysis, supervised pattern recognition techniques). For instance, classification-based methods match food item data against class models in order to determine a value of a single food item characteristic. Food item diagnostics and identity data are successively sent to a Food Journal Manager;

(v) *Food Journal Manager (FJM)* is a food database manager that collects and organizes data coming from FAM. It also provides results of query $q(i, c)$ formulated by a Collective Challenge Solver. Query results consist in a set of values of characteristics c for food items having the same identity properties i;

(vi) *Collective Challenge Solver (CCS)* is an intelligent agent that plays the core role in the collective process for generating reliable food information. It receives from FIB a challenge question consisting in finding the value of the food performance p that is possibly shared by all food items with the same identity properties i. Leveraging on a food knowledge base, it selects food characteristics c that are factors of food performance p. It formulates the query $q(i, c)$ to *FJM* and, once obtained query results, it applies collectively reliable criteria in order to possibly determine the value of the food property shared by food items with same value i. A Reliability Authority establishes these criteria whose application may require the CCS to use specific methods (e.g., statistical methods, machine learning, neural networks) [21, 22];

(vii) *Reliability Authority (RA)* is an organizational entity that is responsible for the process governance. It sets and managesthe criteria that CCS uses to provide reliable information on food performances of some food items belonging to a same food class. These criteria consist of rules that underpin a collective interpretation of food items' characteristics and determine reliability of information on food performances derived from those characteristics.

3.2. The Process Flow. In what follows, we give a description of the process flow that is also visually represented in Figure 1. The process flow consists of two streams, say 1 and 2, which are started by R and C, respectively.

In stream 1, R needs reliable information about a food item performance p. He/she provides FIB with some identity property value *i* and asks FIB for the value of *p* on the food item. FIB controls if the request can be immediately satisfied by consulting a solved challenge database that collects answers given to previous requests. Otherwise, FIB submits a new challenge question to CCS. CCS identifies food characteristics necessary to determine the value of *p* and asks FJM for their values on all food journal items with the same value *i*. CCS controls these data and decides if the value of *p* can be computed and collectively reliable criteria (established by a RA) are applicable. In positive case, CCS determines the value of *p*, and it both inserts the new record in the solved challenge database and sends the challenge answer to FIB that makes it understandable to R.

In stream 2, C examines a food item through his/her own devices (smart food things) in order to acquire measurement data of food item properties. He/she provides FIB with these data and descriptive identity data, say *id*, of that food item. FIB collects and controls them as well as other interaction context data captured by environmental sensors, and it passes the whole data to FAM that determines some food characteristic values, say *c*, by performing a food item diagnosis. The pair (*id, c*) is sent to FJM that stores it a Food Journal.

3.3. Exemplification Scenario. In what follows, we present a scenario to clarify the collective process described above.

A consumer community faces the problem of knowing relevant water performance (e.g., safety) of a branded bottled water. A community member can act as contributor (*C*) and/or recipient (*R*).

Cs are community members that are equipped with lab-on-smartphones (taste-analysis based devices connected to a smartphone), capable to acquire data on electrical impedance of water. Each of them examines a sample of water, acquires electrical impedance data, and transmits them to the FIB with some descriptive identity data (e.g., "product batch number"). FIB collects and controls these data coming from many Cs, and it sends them to the FAM that makes a diagnosis of the sampled water. FAM applies some methods, e.g., multiple regression analysis or principal component analysis to identify chemical compounds (e.g. "magnesium," "calcium," "sodium," poisoning elements as "cyanide," heavy metal pollutants as "copper," and "arsenic") [23] and microbial properties (e.g., pathogenic bacteria as "coliform group" and "escherichia coli") [24]. These water characteristic values of the water sample are permanently stored in the Food Journal.

R is a community member that needs to know performance values (e.g., safety) of a branded bottled water *b*. He/she uses his/her smartphone to scan the label of *b* to acquire the product number of the batch that *b* belongs to, and he/she queries the FIB about the safety of the water contained in *b*. FIB acquires the R's request and determines if it is well formed (e.g., "batch number" correctness, water performance checkability). If this request had not been previously solved, the FIB submits the following challenge to the CCS: "determine if all bottles in the batch of *b* are safe." The CCS selects water characteristics (e.g. cyanide, heavy metal pollutants) that it needs to know in order to solve the challenge. Successively, it queries the FJM to obtain characteristic values referring to previously analysed bottles belonging to the batch of *b*. Once obtained these values, it solves the challenge by applying some methods based on some collectively reliable criteria (established by the RA). In carrying out its activity, the CCS could apply some machine learning or statistical methods to establish:

(i) What is the set of water characteristics (e.g., escherichia coli, cyanide, copper, and arsenic)?

(ii) How they combine in order to obtain category inspect indicators (e.g., pathogenic bacteria, heavy metal pollutants, and chemical contaminants)

(iii) How to use these indicators to determine the water safety performance.

Lastly, the CCS sends the challenge answer to the FIB that could possibly generate a hazard warning for collective awareness of a safety risk related to the water bottles' batch which *b* belongs to.

4. Functional Architecture of a CFA Platform

In what follows we describe a high-level architecture for a CFA platform, as it can support the collective process for sharing reliable food information. The architecture, illustrated in Figure 2, is structured as a classic three-tier architecture commonly found in today's software applications:

(i) An interface layer that enables the user to submit, retrieve, and manipulate data

(ii) An application layer that performs data processing and analysis

(iii) A storage layer where information is stored and retrieved from a persistent database.

In our platform architecture, the interface layer is the front-end interface between the user/consumer and the CFA platform back-end, and it is responsible for interactions with the external environment (user's request formulation, sensor data acquisition, and information presentation/visualization

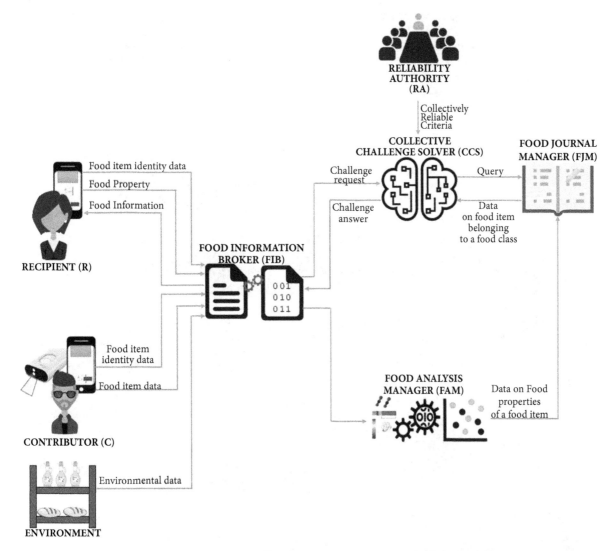

FIGURE 1: A representation of the Collective process for generating reliable food information.

to the user). In particular, the interface layer comprises simple and empowered nodes that are used by the CFA platform to interact with the user, food items and the surrounding environment. A simple node comprises user interface devices while an empowered node include also smart food things, environment sensors and wearable devices, where

(i) *user interface devices* are input-output devices (e.g. smartphone, tablet) that take input from and deliver output to the user in his/hers foreground attention. These devices are able to manage users' requests, manual data entry and acquire data from FIA (e.g. from labels, tables, RFID chips, and NFC tags) and provide human readable food information to users.

(ii) *smart food things* are sensing devices, owned by contributor users that are able to capture implicit signals from food (e.g. food near-infrared emission, food volatile compounds) with or without requiring user's action or attention. Smart food things can be

connected and synchronized to users' interface devices.

(iii) *environmental sensors* are networked sensors that take environment data without requiring user's action or attention. These devices include sensor devices embedded in food packaging, containers, and food appliances and small tools (e.g., kitchen or cooking utensils), as well as ambient sensors;

(iv) *wearable devices* are devices that take input from the user in the background of user's attention (also called, peripheral attention), while he/she is involved in food consumption activities, such as many wearables for food intake monitoring.

The application layer comprises the following:

(i) *Food Information Broker*: this module has the following main functionalities:

(a) It receives unformatted digital data from an empowered node and translates them in a proper

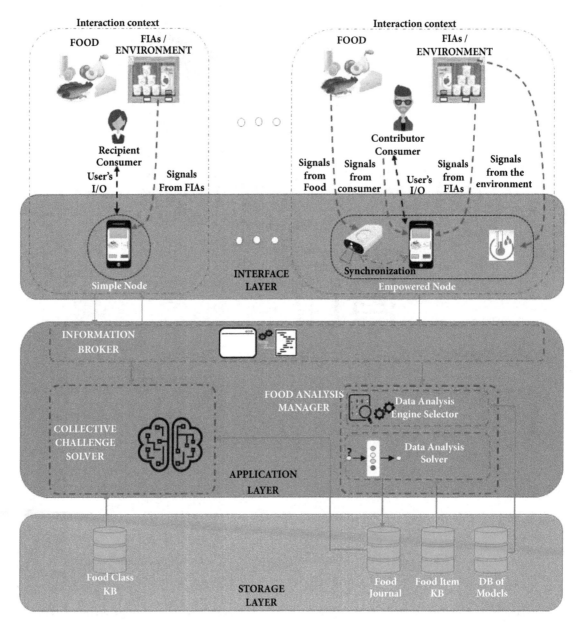

FIGURE 2: A three-tier architecture for the CFA platform.

schema or grammar in order to generate a well-formed digital document (e.g., XML) representing a diagnostic data model and then send it to the FAM so that it can be processed;

(b) It receives data from a simple node and generates a formatted digital document to properly define the challenge to be solved by the CCS;

(c) It verifies if a challenge has been already solved, by querying the *Solved Challenges DB*.

(d) It returns to a simple node challenge results in a formatted document that can be easily processed and converted in human-readable views.

(ii) *FAM Data analysis engine selector*: this submodule receives the formatted diagnostic document from

FIB. By analyzing document entities, it automatically at run-time selects, from the *Model DB*, library software modules for the FAM data analysis solver. They are the implementation of some model/method (statistical, deep learning) for determining food characteristics from sensing data. The selection can be driven by empowered node features contained in the diagnostic document.

(iii) *FAM Data Analysis Solver*: this submodule receives the selected software modules that complete a food diagnosis process engine. By leveraging on an auxiliary database (e.g., a food item training set), the engine produces characteristic values of a single food item and it stores them in the Food Journal.

(iv) *Collective Challenge Solver:* It receives a formatted challenge question from FIB. It leverages on a *Food Class DB* to analyze data coming from Food Journal, in order to determine the challenge results according to some collectively reliable criteria. To perform its analysis it may use complex software libraries such as extreme/deep learning machines, neural networks, classifier algorithms, clustering algorithms, and statistical/regression algorithms.

The storage layer contains persistent food data. In particular, it comprises the following:

(i) *Food Item Training Set:* a database containing data and inference rules to determine food characteristics of a food item.

(ii) *Model DB:* a set of library software modules that can complete a diagnosis process engine.

(iii) *Food Journal:* a public ledger containing data on food characteristics of analyzed food items.

(iv) *Food Class DB:* a set of library software modules that are the systematic representation of collective reliable criteria established by the *RA* and used, on a case by case basis, to determine a class food performance.

(v) *Solved Challenges DB:* a database containing challenge questions already solved by the *CCS*.

5. Entities of the User-CFA Platform Interaction Context

In order to support the collective process, described in Section 2, the CFA platform needs to acquire data from

(a) a user in foreground attention. The user explicitly interacts with platform interface devices that are in the foreground of his/hers attention, i.e. he/she is intentional conscious of interacting with the CFA platform. For instance, he/she could use handheld devices to get data from some food information artifacts, such as labels, RFID, and NFC tags, and, in the place where the artifacts are located, transmits them to the platform. He/she could also interact with smart food things in order to capture and communicate data on some property of a food item.

(b) a user in background attention. The user implicitly interacts with platform interface devices that are in the background of his/hers attention, i.e. they escape the user's observation. For instance, wearable sensors could provide the CFA platform with data for real-time food intake monitoring [25].

(c) a food item or the environment, without requiring any user's action or attention. Some smart things automatically detect food properties and environment conditions, and transmit related data to the platform. They include sensor devices embedded in food packaging, containers, and food appliances and small tools (e.g., kitchen or cooking utensils), as well as environmental sensors.

In what follows we summarize the main entities with their properties (attributes) that are relevant for the CFA process and characterize the CFA platform interaction context.

Context entities:

(i) **user:** a consumer who interacts with the platform through interface devices (including his/her own handheld devices) located in the environment, as he/she participates to the CFA process as recipient or contributor. In the recipient role, he/she asks the platform to give him/her validated information about a food attribute. In the contributor role, he/she can also contribute to the validation process by communicating food item (a class identifier and a food attribute value) and other interaction context information to the platform.

(ii) **food:** it refers to a food item which the user and the platform can interact with. Food related stimuli are perceived by the user and, possibly, smart food things detect signals coming from the food item. Attribute values of the food item can be exchanged during the interaction between the user and the platform;

(iii) **environment:** it is the physical and organizational environment where interactions take place (e.g., a home kitchen, a restaurant, and a food shop). Environmental conditions have direct or indirect influence on the behaviour of both consumer and interface devices during the interaction. Physical properties, like light, humidity, temperature, localization, and spatial layout of the environment, may affect both consumers' perception and instrumental measurements of food item properties. Organizational aspects, like rules, shop opening hours, and working time, may drive the provision of information from the platform.

Context entities attributes are

(i) **Identity.** It refers to properties that identify a context entity or a class the entity belongs to. In particular, the CCS of the platform can build a food class identity by inferring class properties from food item data coming from instrumental evaluations of food item qualities;

(ii) **Time.** It comprises temporal aspects that may range from a current time representation to a complete time history of context entity properties. When referred to a food item, values of this attribute allow the CFA platform to recognize or predict over time qualities of food items in a certain class. For instance, a time series of values of properties, like temperature, pH, or microbial growth, could be used to generate and, share, within a consumer community, information on when food items of a certain class are at their nutritional best and are safe to eat, or on when they should be disposed of to avoid ill health;

(iii) **Location.** Values of this attribute may be quantitative or qualitative. They represent current and previous positions of context entities in absolute or relative terms. When referred to food, location is a fundamental attribute when creating a CFA based on geographical traceability or geographic-based origin determination of food products.

(iv) **Activity**. It refers to fundamental changes of entity attributes that occur when a food activity is performed by a consumer. In particular, changes of food item characteristics, like surface conditions, temperature or size, could be used by the CFA platform to drive a collective awareness on consumption activities (e.g., cooking, or eating) on a certain class of food items.

6. Food Analysis Technologies for a CFA Platform: A Review of Reviews

Food analysis technologies are based on a plethora of quantitative/qualitative food analysis techniques and methodologies investigated by many researchers of various scientific fields. These methods are addressed to automatically acquire food item information (e.g., food quality traits) by using sensor devices, and they can be employed in technical approaches to the development of a CFA platform. Here, we refer to a technical approach as a collection of techniques, tools, devices, and knowledge, that is applied to measure a certain food characteristic (i.e., physical, chemical, biological, and microbiological attributes) in order to determine a certain set of food performances.

In this section, we present a review of review articles that were published from 2012 to 2017 and explicitly referred to technologies capable of nondestructively acquiring and quantifying food characteristics (external and internal quality attributes) for fast, real-time food performance assessment. The intent is to answer the following questions:

(i) Which technical approaches to food-data capture and analysis are investigated in scientific research literature?

(ii) Which food characteristics could be detected by these approaches?

(iii) Which information on food performances could be provided?

According to Kitchenham [26] we have been undertaken a systematic literature review of reviews, in order to provide a complete, exhaustive summary of current literature relevant to our research questions. The steps of the methodology we followed are below described, while Figure 3 shows the workflow we adopted:

(i) *Step 0. Initialization*: we selected Scopus as scientific database where to perform our search. Scopus delivers a comprehensive overview of the world's research output in our domain of reference and it has the ability to handle advanced queries. We initialized a list L of search keywords with English terms related to technologies capable of nondestructively acquiring and quantifying food characteristics (e.g., "spectroscopy," "camera photo," "e-nose," "e-tongue,"and

"machine vision," as well as synonymous, and other broader/wider terms).

(ii) *Step 1. Search process*: We performed a search on Scopus database by using keywords in the list L coupled with term "food" and other terms used for major food groups; then, we filtered retrieved papers by choosing only those indexed as reviews and published since January 2012.

(iii) *Step 2. Screening relevant papers*: We manually analysed metadata (authors, title, source, and year) in order to detect and remove duplicated items. Moreover, we analysed the abstract of each paper in order to determine whether it matched our inclusion criterion:

(a) the paper is classifiable as a research paper review;

(b) the review specifically focuses on research applications for detection and classification of food properties;

Moreover, the list L was possibly extended by adjoining new terms found among the author keywords of each paper.

Steps 1 and 2 were iteratively performed until no newer keywords or new papers were found. At the end of this cycle we obtained the final set R of review papers to be analysed.

(iv) *Step 3. Review papers analysis*. For each review paper $r \in R$ we identified the set $TRP(r)$ of technology research patterns that the paper focuses on. An element of $TRP(r)$ is represented by a triple (t_i, C_i, and P_i), where t_i is a technical approach, C_i is the set of food characteristics measured by t_i, and P_i is the set of food performance determined by t_i from the values of the food characteristics of C_i.

6.1. Results and Discussion. The resulting set R is constituted by 67 review papers whose references are listed in the Appendix. In what follows we present and discuss results with respect to the research question we posed at the beginning of this section. Table 1 shows the set T of technical approaches reported in the literature, Table 2 describes food characteristics that can be detected by these approaches, and Table 3 shows the set of information on food performances that can be determined.

In Table 4, for each technical approach t_i, we summarize the set of technological patterns that comprise t_i, and we indicate the review papers focusing on it.

From these results, it emerges that five class of technologies are promising to be a valued addition to the development of CFA platforms:

(i) **Spectroscopy**. These technologies are mostly based on vibrational spectroscopic data acquisitions and statistical analyses (e.g., principal components analysis, supervised pattern recognition techniques). The first ones collect spectroscopic data (e.g., mid- and near-infrared reflectance or transflectance data) as they measure molecular vibrations either by the

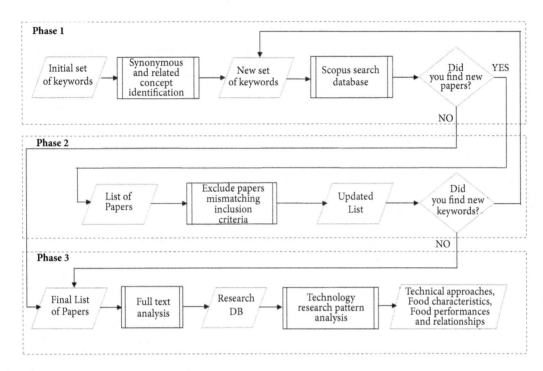

FIGURE 3: Systematic literature review workflow.

TABLE 1: The set T of technical approaches.

Technical Approaches	
t_1: near infrared spectroscopy	t_8: Gas Biosensors
t_2: mid infrared spectroscopy	t_9: Gas Electrochem sensors
t_3: raman spectroscopy	t_{10}: Gas Optical sensors
t_4: fluorescence spectroscopy	t_{11}: Solids and Liquids Gravimetric sensors
t_5: camera image sensors	t_{12}: Solids and Liquids biosensors
t_6: hyperspectral imaging	t_{13}: Solids and Liquids Electrochem sensors
t_7: Gas Gravimetric sensors	t_{14}: Solids and Liquids Optical sensors

TABLE 2: The set C of food characteristics.

	Food Characteristics	
Index	Name	Description
c_1	microbial properties	food kinetic properties that can be measured by microbial detection (e.g., the total count of microorganism in a sample of food)
c_2	chemical properties	food kinetic properties that can be chemically detected (e.g., pH value and total volatile basic nitrogen);
c_3	chemical compounds	chemical compounds' properties (e.g., concentration level);
c_4	surface conditions	visible attributes describing the physical outer aspect of a food item (such as colour, shape);
c_5	mass-volume related properties	physical properties of a food sample (e.g., weight and the volume);
c_6	volatile organic compounds	compounds of organic vapours or gases released into the air by solid or liquid foods.

TABLE 3: The set P of food performances.

Food Performances

Index	Name	Description
p_1	freshness/spoilage	spoilage/edible level of a food product
p_2	hazard	degree of hazard, e.g., presence of illegal ingredients or treatments contaminating or poisoning a food product
p_3	ingredients	edible substances in a dish or a food product
p_4	category	food group (e.g. fruits, dairy, meat, fish) or food type (e.g. apple, orange, apricot) which a food sample belongs to
p_5	variety	variety of a food sample belonging to a food type (e.g. sunstar orange, belladonna orange, tarocco orange)
p_6	nutrients	nutrients (protein, carbs, fat, calories, vitamins, minerals) and their quantities in a food sample
p_7	taste perception	level of tastes (e.g., sourness, saltiness, umami, bitterness, and sweetness)
p_8	quality grade	quality assessment a food sample according to some standardised grading system
p_9	geographical origin	geographical area where a food sample has been originate, according to some geographical classification
p_{10}	adulteration	presence and quantities of improper substances in a food product

TABLE 4: Technological research patterns and related works.

Technical Approach	Food Characteristics	Food Performances	Review Papers
t_1	c_1, c_2, c_3	$p_1, p_2, p_6, p_8, p_{10}$	[r1] [r2] [r3] [r6] [r7] [r8] [r9] [r10] [r11] [r12] [r13] [r14] [r15] [r16] [r17] [r18] [r19] [r20] [r22] [r23] [r24] [r26] [r25] [r28] [r31] [r32] [r55] [r67]
t_2	c_2, c_3	$p_1, p_2, p_3, p_4, p_8, p_9, p_{10}$	[r2] [r10] [r11] [r12] [r13] [r14] [r17] [r19] [r21] [r23] [r31] [r32]
t_3	c_1, c_2, c_3	p_1, p_3, p_8, p_{10}	[r5] [r8] [r9] [r11] [r12] [r13] [r14] [r21] [r23] [r25] [r32]
t_4	c_1, c_2	p_1, p_{10}	[r8] [r11] [r12]
t_5	c_4, c_5	p_1, p_5, p_6, p_8	[r4] [r27] [r35] [r36] [r37] [r39] [r40] [r42] [r44] [r41] [r43] [r45] [r67]
t_6	c_1, c_3, c_4, c_5	$p_1, p_5, p_6, p_8, p_{10}$	[r9] [r12] [r13] [r14] [r15] [r16] [r18] [r21] [r23] [r27] [r28] [r29] [r30] [r33] [r34] [r38]
t_7	c_6	p_1, p_{10}	[r46]
t_8	c_6	p_1, p_{10}	[r46]
t_9	c_1, c_6	$p_1, p_4, p_8, p_9, p_{10}$	[r46] [r47] [r48] [r49] [r50] [r51] [r52] [r53] [r54] [r55] [r56]
t_{10}	c_6	p_1, p_{10}	[r47] [r48] [r49]
t_{11}	c_3	p_1, p_7	[r53] [r62] [r63] [r65]
t_{12}	c_3	p_1, p_5, p_7	[r62] [r63] [r65]
t_{13}	c_1, c_3	$p_1, p_2, p_4, p_7, p_9, p_{10}$	[r54] [r55] [r56] [r57] [r58] [r60] [r61] [r62] [r63] [r64] [r66]
t_{14}	c_1, c_3	p_1, p_7, p_9, p_{10}	[r46] [r53] [r58] [r62] [r63] [r64] [r65]

absorption of light quanta or the inelastic scattering of photons; the second ones are suited to perform targeted and nontargeted screening of ingredients using spectral profiles [27, 28]. They are at the core of food knowledge-based approaches aimed to analyze foods at the molecular level. In most laboratory researches, they are used to collect spectroscopic data coming from scanned training food samples, to build a classification or cluster model according to known values of a certain property, and to determine the property value of a new food sample by matching sample's spectroscopic data against class models [29]. For example, spectroscopic analysis has been successfully applied in food safety analysis and prediction for several food categories, such as meat, fish, fruits and vegetables. In particular, the verification through spectroscopy of the freshness and the presence of any adulterants (or improper substances) in food can be based both on the chemical compounds of food and on the analysis of some properties (such as pH, TVB-N, and K1.), as well as on analytical techniques based on microbial count. Reviews highlight that several methods to assess food freshness have been developed. Such methods are based on the measurement of food deteriorative changes associated with microbial growth and chemical changes.

(ii) **Machine vision**. Recognition methods embedded in computer vision systems can detect visible characteristics by analyzing food images captured with a camera-enabled device (e.g., a smartphone camera photo). They can be employed to determine data relating to the mass, weight and volume of a food product and to identify its food category and subcategory. However, several reviews highlight the existence of substantial obstacles to recognize food in complex cases, such as a home cooked meal or a composite plate [30]. Combinations of these methods in conjunction with databases of food knowledge (e.g., nutritional facts tables) and consumers' profiles can be applied to provide quantitative analysis of various food aspects (e.g., amount of calorie and nutrition in the food), even in a personalized manner. Furthermore, other contextual clues, such as restaurant location and menus, can be also utilized to augment or improve the information provided by the combination of these methods [31–33];

(iii) **Hyperspectral imaging**. Hyperspectral imaging (HSI) is an approach that integrates conventional imaging and spectroscopy to attain both spatial and spectral information from a food object. "The spatial features of HSI enable characterization of complex heterogeneous samples, whereas the spectral features allow a vast range of multiconstituent surface and subsurface features to be identified" [34]. Applications of this technology make it possible to analyze food quality, freshness, and safety, especially for fruits and vegetables Pu et al. [35];

(iv) **Odour analysis (e-noses)**. These technologies mimic the human sense of smell, by identifying and analyzing some food properties on the basis of its odour. The employed methods are based on an array of sensors for chemical detection of analysis of volatile organic compounds (VOCs) and a pattern recognition unit [36]. The sensing system consists of broadly tuned sensors (optical, electrochemical, and gravimetric) that are able to infer a variation of concentration a gas. Optical sensors work by detecting a shift in the emission or absorption of different types of electromagnetic radiation on binding with a desired analyte [37]; electrochemical sensors detect a variation of electrical conductivity of a gas while gravimetric sensors detect a variation of mass of a gas [38]. These technologies are mainly used to discriminate different food varieties for food authenticity and adulteration assessment [39];

(v) **Taste analysis (e-tongues)**. These technologies are based on analytical tools mimicking the functions of human gustatory receptors. Liquid samples are directly analysed without any preparation, while solids require a preliminary dissolution before measurement [40]. Like odour analysis systems, taste analysis tools include an array of nonspecific sensors and a set of appropriate methods for pattern recognition [41]. They are employed to identify variety or geographical origin, to detect adulteration, and to assess authenticity of many food products [42].

7. Conclusions

Today's consumers have more and more need of reliable food information for their food consumption activities to become aware of the wider consequences of decisions they make. Recent cases of adulterations, allegations of fraud and subterfuges that have invested food sector have increased this trend. Current conventional ways of providing food information (e.g., labelling, mass media) have limited chance to satisfy this need, as they are usually product/producer centered and driven by food producers and distributors that tend to reveal only information that suit their marketing approach.

As opposed to that, we have introduced a democratic and bottom-up approach that lets consumers be more food aware as helping them to make more informed decisions in their food related activities. This approach leverages on the superorganism and the capabilities of smart food technologies in determining physical, biochemical, and microbiological properties of food and beverages. At its core, there is a cooperative process that is aimed to foster collective food awareness, as letting a consumers' community share reliable information derived from scientific instrument measurement of food properties.

The main contribution of this paper is to envisage the organization of such a process, as well as a technological platform capable to support it. Moreover, in order to point out significant research outcomes potentially useful for developing the platform, we have conducted a survey of academic papers reviewing technical approaches for determining food characteristics and performances.

We conclude by addressing what we view as limitations and areas for further development of this article.

Firstly, we have presented only a framework in which details of the cooperative process remain unspecified. For instance, how to define a criterion for deriving a food class performance? When do we consider "collectively reliable" such a criterion? How do we empirically assess the cooperative process effectiveness? These are relevant questions when it comes to translating our framework into concrete guidelines for the platform design.

Secondly, all the reviews in our survey have been conducted by scholars and, thus, they have been concerned with research findings oriented to clarify or discover conceptual state of a technology. A more relevant contribution would be given by investigating current gaps between technology research and mobile food diagnostics tools already available. Identifying and understanding knowledge and application gaps is vital for researchers so they can recognize technical challenge, missing insight or pieces of complementary technology in order to move forward from research to development and viability of a platform for collective food awareness.

For us, the above considerations suggest a clear direction for future research. Together with a more extensive exploration of our process model, we need empirical work that reflects both technological and food consumer behaviour perspectives.

Appendix

See Table 5.

TABLE 5

Review Paper	Reference
r1	Qu, J. H., Liu, D., Cheng, J. H., Sun, D. W., Ma, J., Pu, H., & Zeng, X. A. (2015). Applications of near-infrared spectroscopy in food safety evaluation and control: A review of recent research advances. Critical reviews in food science and nutrition, 55(13), 1939-1954.
r2	Barbin, D. F., Felicio, A. L. D. S. M., Sun, D. W., Nixdorf, S. L., & Hirooka, E. Y. (2014). Application of infrared spectral techniques on quality and compositional attributes of coffee: An overview. Food Research International, 61, 23-32.
r3	Wang, L., Sun, D. W., Pu, H., & Cheng, J. H. (2017). Quality analysis, classification, and authentication of liquid foods by near-infrared spectroscopy: A review of recent research developments. Critical reviews in food science and nutrition, 57(7), 1524-1538.
r4	Wu, D., & Sun, D. W. (2013). Colour measurements by computer vision for food quality control–A review. Trends in Food Science & Technology, 29(1), 5-20.
r5	Li, J. L., Sun, D. W., & Cheng, J. H. (2016). Recent advances in nondestructive analytical techniques for determining the total soluble solids in fruits: a review. Comprehensive Reviews in Food Science and Food Safety, 15(5), 897-911.
r6	Fu, X., & Ying, Y. (2016). Food safety evaluation based on near infrared spectroscopy and imaging: a review. *Critical reviews in food science and nutrition, 56*(11), 1913-1924.
r7	Porep, J. U., Kammerer, D. R., & Carle, R. (2015). On-line application of near infrared (NIR) spectroscopy in food production. Trends in Food Science & Technology, 46(2), 211-230.
r8	He, H. J., & Sun, D. W. (2015). Microbial evaluation of raw and processed food products by Visible/Infrared, Raman and Fluorescence spectroscopy. Trends in Food Science & Technology, 46(2), 199-210.
r9	Magwaza, L. S., & Tesfay, S. Z. (2015). A review of destructive and non-destructive methods for determining Avocado fruit maturity. Food and bioprocess technology, 8(10), 1995-2011.
r10	Uríčková, V., & Sádecká, J. (2015). Determination of geographical origin of alcoholic beverages using ultraviolet, visible and infrared spectroscopy: A review. Spectrochimica Acta Part A: Molecular and Biomolecular Spectroscopy, 148, 131-137.
r11	Dai, Q., Cheng, J. H., Sun, D. W., & Zeng, X. A. (2015). Advances in feature selection methods for hyperspectral image processing in food industry applications: a review. Critical reviews in food science and nutrition, 55(10), 1368-1382.
r12	Gowen, A. A., Feng, Y., Gaston, E., & Valdramidis, V. (2015). Recent applications of hyperspectral imaging in microbiology. Talanta, 137, 43-54.
r13	Lohumi, S., Lee, S., Lee, H., & Cho, B. K. (2015). A review of vibrational spectroscopic techniques for the detection of food authenticity and adulteration. Trends in Food Science & Technology, 46(1), 85-98.
r14	Cheng, J. H., & Sun, D. W. (2015). Recent applications of spectroscopic and hyperspectral imaging techniques with chemometric analysis for rapid inspection of microbial spoilage in muscle foods. Comprehensive Reviews in Food Science and Food Safety, 14(4), 478-490.
r15	Xiong, Z., Xie, A., Sun, D. W., Zeng, X. A., & Liu, D. (2015). Applications of hyperspectral imaging in chicken meat safety and quality detection and evaluation: a review. Critical reviews in food science and nutrition, 55(9), 1287-1301.
r16	He, H. J., Wu, D., & Sun, D. W. (2015). Nondestructive spectroscopic and imaging techniques for quality evaluation and assessment of fish and fish products. Critical reviews in food science and nutrition, 55(6), 864-886.
r17	Schmitt, S., Garrigues, S., & de la Guardia, M. (2014). Determination of the mineral composition of foods by infrared spectroscopy: A review of a green alternative. Critical reviews in analytical chemistry, 44(2), 186-197.
r18	Fox, G., & Manley, M. (2014). Applications of single kernel conventional and hyperspectral imaging near infrared spectroscopy in cereals. Journal of the Science of Food and Agriculture, 94(2), 174-179.
r19	Hossain, M. Z., & Goto, T. (2014). Near-and mid-infrared spectroscopy as efficient tools for detection of fungal and mycotoxin contamination in agricultural commodities. World Mycotoxin Journal, 7(4), 507-515.
r20	Chen, G. Y., Huang, Y. P., & Chen, K. J. (2014). Recent advances and applications of near infrared spectroscopy for honey quality assessment. Advance Journal of Food Science and Technology, 6(4), 461-467.
r21	Damez, J. L., & Clerjon, S. (2013). Quantifying and predicting meat and meat products quality attributes using electromagnetic waves: An overview. Meat science, 95(4), 879-896.

TABLE 5: Continued.

Review Paper	Reference
r22	Cattaneo, T. M., & Holroyd, S. E. (2013). The use of near infrared spectroscopy for determination of adulteration and contamination in milk and milk powder: updating knowledge. Journal of Near Infrared Spectroscopy, 21(5), 341-349.
r23	Cheng, J. H., Dai, Q., Sun, D. W., Zeng, X. A., Liu, D., & Pu, H. B. (2013). Applications of non-destructive spectroscopic techniques for fish quality and safety evaluation and inspection. *Trends in Food Science & Technology*, 34(1), 18-31.
r24	Zhang, X. (2013). Application of near infrared reflectance spectroscopy to predict meat chemical compositions: A review. *Spectroscopy and Spectral Analysis*, 33(11), 3002-3009.
r25	Yibin, F. X. Y. (2013). Application of NIR and Raman Spectroscopy for Quality and Safety Inspection of Fruits and Vegetables: A Review [J]. *Transactions of the Chinese Society for Agricultural Machinery*, 8, 027.
r26	López, A., Arazuri, S., García, I., Mangado, J., & Jarén, C. (2013). A review of the application of near-infrared spectroscopy for the analysis of potatoes. Journal of agricultural and food chemistry, 61(23), 5413-5424.
r27	Chen, L., & Opara, U. L. (2013). Texture measurement approaches in fresh and processed foods—A review. *Food Research International*, 51(2), 823-835.
r28	Dale, L. M., Thewis, A., Boudry, C., Rotar, I., Dardenne, P., Baeten, V., & Pierna, J. A. F. (2013). Hyperspectral imaging applications in agriculture and agro-food product quality and safety control: a review. *Applied Spectroscopy Reviews*, 48(2), 142-159.
r29	Feng, Y. Z., & Sun, D. W. (2012). Application of hyperspectral imaging in food safety inspection and control: a review. Critical reviews in food science and nutrition, 52(11), 1039-1058.
r30	ElMasry, G., Kamruzzaman, M., Sun, D. W., & Allen, P. (2012). Principles and applications of hyperspectral imaging in quality evaluation of agro-food products: a review. *Critical reviews in food science and nutrition*, 52(11), 999-1023.
r31	Cozzolino, D. (2012). Recent trends on the use of infrared spectroscopy to trace and authenticate natural and agricultural food products. Applied Spectroscopy Reviews, 47(7), 518-530.
r32	Ellis, D. I., Brewster, V. L., Dunn, W. B., Allwood, J. W., Golovanov, A. P., & Goodacre, R. (2012). Fingerprinting food: current technologies for the detection of food adulteration and contamination. *Chemical Society Reviews*, 41(17), 5706-5727.
r33	Zhang, R., Ying, Y., Rao, X., & Li, J. (2012). Quality and safety assessment of food and agricultural products by hyperspectral fluorescence imaging. *Journal of the Science of Food and Agriculture*, 92(12), 2397-2408.
r34	ElMasry, G., Barbin, D. F., Sun, D. W., & Allen, P. (2012). Meat quality evaluation by hyperspectral imaging technique: an overview. *Critical Reviews in Food Science and Nutrition*, 52(8), 689-711.
r35	Martin, C. K., Nicklas, T., Gunturk, B., Correa, J. B., Allen, H. R., & Champagne, C. (2014). Measuring food intake with digital photography. Journal of Human Nutrition and Dietetics, 27, 72-81.
r36	Sharp, D. B., & Allman-Farinelli, M. (2014). Feasibility and validity of mobile phones to assess dietary intake. *Nutrition*, 30(11-12), 1257-1266.
r37	Ma, J., Sun, D. W., Qu, J. H., Liu, D., Pu, H., Gao, W. H., & Zeng, X. A. (2016). Applications of computer vision for assessing quality of agri-food products: a review of recent research advances. *Critical reviews in food science and nutrition*, 56(1), 113-127.
r38	Pu, Y. Y., Feng, Y. Z., & Sun, D. W. (2015). Recent progress of hyperspectral imaging on quality and safety inspection of fruits and vegetables: a review. *Comprehensive Reviews in Food Science and Food Safety*, 14(2), 176-188.
r39	Devi, P. V., & Vijayarekha, K. (2014). Machine vision applications to locate fruits, detect defects and remove noise: a review. *Rasayan J. Chem*, 7(1), 104-113.
r40	Zhang, B., Huang, W., Li, J., Zhao, C., Fan, S., Wu, J., & Liu, C. (2014). Principles, developments and applications of computer vision for external quality inspection of fruits and vegetables: A review. *Food Research International*, 62, 326-343.
r41	Dowlati, M., de la Guardia, M., & Mohtasebi, S. S. (2012). Application of machine-vision techniques to fish-quality assessment. *TrAC Trends in Analytical Chemistry*, 40, 168-179.
r42	Rady, A. M., & Guyer, D. E. (2015). Rapid and/or nondestructive quality evaluation methods for potatoes: A review. *Computers and electronics in agriculture*, 117, 31-48.
r43	Steele, R. (2015). An overview of the state of the art of automated capture of dietary intake information. *Critical reviews in food science and nutrition*, 55(13), 1929-1938.
r44	Mahajan, S., Das, A., & Sardana, H. K. (2015). Image acquisition techniques for assessment of legume quality. *Trends in Food Science & Technology*, 42(2), 116-133.

TABLE 5: Continued.

Review Paper	Reference
r45	Zhang, B., Huang, W., Li, J., Zhao, C., Fan, S., Wu, J., & Liu, C. (2014). Principles, developments and applications of computer vision for external quality inspection of fruits and vegetables: A review. *Food Research International, 62*, 326-343.
r46	Banerjee, R., Tudu, B., Bandyopadhyay, R., & Bhattacharyya, N. (2016). A review on combined odor and taste sensor systems. *Journal of Food Engineering, 190*, 10-21.
r47	Beltran Ortega, J., Martinez Gila, D. M., Aguilera Puerto, D., Gamez Garcia, J., & Gomez Ortega, J. (2016). Novel technologies for monitoring the in-line quality of virgin olive oil during manufacturing and storage. *Journal of the Science of Food and Agriculture, 96*(14), 4644-4662.
r48	Jha, S. N., Jaiswal, P., Grewal, M. K., Gupta, M., & Bhardwaj, R. (2016). Detection of adulterants and contaminants in liquid foods—a review. *Critical reviews in food science and nutrition, 56*(10), 1662-1684.
r49	Wang, Y., Li, Y., Yang, J., Ruan, J., & Sun, C. (2016). Microbial volatile organic compounds and their application in microorganism identification in foodstuff. *TrAC Trends in Analytical Chemistry, 78*, 1-16.
r50	Balasubramanian, S., Amamcharla, J., & Shin, J. E. (2016). Possible application of electronic nose systems for meat safety: An overview. In *Electronic Noses and Tongues in Food Science*(pp. 59-71).
r51	Wiśniewska, P., Dymerski, T., Wardencki, W., & Namieśnik, J. (2015). Chemical composition analysis and authentication of whisky. *Journal of the Science of Food and Agriculture, 95*(11), 2159-2166.
r52	Loutfi, A., Coradeschi, S., Mani, G. K., Shankar, P., & Rayappan, J. B. B. (2015). Electronic noses for food quality: A review. *Journal of Food Engineering, 144*, 103-111.
r53	Sliwinska, M., Wisniewska, P., Dymerski, T., Namiesnik, J., & Wardencki, W. (2014). Food analysis using artificial senses. *Journal of agricultural and food chemistry, 62*(7), 1423-1448.
r54	Peris, M., & Escuder-Gilabert, L. (2013). On-line monitoring of food fermentation processes using electronic noses and electronic tongues: a review. *Analytica chimica acta, 804*, 29-36.
r55	Smyth, H., & Cozzolino, D. (2012). Instrumental methods (spectroscopy, electronic nose, and tongue) as tools to predict taste and aroma in beverages: advantages and limitations. *Chemical reviews, 113*(3), 1429-1440.
r56	Ponzoni, A., Comini, E., Concina, I., Ferroni, M., Falasconi, M., Gobbi, E., Sberveglieri, V., Sberveglieri, G. (2012). Nanostructured metal oxide gas sensors, a survey of applications carried out at sensor lab, Brescia (Italy) in the security and food quality fields. Sensors, 12(12), 17023-17045.
r57	Cetó, X., Voelcker, N. H., & Prieto-Simón, B. (2016). Bioelectronic tongues: New trends and applications in water and food analysis. *Biosensors and bioelectronics, 79*, 608-626.
r58	Wadehra, A., & Patil, P. S. (2016). Application of electronic tongues in food processing. *Analytical Methods, 8*(3), 474-480.
r59	Alessio, P., Constantino, C. J. L., Daikuzono, C. M., Riul, A., & de Oliveira, O. N. (2016). Analysis of Coffees Using Electronic Tongues. In *Electronic Noses and Tongues in Food Science* (pp. 171-177).
r60	Jiménez-Jorquera, C., & Gutiérrez-Capitán, M. (2016). Electronic Tongues Applied to Grape and Fruit Juice Analysis. In *Electronic Noses and Tongues in Food Science* (pp. 189-198).
r61	Ha, D., Sun, Q., Su, K., Wan, H., Li, H., Xu, N., Sun, F., Zhuang, L., Hu, N., Wang, P. (2015). Recent achievements in electronic tongue and bioelectronic tongue as taste sensors. *Sensors and Actuators B: Chemical, 207*, 1136-1146.
r62	Tahara, Y., & Toko, K. (2013). Electronic tongues–a review. *IEEE Sensors Journal, 13*(8), 3001-3011.
r63	Yasuura, M., & Toko, K. (2015). Review of development of sweetness sensor. *IEEJ Transactions on Sensors and Micromachines, 135*(2), 51-56.
r64	Gutiérrez-Capitán, M., Capdevila, F., Vila-Planas, J., Domingo, C., Büttgenbach, S., Llobera, A., Puig-Pujol, A., Jiménez-Jorquera, C. (2014). Hybrid electronic tongues applied to the quality control of wines. *Journal of Sensors, 2014*.
r65	Chen, Z., Wu, J., Zhao, Y., Xu, F., & Hu, Y. (2012). Recent advances in bitterness evaluation methods. *Analytical Methods, 4*(3), 599-608.
r66	Latha, R. S., & Lakshmi, P. K. (2012). Electronic tongue: an analytical gustatory tool. *Journal of advanced pharmaceutical technology & research, 3*(1), 3.
r67	Rateni, G., Dario, P., & Cavallo, F. (2017). Smartphone-based food diagnostic technologies: a review. *Sensors, 17*(6), 1453.

References

[1] European Commission, "ICT research area on "Collective Awareness Platforms for Sustainability and Social Innovation"," http://ec.europa.eu/information_society/activities/collectiveaware-ness, 2012.

[2] F. Bellini, A. Passani, M. Klitsi, and W. Vanobberger, *Exploring Impacts of Collective Awareness Platforms for Sustainability and Social Innovation*, Eurokleis Press, Rome, Italy, 2016.

[3] F. Sestini, "Collective awareness platforms: Engines for sustainability and ethics," *IEEE Technology and Society Magazine*, vol. 31, no. 4, pp. 54–62, 2012.

[4] A. P. Volpentesta, A. M. Felicetti, and S. Ammirato, "Intelligent Food Information Provision to Consumers in an Internet of Food Era," in *Collaboration in a Data-Rich World*, vol. 506 of *IFIP Advances in Information and Communication Technology*, pp. 725–736, Springer International Publishing, 2017.

[5] L. Atzori, A. Iera, G. Morabito, and M. Nitti, "The social internet of things (SIoT)—when social networks meet the internet of things: concept, architecture and network characterization," *Computer Networks*, vol. 56, no. 16, pp. 3594–3608, 2012.

[6] C. Evers, R. Kniewel, K. Geihs, and L. Schmidt, "The user in the loop: enabling user participation for self-adaptive applications," *Future Generation Computer Systems*, vol. 34, pp. 110–123, 2014.

[7] A. Botta, W. de Donato, V. Persico, and A. Pescapé, "Integration of cloud computing and internet of things: a survey," *Future Generation Computer Systems*, vol. 56, pp. 684–700, 2016.

[8] J. Surowiecki, *The Wisdom of Crowds*, Doubleday, 2004.

[9] N. Bicocchi, A. Cecaj, D. Fontana, M. Mamei, A. Sassi, and F. Zambonelli, "Collective awareness for human-ICT collaboration in smart cities," in *Proceedings of the IEEE 22nd International Workshop on Enabling Technologies: Infrastructure for Collaborative Enterprises (WETICE '13)*, pp. 3–8, 2013.

[10] C.-W. Tsai, C.-F. Lai, and A. V. Vasilakos, "Future internet of things: open issues and challenges," *Wireless Networks*, vol. 20, no. 8, pp. 2201–2217, 2014.

[11] K. Zia, D. K. Saini, A. Muhammad, and A. Ferscha, "Nature-Inspired Computational Model of Population Desegregation Under Group Leaders Influence," *IEEE Transactions on Computational Social Systems*, vol. 5, no. 2, pp. 532–543, 2018.

[12] E. Bonabeau, M. Dorigo, and G. Theraulaz, *Swarm Intelligence: from Natural to Artificial Systems*, Oxford University Press, London, UK, 1998.

[13] N. Bicocchi, D. Fontana, M. Mamei, and F. Zambonelli, "Collective awareness and action in urban superorganisms," in *Proceedings of the 2013 IEEE International Conference on Communications Workshops, (ICC '13)*, pp. 194–198, 2013.

[14] X.-S. Yang and M. Karamanoglu, "Swarm Intelligence and Bio-Inspired Computation: An Overview," *Swarm Intelligence and Bio-Inspired Computation*, pp. 3–23, 2013.

[15] P. Arpaia, C. Manna, G. Montenero, and G. D'Addio, "In-time prognosis based on swarm intelligence for home-care monitoring: A case study on pulmonary disease," *IEEE Sensors Journal*, vol. 12, no. 3, pp. 692–698, 2012.

[16] M. Kumawat, N. Gupta, N. Jain, and R. C. Bansal, "Swarm-Intelligence-Based Optimal Planning of Distributed Generators in Distribution Network for Minimizing Energy Loss," *Electric Power Components and Systems*, vol. 45, no. 6, pp. 589–600, 2017.

[17] D. Pradeepkumar and V. Ravi, "Forecasting financial time series volatility using Particle Swarm Optimization trained Quantile Regression Neural Network," *Applied Soft Computing*, vol. 58, pp. 35–52, 2017.

[18] A. P. Volpentesta and A. M. Felicetti, "Research Investigation on Food Information User's Behaviour," in *Collaborative Networks of Cognitive Systems*, L. M. Camarinha-Matos, H. Afsarmanesh, and Y. Rezgui, Eds., vol. 534 of *IFIP Advances in Information and Communication Technology*, pp. 190–202, Springer International Publishing, Heidelberg, Germany, 2018.

[19] F. J. Xu, V. P. Zhao, L. Shan, and C. Huang, "A Framework for Developing Social Networks Enabling Systems to Enhance the Transparency and Visibility of Cross-border Food Supply Chains," *GSTF Journal on Computing (JoC)*, vol. 3, no. 4, p. 132, 2014.

[20] B. Smith and W. Ceusters, "Aboutness: Towards foundations for the information artifact ontology," in *Proceedings of the Sixth International Conference on Biomedical Ontology (ICBO '15)*, pp. 47–51, Lisbon, Portugal, 2015.

[21] L.-G. Zhang, X. Zhang, L.-J. Ni, Z.-B. Xue, X. Gu, and S.-X. Huang, "Rapid identification of adulterated cow milk by nonlinear pattern recognition methods based on near infrared spectroscopy," *Food Chemistry*, vol. 145, pp. 342–348, 2014.

[22] V. Corvello and A. M. Felicetti, "Factors affecting the utilization of knowledge acquired by researchers from scientific social networks: An empirical analysis," *Knowledge Management*, vol. 13, no. 3, pp. 15–26, 2014.

[23] K. Toko, "Taste sensor," *Sensors and Actuators B: Chemical*, vol. 64, no. 1–3, pp. 205–215, 2000.

[24] L. França, A. Lopéz-Lopéz, R. Rosselló-Móra, and M. S. da Costa, "Microbial diversity and dynamics of a groundwater and a still bottled natural mineral water," *Environmental Microbiology*, vol. 17, no. 3, pp. 577–593, 2015.

[25] T. Vu, F. Lin, N. Alshurafa, and W. Xu, "Wearable Food Intake Monitoring Technologies: A Comprehensive Review," *The Computer Journal*, vol. 6, no. 1, p. 4, 2017.

[26] B. Kitchenham, *Procedures for Performing Systematic Reviews*, Keele University, Keele, UK, 2004.

[27] D. Cozzolino, "The role of vibrational spectroscopy as a tool to assess economically motivated fraud and counterfeit issues in agricultural products and foods," *Analytical Methods*, vol. 7, no. 22, pp. 9390–9400, 2015.

[28] G. Downey, *Advances in Food Authenticity Testing*, Woodhead Publishing Series in Food Science, Technology and Nutrition, 2016.

[29] M. Casale and R. Simonetti, "Review: Near infrared spectroscopy for analysingolive oils," *Journal of Near Infrared Spectroscopy*, vol. 22, no. 2, pp. 59–80, 2014.

[30] R. Steele, "An Overview of the State of the Art of Automated Capture of Dietary Intake Information," *Critical Reviews in Food Science and Nutrition*, vol. 55, no. 13, pp. 1929–1938, 2015.

[31] F. Kong and J. Tan, "DietCam: Automatic dietary assessment with mobile camera phones," *Pervasive and Mobile Computing*, vol. 8, no. 1, pp. 147–163, 2012.

[32] Y. Kawano and K. Yanai, "FoodCam: A real-time food recognition system on a smartphone," *Multimedia Tools and Applications*, vol. 74, no. 14, pp. 5263–5287, 2015.

[33] O. Beijbom, N. Joshi, D. Morris, S. Saponas, and S. Khullar, "Menu-match: Restaurant-specific food logging from images," in *Proceedings of the 2015 IEEE Winter Conference on Applications of Computer Vision, (WACV '15)*, pp. 844–851, IEEE, 2015.

[34] S. Lohumi, S. Lee, H. Lee, and B.-K. Cho, "A review of vibrational spectroscopic techniques for the detection of food authenticity and adulteration," *Trends in Food Science & Tech-*

nology, vol. 46, no. 1, pp. 85–98, 2015.

[35] Y.-Y. Pu, Y.-Z. Feng, and D.-W. Sun, "Recent progress of hyperspectral imaging on quality and safety inspection of fruits and vegetables: A review," *Comprehensive Reviews in Food Science and Food Safety*, vol. 14, no. 2, pp. 176–188, 2015.

[36] M. Peris and L. Escuder-Gilabert, "A 21st century technique for food control: electronic noses," *Analytica Chimica Acta*, vol. 638, no. 1, pp. 1–15, 2009.

[37] J. E. Fitzgerald, E. T. H. Bui, N. M. Simon, and H. Fenniri, "Artificial Nose Technology: Status and Prospects in Diagnostics," *Trends in Biotechnology*, vol. 35, no. 1, pp. 33–42, 2017.

[38] A. D. Wilson and M. Baietto, "Applications and advances in electronic-nose technologies," *Sensors*, vol. 9, no. 7, pp. 5099–5148, 2009.

[39] S. N. Jha, P. Jaiswal, M. K. Grewal, M. Gupta, and R. Bhardwaj, "Detection of Adulterants and Contaminants in Liquid Foods—A Review," *Critical Reviews in Food Science and Nutrition*, vol. 56, no. 10, pp. 1662–1684, 2016.

[40] K. Toko, Y. Tahara, M. Habara, Y. Kobayashi, and H. Ikezaki, "Taste Sensor: Electronic Tongue with Global Selectivity," *Essentials of Machine Olfaction and Taste*, pp. 87–174, 2016.

[41] R. Banerjee, B. Tudu, R. Bandyopadhyay, and N. Bhattacharyya, "A review on combined odor and taste sensor systems," *Journal of Food Engineering*, vol. 190, pp. 10–21, 2016.

[42] M. Peris and L. Escuder-Gilabert, "Electronic noses and tongues to assess food authenticity and adulteration," *Trends in Food Science & Technology*, vol. 58, pp. 40–54, 2016.

8

Tangible User Interface for Social Interactions for the Elderly

Way Kiat Bong ⓘ, Weiqin Chen, and Astrid Bergland

Department of Computer Science, Faculty of Technology, Art and Design, OsloMet-Oslo Metropolitan University, Pilestredet 35, 0166 Oslo, Norway

Correspondence should be addressed to Way Kiat Bong; way-kiat.bong@hioa.no

Academic Editor: Thomas Mandl

The global population is ageing rapidly. The ageing population faces not only the risk of health-related problems but also the challenge of social isolation and loneliness. While mainstream technology is designed to improve daily life, elderly people's unique needs are often neglected. These technology designs can be difficult for older adults to learn and use. Tangible user interface (TUI) gives physical form to digital information, with the aim of bridging the gap between the digital world and the physical world. Thus, it can be a more natural and intuitive interface for the older adults. The objective of this research is to review the existing research on TUI for enhancing the social interactions of elderly people. Results show that very little research has been published, given that the TUI concept was introduced 20 years ago. Our systematic literature review also resulted in several recommendations for future research, which includes getting elderly people involved in the process, from designing to evaluating the prototype and investigating the effect of TUI on older adults' social interactions and health.

1. Introduction

According to DESA, the United Nations Department of Economic and Social Affairs [1], the number of adults who are 60 and above will grow from 901 million to 1.4 billion between 2015 and 2030. This number is projected to grow to 2.1 billion by 2050 and 3.2 billion in 2100. Due to socioeconomic developments, people tend to live better, have better healthcare, and thus, are living longer [2]. Life expectancies are increasing, while fertility rates remain low, and this condition is expected to continue in the coming decades. However, evidence is scarce as to whether these added years are lived in good health and function [3, 4]. Thus, since the world population is ageing rapidly, it is essential to identify determinants of healthy ageing so one can maintain his or her function and preserve health as long as possible [5].

Healthy lifestyles have a strong association with healthy ageing and maintenance of social and physical function [6]. According to World Health Organization (WHO) [7], social well-being is one of the elements required for a person to be healthy. In Europe, at least one-third of the elderly people live alone [8], who tend to be socially excluded. This number is growing according to recent statistics [9]. Being socially active, which means having good social interactions, can contribute to our well-being and feelings of belonging, which makes us happy [10]. Social relationships are found to be a significant predictor of well-being across the course of life [11–13] which is perhaps particularly salient for older adults [14, 15].

While information and communication technologies (ICT) tools designed to improve daily life are expanding widely, the special needs of elderly people have always been neglected in the design of technology tools such as mobile applications and social media [16, 17]. Older adults might not be as good as younger people when it comes to physical and cognitive abilities, and every elderly person is different. As a result, older adults need a better design for interaction while using technology tools.

Tangible user interface (TUI) can be defined as an interface where everyday physical objects play a central role as both physical representations and controls for digital information [18, 19]. In short, TUI makes no distinction between "input" and "output." TUI offers an intuitive design that allows tactile manipulation and physical expressiveness by coupling digital information with physical objects and environments [20]. It merges physical objects with digital information. By using physical objects to represent digital output, TUI eliminates the need to have intangible output devices such as monitors and speakers [21]. Thus, TUI has been identified by Spreicer [21] as having great potential to improve older adults' acceptance of technology acceptance. This can be a more natural, intuitive, and easier interaction for elderly people, which might also result in less cognitive and physical efforts required from them.

Therefore, TUI has potential to make technology tools more accessible to elderly people. The objective of our review is to gain an overview of the evidence. By conducting this systematic literature review, we wish to summarize the current research evidence where elderly people are involved in TUI design process and TUI has an impact on the social interactions of older adults. We identify possible shortcomings of the current research in this area and suggest improvements. This paper is organized as follows. After the Introduction, we present the background, covering loneliness and social interactions of older adults and TUI. We present methods and process of the literature review in Section 3, from planning, conducting a review, and studying the selection, to reporting on the review. Results are discussed in Section 4. In Sections 5 and 6, we present our recommendations and conclude the paper by reflecting on the process and outcome.

2. Background

2.1. Loneliness and Social Interactions of Elderly People. Loneliness can be defined as a feeling or emotional state of individuals who are dissatisfied with their social relationships. This dissatisfaction occurs when they face a difference between what they expect or want and what they get when it comes to their social lives [22]. Social interaction is defined as *"two or more autonomous agents co-regulating their coupling with the effect that their autonomy is not destroyed and their relational dynamics acquire an autonomy of their own. Examples: conversations, collaborative work, arguments, collective action, dancing and so on"* [23]. Thus, any form of socialization between two or more agents, for instance, between elderly people with their friends and families, health personnel, or even new people who they have never talked to, is considered as social interaction as long as it is done with their own will. Social interaction varies across gender and age [24]. Due to transitions in one's life cycle, for instance, from schooling to working then retirement, from being single to getting married, and so on, the social interaction changes.

Elderly people who are dissatisfied or inactive in their social interactions would feel lonely and socially isolated. Loneliness and social isolation among the ageing population are significant concerns as they have varied negative impacts on elderly people's health [25–31]. Socially disconnected older adults (e.g., having small social networks and infrequent participation in social activities) face the possibilities of having inferior physical and mental health because of being isolated [32]. Studies have also demonstrated associations between loneliness and diseases such as heart disease, hypertension, stroke, lung disease, and metabolic disorders [29]. Being

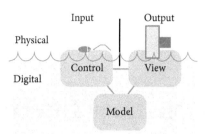

FIGURE 1: Interaction model of GUI: Model-view-control model from Smalltalk-80 [35].

active in social interaction can contribute in less cognitive decline and better physical well-being [24]. Thus, having good social interactions is essential, as active social lives can help maintain a good quality of life, health, and physical functioning [33, 34].

Many studies have been conducted regarding the use of ICT tools to prevent or reduce the social isolation of elderly people, but the outcomes are ambiguous. Social isolation has been identified by Chen and Schulz [17] as an untested concept in these studies since most studies only evaluated loneliness, social network size, and social support. Thus, the effects of these ICT interventions on the overall perception of social isolation remain largely unknown. They also suggested that the ICT solutions are not "one for all." The benefits of ICT interventions to improve older adults' social interactions can only be maximized if the potential elderly users can be identified.

2.2. Tangible User Interface (TUI). Much of our daily life has become digitalized. From physical walk-in banks to electronic banking (e-banking), from abacus and physical calculator to calculator in computers and mobile phones, more of our physical surroundings are being replaced by the digital world. With the intention of rejoining the richness of physical world in Human Computer Interaction (HCI), Ishii and Ullmer [18] introduced the vision "Tangible Bits." By coupling digital information (bits) with everyday physical objects and architectural surfaces, the interaction between humans and digital information can be enhanced from its traditional Graphical User Interface (GUI).

The traditional GUI obtains input from control and displays the output in the forms of "digital representations" [19]. As illustrated in Figure 1, this interaction model was developed in conjunction with Smalltalk-80 programming language [35]. The difference between the traditional GUI interaction model and TUI is that TUI does not make a distinction between input and output (Figure 2).

According to Ullmer and Ishii [19], TUI has three main characteristics, as shown in Figure 2. They are as follows:

(1) Physical representations *(rep-p)* are computationally coupled to underlying digital information *(model)*.

(2) Physical representations embody mechanisms for interactive control *(control)*.

(3) Physical representations are perceptually coupled to actively mediated digital representations *(rep-d)*.

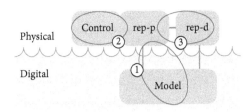

FIGURE 2: Interaction model of TUI by Ullmer and Ishii [19].

Besides that Ullmer and Ishii [19] suggest five types of tasks which TUI is good for. They are as follows:

(1) Information storage, retrieval, and manipulation.

(2) Information visualization.

(3) Modelling and simulation.

(4) Systems management, configuration, and control.

(5) Education, entertainment, and programming systems.

Tangible Bits aim to eliminate the gaps between the physical and digital world, as well as the foreground and background of human activities. Ishii and Ullmer [18] presented three key concepts of Tangible Bits:

(1) Interactive surfaces: surfaces such as walls, ceilings, doors, and windows are transformed into active surfaces between physical and digital worlds.

(2) The coupling of bits with graspable physical objects: everyday graspable objects such as cups, books, and cards are coupled with digital information.

(3) Ambient media for background awareness: ambient media such as sound, light, airflow, and water movement serve as the background interfaces for digital worlds where a human being can perceive them.

Due to its advantage in using haptic interaction to interact with the digital world, TUI has been used in fields such as learning, problem solving and planning, information visualization, tangible programming, entertainment, and social communication [36]. Urban Planning Workbench (Urp) was developed by Underkoffler and Ishii [37] as the first generation of TUI. Scaled physical models of buildings were used as representations of digital models of the buildings, so users can manipulate them physically to change location and simulate shadow, light reflection, and more.

From Urp, it is clear that collaboration, learning, and decision making though digital technology could be enhanced by having a human being physically touch and interact with the physical objects [38]. Although TUI provides an excellent platform for collaboration and makes users feel "situated" in the real world with digital information, it faces the problem of scalability and versatility [36]. The more digital information users must deal with, the more complex the TUI must be. Digital objects are easy to create and modify, but physical objects cannot be transformed as easily as digital objects.

3. Method and Results

The methodology of this review has been derived by referencing other published literature review and refers to the systematic literature review guidelines by Keele [39]. Our review methodology consists of three main phases.

3.1. Planning the Review. During this phase, we identified the needs for this literature review, which we clarified and presented in our introduction. To identify the gaps and give recommendations for future research directions [39, 40], we reviewed the state-of-the-art existing literature in this area. The research questions were generated accordingly, and they are listed as follows:

(1) How does TUI impact the social interactions of elderly people?

(2) Have elderly people been involved in the process of design and development of TUI prototype, and if so, in which way?

3.2. Conducting the Review. From the research questions, we identified three main search terms, and they were "elderly," "tangible user interface," and "social." Before performing the search, the inclusion and exclusion criteria were defined.

(1) The target group of the paper must be older adults who are generally above 50.

(2) Papers must focus on TUI.

(3) Papers must focus on the social aspect.

(4) Papers where TUI focuses on robot, mobile, computer and tablet-based applications, ambient intelligence, and smart homes are excluded. Our primary focus on TUI is using everyday objects and not a whole environment or unfamiliar object. Robot, mobile, computer and tablet-based applications, ambient intelligence, and smart homes do not fulfil the condition of using an everyday object as TUI. Mobile phones, computers, and tablets also have a certain level of difficulty in use for the elderly people. Both ambient intelligence and smart homes work as an environment and not a single object. Therefore, they are also excluded.

(5) Only published or peer-reviewed works are included. Dissertations and theses are excluded.

(6) Non-English papers are excluded.

The search was conducted from 20 June 2017 to 10 July 2017 by two researchers, separately. Four electronic databases recommended by Brereton et al. [41] and one by Keele [39] were used in performing the search. Combining the main search terms and inclusion and exclusion criteria, the generated search string was *elderly AND "tangible user interface" AND social AND NOT robot AND NOT "smart home" AND NOT "ambient intelligence"*. A supplement search using the same search string was conducted on Google Scholar (also recommended by Brereton et al. [41]) from 29 January 2018 to 31 January 2018.

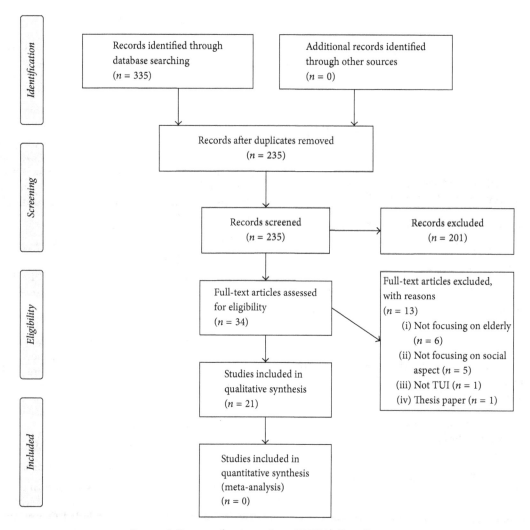

FIGURE 3: Process of review using a PRISMA flow diagram.

TABLE 1: Summary of electronic databases and number of search results.

Electronic database	Number of search results
ACM	66
Springer	69
Science Direct	14
Engineering Village	8
IEEE	10
Google Scholar	168
Total	335

We did not exclude mobile, computer, and tablet at this stage because we considered the possibility of researchers using these technologies in developing their TUI prototypes. The results from each electronic database are summarized in Table 1.

Total records identified through database search and other sources from two searches are 335 papers. Records after removing duplicates are 235 papers. After removing duplicates, abstracts of the papers were read, and the content of the papers was screened by both researchers to determine if the papers fulfilled all the inclusion criteria and exclusion criteria.

Synonym terms for "elder" such as aged, old, and senior were searched throughout the papers to check if they fulfilled criteria (1). The papers were also checked to determine if they fulfilled the definition of TUI. A TUI makes no distinction between input and output, just like an abacus [19]. Prototypes that were purely mobile, computer, or tablet-based were also excluded. The screening resulted in 34 papers. 201 papers were excluded at this stage due to the fact that they did not fulfil all of our inclusion and exclusion criteria as stated in Section 3.2.

After screening, the papers were assessed and read in full-text for eligibility, to check if they fulfilled all the inclusion and exclusion criteria. 21 papers were included as relevant papers that use the concept of TUI in enhancing social interactions of elderly people. Figure 3 illustrates the process using a PRISMA flow diagram [42]. There were no studies included in quantitative synthesis due to no common data being measured in the selected papers.

3.3. Studying the Selection and Reporting the Results. The 21 selected papers were studied and reviewed. The research questions guided the review process, and the review was based on the following criteria:

(1) Objective of the study.

(2) Discipline in which the author and coauthors of the papers worked.

(3) Methodology guiding the design and development of the prototype.

(4) Methodology guiding the evaluation processes.

(5) User involvement (user here means elderly people. Involvement means involvement at any stage of the research).

(6) Sample size and demographics (during evaluation).

(7) Evaluation method and data capture.

Most of the papers aimed at designing, developing, and evaluating their prototypes which targeted to address loneliness and social exclusion among elderly people. Most of the authors and coauthors of the papers worked within the technology field, while a few worked in art and design. Regarding methodology for design and development of the prototypes, six papers [43–48] adopted a user-centered approach which involves users in the iterative process of requirement gathering, design, development, and testing. Although other papers did not use user-centered approach, some of them did involve users to identify their requirements. For instance, Zhao et al. [49] conducted interviews with 10 elderly people in their first design study, while Davidoff et al. [50] used semistructured interviews with six email-using elderly participants.

In terms of methodology for evaluating the prototypes, one paper [51] did not present any testing or evaluation of their proposed TUI. The other 20 papers used empirical approach. All 21 papers presented their prototypes and all but two [51, 52] involved users in their evaluations. Four papers [44, 46, 53, 54] reported that they had evaluation but did not present information about their sample. Thus combining the two papers that did not involve users in their evaluation, a total of six papers had no sample. The summary of the review is presented in Table 2.

4. Discussion

4.1. Evidence and Number of Relevant Papers. The review results indicate very little use of TUI to enhance older adults' social interactions. Our search using six electronic databases resulted in 167 search results, and out of these 167 search results, only 21 papers fulfilled all the inclusion and exclusion criteria. The number of papers selected after all screening processes shows the lack of research in using TUI for elderly people's social interactions.

The search results include many research works using touch gestures, such as mobile applications and tablet-based applications since touch gestures are also a kind of "tangible" user interface. However, this review only targets on the TUI

that uses Tangible Bits, where digital bits are coupled with everyday physical objects and architectural surfaces [18]. Elderly people do have problems using touch-gesture devices [16, 64, 65]. As a result, researches where the prototype was mobile, tablet, and even computer-based were excluded and we only considered TUI that adopted everyday physical objects in our review.

No time range was applied during the search in order to include as many search results as possible. Although the TUI was introduced by Ishii and Ullmer [18] nearly 20 years ago, our review only managed to identify 21 relevant papers using TUI to improve the social interactions of the older adults. Three out of 21 papers [44, 46, 47] were on same project, kommTui. Thus the number of individual studies was even smaller. The small number of papers indicated little evidence of research work done in this field.

In terms of data capture by the 21 reviewed papers, most of them focused on the usability aspect of the prototype. Only seven papers focused on the social interaction of the elderly people. Foverskov and Binder [43] studied the possibilities for elderly people to have more active interactions and dialogues; workshop series conducted by Ehrenstrasser and Spreicer [47] in 2010 explored on the communication habits of elderly people; Meza-Kubo et al. [56] studied interactions of elderly people within cognitive stimulation sessions and the factors affecting the relationships of them with their family through case study; Huldtgren et al. [58] observed the interactions of the elderly participants with a tangible multimedia book and interactions between people during reminiscence sessions; Marques et al. [53] conducted usability testing to observe how elderly people used tangible objects and interacted with other players while playing tabletop game; using tangible objects and tabletop surface, Murko and Kunze [62] studied the well-being of the dementia patients in terms of social interactions between caregivers and patients; and lastly, Angelini et al. [63] evaluated whether elderly participants managed communicate with the person on the other side of the prototype, a tangible window. The small amount of reviewed papers focusing on social interaction of the elderly people clearly shows the lack of evidence in using TUI to make an impact on the social interactions of older adults.

4.2. The Objectives of the Papers. The majority of the papers in our review focused on usability, accessibility. and user experience, as they effect the elderly people's acceptance of the newly introduced technology. However, some focused more on other aspects. For example, Fu et al. [55] targeted to provide elderly people a tangible self-health management system. In the mean time they acknowledge that health and social interaction are very much related. Thus, the system linked the elderly people with their family, friends, and doctors by cross-media platform and social network.

Meza-Kubo et al. [56] designed a TUI pervasive cognition simulation collaboration system. The system aimed at not only reducing the risks of suffering a cognitive decline related condition, but also addressing the technical, social family networks and illiteracy gaps of the elderly people. Augmented reality cubes were designed by Boletsis and McCallum [57] to

TABLE 2: Summary of review results.

Paper #	Objective of the paper	Discipline	Design & development methodology	Evaluation methodology	User involvement	Sample size & demographics	Evaluation method & data capture
[50]	To design and conduct a preliminary evaluation of a "the book as user interface"-based email system for elderly people	Human-Computer Interaction	Semistructured interviews with email using elderly participants	Yes. Empirical	Yes	Six participants (five were using a computer for the first time, while one was a complete beginner)	Questionnaire. Perceived ease of use and feelings of independence
[45]	To promote reminiscence and memory sharing activities by explore the suitability of using digital media with tangible scrapbook application	Information Technologies, Computer Science and Informatics	User-centered	Yes. Empirical	Yes	Not elderly participants	User study experiment and questionnaire. Usability in terms of performance results, ease of use, usefulness, and so on
[44]	To better design usable and user-sensitive interaction for the elderly people, with the purpose to increase their acceptance using ICT for communications	Technology Assessment & Design, Inclusive Design and Research	User-centered	Yes. Empirical	Yes	Not mentioned	Workshop. Usability
[49]	To design and evaluate a TUI embedding asynchronous voice message systems to address elderly people's intergenerational communication	Bioengineering, Computer Science and Engineering, Art	Research through study approach with engaging users	Yes. Empirical	Yes	Not elderly participants	Qualitative evaluation. Usability and user engagement
[43]	To study how to create possibilities of interaction and dialogues using tangible social media via the design concept of Super Dots	Centre for Theory & Method/Co-Design	User-centered	Yes. Empirical	Yes	Age was not clearly mentioned. One participant was 82 years old. A total of six elderly participants were mentioned throughout the paper	Workshops. Possibility for interaction and dialogues
[46]	To apply and analyze different multimodality (aural, visual, tactile, gesture, posture, and space) in designing tangible communication systems for elderly, with the purpose to support communication and social interaction among elderly people. Prototypes were implemented and evaluated	Informatics & Design, Inclusive Design and Research	User-centered	Yes. Empirical	Yes	Not mentioned	Workshops with use cases. Observation on how players interacted with the TUI in terms of different modalities

TABLE 2: Continued.

Paper #	Objective of the paper	Discipline	Design & development methodology	Evaluation methodology	User involvement	Sample size & demographics	Evaluation method & data capture
[55]	To design more accessible and enjoyable chronic disease self-health management system for the elderly people	Information Art & Design, Computer Science and Technology	User research (interview, observation, persona)	Yes. Empirical	Yes	10 participants (only details of seven of them were given). Age ranged from 60 to 90, with different diseases like hypertension, bronchitis, diabetes, and disabilities such as poor memory, visual impairment, motor impairment, and so on	Role-play to access the elderly people's interaction pattern; cord sorting to understand mental model. Visual interface was also tested
[47]	To design accessible, functional and acceptable TUI for elderly people's digital inclusion through user involvement	Informatics & Design, Inclusive Design and Research	User-centered	Yes. Empirical	Yes	Series of workshop were conducted from year 2010 to 2012 but sample size and demographics of the participants were not mentioned	Workshops with interviews, design sessions, focus groups, usability testing, and feedback rounds. Multimodal analysis frames were also used as evaluation tools for redesign process. Workshop series in 2010: focus on the exploration of communication habits of elderly people. Workshop series in 2011: focus on the interaction design. Workshop series in 2012: focus on the usability
[56]	To design and evaluate a TUI pervasive cognition simulation collaborative system, with the aim of addressing technological, social family networks, and illiteracy gaps regardless of physical location for elderly people	Computer Sciences	Case studies (identifying and understanding users, roles, interactions, and identifying factors that affect relationships of elderly people with their family)	Yes. Empirical	Yes	Six healthy elderly participants with one relative each (five adult children, age ranged from 33 to 55 & one grandchildren aged 21)	Observation and questionnaire to study perception of use (ease of use, usefulness, enjoyment, and anxiety) and projected use (intention of use and expected use). Open questions to study communication practices and cognition simulation activities

TABLE 2: Continued.

Paper #	Objective of the paper	Discipline	Design & development methodology	Evaluation methodology	User involvement	Sample size & demographics	Evaluation method & data capture
[57]	To design a serious game for cognitive training and screening for elderly people by utilising augmented reality and tangible objects	Computer Sciences	Based on design principles, design, and usability suggestion from other studies and collaboration with physician	Yes. Empirical	Yes	Five elderly participants who were 60 years old and above, independently performing activities of daily living, not diagnosed with any kind of dementia, familiar with technology (i.e., using or having used laptop, tablet PC, and smartphone) and video games (i.e., playing or having played video games before) and would be novice augmented reality users	In-Game Experience Questionnaire to evaluate the game experience. System Usability Scale to evaluate the usability and interaction. Open, semistructured interviews to study participants' personal playing experience
[58]	To employ tangible multimedia artifact to support reminiscence sessions	Media, Design, Innovation Sciences	Field research	Yes. Empirical	Yes	Eight people with dementia (7 women and 1 man. Age above 80) suffered from different levels of Alzheimer's with handicaps such as mobility problems, hearing problems, speech impairments (related to strokes), and four caregivers	Sound recording for transcripts and observations to study the interactions with a tangible multimedia book, interactions between people, and physical reactions of participants during reminiscence sessions. Focus group to get feedback from caregivers about the reminiscence sessions

TABLE 2: Continued.

Paper #	Objective of the paper	Discipline	Design & development methodology	Evaluation methodology	User involvement	Sample size & demographics	Evaluation method & data capture
[59]	To design an immersive interface focusing on edutainment contents, with the aim for elderly people to enjoy themselves and improve their health and quality of lives	Internet & Multimedia Engineering, Advanced Fusion Technology, Game Engineering,	Not mentioned	Yes. Empirical	Yes	Experiment 1: 30 people (five age groups (20, 30, 40, 50, and 60) and each age group consists of three men and three women). Experiment 2: 8 subjects (three women & five men. Age ranged from 50 to 70)	Experiment 1: performances of playing the games were evaluated to measure the effects of familiarity to the interaction metaphor. Learning curves of the digitalized game were tested to measure the effects of familiar interaction metaphor. Experiment 2: time required to complete each game was measured to see the effects of believable interaction metaphor. Subjects were interviewed with questionnaire to measure user satisfaction
[48]	To develop a tangible intergenerational collaborative game for elderly people	Embedded Interaction, Informatics	User-centered	Yes. Empirical	Yes	Two elderly women (age ranged from 56 to 65) who did not have grandchildren and described themselves as advanced computer users, and one boy (age 8) who played computer games frequently	Observations and comments from the participants. The acceptance, the handling with the game and suggestions to improve the games and to adapt the players' requirements
[52]	To bridge intergenerational gap between elderly and young people with the aim of engaging elderly people in social media through photos and solving social isolation barrier	Imaging Media	Not mentioned	Yes. Empirical	No	N/A	Comparing with other existing systems (Sound Shot, AudioBoom, and Yappie) and the previous work (audio enhanced paper photos) in terms of functionality and performance of system
[60]	To design and evaluate a tabletop game especially created for senior citizens, with the aim of providing leisure and fun	Industrial Design, Communication and Information Sciences	Field study (observation, interview)	Yes. Empirical	Yes	Eight elderly participants (three women & five men. Age ranged from 65 to 73)	Questionnaire and interview. Game experience of the elderly players

TABLE 2: Continued.

Paper #	Objective of the paper	Discipline	Design & development methodology	Evaluation methodology	User involvement	Sample size & demographics	Evaluation method & data capture
[61]	To design a tabletop solution that provides a pleasant social cognitive training, with the aim of preserving cognitive functions in elderly people	General Psychology, Bioengineering and Technology	A series of stages including identification of requirements, planning and development of initial concepts, and usability and acceptance analysis	Yes. Empirical	Yes	Usability evaluation: three different groups of four elderly players (age ranged from 64 to 75, mean age 68.083, standard deviation 3.34); trial managers and usability experts. Level of acceptance of the prototype: 107 elderly users in three trial centers (Spain 46%, England 14%, and Norway 40%) and a group of 21 experienced users. Consistency of the monitoring module: 59 elderly players	Usability evaluation: video-analysis and observation for elderly players to identify requests for help. Checklists for trial managers and usability experts to test usability. Level of acceptance of the prototype: questionnaires and focus groups to evaluate acceptance. Consistency of the monitoring module: statistic comparison of the scores by Eldergames with those obtained with the Wechsler Abbreviated Scale of Intelligence to validate the scoring system
[54]	To study the guidelines for making users feel playful and engaged while playing game by developing an application	Computer Sciences	Based on guidelines	Yes. Empirical	Yes	Not mentioned	Observation and comments from participants. The impact of games in terms of user experience
[51]	To present a multitouch social interaction system for elderly people that enables them to engage the benefits of ICT and enhance their social interaction	Industrial Design, Computer Science and Information Engineering	Not mentioned	No	No	N/A	N/A
[53]	To improve the quality of elderly people's life by providing a better and richer gaming experience with the use of real objects while interacting with digital games	Computer Engineering	Not mentioned	Yes. Empirical	Yes	Not mentioned	Observation during usability testing. The use of tangible objects and the interactions of elderly people with them while playing the game

TABLE 2: Continued.

Paper #	Objective of the paper	Discipline	Design & development methodology	Evaluation methodology	User involvement	Sample size & demographics	Evaluation method & data capture
[62]	To explore the use of surface computing and TUI for people with dementia by developing three prototypes	Human and Technology Interaction	Interviews and workshop with experts, use of personas and referencing books and material collections for occupational therapy in dementia	Yes. Empirical	Yes	14 participants (nine women & five men. Age ranged from 77 to 93) representing all degrees of dementia	Observation, system log, and interview with occupational therapists. User experience and system usability, well-being of the dementia patients in terms of social interactions between caregivers and patients
[63]	To design a system where the technology is hidden behind a well-known metaphor so that system accessibility and user acceptance of elderly people can be improved	Technology for Human Well-being, Hospital & Health Care, Technology	Based on guidelines, feedback from lab users and visitors	Yes. Empirical	Yes	Eight participants (five women & three men. Age ranged from 69 to 100) with different health conditions. Had primary education level and rarely used new ICT. Social interactions varied from weekly visit to yearly visit and from receiving calls from family and friends to no calls	Observation to study task-based analysis (communication task, recognition task, and opening/closing task) and interaction analysis (proximity in terms of distance where people stand from each other while interacting, participants' gestures and actions, and emotions). Semistructured interview to study user experience

use in games for cognitive training and screening for elderly people. They also emphasized the social interaction aspect while studying the game mechanics.

4.3. Study Design and Involvement of Elderly Users. Due to cultural differences, we did not specify the older adults' age since the definition may vary from country to country. Out of the 21 papers, 19 involved elderly user involvement throughout their research while two papers [51, 52] did not mention anything about involving elderly participants.

The study design of these 21 papers did not give enough detail in terms of the elderly user involvement. Spreicer et al. [44], Tellioğlu et al. [46], Marques et al. [53], and De la Guía et al. [54] did not provide much information about their participants throughout the paper. This made it difficult for us to understand more about their study design.

Although Zhao et al. [49] interviewed six women and four men whose ages ranged from 70 to 86 for their design study, they did not include them in testing. Instead, they only had a qualitative evaluation where they involved around 200 people that visited their exhibition and seven instructors from universities. These evaluation results would be able to tell us more about the impact of using TUI in enhancing social interactions of the older adults if the evaluations had been done by their target users, the elderly people. West et al. [45] did the same thing. 14 elderly participants whose ages ranged from 63 to 81 were involved in their design process. However, seven users whose ages ranged from 20 to 40 were asked to evaluate the prototype.

Nevertheless, six out of 21 papers [43–48] used a user-centered approach. These studies showed that involving the elderly users at an early stage, such as gathering input, could determine more specific and precise user requirements while designing the prototype. Elderly people tend to need more time to learn how to use new technology. Thus, taking into the older adults' needs into consideration is vital while designing new technology for them [16, 66].

Another finding is that West et al. [45] and Ehrenstrasser and Spreicer [47] utilised cultural probes to provoke inspiring responses from the elderly participants; they came out with a design that suited the end users. Cultural probes can result in a design process which is more responsive, and they are suitable to be used when target users are unfamiliar [67].

4.4. The Disciplines Where Researchers Worked. In terms of disciplines where the papers' writers and cowriters worked, the review shows that the idea of adopting TUI in improving social interactions of elderly people has not been widely explored in academic disciplines. There were some collaborations between technology and art, but very little with other related disciplines such as health sciences and social sciences. Only three papers [49, 61, 63] demonstrated multidisciplinary collaborations. Collaborations between technology and other disciplines such as health sciences and social sciences might tell us more about the benefits of using TUI to enhance social interactions of elderly people.

5. Recommendations

5.1. Precise Use of the Term "Tangible User Interface". Ishii and Ullmer [18] define TUI as a user interface that augments the real physical world by coupling digital information to everyday physical objects. Not all tangible objects are everyday physical objects. Thus, there is definitely a difference between a user interface that is tangible and tangible user interface. Many researchers quote works which use touch devices such as tablets and smartphones as TUI. However, these devices are not everyday physical objects.

5.2. Elderly Users' Involvement throughout the Whole Research Process. Out of 21 papers in our review, Spreicer et al. [44] Tellioğlu et al. [46], Marques et al. [53], and De la Guía et al. [54] did not provide clear information about their elderly participants, while West et al. [45] and Zhao et al. [49] only involved elderly participants during their design process and not in the testing or evaluation process. Having elderly participants before or during design can ensure more precise user requirements from the actual users: elderly people. Without having them test the prototype, it cannot lead researchers to a more accurate evaluation and validation of the prototype. As a result, we see the importance of involving older adults through the whole research study, from designing the new technology for them to having them test the new technology.

5.3. More Research on Using TUI to Enhance Elderly People's Social Interactions. From this review, we can see that TUI has indeed been adopted to enhance elderly people's social interactions, but only to a minimal extent. The review resulted in 235 relevant papers after eliminating the duplicate ones, and then only 21 papers were selected after all the screening with full-text reading. Out of these 21 papers, three papers [44, 46, 47] presented the same prototype, kommTui. Given that TUI was introduced 20 years ago, our findings with only 21 papers indicate the limited amount of research studies in this field. During our review process, we came across a few papers which only focused on aspects such as learning and training. These papers are not included in our review.

5.4. More Focus on the Social Interaction Aspect in addition to Usability during Evaluation. During the evaluations, usability aspects were studied in most of the papers, and in their evaluation, social aspects were completely neglected. Out of the 21 papers, only seven papers [43, 47, 53, 56, 58, 62, 63] focused on the social interaction aspect during their evaluation. Other papers like Davidoff et al. [50], West et al. [45], Spreicer et al. [44], and Zhao et al. [49] focused on usability aspects, such as ease of use, performance results in using the prototype, and feelings of independence. Because there were so few papers, we decided to include them nevertheless. As a result, we did not define quality criteria, and only presented the works they had done. While introducing a new technology for older adults to improve their social interactions, it is important to evaluate the impact of their social interactions and not just the usability of the prototype. A prototype that scores high in the usability aspect might turn out to be not useful to the target users, thus not improving their social interactions.

5.5. Interdisciplinary Collaboration. As shown in Section 4.4, there was very little collaboration in terms of disciplines. There is a definite strong relationship between health and social well-being in the elderly population. By using easy, accessible technology tools, the elderly people can benefit from having a more active social life, which leads to better health too. Only three papers [49, 61, 63] showed collaborations with other disciplines. While most of the papers did not emphasize the relationship between technology, health, and social aspects, we would like to highlight the importance of interdisciplinary collaboration, and hopefully, more research studies can be carried out together by researchers with different yet related backgrounds.

5.6. Longitudinal Study on Impact in a Larger Scale. The impact of using TUI to enhance social interactions in older adults is significant; it can be even greater if interdisciplinary research study can be conducted over a more extended period to see its impact from a health perspective, such as the quality of life and health of older adults. A longitudinal study can be conducted. This will be a more precise measure since it can serve as a follow-up after introducing the prototype to older adults. All in all, we hope to see our literature review inspire more research work in this field. This research work can be extended to more collaboration with researchers from other countries. It is certainly worthwhile to see how TUI can improve the social interactions of older adults in both a longer period and a larger geographical picture.

5.7. Guidelines for Developing and Evaluating TUI for Older Adults. Lastly, while we have guidelines for developing and evaluating mobile application such as The World Wide Web Consortium (W3C) Web Accessibility Initiative's (WAI's) accessibility guidelines, we do not have a set of guidelines specifically created for TUI. Needless to say, we do not have the guidelines to design and evaluate a TUI that are targeted for older adults. These guidelines which can be used both in developing and in evaluating can help researchers, designers, and developers to provide TUI that is accessible, usable, and easy to learn and use and keep the elderly users motivated while using it. Lack of guidelines can result in a system that is neither accessible nor useful to users. Some existing guidelines for mobile applications and technology targeted to elderly people could be applicable. However, further study has to be conducted to verify this.

6. Conclusion

With the fast growth of ageing population, lack of social interaction among elderly people is becoming an increasing social and economic challenge in many countries. The objective of our systematic literature review is to gain an overview of the state of the art research and evident effects of TUI as an intervention on social interactions of older adults. This research is therefore timely and important both to the research communities related to elderly, health, and TUI but also have implications for the society.

At the early stage of the review we found out that many researchers referred to their touch screen, mobile-based, and computer-based prototypes as a "tangible" user interface. By adopting the definition of TUI by Ishii and Ullmer [18], we managed to make a clear distinction between user interface that is tangible and tangible user interface. Doing so helped us develop the exclusion criteria used in our search and screening process.

We acknowledge that the quality of the research in the reviewed papers varies. Data captured by the 21 relevant papers were very different, and there were no criteria in common where we could evaluate these papers. All of them focused on very different aspects and thus, it was impossible to come out with a quality score. As a result, we could only present what has been done, and where there is a gap.

Although the papers aimed at designing, developing, and evaluating prototypes to address the loneliness and social exclusion among elderly people, most papers only evaluated the usability aspect of the prototype. Collaborations between technology and other disciplines such as health and psychology have been low among the researchers. There is a lack of user involvement, both in designing TUI for the elderly people and in testing and evaluating the prototype.

The process of this systematic literature review has been fruitful. Referring to the guidance by Keele [39] and referencing other published literature reviews, we have conducted this literature review to address our research questions. The literature review resulted in 21 papers that fulfil all the inclusion and exclusion criteria. As three out of these 21 papers presented the same prototype, this makes the amount of prototypes even fewer. The results from the literature review clearly indicate very little use of TUI in making an impact in elderly people's social interactions, especially since TUI was introduced by Ishii and Ullmer [18] 20 years ago.

We acknowledge that research conducted in different countries defines the age group differently. Some research might have also adopted TUI but did not use the exact term, so they did not appear in our search results. Thus, we might have overlooked some papers. All in all, by conducting this literature review, we hope that more researchers can be inspired to develop and evaluate TUI for enhancing elderly people's social interactions. Our future work will focus on designing and evaluating a TUI system for social interaction among elderly people. We will adopt a user-centered approach. By including the elderly people throughout our design, development and testing iterations, and collaborating with researcher from health sciences, we hope to gain more evidence on how TUI can contribute to enhancing the social interactions among elderly people and consequently improve their general well-being.

References

[1] U. DESA, "World population prospects: The 2015 revision, key findings and advance tables," Working Paper No, 2015.

[2] WHO, *World report on ageing and health*, World Health Organization, 2015.

[3] J. R. Beard, A. Officer, I. A. De Carvalho et al., "The World report on ageing and health: a policy framework for healthy ageing," *The Lancet*, vol. 387, no. 10033, pp. 2145-2154, 2016.

[4] S. Chatterji, J. Byles, D. Cutler, T. Seeman, and E. Verdes, "Health, functioning, and disability in older adults—present status and future implications," *The Lancet*, vol. 385, no. 9967, pp. 563-575, 2015.

[5] N. M. Peel, R. J. McClure, and H. P. Bartlett, "Behavioral determinants of healthy aging," *American Journal of Preventive Medicine*, vol. 28, no. 3, pp. 298-304, 2005.

[6] H. Kendig, C. J. Browning, S. A. Thomas, and Y. Wells, "Health, lifestyle, and gender influences on aging well: an Australian longitudinal analysis to guide health promotion," *Frontiers in Public Health*, vol. 2, article 70, 2014.

[7] WHO, *WHO — Mental Health: A State of Well-Being*, 2014.

[8] Eurostat, "Eurostat—A look at the lives of the elderly in the EU today," 2017.

[9] A. Machielse, "Profiles of socially isolated elderly: a typology with intervention implications," *Innovation in Aging*, vol. 1, supplement 1, pp. 1089-1089, 2017.

[10] G. M. Sandstrom and E. W. Dunn, "Social interactions and well-being: the surprising power of weak ties," *Personality and Social Psychology Bulletin*, vol. 40, no. 7, pp. 910-922, 2014.

[11] E. Diener and S. Oishi, "The nonobvious social psychology of happiness," *Psychological Inquiry*, vol. 16, no. 4, pp. 162-167, 2005.

[12] E. Diener and M. E. P. Seligman, "Very happy people," *Psychological Science*, vol. 13, no. 1, pp. 81-84, 2002.

[13] P. Dolan, R. Layard, and R. Metcalfe, "Measuring subjective well-being for public policy," 2011.

[14] A. Bowling, Z. Gabriel, J. Dykes et al., "Let's ask them: a national survey of definitions of quality of life and its enhancement among people aged 65 and over," *International Journal of Aging & Human Development*, vol. 56, no. 4, pp. 269-306, 2003.

[15] S. C. White and C. Blackmore, *Measuring National Wellbeing: Measuring What Matters*, vol. 2, Office of National Statistics, London, UK, 2011.

[16] B. W. Kiat and W. Chen, "Mobile instant messaging for the elderly," in *Proceedings of the 6th International Conference on Software Development and Technologies for Enhancing Accessibility and Fighting Info-exclusion*, pp. 28-37, June 2015.

[17] Y.-R. R. Chen and P. J. Schulz, "The effect of information communication technology interventions on reducing social isolation in the elderly: a systematic review," *Journal of Medical Internet Research*, vol. 18, no. 1, p. e18, 2016.

[18] H. Ishii and B. Ullmer, "Tangible bits: Towards seamless interfaces between people, bits and atoms," in *Proceedings of the 1997 Conference on Human Factors in Computing Systems (CHI '97)*, pp. 234-241, ACM, March 1997.

[19] B. Ullmer and H. Ishii, "Emerging frameworks for tangible user interfaces," *IBM Systems Journal*, vol. 39, no. 3-4, pp. 915-930, 2000.

[20] M. E. Cho, M. J. Kim, and J. T. Kim, "Design Principles of User Interfaces for the Elderly in Health Smart Homes," 2013.

[21] W. Spreicer, "Tangible interfaces as a chance for higher technology acceptance by the elderly," in *Proceedings of the 12th International Conference on Computer Systems and Technologies (CompSysTech '11)*, pp. 311-316, ACM, June 2011.

[22] D. W. Russell, C. E. Cutrona, C. McRae, and M. Gomez, "Is loneliness the same as being alone?" *The Journal of Psychology: Interdisciplinary and Applied*, vol. 146, no. 1-2, pp. 7-22, 2012.

[23] H. De Jaegher, E. Di Paolo, and S. Gallagher, "Can social interaction constitute social cognition?" *Trends in Cognitive Sciences*, vol. 14, no. 10, pp. 441-447, 2010.

[24] S. Ristau, "People do need people: Social interaction boosts brain health in older age," *Generations*, vol. 35, no. 2, pp. 70-76, 2011.

[25] J. T. Cacioppo, L. C. Hawkley, L. E. Crawford et al., "Loneliness and health: potential mechanisms," *Psychosomatic Medicine*, vol. 64, no. 3, pp. 407-417, 2002.

[26] K. Holmén and H. Furukawa, "Loneliness, health and social network among elderly people - A follow-up study," *Archives of Gerontology and Geriatrics*, vol. 35, no. 3, pp. 261-274, 2002.

[27] B. Nausheen, Y. Gidron, A. Gregg, H. S. Tissarchondou, and R. Peveler, "Loneliness, social support and cardiovascular reactivity to laboratory stress," *Stress*, vol. 10, no. 1, pp. 37-44, 2007.

[28] A. C. Patterson and G. Veenstra, "Loneliness and risk of mortality: a longitudinal investigation in Alameda County, California," *Social Science & Medicine*, vol. 71, no. 1, pp. 181-186, 2010.

[29] T. Petitte, J. Mallow, E. Barnes, A. Petrone, T. Barr, and L. Theeke, "A systematic review of loneliness and common chronic physical conditions in adults," *The Open Psychology Journal*, vol. 8, no. 1, pp. 113-132, 2015.

[30] L. A. Theeke and J. Mallow, "Original research: Loneliness and quality of life in chronically ILL rural older adults," *American Journal of Nursing*, vol. 113, no. 9, pp. 28-37, 2013.

[31] J. Tomaka, S. Thompson, and R. Palacios, "The relation of social isolation, loneliness, and social support to disease outcomes among the elderly," *Journal of Aging and Health*, vol. 18, no. 3, pp. 359-384, 2006.

[32] E. Y. Cornwell and L. J. Waite, "Social disconnectedness, perceived isolation, and health among older adults," *Journal of Health and Social Behavior*, vol. 50, no. 1, pp. 31-48, 2009.

[33] A. Bergland, I. Meaas, J. Debesay et al., "Associations of social networks with quality of life, health and physical functioning," *European Journal of Physiotherapy*, vol. 18, no. 2, pp. 78-88, 2016.

[34] L. F. Berkman and T. Glass, "Social integration, social networks, social support, and health," *Social Epidemiology*, vol. 1, pp. 137-173, 2000.

[35] A. Goldberg, *SMALLTALK-80: the interactive programming environment*, Addison-Wesley Longman Publishing Co., Inc, 1984.

[36] O. Shaer and E. Hornecker, "Tangible user interfaces: past, present, and future directions," *Foundations and Trends in Human-Computer Interaction*, vol. 3, no. 1-2, pp. 1-137, 2009.

[37] J. Underkoffler and H. Ishii, "Urp: A luminous-tangible workbench for urban planning and design," in *Proceedings of the SIGCHI Conference on Human Factors in Computing Systems (CHI '99)*, pp. 386-393, ACM, Pittsburgh, PA, USA, May 1999.

[38] H. Ishii, "The tangible user interface and its evolution," *Communications of the ACM*, vol. 51, no. 6, pp. 32-36, 2008.

[39] S. Keele, "The analysis of EBSe programs for effective use of EBSe in elementary English classrooms," Tech. Rep. 2, EBSE, 2007.

[40] C. Fuentes, C. Gerea, V. Herskovic, M. Marques, I. Rodríguez, and P. O. Rossel, "User interfaces for self-reporting emotions: a systematic literature review," in *Proceedings of the International Conference on Ubiquitous Computing and Ambient Intelligence*, vol. 9454, pp. 321–333, Springer, 2015.

[41] P. Brereton, B. A. Kitchenham, D. Budgen, M. Turner, and M. Khalil, "Lessons from applying the systematic literature review process within the software engineering domain," *The Journal of Systems and Software*, vol. 80, no. 4, pp. 571–583, 2007.

[42] D. Moher, A. Liberati, J. Tetzlaff, and D. G. Altman, "Preferred reporting items for systematic reviews and meta-analyses: the PRISMA statement," *PLoS Medicine*, vol. 6, no. 7, Article ID e1000097, 2009.

[43] M. Foverskov and T. Binder, "Super Dots: making social media tangible for senior citizens," in *Proceedings of the 2011 Conference on Designing Pleasurable Products and Interfaces (DPPI '11)*, p. 65, ACM, June 2011.

[44] W. Spreicer, L. Ehrenstrasser, and H. Tellioğlu, "kommTUi: designing communication for elderly," in *Proceedings of the International Conference on Computers for Handicapped Persons*, vol. 7382, pp. 705–708, Springer, 2012.

[45] D. West, A. Quigley, and J. Kay, "MEMENTO: a digital-physical scrapbook for memory sharing," *Personal and Ubiquitous Computing*, vol. 11, no. 4, pp. 313–328, 2007.

[46] H. Tellioğlu, L. Ehrenstrasser, and W. Spreicer, "Multimodality in design of tangible systems," *I-Com Zeitschrift Für Interaktive Und Kooperative Medien*, vol. 11, no. 3, pp. 19–23, 2012.

[47] L. Ehrenstrasser and W. Spreicer, "kommTUi—a design process for a tangible communication technology with seniors," in *Human Factors in Computing and Informatics*, vol. 7946, pp. 625–632, Springer, 2013.

[48] D. Kern, M. Stringer, G. Fitzpatrick, and A. Schmidt, "Curball—a prototype tangible game for inter-generational play," in *Proceedings of the 15th IEEE International Workshops on Enabling Technologies: Infrastructure for Collaborative Enterprises (WETICE '06)*, pp. 412–417, June 2006.

[49] M. Zhao, Z. Chen, K. Lu, C. Li, H. Qu, and X. Ma, "Blossom: design of a tangible interface for improving intergenerational communication for the elderly," in *Proceedings of the International Symposium on Interactive Technology and Ageing Populations (ITAP '16)*, pp. 87–98, ACM, Kochi, Japan, October 2016.

[50] S. Davidoff, C. Bloomberg, I. A. R. Li, J. Mankoff, and S. R. Fussell, "The book as user interface: lowering the entry cost to email for elders," in *Proceedings of the Conference on Human Factors in Computing Systems (CHI EA '05)*, pp. 1331–1334, ACM, April 2005.

[51] T.-H. Tsai and H.-T. Chang, "Sharetouch: A multi-touch social platform for the elderly," in *Proceedings of the 2009 11th IEEE International Conference on Computer-Aided Design and Computer Graphics (CAD/Graphics '09)*, pp. 557–560, IEEE, August 2009.

[52] R. Sarki, J. Haeun, and Y.-M. Kwon, "Design and implementation of web-based elderly friendly tangible photo technique," in *Proceedings of the 10th International Conference on Digital Information Management (ICDIM '15)*, pp. 194–197, IEEE, October 2015.

[53] T. Marques, F. Nunes, P. Silva, and R. Rodrigues, "Tangible interaction on tabletops for elderly people," in *Proceedings of the International Conference on Entertainment Computing*, vol. 6972, pp. 440–443, Springer, 2011.

[54] E. De La Guía, M. D. Lozano, and V. M. R. Penichet, "Increasing engagement in elderly people through tangible and distributed user interfaces," in *Proceedings of the Workshop on REHAB 2014*, pp. 390–393, Institute for Computer Sciences, Social-Informatics and Telecommunications Engineering, 2014.

[55] Z. Fu, D. Yu, and S. Zhang, "Feeling in control: design tangible self-health management service touch ponits for the elderly with holistic experience," *Korea Conference HCI*, pp. 453–461, 2013.

[56] V. Meza-Kubo, A. L. Morán, and M. D. Rodríguez, "Bridging the gap between illiterate older adults and cognitive stimulation technologies through pervasive computing," *Universal Access in the Information Society*, vol. 13, no. 1, pp. 33–44, 2014.

[57] C. Boletsis and S. McCallum, "Augmented reality cubes for cognitive gaming: preliminary usability and game experience testing," *International Journal of Serious Games*, vol. 3, no. 1, pp. 3–18, 2016.

[58] A. Huldtgren, F. Mertl, A. Vormann, and C. Geiger, "Reminiscence of people with dementia mediated by multimedia artifacts," *Interacting with Computers*, vol. 29, no. 5, pp. 679–696, 2017.

[59] H. Kim, Y. Roh, and J. Kim, "An immersive motion interface with edutainment contents for elderly people," in *International Workshop on Motion in Games*, vol. 5277 of *Lecture Notes in Computer Science*, pp. 154–165, Springer Berlin Heidelberg, Berlin, Heidelberg, 2008.

[60] A. A. Mahmud, O. Mubin, S. Shahid, and J.-B. Martens, "Designing and evaluating the tabletop game experience for senior citizens," in *Proceedings of the NordiCHI 2008: Building Bridges—5th Nordic Conference on Human-Computer Interaction*, pp. 403–406, October 2008.

[61] L. Gamberini, F. Martino, B. Seraglia et al., "Eldergames project: an innovative mixed reality table-top solution to preserve cognitive functions in elderly people," in *Proceedings of the 2009 2nd Conference on Human System Interactions (HSI '09)*, pp. 164–169, May 2009.

[62] P. Murko and C. Kunze, "Tangible memories: exploring the use of tangible interfaces for occupational therapy in dementia care," in *Proceedings of the 3rd European Conference on Design4Health*, p. 16, 2015.

[63] L. Angelini, F. Carrino, M. Caon et al., "Testing the tangible interactive window with older adults," *GeroPsych*, vol. 29, no. 4, pp. 215–224, 2016.

[64] W. Chen, "Gesture-Based Applications for Elderly People," in *Human-Computer Interaction. Interaction Modalities and Techniques*, vol. 8007 of *Lecture Notes in Computer Science*, pp. 186–195, Springer Berlin Heidelberg, Berlin, Heidelberg, 2013.

[65] V. Teixeira, C. Pires, F. Pinto, J. Freitas, M. S. Dias, and E. M. Rodrigues, "Towards elderly social integration using a multimodal human-computer interface," in *Proceedings of the 2nd International Living Usability Lab Workshop on AAL Latest Solutions, Trends and Applications*, pp. 3–13, Vilamoura, Algarve, Portugal, Feburary 2012.

[66] J. Vermeulen, J. C. L. Neyens, M. D. Spreeuwenberg et al., "User-centered development and testing of a monitoring system that provides feedback regarding physical functioning to elderly people," *Patient Preference and Adherence*, vol. 7, pp. 843–854, 2013.

[67] B. Gaver, T. Dunne, and E. Pacenti, "Design: cultural probes," *Interactions*, vol. 6, no. 1, pp. 21–29, 1999.

9

A Text-Based Chat System Embodied with an Expressive Agent

Lamia Alam and Mohammed Moshiul Hoque

Department of Computer Science & Engineering, Chittagong University of Engineering & Technology, Chittagong 4349, Bangladesh

Correspondence should be addressed to Mohammed Moshiul Hoque; moshiulh@yahoo.com

Academic Editor: Carole Adam

Life-like characters are playing vital role in social computing by making human-computer interaction more easy and spontaneous. Nowadays, use of these characters to interact in online virtual environment has gained immense popularity. In this paper, we proposed a framework for a text-based chat system embodied with a life-like virtual agent that aims at natural communication between the users. To achieve this kind of system, we developed an agent that performs some nonverbal communications such as generating facial expression and motions by analyzing the text messages of the users. More specifically, this agent is capable of generating facial expressions for six basic emotions such as happy, sad, fear, angry, surprise, and disgust along with two additional emotions, irony and determined. Then to make the interaction between the users more realistic and lively, we added motions such as eye blink and head movements. We measured our proposed system from different aspects and found the results satisfactory, which make us believe that this kind of system can play a significant role in making an interaction episode more natural, effective, and interesting. Experimental evaluation reveals that the proposed agent can display emotive expressions correctly 93% of the time by analyzing the users' text input.

1. Introduction

The ability to express emotions or displaying expression is essential characteristic for both the human-human and human-agent interactions. To simulate emotional expressions in an interactive environment, an intelligent agent needs both a model for generating persuasive responses and a visualization model for mapping emotions into facial expressions. Expressive behavior in intelligent agents provides several important purposes. First, it permits an entity to interact effectively with other expressive beings in social contexts. Second, expressive behavior may provide a visualization tool for monitoring the complex internal states of a computer system. Moreover, displaying emotions play a positive role in several applications that allow users to have a more fruitful and enjoyable experience with the system [1].

Face is the part of human body that is most closely observed during the interaction. When the people interact with one another, they tend to adapt their head movements and facial expressions in response to each other [2]. However, this is not the same when people interact with each other through computer nonverbally. A major challenge here is to develop an expressive intelligent agent that can generate facial expressions and motions, while people are interacting through it. In order to do so, the agent should understand the emotional content of the user's input that is expressed through his/her text message and should respond accordingly to that text. It requires both the model to recognize the emotions and the model to generate the facial expressions to produce the appropriate emotional response.

People's thoughts, feelings, or intents are not expressed completely while communicating with each other by exchanging text messages (especially in chatting scenario) through computer. Moreover, communicating via text messages alone often seems boring to interacting partners. In order to make the chatting interaction amusing, few systems use virtual characters to represent chatting partners. These are mostly 2D or 3D models of human, cartoon, or animal like characters. But most people find these kinds of virtual characters unrealistic and incompatible with their personality because of their static and unsuitable representations.

In this paper, we developed a system embodied with an intelligent agent that can exhibit various emotions by generating appropriate facial expressions and motions. According to El-Nasr et al. [3], this type of agent requires a visual interface, typically a human face, which is familiar and nonintimidating, making users feel comfortable when interacting with a computer. We have decided to use six basic expressions (i.e., happy, sad, fear, surprise, anger, and disgust) due to their universality [4] and two more expressions, determined and irony. In order to visualize these emotions through facial expression, we developed a life-like character that understands the emotional intent of user that expressed through textual input (as a form of words or sentence) [5]. In addition to these emotions, we adopted eye blinks and head movements to make the interaction more engaging and to maintain more natural communication.

2. Related Work

A few research activities have been conducted on life-like characters. There are some 2D or 3D virtual agents with very limited ability to demonstrate nonverbal behavior such as displaying predefined facial expression controlling through emotion wheel [6], movement of face components (lips, eye brows, etc.) to conduct input speech [7], and low level communication like gaze direction [8]. Other interactive animated creatures called woggles are autonomous and self-controlled and have the ability to jump, slide, move eyes, and change body and eye shape while interacting among themselves and with the outside world [9]. Most of these studies are focused on generating static facial expressions, while the motions of some of the face components have been neglected, in particular the eyes and the rigid motion of the head. Another aspect that is not addressed in these previous works is adaption of expressions with intermediate states.

Not only these virtual agents are used for entertainment, but also these agents are widely used for customer service functionality. Two such types of agents are Anna (virtual assistant) [10] and Rea (the real estate agent) [11]. These agents interact with the users in a human-like way with a very limited emotion.

Another facial animation system LUCIA is developed by Riccardo and Peiro [12] works on standard Facial Animation Parameters and speaks with the Italian version of FESTIVAL TTS and can copy a real human by reproducing the movements of passive markers positioned on his face and recorded by the ELITE device or can be driven by an emotional XML tagged input text.

Kramer et al. [13] explored design issues of the conversational virtual human as a socially acceptable autonomous assistive system for elderly and cognitively impaired users.

Ameixa et al. [14] introduced Filipe, a chatbot that answers users' request by taking advantage of a corpus of turns obtained from movies subtitles (the Subtle corpus). Filipe is based on Say Something Smart, a tool responsible for indexing a corpus of turns and selecting the most appropriate answer.

Youssef et al. [15] presented a *socially adaptive virtual agent* that can adapt its behavior according to social constructs (e.g., attitude and relationship) that are updated depending on the behavior of its interlocutor. They considered the context of job interviews with the virtual agent playing the role of the recruiter.

In their work, Straßmann et al. [16] tested four different categories of nonverbal behavior: dominant, submissive, cooperative, and noncooperative nonverbal behavior. Most of the behaviors were created using motion capturing with a postprocessing of bones, gaze, and hand shape and were mapped onto the embodied conversational agent Billy (Social Cognitive System Group, Citec Bielefeld Germany), while some behaviors were created with a key-frame editor. The virtual agent Billie is humanoid, male, more childish-looking and has a medium degree of realism (between cartoon and photo-realistic)

Kopp et al. [17] describe an application of the conversational agent Max in a real-world setting. The agent is employed as guide in a public computer museum, where he engages with visitors in natural face-to-face communication, provides them with information about the museum or the exhibition, and conducts natural small talk conversations

In their work, Vosinakis and Panayiotopoulos [18] presented SimHuman, a platform for the generation of real-time 3D environments with virtual agents. SimHuman is highly dynamic and configurable, as it is not based on fixed scenes and models and has an embedded physically based modeling engine. Its agents can use features such as path finding, inverse kinematics, and planning to achieve their goals.

Formolo and Bosse [19] developed a new system that captures emotions from human voice and, combined with the context of a particular situation, uses this to influence the internal state of the agent and change its behavior.

Gratch et al. [20] describe a system, based on psycholinguistic theory, designed to create a sense of rapport between a human speaker and virtual human listener.

In order to deal with the problems of managing chat dialogues in the standard 2D text-based chat, Kim et al. [21] proposed a more realistic communication model for chat agents in 3D virtual space. In their work, they measure the capacity of communication between chat agents by considering the spatial information and applied a novel visualization method to depict the hierarchical structure of chat dialogues. They also proposed a new communication network model to reveal the microscopic aspect of a social network. But their work is limited to only seven users.

Weise et al. [22] presented a system for performance-based character animation that enables any user to control the facial expressions of a digital avatar in real-time. The user is recorded in a natural environment using a nonintrusive, commercially available 3D sensor Kinect.

mocitoTalk! [23] is a solution to stream videos in real-time for instant messaging and/or video-chat applications developed by a company named Charamel. It provides real-time 3D avatar rendering with direct video-stream output and automatic lip synchronization live via headset. It is widely used for messaging services, video production, server-side video generating, e-mail marketing, and interactive digital assistants (IDA).

Alam and Hoque [24] focused on developing a human-like virtual agent that produces facial expressions with motions (such as head movement and eye blinks) during human-computer interaction scenarios through analyzing the input text messages of users. This agent is able to display six facial expressions, namely, happy, sad, angry, disgust, fear, and surprise, based on the chatting partner's input text that makes the interaction enjoyable. Table 1 summarizes the works.

Sentiment analysis or opinion mining is one of the most popular research topics today. Sentiment analysis has its roots in natural language processing and linguistics and has become popular due to widespread Internet usage and the texts freely available online on social media. Sentiment analysis or opinion mining deals with using automatic analysis to find sentiments, emotions, opinions, and attitudes from a written text towards a subject. This subject may be a product, an organization, a person, a service, or their attributes. On the other hand, for a successful and effective human-human communication, emotion plays a very significant role. In fact, for an engaging interaction, sometimes emotion is more important than IQ. According to the study of Cambria et al. [25], affective computing and sentiment analysis are key for the advancement of AI and all the research fields that stem from it. In their work, they pointed out various application areas where affective computing and sentiment analysis has great potentials. They also described the existing approaches to affective computing and sentiment analysis.

Chandra and Cambria [26] developed a system to enhance the chat experience by using an intelligent adaptive user interface (UI) that exploits semantics and sentics, which is the cognitive and affective information, associated with the ongoing communication. In particular, their approach leverages sentiment analysis techniques to process communication content and context and, hence, enable the interface to be adaptive in order to offer users a richer and more immersive chat experience. For example, if the detected mood of the conversation is "happy," the UI will reflect a clear sunny day. Similarly, a gloomy weather reflects a melancholy tone in the conversation. Anusha and Sandhya [27] proposed an approach which adds natural language processing techniques to improve the performance of learning based emotion classifier by considering the syntactic and semantic features of text. They added an extra module to traditional learning system architecture. This extra module (NLP module) focuses on analyzing syntactic and semantic information using NLP techniques. Mohammad [28] summarized the diverse landscape of problems and applications associated with automatic sentiment analysis. He also explained several manual and automatic approaches to creating valence- and emotion-association lexicons and described work on sentence-level sentiment analysis.

Dai et al. [29] proposed a computational method for emotion recognition and affective computing on vocal social media to estimate complex emotion as well as its dynamic changes in a three-dimensional PAD (Position-Arousal-Dominance) space; furthermore, this paper analyzes the propagation characteristics of emotions on the vocal social media site WeChat. Poria et al. [30] propose a novel methodology for multimodal sentiment analysis to harvest sentiments from Web videos by demonstrating a model that uses audio, visual, and textual modalities as sources of information. They used both feature- and decision-level fusion methods to merge affective information extracted from multiple modalities. For their textual sentiment analysis module they have used sentic-computing-based features. In his work, Younis [31] presented an open source approach, throughout which twitter Microblogs data has been collected, preprocessed, analyzed, and visualized using open source tools to perform text mining and sentiment analysis for analyzing user contributed online reviews about two giant retail stores in the UK, namely, Tesco and Asda stores, over Christmas period 2014.

In this work, sentiment analysis refers to perhaps the most basic form, which is detecting emotions such as joy, fear, and anger. from a text and to determine if a text or sentence is positive or negative. We mainly focused on developing an expressive agent that displays different facial expressions by analyzing textual contents of the user.

3. Proposed System Framework

A schematic representation of the proposed system is shown in Figure 1. The proposed system consists of some main modules: text processing, database, emotion recognition, intensity determination, facial expression visualization, and movement generation. A brief overview of these modules follows.

3.1. Text Processing. In order to produce facial expression, the module recognizes the emotional word of sender's text. The module tokenizes the sender's input text into tokens by splitting the input sentence on specified delimiter characters (such as " ",",",".","?" etc.).

For example, consider a text message: "Hi, How are you doing today?"

Our system will at first take this message as text input and will tokenize the input based on delimiters " " (space), "," and "?". Output from this module will be tokens: "Hi," "How," "are," and "you" which will be sent as input to the next module.

3.2. Recognizing Emotion. From a set of tokens, it searches for keywords and related modifiers by matching each token with the keywords and modifiers stored in the database. After recognition of keywords and modifiers, the module will represent the emotional state against each word. But in case no keyword or modifier is recognized, it assumes that it is a normal text and maintains a neutral emotional state.

In the current implementation, we have used eight emotional states: happy, sad, anger, surprise, fear, disgust, irony, and determined. The recognized words are mainly adjectives (like happy, sad, furious, serious, horrid, etc.) that give a clearer idea of emotion. For example, consider two people who are chatting to each other and trying to express their feelings:

User A: My friend met a *terrible* accident today.

User B: *Sorry* to hear about the accident.

TABLE 1: Summarized related works in the literature.

Article	Agent's appearance	Inputs/sensors	Actions	Agent's communication type	Application
Kurlander et al. [6]	2D comic characters	Text; emotional wheel	Display gesture; generate text balloons	Both verbal and nonverbal	Entertainments
Nagao and Takeuchi [7]	3D face model	Human voice	Displays facial expressions and gestures; generates voice	Both verbal and nonverbal	Entertainments
Vilhjalmsson and Cassell [8]	3D upper body of a cartoon like character	Cursor key; mouse; text	Generates gestures: glance, smile, wave, head nod, raising brows	Nonverbal	Chatting
Loyall and Bates [9]	An ellipsoid with eyes	Observes the virtual environment	Jump, turn, squash, puff up, slide, change color, move eyes, and so on	Nonverbal	Entertainment
Mount [10]	Photo unreal representation of a female	Text input (queries by customer or visitors)	Answers queries; generates gestures: blink eyes, raising eye brows, smiles, tilts, and so on	Both verbal and nonverbal	Virtual customer care agent (Anna) in IKEA.com
Cassell et al. [11]	Computer generated human	Camera; audio; input text	Generates voice; displays facial expression and gestures	Both verbal and nonverbal	Virtual real estate agent (REA)
Riccardo and Peiro [12]	3D female facial model	Input text; camera; human voice	Speaks Italian language; copies human movement	Both verbal and nonverbal	Research
Kramer et al. [13]	Virtual male agent	Audio	Speak; displays appointments	Both verbal and nonverbal	Assistive system for elderly and cognitively impaired users
Ameixa et al. [14]	Animated agent	Input text (user requests)	Replies using knowledge based system	Verbal	Research
Youssef et al. [15]	Female animated agent	Camera; audio	Leads discussions; proposes conversations; reacts in response to interviewee	Both verbal and nonverbal	Virtual recruiter
Straßmann et al. [16]	Humanoid male agent	-	Displays nonverbal behavior: dominant, submissive, cooperative, and noncooperative	Nonverbal	Research
Kopp et al. [17]	Animated agent	Keyboard; camera; audio	Generates voice; displays nonverbal behavior	Both verbal and nonverbal	Virtual guide in a public computer museum
Vosinakis and Panayiotopoulos [18]	3D model of an agent/avatar or any object	-	Can use features such as path finding, inverse kinematics, and planning to achieve their goals	Nonverbal	Research
Formolo and Bosse [19]	Animated agent	Audio; input text	Changes behavior	Nonverbal	Research
Gratch et al. [20]	Animated agent	Camera; audio	Speaks German language; copies the gesture of one user and shows it to the other user	Both verbal and nonverbal	Entertainment

TABLE 1: Continued.

Article	Agent's appearance	Inputs/sensors	Actions	Agent's communication type	Application
Kim et al. [21]	3D humanoid agent	Input text	Generates movements and dialogues; generates gaze	Both verbal and nonverbal	Social interaction
Weise et al. [22]	Digital character	Kincct; audio	Copies the user gesture and voice	Both verbal and nonverbal	Digital game play; social interaction
mocitotalk [23]	Animated agent	Camera; audio	Generates an animate agent, copies action, and so on	Both verbal and nonverbal	Entertainment
Alam and Hoque [24]	Male and female agent	Input text	Generates facial expressions with motions (such as head movement and eye blinks)	Nonverbal	Chatting

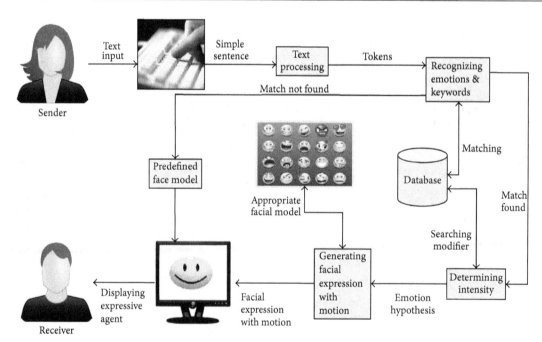

FIGURE 1: Proposed framework for the system.

Here the sentence "My friend met a terrible accident today" is first divided into tokens: "My," "friend," "met," "a," "terrible," "accident," and "today." Then the keyword "terrible" is extracted from these tokens to characterize User A's emotional state. Similarly, User B's emotional state is characterized with the word "Sorry."

3.3. Determining Intensity. This module will assign the level of intensity with the corresponding emotional state. Consider another example: User B's statement with different emotional intensity:

    User B: *Very sorry* to hear about the accident.

In this case, the modifier "very" is used to determine the intensity level for this emotional state. The intensity level for the emotional state "very sorry" and "sorry" is different.

Therefore, their corresponding facial expression and intensity level will change with high to low values. Once the emotional strength of a particular category passes a certain threshold, then user's agents' representation can be changed to show the appropriate expression. This system also generates facial motions such as eye blink and head movements based on certain text input such as yes, ya, no, and nope.

3.4. Database. Database is an important module of our system. It contains keywords which are used to characterize different emotional states and to express acceptance and rejection. It also contains modifiers to define the intensity level of emotion. Each token found from text processing module is matched with database in order to identify the emotional state and its density. Table 2 contains some sample keywords used to identify the emotional state from text message of user.

TABLE 2: Example of keywords used to identify emotional state.

Emotional state	Happy	Sad	Anger	Surprise	Disgust	Fear	Irony	Determined
Keywords	Glad, delighted, amazing	Unhappy, poor, sorry	Crazy, annoying, furious	Amazed, unexpected, wonder	Outrageous, disgusting, dislike	Fearful, horrified, direful	Humorous, contempt, twisted	Serious, determined, intended

TABLE 3: Example of keywords to express acceptance and rejection.

Express	Acceptance	Rejection
Keywords	Yes, yeah, ya	No, nope, never

Some keywords which are used to express acceptance and rejection in form of head nodding and shaking are shown in Table 3.

Some examples of modifiers used to determine the intensity levels of an emotion are *so, very, extremely, highly,* and so on.

3.5. Generating Facial Expression with Motion.

We have designed this module by dividing it into two steps as follows.

3.5.1. Facial Expression Visualization.

In our work, we mainly focused on **generating facial** expression for eight emotions: happy, sad, fear, **surprise, anger,** disgust, irony, and determined. According to El-Nasr et al. [3], facial expression is controlled through the action of sixteen parameters. Five of these control the eyebrows. Four control the eyes. Five control the mouth and two control face orientation. We manipulated these parameters using the cues for facial expression of six basic emotions as suggested by Ekman and Friesen [32].

To visualize expression, we created two 3D life-like human characters both a male and a female using software MakeHuman [33]. We designed the characteristic of the agents in a way so that an Asian can easily relate him/herself to the characters.

Blender [34] is used to make these agents more realistic and to generate the facial expressions for each emotion. In order to make the agents more natural, we manipulated the texture of the agent and performed cloth simulation.

We generated eight facial expressions and motions (i.e., eye blinks and head movements) by manipulating the facial parameters based on the involvement of facial muscles and other nonverbal behaviors. A brief description of these emotions is given bellow along with the cues of facial parameters used to generate facial expression:

(i) *Happy* is an emotion of feeling or showing pleasure or contentment. When we are happy corners of our lips are pulled up, mouth may or may not be parted with teeth exposed or not, corners of cheeks are raised, and lower eyelid shows wrinkles below it and maybe raised but not tense.

(ii) *Sad* is an emotion of being affected with or expressive of grief or unhappiness. For sad inner corners of eyebrows are drawn up, skin below the eyebrow is triangulated, corners of the lips are drawn, or lip is trembling.

(iii) *Angry* is an emotion that highly contrasts and disagrees with the emotion happy. When angry, brows are lowered and drawn together, vertical lines appear between brows, eyes have a hard stare and may have a bulging appearance, and lips are either pressed firmly together with corners straight or down or open.

(iv) *Fear* is an unpleasant emotion caused by the threat of danger, pain, or harm. We can define the expression fear by brows raised and drawn together and forehead wrinkles drawn to the center, mouth is open, and lips are slightly tense or stretched and drawn back.

(v) *Surprise* is an emotion to strike or occur with a sudden feeling of wonder or astonishment, as through unexpectedness. Brows are raised, eyelids are opened and more of the white of the eye is visible, and jaw drops open without tension or stretching of the mouth in case of surprise.

(vi) *Irony* is the expression of one's meaning by using language that normally signifies the opposite, typically for humorous or emphatic effect. It involves neutral eyebrows and upper lips stretched.

(vii) *Determined* is the emotion of having made a firm decision and being resolved not to change it. We can define the expression determined by inner brows raised and lips rolled.

Figure 2 shows the facial expression of eight emotions along with neutral expression for both male and female character. From this figure, we can easily understand the difference between the expressions of each emotion.

3.5.2. Facial Motion and Head Movements.

Humans prefer to interact with virtual agents as naturally as they do with other. To facilitate this kind of interaction, agent behavior should reflect life-like qualities. For naturalness, we included three kinds of movements in facial components: eye blinks, head nodding, and head shaking.

(i) *Eye blink* is defined as a temporary closure of both eyes, involving movements of the upper and lower eyelids. Figure 3 shows the frames used to generate eye blink. We choose to blink every 3 seconds and one blink lasts about 1/3 seconds.

(ii) *Head movements* in human mainly involve motion in head. There are two major kinds of head movements:

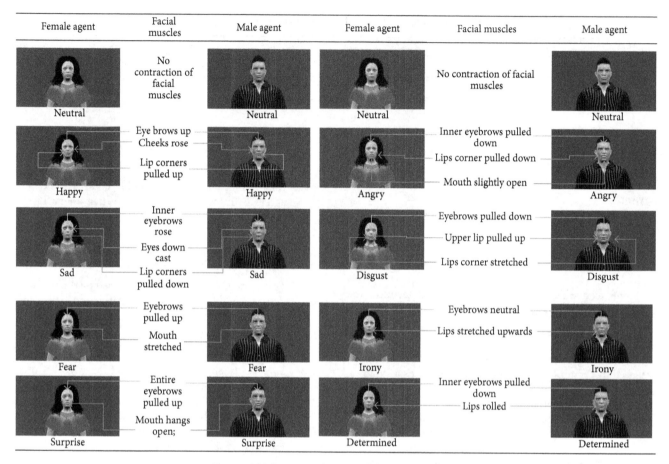

FIGURE 2: A fragment of generated facial expressions.

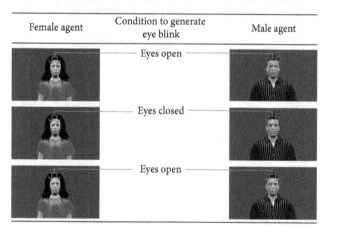

FIGURE 3: Example of typical frames used to generate eye blinks.

(a) *Nodding*: head is tilted in alternating up and down arcs along the sagittal plane. Nodding of head is used to indicate acceptance.

(b) *Shaking*: head is turned left and right along the transverse plane repeatedly in a quick succession. Shaking of head is used to indicate disagreement, denial, or rejection.

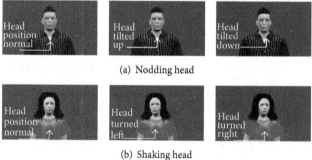

FIGURE 4: Frames used to generate head movements.

In order to generate the head movements, we manipulated the bone group of neck. To achieve these head movements, frame-by-frame animation technique is used. Figure 4 shows the frames used to generate head movements.

4. Graphical User Interface

In our project, designing the GUI is the most important part of the system as through this the users will interact with each other by text message and will be able to see the facial expressions and facial motion generated by the agents. Three graphical user interfaces for this system are as follows:

(i) *Login window:* this is the main interface that user's see when the application is launched. This window requires users to input a user name and server IP address and to specify user's gender in order to select suitable avatar representation for the user. This interface checks if the user name already exists in the network and also generates error message in case of blank input, unspecified gender, and wrong server address. For correct input information, this interface establishes a connection with the server and directs users to user homepage. From this window, user first gets access to the database.

(ii) *User homepage:* a successful connection to the server leads the user to this window. This interface allows users to change his/her availability (Available/Away/Busy/Offline) and to update his/her status. This interface also shows the other users who are currently online and available for chat. The interface runs updates periodically for all kind of changes to take place and to make it visible to the user, for example, change in availability by other user or user itself and any user leaving or joining the list. Changes are also made to the database from this interface. User can select any user from the list to initiate a personal chat and this will open a chat window. This interface also offers the feature to logout which in turn requests the server to remove the user from active user list and to close the connection with the corresponding user.

(iii) *Chat window:* this window is opened when a user wishes to chat with another user in the network whose name is visible in the online friend list of the user who initiated the chat.

Figure 5 shows the graphical user interfaces of our system.

5. Experimental Results and Analysis

To evaluate the system, we conducted two experiments. The purpose of first experiment is to evaluate the appropriate expression for each basic emotion. In the second experiment, we evaluated the overall performance of our proposed system by comparing the system with other emoticon-based systems.

5.1. Experiment 1: To Evaluate Appropriate Expressions. To evaluate the system, we conducted an experiment to achieve the appropriate expression for each basic emotion. A total of ten participants participated in this experiment. The average age of participants is 32.4 years (SD = 4.45).

5.1.1. Experimental Design. To select the appropriate facial expression, we designed different types of expressions of each. For happy, sad, angry, fear, and disgust, we designed five different types of expression and for surprise, irony, and determined we used three types. Before the experiment, we explained that the purpose of this experiment is to

Home page

Login window   Chat window

FIGURE 5: GUI of our proposed system.

evaluate the suitable expression for each emotion. Each trial was started with showing the participants different types of expressions for each emotion twice. Each participant interacted with both male and female agents and each session took approximately 45 minutes. After experiencing all expressions, participants were asked to rate their feelings for each type in terms of 1-to-7-point Likert scale.

5.1.2. Evaluation Measures. We measured the following two items in this experiment:

(i) *Appropriateness:* we asked a question *("Which type of expression do you like most preferable to represent an emotion?")* to all participants.

(ii) *Accuracy:* to evaluate the system performance, we counted total number of emotive keywords in the texts (N), total number of emotive words that are correctly recognized (C), and total number of incorrect emotive words (M). We used the following equations to measure the accuracy (A) in recognizing emotion:

$$A = \frac{N - M}{N} \times 100\%. \tag{1}$$

5.1.3. Results. The results of the experiments conducted to measure the appropriateness of each facial expression and the overall accuracy of the system are explained as follows.

(1) Appropriate Expressions. We collected a total of 800 (10 [participants] × 8 [expressions] × 5 [types] × 2 [agents]) interaction responses for both agents. We conducted a repeated measure of analysis of variance (ANOVA) on the participants' scores for both male and female agents. Figure 6 shows the results of analysis.

For happy expression of female agent, the results show that the differences among conditions were statistically significant [$F(4, 49) = 31.5$, $p < 0.0001$, $\eta^2 = 0.75$]. Results also indicate that type 3 expression gained the higher scores than

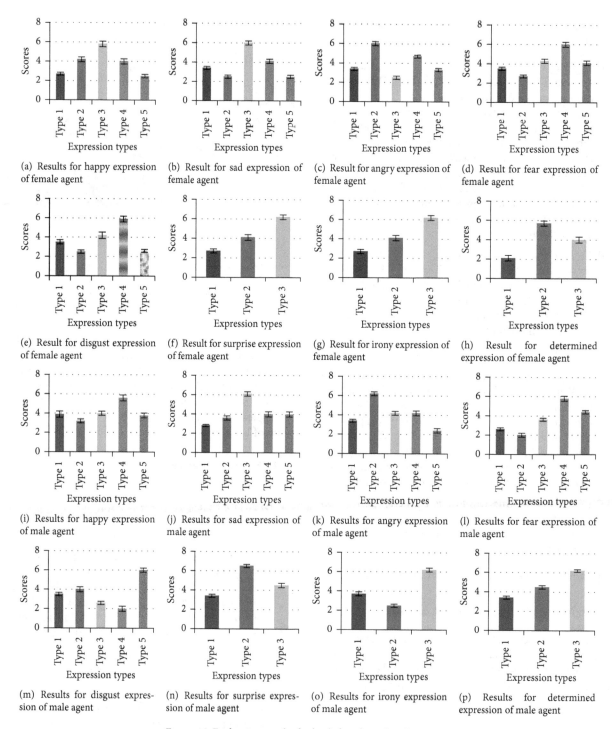

FIGURE 6: Evaluation results for both female and male agents.

other types (Figure 6(a)). Thus, we chose type 3 expression for happy expression of female agent. On the other hand, for same expression of male agent, we also found significant differences among conditions [$F(4, 49) = 11.8$, $p < 0.0001$, $\eta^2 = 0.51$]. The result also reveals that type 4 expression gained the higher scores than other types (Figure 6(i)). Thus, we have to decide to use expression type 4 for producing the happy expression of male agent.

In case of sad expression of female agent [$F(4, 49) = 58.1$, $p < 0.0001$, $\eta^2 = 0.83$] and male agent [$F(4, 49) = 29.3$, $p < 0.0001$, $\eta^2 = 0.72$], the results show that the differences among conditions were statistically significant. Results (Figures 6(b) and 6(j)) also indicate that for both female and male agent the expression type 3 gained the higher scores than other types. Thus, we chose type 3 expression for sad expression of both female and male agents.

TABLE 4: Summarization of analysis results for male and female agents.

Expression types	Type 1		Type 2		Type 3		Type 4		Type 5	
	Female	Male	Female	Male	Female	Male	Female	Male	Female	Male
Happy	2.7	3.9	4.2	3.2	**5.8**	4.0	4.0	**5.6**	2.5	3.8
Sad	3.4	2.8	2.5	3.6	**6.0**	**6.1**	4.1	4.0	2.5	4.0
Angry	3.4	3.4	**6.0**	**6.2**	2.5	4.2	4.7	4.2	3.3	2.4
Fear	3.5	2.6	2.7	2.0	4.3	3.6	**6.0**	**5.8**	4.1	4.4
Disgust	3.5	3.5	2.5	4.0	4.2	2.6	**5.9**	2.0	2.6	**6.0**
Surprise	2.7	3.4	4.1	**6.5**	6.2	4.5	-	-	-	-
Irony	3.4	3.7	3.9	2.5	**5.6**	**6.2**	-	-	-	-
Determined	2.1	3.4	**5.7**	4.5	4.0	**6.2**	-	-	-	-

Similarly for angry expression of female agent [$F(4, 49)$ = 65.2, $p < 0.0001$, $\eta^2 = 0.85$] and male agent [$F(4, 49)$ = 44.8, $p < 0.0001$, $\eta^2 = 0.80$], the results show that the differences among conditions were statistically significant. Results (Figures 6(c) and 6(k)) revealed that type 2 expression gained the higher scores than other types for both female and male agents. Thus, we have to decide to use expression type 2 for producing the angry expression.

In case of fear expression of female agent [$F(4, 49)$ = 34.3, $p < 0.0001$, $\eta^2 = 0.75$] and male [$F(4, 49)$ = 60.3, $p < 0.0001$, $\eta^2 = 0.80$] agent, the results (Figures 6(d) and 6(l)) show that the differences among conditions were statistically significant and indicate that type 4 expression gained the higher scores than other types for both agents. Thus, we chose type 4 expression for fear expression.

For disgust expression, the results show statistically significant differences among female [$F(4, 49)$ = 31.3, $p < 0.0001$, $\eta^2 = 0.74$] and male agents [$F(4, 49)$ = 51.1, $p < 0.0001$, $\eta^2 = 0.82$]. The results also indicate that type 4 expression gained the higher scores than other types for female agent (Figure 6(e)). On the other hand, for the same expression of male agent, the result indicates that type 5 expression gained the higher scores than the other types (Figure 6(m)).

For surprise expression, the results show statistically significant differences among conditions for female [$F(2, 29)$ = 50.4, $p < 0.0001$, $\eta^2 = 0.78$] and male [$F(2, 29)$ = 32.8, $p < 0.0001$, $\eta^2 = 0.84$] agents. The results also indicate that type 3 expression gained the higher scores than the other types for female agent (Figure 6(f)) and type 2 expressions gained the higher scores than the other types for male agent (Figure 6(n)). Thus, we have to decide to use expression types 3 and 2 for producing the surprise expression of female and male agent, respectively.

For irony expression, the results show statistically significant differences among conditions for female [$F(2, 29)$ = 30.69 $p < 0.0001$, $\eta^2 = 0.69$] and male [$F(2, 29)$ = 34.32, $p < 0.0001$, $\eta^2 = 0.87$] agents. The results also indicate that type 3 expression gained the higher scores than the other types for both female and male agents (Figures 6(g) and 6(o)).

For determined expression, the results show statistically significant differences among conditions for female [$F(2, 29)$ = 41.7, $p < 0.0001$, $\eta^2 = 0.75$] and male

TABLE 5: Accuracy of recognizing emotive words.

Number of emotive keywords (N)	Correctly recognizes emotive words	Incorrectly recognized words (M)
100	93	7

[$F(2, 29)$ = 32.4, $p < 0.0001$, $\eta^2 = 0.86$] agents. The results also indicate that type 2 expression gained higher scores than other types for female agent (Figure 6(h)) and type 3 expressions gained higher scores than the other types for male agent (Figure 6(p)). Thus, we have to decide to use expression types 2 and 3 for producing the surprise expression of female and male agents, respectively.

Table 4 summarizes the results of analysis. It shows the mean score for different expression types for both male and female agent. For angry, sad, fear, and irony, the same expression type for both male and female agents was chosen, that is, type 2, type 3, type 4, and type 3, respectively. For happy, disgust, surprise, and irony, different expression type was selected. It is due to the fact that in some cases intensity of facial expression shown by male and female is different.

(2) Accuracy. Table 5 summarizes the results of data analysis. We calculated the accuracy of the system in recognizing emotions and generating corresponding expressions using (1). This result revealed that the system is about 93% accurate in recognizing emotion from the input texts. From Table 5 we can see that some sentences produce wrong output expressions, because expressions are generated using the adjective detected first. For example, for the sentence "His sudden death made everyone sad," the keyword "sudden" is detected first and the system produced the expression *surprise* rather than the expression *sad*.

5.2. Experiment 2: To Evaluate Overall System. In order to measure the acceptability and usability of the system, we design experiment and compared the proposed system with other emoticon-based systems (such as Yahoo Messenger).

5.2.1. Experimental Design. A total of 10 participants interacted with different professions that have experienced using emoticon-based chatting system [mean = 38, SD = 9.56]. We

TABLE 6: Comparative analysis based on the subjective evaluation between the proposed and emoticon based approaches.

Questionnaire items	Proposed method Mean (Std.)	Emoticon based method Mean (Std.)	Significant level (p)
Ease of operation	5.4 (0.87)	3.9 (0.84)	$p = 0.0003$
Reliability	5 (0.48)	1.7 (0.47)	$p < 0.0001$
Expressiveness	5.7 (0.82)	2.3 (0.48)	$p < 0.0001$
Suitability	4.4 (0.42)	1.2 (1.07)	$p < 0.0001$
Effectiveness	5.6 (0.82)	2.7 (0.51)	$p < 0.0001$
Appropriateness	5.6 (0.94)	2.7 (0.69)	$p < 0.0001$
Interestingness	6.3 (1.2)	3.5 (0.48)	$p < 0.0001$

FIGURE 7: A scene where the participant is interacting with the proposed system.

explained to the participants that the purpose of experiment was to evaluate the performance agent's behaviors to make them feel that the agent can effectively display its expression. The experiment had a within-subject design, and the order of all experimental trials was counterbalanced. We asked the participants in pairs (i.e., 10 participants are paired into 5 groups) to use the proposed system and also an existing emoticon-based system to chat with their respective partners. There was no remuneration for participants. Figure 7 illustrates a scene, where a participant is interacting with the proposed agent.

During their communication through the system, they interacted with each other using the agents and emoticons. Figure 8 shows the conversation window.

5.2.2. Measurements. After interacting, we asked participants to fill out a questionnaire for each condition. The measurement was a simple rating on a Likert scale of 1-to-7 where 1 stands for the lowest and 7 for the highest. The questionnaire had the following items:

(i) *Ease of operation*: how easy was it to interact with the agent?

(ii) *Reliability*: how reliable was the agent in generating the expression?

(iii) *Expressiveness*: do you think that the agent is able to display emotions according to your emotive word(s)?

(iv) *Suitability*: was the agent suitable for your interaction?

(v) *Effectiveness*: was the agent effective in replicating your textual emotion into its facial expression?

(vi) *Appropriateness*: are the expressions generated by the agent appropriate against your input emotive text?

(vii) *Interestingness*: was the agent interesting or boring?

5.2.3. Results. Table 6 shows the results of the questionnaire assessment. We compared the 10 resultant pairs for each questionnaire item using t-test. The result shows significant differences for all items between proposed and traditional emoticon-based methods.

Figure 9 also illustrates these results. For ease of operation, the result shows the significant differences between two methods $[t(9) = 5.58, p = 0.0003]$. For reliability, the result indicates the significant differences between two methods $[t(9) = 21.6, p < 0.0001]$. In case of expressiveness, we also found the significant differences between methods $[t(9) = 12.7, p < 0.0001]$. Concerning suitability, analysis reveals that there is significant differences between two methods $[t(9) = 7.6, p < 0.0001]$. Significant differences between two methods are also found for effectiveness $[t(9) = 10.4, p < 0.0001]$ as well as for interestingness $[t(9) = 8.3, p < 0.0001]$. For appropriateness, the result shows the significant differences between two methods $[t(9) = 7.2, p < 0.0001]$.

Although the current system has limited capabilities, the above analysis revealed that the proposed system outperforms the traditional emoticon-based system.

6. Discussion

The primary focus of our work is to develop a life-like character that can generate facial expressions with some facial movements as a means of communication. For this purpose, we developed an agent that can display eight facial expressions and three motions (eye blinks, head shaking, and head nodding) depending on the textual input of the users. This agent can be used in chatting scenarios in place of emoticons that will make the text-based chatting more interesting and enjoyable.

Results from experiment 1 were used to map appropriate facial expressions for corresponding emotions. Here, we carried out an evaluation of expression as psychological satisfaction is relative mater and varies from man to man.

Experiment 2 was conducted in order to measure the acceptability and usability of the system in terms of ease of operation, reliability, expressiveness, suitability, effectiveness, appropriateness, interestingness, and overall evaluation.

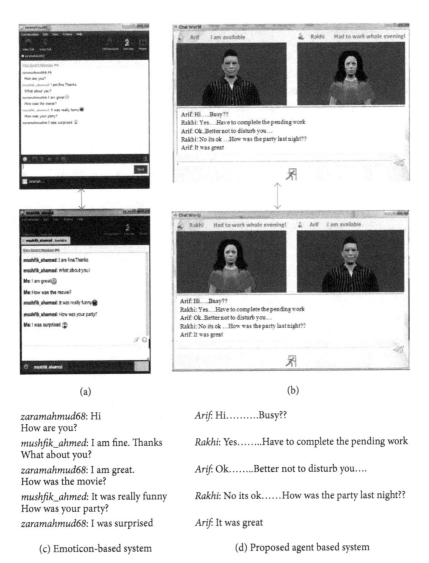

(a)   (b)

zaramahmud68: Hi
How are you?

mushfik_ahmed: I am fine. Thanks
What about you?

zaramahmud68: I am great.
How was the movie?

mushfik_ahmed: It was really funny
How was your party?

zaramahmud68: I was surprised

Arif: Hi..........Busy??

Rakhi: Yes........Have to complete the pending work

Arif: Ok........Better not to disturb you....

Rakhi: No its ok......How was the party last night??

Arif: It was great

(c) Emoticon-based system   (d) Proposed agent based system

FIGURE 8: An example scenario of user's chatting through (a) existing emoticon-based system and (b) our proposed system and a sample of conversation between participants interacting through (c) emoticon-based system and (d) our proposed system.

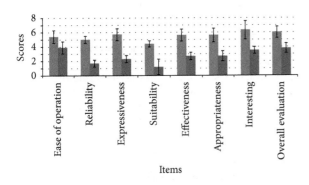

- ■ Proposed system
- ■ Existing emoticon-based system

FIGURE 9: Results of questionnaire assessment based on the subjective evaluation.

Results revealed that the system is quite satisfactory to serve its purpose.

Although the current version of the agent has some limitations, it can be a better way of recreation for people and may represent themselves via this agent online. Full body embodiment with various gestures will enhance the interaction quality of the agent. Moreover, the relationship between cognition and expression is not yet well understood in the current work. These are left as future issues.

7. Conclusion

Virtual agent plays an important role in human-machine interaction, allowing users to interact with a system. In this paper, we focused on developing a virtual agent with expressive capability. To increase life-likeness of the agent, we tried to combine a model of emotions with a facial model, by providing a mapping from emotional states onto facial expressions. It is extremely complex and difficult to model. Moreover, emotions are quite important in human interpersonal relations and individual development. Our proposed framework may not express a vast range of expression but the expression with some facial motion made by the agent is quite satisfactory. The overall experimental results show that the project is functioning quite well. Finally, we can say that the people using the system get some mental satisfaction for a moment. So the main motivation of providing an expressive intelligent is quite fulfilled. Adding chat sounds and animated emoticon may improve the quality and enjoyment of interaction in chatting scenario. These are left as future issues of this work.

References

[1] K. Höök, A. Bullock, A. Paiva, M. Vala, R. Chaves, and R. Prada, "FantasyA and SenToy," in *Proceedings of the Conference on Human Factors in Computing Systems, CHI EA 2003*, pp. 804-805, ACM Press, Lauderdale, Fla, USA, April 2003.

[2] S. M. Boker, J. F. Cohn, B.-J. Theobald, I. Matthews, T. R. Brick, and J. R. Spies, "Effects of damping head movement and facial expression in dyadic conversation using real-time facial expression tracking and synthesized avatars," *Philosophical Transactions of the Royal Society B: Biological Sciences*, vol. 364, no. 1535, pp. 3485–3495, 2009.

[3] M. El-Nasr, T. Ioerger, J. Yen, D. House, and F. Parke, "Emotionally expressive agents," in *Proceedings of the Computer Animation 1999*, pp. 48–57, Geneva, Switzerland.

[4] P. Ekman, E. R. Sorenson, and W. V. Friesen, "Pan-cultural elements in facial displays of emotion," *Science*, vol. 164, no. 3875, pp. 86–88, 1969.

[5] S. Helokunnas, *Neural responses to observed eye blinks in normal and slow motion: an MEG study [M.S. Thesis]*, Cognitive Science, Institute of Behavioural Sciences, University of Helsinki, Finland, 2012.

[6] D. Kurlander, T. Skelly, and D. Salesin, "Comic chat," in *Proceedings of the 1996 Computer Graphics Conference, SIGGRAPH*, pp. 225–236, August 1996.

[7] K. Nagao and A. Takeuchi, "Speech dialogue with facial displays: multimodal human-computer conversation," in *Proceedings of the Annual Meeting of the Association for Computational Linguistics*, pp. 102–109, USA, June 1994.

[8] H. H. Vilhjalmsson and J. Cassell, "BodyChat: Autonomous communicative behaviors in avatars," in *Proceedings of the 1998 2nd International Conference on Autonomous Agents*, pp. 269–276, Minneapolis, USA, May 1998.

[9] A. B. Loyall and J. Bates, "Real-time control of animated broad agents," in *Proceedings of Conference of the Cognitive Science Society*, USA, 1993.

[10] I. Mount, "Cranky consumer: testing online service reps," *The Wall Street Journal*, 2005, https://www.wsj.com/articles/SB110721706388041791.

[11] J. Cassell, T. Bickmore, M. Billinghurst et al., "Embodiment in conversational interfaces: Rea," in *Proceedings of the SIGCHI Conference on Human Factors in Computing Systems, CHI 1999*, pp. 520–527, USA, May 1999.

[12] L. Riccardo and C. Peiro, "A Facial Animation Framework with Emotive/Expressive Capabilities," in *Proceeding of IADIS International Conference Interfaces and Human Computer Interaction*, pp. 49–53, Italy, 2011.

[13] K. Kramer, R. Yaghoubzadeh, S. Kopp, and K. Pitsch, "A conversational virtual human as autonomous assistant for elderly and cognitively impaired users? Social acceptability and design

[14] D. Ameixa, L. Coheur, P. Fialho, and P. Quaresma, "Luke, I am your father: Dealing with out-of-domain requests by using movies subtitles," in *Proceedings of the 14th International Conference*, vol. 8637 of *on Intelligent Virtual Agents (IVA)*, pp. 13–21, Boston, MA, USA, August 27–29, 2014.

[15] A. B. Youssef, M. Chollet, H. Jones, N. Sabouret, C. Pelachaud, and M. Ochs, "Towards a socially adaptive virtual agent," in *Proceedings of the 15th International Conference*, vol. 9238 of *on Intelligent Virtual Agents (IVA)*, p. 3, Delft, Netherlands, August 26–28, 2015.

[16] C. Straßmann, A. R. Von Der Pütten, R. Yaghoubzadeh, R. Kaminski, and N. Krämer, "The effect of an intelligent virtual agent's nonverbal behavior with regard to dominance and cooperativity," in *Proceedings of the 16th International Conference on Intelligent Virtual Agents (IVA)*, vol. 10011, 28 pages, Los Angeles, CA, USA, September 20–23, 2016.

[17] S. Kopp, L. Gesellensetter, N. C. Krämer, and I. Wachsmuth, "A conversational agent as museum guide: design and evaluation of a real-world application," in *Lecture Notes in Computer Science*, T. Rist, T. Panayiotopoulos, J. Gratch, R. Aylett, D. Ballin, and P. Olivier, Eds., pp. 329–343, Springer-Verlag, London, UK, 2005.

[18] S. Vosinakis and T. Panayiotopoulos, "SimHuman: A Platform for Real-Time Virtual Agents with Planning Capabilities," in *Proceedings of the of International Workshop on Intelligent Virtual Agents (IVA)*, vol. 2190 of *Lecture Notes in Computer Science*, pp. 210–223, Madrid, Spain, September 10-11, 2001.

[19] D. Formolo and T. Bosse, "A Conversational Agent that Reacts to Vocal Signals," in *Proceedings of the 8th International Conference on Intelligent Technologies for Interactive Entertainment (INTETAIN 2016)*, vol. 178, Springer International Publishing, Utrecht, Netherlands, June 28–30, 2016.

[20] J. Gratch, A. Okhmatovskaia, F. Lamothe et al., "Virtual Rapport," in *Proceedings of the 6th International Conference of Intelligent Virtual Agents (IVA)*, vol. 4133, pp. 14–27, Marina Del Rey, CA; USA, August 21–23, 2006.

[21] J.-W. Kim, S.-H. Ji, S.-Y. Kim, and H.-G. Cho, "A new communication network model for chat agents in virtual space," *KSII Transactions on Internet and Information Systems*, vol. 5, no. 2, pp. 287–312, 2011.

[22] T. Weise, S. Bouaziz, H. Li, and M. Pauly, "Realtime performance-based facial animation," *ACM Transactions on Graphics*, vol. 30, no. 4, p. 1, 2011.

[23] https://www.charamel.com/en/solutions/avatar_live_chat_mocitotalk.html.

[24] L. Alam and M. M. Hoque, "The design of expressive intelligent agent for human-computer interaction," in *Proceedings of the 2nd International Conference on Electrical Engineering and Information and Communication Technology, iCEEiCT 2015*, Bangladesh, May 2015.

[25] E. Cambria, D. Das, S. Bandyopadhyay, and A. Feraco, "Affective computing and sentiment analysis," in *A Practical Guide to Sentiment Analysis*, vol. 5 of *Socio-Affective Computing*, pp. 1–10, Springer, Cham, Switzerland, 2017.

[26] P. Chandra and E. Cambria, "Enriching social communication through semantics and sentics," in *Proceedings of the Workshop on Sentiment Analysis where AI meets Psychology (SAAIP)*, pp. 68–72, Chiang Mai, Thailand, November 13, 2011.

[27] V. Anusha and B. Sandhya, "A learning based emotion classifier with semantic text processing," *Advances in Intelligent Systems and Computing*, vol. 320, pp. 371–382, 2015.

[28] S. M. Mohammad, "Sentiment analysis: detecting valence, emotions, and other affectual states from text," *Emotion Measurement*, pp. 201–237, 2016.

[29] W. Dai, D. Han, Y. Dai, and D. Xu, "Emotion recognition and affective computing on vocal social media," *Information Management*, vol. 52, pp. 777–788, 2015.

[30] S. Poria, E. Cambria, N. Howard, G.-B. Huang, and A. Hussain, "Fusing audio, visual and textual clues for sentiment analysis from multimodal content," *Neurocomputing*, vol. 174, pp. 50–59, 2016.

[31] E. M. G. Younis, "Sentiment analysis and text mining for social media microblogs using open source tools: an empirical study," *International Journal of Computer Applications*, vol. 112, no. 5, 2015.

[32] P. Ekman and W. Friesen, *Unmasking the face: A Guide to Recognizing Emotions from Facial Clues*, Prentice-Hall, 1975.

[33] MakeHuman. http://www.makehuman.org/.

[34] Blender. http://www.blender.org/.

10

Lower Order Krawtchouk Moment-Based Feature-Set for Hand Gesture Recognition

Bineet Kaur and Garima Joshi

Department of Electronics and Communication Engineering, University Institute of Engineering and Technology, Panjab University, Sector 25, Chandigarh 160036, India

Correspondence should be addressed to Bineet Kaur; bineetkaur91@gmail.com

Academic Editor: Marco Mamei

The capability of lower order Krawtchouk moment-based shape features has been analyzed. The behaviour of 1D and 2D Krawtchouk polynomials at lower orders is observed by varying Region of Interest (ROI). The paper measures the effectiveness of shape recognition capability of 2D Krawtchouk features at lower orders on the basis of Jochen-Triesch's database and hand gesture database of 10 Indian Sign Language (ISL) alphabets. Comparison of original and reduced feature-set is also done. Experimental results demonstrate that the reduced feature dimensionality gives competent accuracy as compared to the original feature-set for all the proposed classifiers. Thus, the Krawtchouk moment-based features prove to be effective in terms of shape recognition capability at lower orders.

1. Introduction

Gesture recognition system identifies gestures using shape features. These systems are applied in video-surveillance, 3D animation, sign language interpretation, and Human Computer Interaction (HCI) systems. Sign language is a nonverbal way of communication among the deaf through hand gestures. In sign language, different signs are created by the combination of hand movements and facial expressions. Sign language has its own grammar and syntax which is different than the grammar used in spoken or written language. Every country has its own sign language with its own phonetics. Some of the sign languages are American Sign Language (ASL), British Sign Language (BSL), Japanese Sign Language (JSL), Korean Sign Language (KSL), and so on. Indian Sign Language (ISL) has a well-structured phonology, morphology, syntax, and grammar. ISL provides information through movements of hands, arms, face, and head. It can produce an isolated sign (single hand gesture) and continuous sign (movement of hands in series). The aim is to create an application which understands ISL alphabets by interpreting gestures of hands which can then be produced in the textual form on the computer screen. This will make interaction with the deaf people easy without the need for an interpreter, thereby developing Human Computer Interaction (HCI) system in terms of ISL. The block diagram of ISL recognition system is illustrated in Figure 1.

For a gesture recognition system to be effective, features play an important role in extracting information about the image. Therefore, moments are widely used shape descriptors because they are capable of extracting local as well as global information. These have been used in various applications like pattern recognition [1], face recognition [2, 3], image watermarking [4], medical image analysis [5], and gesture recognition [6, 7]. Hu proposed moments for the first time [8]. These were seven moments, which were invariant to scale, rotation, and translation. Since then, a lot of research has been done on its applicability in various domains. After this, Teague introduced continuous orthogonal moments, Zernike and Legendre [9]. Being orthogonal in nature, they had minimum information redundancy. So, image reconstruction was easier as compared to Hu moments which were nonorthogonal in nature. However, these moments require image coordinate space transformation. Moreover, the numerical approximation of continuous moment integrals results in discretization error, thus reducing the recognition accuracy. However, Khotanzad and Hong used Zernike moments for pattern recognition because of its rotational

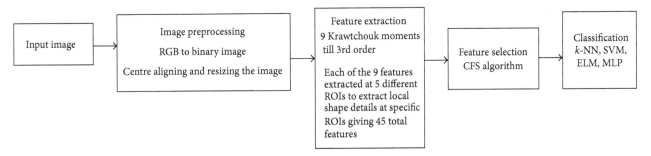

FIGURE 1: Block diagram of ISL recognition system.

invariance property [10]. To rectify the problems encountered in continuous orthogonal moments, discrete orthogonal moments like Tchebichef and Krawtchouk were proposed.

Yap et al. analyzed Krawtchouk moments for the first time on 2D images [11]. One benefit of Krawtchouk moments is that they are defined in image coordinate space and hence do not have a discretization error. Another benefit is that they not only extract global information like Zernike moments but also have the ability to represent local information from any Region of Interest (ROI) in an image. Wang et al. compared Krawtchouk (till 4th order, with ROI at centre), Legendre, and Zernike moments for handwritten Chinese character recognition [12]. It was concluded that Krawtchouk moments outperformed other moments in terms of recognition accuracy. Moreover, Krawtchouk moments proved to be best feature descriptors in face recognition systems also. Noraini analyzed the performance of Krawtchouk and Tchebichef moments on a database of facial expressions [2]. It was studied that Krawtchouk moments gave better accuracy. In the context of hand gestures, Priyal and Bora evaluated the performance of Krawtchouk moments (till 80th order, with ROI at centre) on single handed 10 gesture signs of digits "0" to "9," taken from 23 users, with 423 samples for each gesture [7]. The gestures were taken at different angles, scales, and orientations. It was concluded that Krawtchouk moments were user-invariant as compared to Geometric and Zernike moments. The paper focuses on following objectives:

(1) A Krawtchouk moment-based feature-set till 3rd order is extracted. To include local shape characteristics, the feature vector is increased by varying the ROI.

(2) The performance of proposed features is analysed for different classifiers.

(3) The recognition accuracy of original feature-set is compared with the reduced feature-set. An optimal feature-set and classifier combination that gives good recognition accuracy is proposed.

(4) For comparative analysis the performance of proposed feature vector is also analysed on standard Jochen-Triesch's database.

The paper is organized as follows: Section 2 gives the introduction of classical Krawtchouk polynomials, Krawtchouk invariant moments for feature extraction, and spatial behaviour of 1D and 2D Krawtchouk polynomials. Section 3 presents the detail of proposed methodology. The details about the database, feature extraction technique, feature selection algorithm, and classifiers used in this work are detailed in this section. Section 4 discusses the results and comparison of results for original as well as reduced feature-set. Section 5 gives conclusion and scope of future work.

2. Krawtchouk Moment-Based Features

Krawtchouk moments are derived from Krawtchouk polynomials. These are discrete in nature and are associated with binomial functions [13]. This section gives an introduction to the classical Krawtchouk polynomials and weighted Krawtchouk polynomials. The spatial behaviour of 1D and 2D Krawtchouk polynomials with varying ROI is also presented.

2.1. Krawtchouk Polynomials. The 1D weighted Krawtchouk polynomials of rth order are defined as [11]

$$\overline{K}_r(i; p, X) = K_r(i; p, X) \sqrt{\frac{w(i; p, X)}{\rho(r; p, X)}}. \tag{1}$$

The parameter "p" can be used to vary the position of peak. In 1D it can be varied from 0 to 1. In the classical Krawtchouk polynomials increasing the order results in numerical fluctuations. So, weighted Krawtchouk polynomials are used to achieve numerical stability. The Krawtchouk polynomials are defined as

$$K_r(i; p, X) = \sum_{k=0}^{\infty} \frac{(-r)_k (-i)_k (1/p)^k}{(-X)_k (k!)}, \tag{2}$$

where $(m)_k$ is the pochhammer symbol which is given by

$$(m)_k = m(m+1)\cdots(m+k-1) = \frac{\Gamma(m+k)}{\Gamma(m)}. \tag{3}$$

The weight functions used in (1) are given by

$$w(i; p, X) = \binom{X}{i} p^i (1-p)^{X-i},$$

$$\rho(r; p, X) = (-1)^r \left(\frac{1-p}{p}\right)^r \frac{r!}{(-X)_r}. \tag{4}$$

In weighted Krawtchouk polynomials, as the order increases, the numbers of zero crossings also increase. Figure 2 shows the 1D weighted Krawtchouk polynomials plot at 0th, 1st, 2nd, and 3rd order. In these plots, ROI is varied by varying parameter p = 0.3, 0.5, and 0.7, respectively. The parameter p deviates from 0.5 by Δp. For example, if p = 0.5, the ROI lies at the centre of the image. For $p > 0.5$, the ROI is shifted towards the positive x-direction and, with $p < 0.5$, it is shifted to the negative x-direction. It can be observed that the value of weighted Krawtchouk polynomials lies within the range of $(-1, 1)$.

2.2. Krawtchouk Moment Invariants. For an image intensity function $f(i, j)$, the 2D Krawtchouk moments of order $(r + q)$ is

$$Q_{rq}$$
$$= \sum_{i=0}^{X-1} \sum_{j=0}^{Y-1} \overline{K}_r(i; p_1, X-1) \overline{K}_q(j; p_2, Y-1) f(i, j), \quad (5)$$

where the size of $f(i, j)$ is (X, Y). In case of 2D Krawtchouk polynomial plots, parameters p_1 and p_2 shift the ROI horizontally and vertically, respectively. $p_1 > 0.5$ shifts ROI horizontally to the positive x-direction while $p_1 < 0.5$ shifts the ROI horizontally to the negative x-axis. Similarly, for $p_2 > 0.5$, shifting of ROI takes place vertically to the negative y-direction and, for $p_2 < 0.5$, the ROI shifts to the positive y-direction. Figure 3 shows the top view of 2D Krawtchouk moment plots at lower orders. Here, ROI is focused to the centre with $p_1 = p_2 = 0.5$. The ROIs with different values of p_1 and p_2 are shown in Figure 4, covering different ROIs in an image which are used as features in this paper. The white colour shows positive peaks whereas black colour shows negative peaks. It shows that the Krawtchouk moments are very good local descriptors.

For an image, various lower orders of Krawtchouk moments can be calculated as shown in Figure 3. Further, the ROIs are defined at different positions of the image, thus covering the entire image. The ROI is shifted horizontally and vertically by taking values of (p_1, p_2) as (0.5, 0.5), (0.3, 0.3), (0.4, 0.7), (0.6, 0.3), and (0.6, 0.7) as shown in Figure 4. At each ROI, till 3rd order 9 features are calculated. Thus, a total of 45 Krawtchouk moment-based local features are extracted to study the recognition accuracy of ISL alphabets.

The shape-based local features invariant to rotation, scale, and translation are calculated from Krawtchouk moments. These invariant Krawtchouk moments are listed in the following:

$$\widetilde{Q}_{00} = \Omega_{00} \widetilde{v}_{00},$$

$$\widetilde{Q}_{10} = \Omega_{10} \left[\widetilde{v}_{00} - \frac{1}{(X-1) p_1} \widetilde{v}_{10} \right],$$

$$\widetilde{Q}_{01} = \Omega_{01} \left[\widetilde{v}_{00} - \frac{1}{(Y-1) p_2} \widetilde{v}_{01} \right],$$

$$\widetilde{Q}_{11} = \Omega_{11} \left[\widetilde{v}_{00} - \frac{1}{(X-1) p_1} \widetilde{v}_{10} - \frac{1}{(Y-1) p_2} \widetilde{v}_{01} \right.$$
$$\left. + \frac{1}{(X-1)(Y-1) p_1 p_2} \widetilde{v}_{11} \right], \quad (6)$$

where

$$\Omega_{rq} = \left[\rho(r; p_1, X-1) \rho(q; p_2, Y-1) \right]^{-(1/2)}. \quad (7)$$

The Krawtchouk moments can also be written in terms of geometric moments as follows:

$$\widetilde{v}_{rq} = \sum_{i=0}^{X-1} \sum_{j=0}^{Y-1} \left[\frac{\{(X \times Y)/2\}}{M_{00}} \right] f(i, j)$$

$$\cdot \left\{ \left[(i - \bar{i}) \cos \theta + (j - \bar{j}) \sin \theta \right] \sqrt{\frac{\{X^2/2\}}{M_{00}}} + \frac{X}{2} \right\}^r \quad (8)$$

$$\cdot \left\{ \left[(j - \bar{j}) \cos \theta - (i - \bar{i}) \sin \theta \right] \sqrt{\frac{\{Y^2/2\}}{M_{00}}} + \frac{Y}{2} \right\}^q,$$

where geometric moments of order $(r + q)$ are given by

$$M_{rq} = \sum_{i=0}^{X-1} \sum_{j=0}^{Y-1} i^r j^q f(i, j),$$

$$\gamma = \frac{r+q}{2} + 1,$$

$$\bar{i} = \frac{M_{10}}{M_{00}}, \quad (9)$$

$$\bar{j} = \frac{M_{01}}{M_{00}},$$

$$\theta = 0.5 \tan^{-1} \left(\frac{2\mu_{11}}{\mu_{20} - \mu_{02}} \right),$$

where θ is in the range of $-45° \leq \theta \leq 45°$. To define it in the range of $0°$ to $360°$, make modifications as done by Teague [9]. μ_{rq} is central moment. The Krawtchouk moments thus obtained in (8) are invariant to rotation, scale, and translation:

$$\widetilde{Q}_{rq} = \left[\rho(r) \rho(q) \right]^{-0.5} \sum_{R=0}^{r} \sum_{Q=0}^{q} a_{R,r,p_1} a_{Q,q,p_2} \widetilde{v}_{RQ}. \quad (10)$$

3. Proposed Methodology

3.1. ISL Database. The database consists of 10 hand gestures of ISL alphabets "A," "B," "F," "I," "K," "M," "P," "Q," "U," and "W." Each gesture is collected from 72 subjects. A total of 720 gesture images are constructed from different signers as shown in Figure 5. A total of 720 gesture images are constructed from different signers. The signs are selected

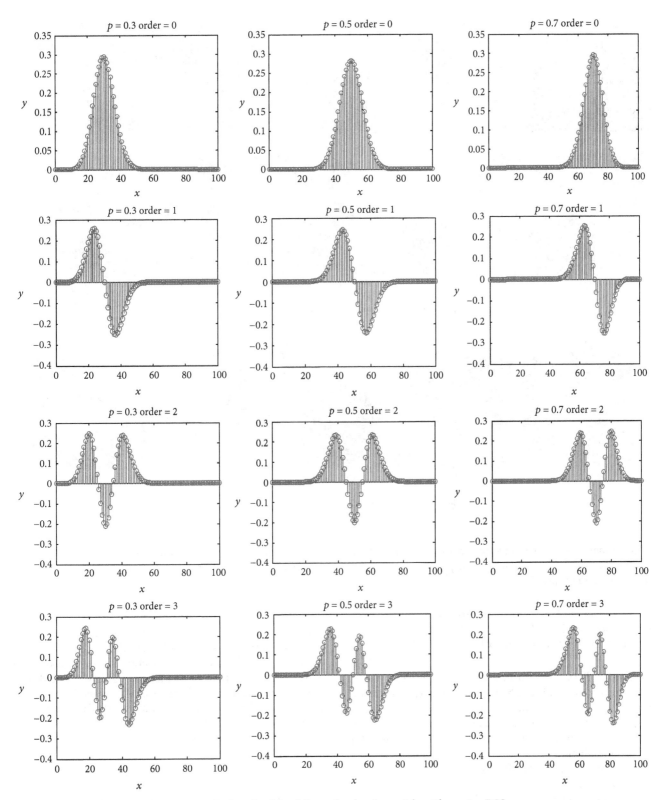

FIGURE 2: 1D plot of weighted Krawtchouk polynomials, with varying ROI.

such that they have identical shapes like, "A," "B," "P," "Q," "U," and "W," high occlusion as in "M" and "W," and one gesture being subgesture of the other as in "I" and "K." In most of signs both hands are used, which leads to complexity.

The images have a resolution of 640 × 480 pixels, taken on a uniform (black) background, with varying illumination, at a fixed distance from the camera. These go through preprocessing stage, where each image is converted from

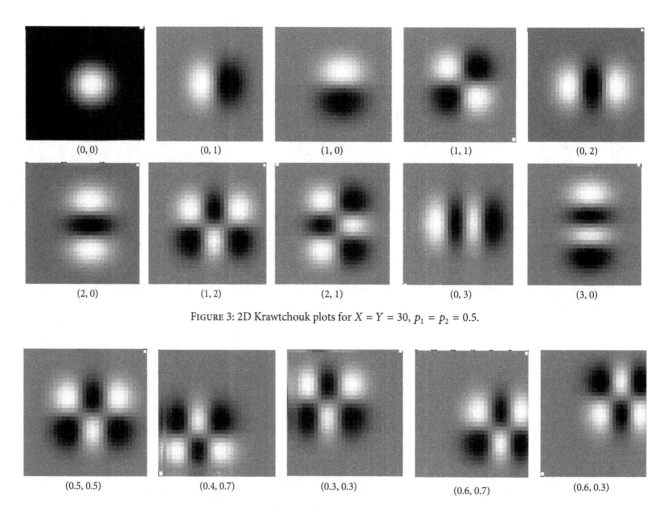

FIGURE 3: 2D Krawtchouk plots for $X = Y = 30$, $p_1 = p_2 = 0.5$.

FIGURE 4: Different ROIs used for feature extraction.

RGB to binary form. Edge detectors are used and each image is resized to form 30×30 binary images, while preserving their edges and shape.

3.2. Jochen-Triesch's Database.
The database consists of 10 static hand postures collected from 24 subjects in uniform dark, uniform light, and complex background [14].

3.3. Feature Extraction.
In this work, the moments till 3rd order are selected. This can be viewed in Figure 6, where the reconstruction results show that they cover the entire image giving local shape features. Thus, the lower order Krawtchouk moments of 3rd order are more suitable for classification [15]. On the other hand, the higher order moments result in more computational complexity with the increase in the number of Krawtchouk coefficients.

The Krawtchouk features up to 3rd order are extracted by varying values of p_1 and p_2. Lower orders have the ability to characterize shape details, thus providing local information from a specific ROI. The features calculated for various ROIs are shown in Figure 7. The 9-dimensional feature-set extracted for each ROI includes

$$\widetilde{Q}_{rq} = \left[\widetilde{Q}_{01}, \widetilde{Q}_{10}, \widetilde{Q}_{11}, \widetilde{Q}_{02}, \widetilde{Q}_{20}, \widetilde{Q}_{12}, \widetilde{Q}_{21}, \widetilde{Q}_{03}, \widetilde{Q}_{30}\right]. \quad (11)$$

As shown in Figure 7, for 5 values of (p_1, p_2), a total of 45 Krawtchouk moment-based local features are calculated for image.

3.4. Feature Selection.
Feature selection is useful in removing irrelevant and redundant features. In this paper, correlation-based feature selection (CFS) algorithm is used. CFS is considered as the most stable feature selection algorithm which selects feature subsets that are highly correlated with the class, but uncorrelated with each other [16, 17]. CFS uses Pearson correlation coefficient which is calculated as follows [18]:

$$M_s = \frac{k\bar{r}_{\mathrm{cf}}}{\sqrt{k + k(k-1)\,\bar{r}_{\mathrm{ff}}}}, \quad (12)$$

where M_s is the merit of the current subset of features, k is the number of features, $\bar{r}_{\mathrm{cf}}$ is the mean of the correlations between each feature and the class, and $\bar{r}_{\mathrm{ff}}$ is the mean of the pairwise correlations between every two features. The numerator increases when the features can classify the data accurately and the denominator increases when there exists redundancy between the features. Larger M_s gives the best feature subset. The feature subset is chosen on the basis of

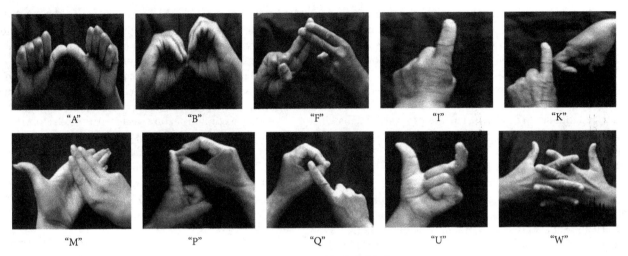

"A"   "B"   "F"   "I"   "K"

"M"   "P"   "Q"   "U"   "W"

FIGURE 5: Database of 10 ISL alphabets.

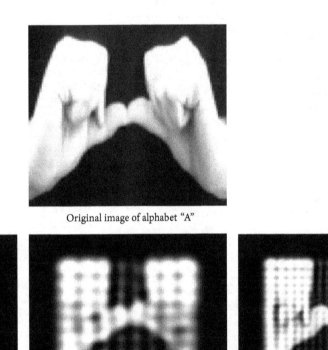

Original image of alphabet "A"

1st order   2nd order   3rd order

FIGURE 6: Reconstruction of original image using Krawtchouk moments with ROI at centre.

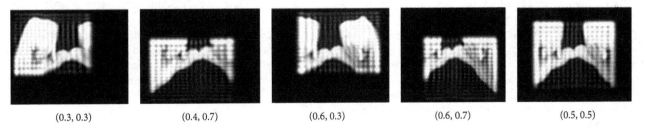

(0.3, 0.3)   (0.4, 0.7)   (0.6, 0.3)   (0.6, 0.7)   (0.5, 0.5)

FIGURE 7: Reconstruction of original image using Krawtchouk moments with varying ROIs.

highest M_s value. For this, greedy stepwise algorithm is used, where one feature is added at a time into an empty matrix at each stage. Each feature subset is ranked on the basis of M_s until a subset is selected on the basis of the best correlation coefficient value (M_s) [19].

CFS has been used for large databases to reduce the problems of class imbalance, high dimensionality, and information redundancy [17, 20, 21]. For the proposed database in this paper, it reduces the feature-set from 45 to 22. A comparison of original and reduced feature-set is done in terms of recognition accuracy at various classifiers.

3.5. Classifiers. The performance of k-Nearest Neighbour (k-NN) using Manhattan (MD), k-NN using Euclidean distance (ED) (with value of $k = 1$, in both cases), Multilayer Perceptron (MLP), Support Vector Machine (SVM), and Extreme Learning Machines (ELM) is analyzed [22, 23]. A comparison of performance of these classifiers in terms of recognition accuracy with variation of feature-set dimensionality is studied. For SVM, the performance of PUK, RBF, and Poly kernel is deliberated. For ELM, linear, Poly, and RBF kernels are taken into consideration. SVM with PUK has the strongest mapping power and better generalization as compared to other kernel functions like polynomial, linear, and RBF [24]. They outperformed in terms of recognition accuracy as compared to other kernels and classifiers like k-NN, MLP, and SVM with polynomial and RBF kernels [17, 25]. ELM is used in various multiclass classification applications and gives similar or better generalizations at faster learning speed as compared to SVM which has high computational complexity [23]. In each case, the results for raw feature vector and feature vector after normalization are also compared.

4. Results and Discussions

The accuracy is defined as total number of correctly recognized images to total number of test images:

Accuracy

$$= \frac{\text{Total number of correctly recognized images}}{\text{Total number of test images}} \quad (13)$$

$$\times 100\%.$$

To ensure the recognition ability of Krawtchouk moments, the comparison with Hu moments and Zernike moments is done. Table 1 shows the recognition accuracy for ISL alphabets for these three moments. For a small feature vector up to 3rd order, Krawtchouk moments show the best results for all the classifiers except for ELM. On normalization, the best accuracy of 85.9% is observed with Krawtchouk moments by SVM PUK, SVM polynomial, and k-NN using Manhattan distance. In case of Hu and Zernike moments, the best recognition accuracies are observed in SVM PUK and ELM polynomial kernel.

In Tables 2 and 3, a comparison of accuracies is carried out for increased feature vector of Krawtchouk moments for

ISL database and the standard Jochen-Triesch's dataset. With an increase in the feature-set at different ROIs, recognition accuracy improves gradually for different classifiers. A total of five ROIs are taken, from center, top-left, top-right, bottom-left, and bottom-right of an image. The aim is to find a combination of feature-set and a classifier that gives the best recognition accuracy.

For the maximum feature vector size of 45, ELM with polynomial kernel gives the best recognition of 88.1% followed by SVM with PUK and ELM with linear kernel both giving 87.9%. ELM with RBF gives 87.7% accuracy. Some classifiers like k-NN using Euclidean and Manhattan distance show good recognition accuracy even with a smaller feature vector size. For other classifiers like SVM and MLP, a larger feature-set results in better accuracy.

However, after normalizing the feature-set, improvement in accuracy is observed. Normalization maps the feature values into a specific range. In this paper, the normalized feature values lie within $[-1, 1]$. It helps in improving the recognition accuracy as it accelerates the training step [29, 30]. For normalized feature vector, SVM with PUK shows best recognition accuracy of 90%. It is followed by ELM with polynomial kernel giving 89.3%. SVM with RBF and ELM with RBF kernel both show 89.2%.

On applying CFS technique, the feature-set reduces to 22 features. Table 4 shows the recognition accuracies at different classifiers for selected feature-set. For some classifiers the performance of accuracy reduces slightly but for others the recognition accuracy improves. The best performance is shown by ELM with polynomial kernel giving 89.6%. Also, SVM with RBF, ELM with RBF, and MLP show the comparable results. On normalization of reduced feature vector, SVM PUK and ELM polynomial both show the best accuracy at 90% at 22 features. This is equivalent to maximum accuracy achieved by normalized 45 features. ELM linear kernel gives 89.9%, followed by 89.8% shown by both SVM RBF and ELM RBF. Overall, the feature-reduction algorithm proves to be effective, as accuracies obtained at smaller feature-sets are either better or comparable.

5. Conclusion

In this paper, the spatial behavior of 1D and 2D Krawtchouk polynomials at lower orders has been studied. Reconstruction results ensure that the lower order moments give local characteristics of an image. Krawtchouk-based moment invariants are extracted till 3rd order to represent their shape details. The ROI is varied by changing parameters p_1 and p_2, and features are calculated from different regions in an image. It is concluded that lower order Krawtchouk moment proves to be effective shape descriptors. The performance of these in terms of recognition accuracy is analyzed for different classifiers. It is observed that ELM polynomial kernel gives the best recognition accuracy of 88.1% at 45 features followed by SVM PUK and ELM linear kernel with 87.9%.

However, on normalizing features, 90% accuracy is observed in SVM PUK followed by 89.3% in ELM polynomial kernel.

TABLE 1: Comparison of recognition accuracies of Hu moments, Zernike moments, and Krawtchouk moment.

Feature set (up to 3rd order)	k-NN using ED (k = 1)	k-NN using MD (k = 1)	SVM Poly	RBF	PUK	MLP	ELM Poly	RBF	Linear
Raw feature-set for ISL database									
Hu moments (7 features)	66.9%	67.8%	67.9%	70%	**71.1%**	70.2%	70.2%	69.2%	70%
Zernike moments (6 features)	77.6%	74.3%	73.5%	76%	**78%**	75.1%	76.2%	76%	75.4%
Krawtchouk moments (9 features)	**84.9%**	85.3%	82.9%	83.5%	**84.9%**	84.5%	66.2%	65.4%	66.1%
Normalized feature-set for ISL database									
Hu moments (7 features)	68%	68.3%	70.2%	70.4%	**71.9%**	70.1%	70.8%	70.2%	70.2%
Zernike moments (6 features)	78.2%	75.7%	79%	79.4%	79.6%	78%	**79.7%**	79%	78.4%
Krawtchouk moments (9 features)	85.5%	**85.9%**	85.9%	84.8%	85.9%	85.2%	70.7%	70.2%	70.1%

TABLE 2: Recognition accuracies at Jochen-Triesch images taken at different values of p_1 and p_2.

Values of p_1 and p_2	Total FV	k-NN using ED	k-NN using MD	SVM Poly	RBF	PUK	ELM Poly	RBF	Linear	MLP
Raw feature-set for Jochen-Triesch										
$p_1 = 0.5$ $p_2 = 0.5$	9	60%	61.1%	58.4%	59.2%	62.2%	65.2%	62.3%	**66.1%**	63.3%
$p_1 = 0.4$ $p_2 = 0.7$	18	65.6%	66.6%	67%	69.3%	70.7%	73.3%	72.1%	**79.6%**	68.3%
$p_1 = 0.3$ $p_2 = 0.3$	27	67.9%	67.2%	76%	77.1%	79.1%	80.2%	79.9%	**80.4%**	78.4%
$p_1 = 0.6$ $p_2 = 0.3$	36	75.7%	78.9%	78.4%	79%	80.9%	82.7%	81.7%	**82.4%**	81.1%
$p_1 = 0.6$ $p_2 = 0.7$	45	80%	81.1%	82.2%	82.7%	82.9%	83.5%	82.9%	**83%**	82.5%
Normalized feature-set for Jochen-Triesch										
$p_1 = 0.5$ $p_2 = 0.5$	9	60%	61.5%	58.5%	61.4%	63.7%	69.2%	66.6%	**69.2%**	65%
$p_1 = 0.4$ $p_2 = 0.7$	18	65.8%	66.9%	67.2%	72%	72%	**75%**	74%	74.2%	69%
$p_1 = 0.3$ $p_2 = 0.3$	27	67.9%	67.9%	76.7%	79.1%	80.6%	**82.6%**	81.2%	82.1%	79.6%
$p_1 = 0.6$ $p_2 = 0.3$	36	75.9%	78.9%	79%	80.3%	83.2%	**83.9%**	82.8%	83.3%	82.5%
$p_1 = 0.6$ $p_2 = 0.7$	45	80.1%	81.8%	83.9%	83.9%	84.5%	**84.9%**	84%	84.5%	83.5%

TABLE 3: Recognition accuracies at different classifiers for ISL images taken at different values of p_1 and p_2 with raw feature-set.

Values of p_1 and p_2	Total F.V.	k-NN using ED	k-NN using MD	SVM Poly	RBF	PUK	ELM Poly	RBF	Linear	MLP
Raw feature-set for ISL database										
$p_1 = 0.5$ $p_2 = 0.5$	9	84.9%	**85.3%**	82.9%	83.5%	84.9%	66.2%	65.4%	66.1%	84.5%
$p_1 = 0.4$ $p_2 = 0.7$	18	85%	**86.1%**	83%	84.3%	85.4%	76%	75.8%	76.4%	85.3%
$p_1 = 0.3$ $p_2 = 0.3$	27	86.1%	86.1%	84.1%	84.7%	86.4%	84.5%	82.7%	84.2%	**86.9%**
$p_1 = 0.6$ $p_2 = 0.3$	36	86.9%	86.3%	84.1%	86.6%	86.8%	85.3%	84.47%	84.9%	**86.9%**
$p_1 = 0.6$ $p_2 = 0.7$	45	86.9%	86.9%	86.1%	87.4%	87.9%	**88.1%**	87.7%	87.9%	87.3%
Normalized feature-set for ISL database										
$p_1 = 0.5$ $p_2 = 0.5$	9	85.5%	**85.9%**	85.9%	84.8%	**85.9%**	70.7%	70.2%	70.1%	85.2%
$p_1 = 0.4$ $p_2 = 0.7$	18	86%	86.5%	87.4%	87.4%	**87.5%**	80%	79.2%	80.4%	85.8%
$p_1 = 0.3$ $p_2 = 0.3$	27	87.6%	88.1%	**88.5%**	87.3%	87.7%	86.2%	87.8%	85.9%	86%
$p_1 = 0.6$ $p_2 = 0.3$	36	88.2%	88.1%	88.6%	88.2%	**88.9%**	87.5%	87.9%	86.8%	86.3%
$p_1 = 0.6$ $p_2 = 0.7$	45	88.2%	88.2%	88.9%	89.2%	**90%**	89.3%	89.2%	88.9%	87.6%

TABLE 4: Recognition accuracies for original and reduced feature-sets for ISL database.

CFS (22 features)	k-NN using ED	k-NN using MD	SVM Poly	RBF	PUK	ELM Poly	RBF	Linear	MLP
Raw features	84.5%	86.5%	84.8%	89.5%	89.2%	**89.6%**	89.4%	85.6%	89.3%
Normalized features	87.9%	87.9%	87.4%	89.8%	**90%**	90%	89.8%	89.9%	89.3%

TABLE 5: Comparison of results for Jochen-Triesch's dataset.

Reference	Feature extraction method	Recognition accuracy
[14]	Elastic graph matching	92.9%
[26]	Modified census transform	89.9%
[27]	Weighted Eigen-space size functions	85.1%
[28]	Tchebichef (till 9th order), Hu, and Geometric features	84.63% (dark background) 95.55% (light background)
Proposed method	*Krawtchouk features till 3rd order (45 features)*	**84.9%**

Other classifiers also show encouraging results. However, the feature-set is reduced from 45 to 22 by CFS algorithm. The best performance is shown by ELM with polynomial kernel giving 89.6% from 88.1% at 45 features. With normalization of features, the accuracy improves further on feature selection. SVM PUK and ELM polynomial kernel both show the best accuracy at 90% at 22 features. ELM and SVM both perform best when the feature-set is increased and normalized. k-NN shows best performance with a lower feature vector size.

Overall, it can be concluded that the normalized feature-set of 22 features is capable of classifying the images with maximum accuracy of 90% in case of SVM PUK and ELM-Poly classifiers for ISL dataset. For Jochen-Triesch dataset, it is 84.9% for ELM with Poly kernel.

Table 5 shows the comparison of results of proposed feature-set for Jochen-Triesch's dataset. It is concluded that Krawtchouk moment-based features prove to be effective in shape recognition capability even with a smaller feature vector size as compared to other methods used which involve a large feature vector size. The feature-set for this database can be increased by extracting Krawtchouk moment features at higher orders. The technique employed for feature extraction can be based on image partitioning, with Krawtchouk moment features calculated at different subimages.

Competing Interests

The authors declare that there are no competing interests regarding the publication of this paper.

References

[1] Y. S. Abu-Mostafa and D. Psaltis, "Recognitive Aspects of Moment Invariants," *IEEE Transactions on Pattern Analysis and Machine Intelligence*, vol. 6, no. 6, pp. 698–706, 1984.

[2] A. J. Noraini, "A comparative study of face recognition using discrete orthogonal moments," in *Proceedings of the10th International Conference on Information Sciences Signal Processing and their Applications (ISSPA '10)*, pp. 197–200, Kuala Lumpur, Malaysia, May 2010.

[3] J. S. Rani and D. Devaraj, "Face recognition using Krawtchouk moment," *Sadhana*, vol. 37, no. 4, pp. 441–460, 2012.

[4] E. D. Tsougenis, G. A. Papakostas, D. E. Koulouriotis, and V. D. Tourassis, "Performance evaluation of moment-based watermarking methods: a review," *Journal of Systems and Software*, vol. 85, no. 8, pp. 1864–1884, 2012.

[5] X. B. Dai, H. Z. Shu, L. M. Luo, G. N. Han, and J. L. Coatrieux, "Reconstruction of tomographic images from limited range projections using discrete Radon transform and Tchebichef moments," *Pattern Recognition*, vol. 43, no. 3, pp. 1152–1164, 2010.

[6] A. Sit and D. Kihara, "Comparison of image patches using local moment invariants," *IEEE Transactions on Image Processing*, vol. 23, no. 5, pp. 2369–2379, 2014.

[7] S. P. Priyal and P. K. Bora, "A robust static hand gesture recognition system using geometry based normalizations and Krawtchouk moments," *Pattern Recognition*, vol. 46, no. 8, pp. 2202–2219, 2013.

[8] M. K. Hu, "Visual pattern recognition by moment invariants," *IRE Transactions on Information Theory*, vol. 8, no. 2, pp. 179–187, 1962.

[9] M. R. Teague, "Image analysis via the general theory of moments," *Journal of the Optical Society of America*, vol. 70, no. 8, pp. 920–930, 1980.

[10] A. Khotanzad and Y. H. Hong, "Invariant image recognition by Zernike moments," *IEEE Transactions on Pattern Analysis and Machine Intelligence*, vol. 12, no. 5, pp. 489–497, 1990.

[11] P.-T. Yap, R. Paramesran, and S.-H. Ong, "Image analysis by Krawtchouk moments," *IEEE Transactions on Image Processing*, vol. 12, no. 11, pp. 1367–1377, 2003.

[12] X. Wang, B. Xie, and Y. Yang, "Combining krawtchouk moments and HMMs for offline handwritten chinese character recognition," in *Proceedings of the 3rd International IEEE Conference on Intelligent Systems*, pp. 661–665, London, UK, September 2006.

[13] G. Y. Pryzva, "Kravchuk orthogonal polynomials," *Ukrainian Mathematical Journal*, vol. 44, no. 7, pp. 792–800, 1992.

[14] J. Triesch and C. Von der Malsburg, "Classification of hand postures against complex backgrounds using elastic graph matching," *Image and Vision Computing*, vol. 20, no. 13-14, pp. 937–943, 2002.

[15] S. Liu, Y. Liu, J. Liu, and Z. Wang, "A static hand gesture recognition algorithm based on krawtchouk moments," in *Pattern Recognition: 6th Chinese Conference, CCPR 2014, Changsha, China, November 17–19, 2014. Proceedings, Part II*, vol. 484 of *Communications in Computer and Information Science*, pp. 321–330, Springer, Berlin, Germany, 2014.

[16] H. Wang, T. M. Khoshgoftaar, and A. Napolitano, "Stability of filter- and wrapper-based software metric selection techniques," in *Proceedings of the IEEE 15th International Conference on Information Reuse and Integration (IRI '14)*, pp. 309–314, Redwood City, Calif, USA, August 2014.

[17] S. Chapaneri, R. Lopes, and D. Jayaswal, "Evaluation of music features for PUK kernel based genre classification," *Procedia Computer Science*, vol. 45, pp. 186–196, 2015.

[18] J. L. Rodgers and W. A. Nicewander, "Thirteen ways to look at the correlation coefficient," *The American Statistician*, vol. 42, no. 1, pp. 59–66, 1988.

[19] D. J. Dittman, T. M. Khoshgoftaar, R. Wald, and A. Napolitano, "Simplifying the utilization of machine learning techniques for bioinformatics," in *Proceedings of the 12th International Conference on Machine Learning and Applications (ICMLA '13)*, pp. 396–403, IEEE, Miami, Fla, USA, December 2013.

[20] R. Wald, T. M. Khoshgoftaar, and A. Napolitano, "Using correlation-based feature selection for a diverse collection of bioinformatics datasets," in *Proceedings of the IEEE International Conference on Bioinformatics and Bioengineering (BIBE '14)*, pp. 156–162, IEEE, Boca Raton, Fla, USA, November 2014.

[21] X. Xu, A. Li, and M. Wang, "Prediction of human disease-associated phosphorylation sites with combined feature selection approach and support vector machine," *IET Systems Biology*, vol. 9, no. 4, pp. 155–163, 2015.

[22] X. Chen and M. Koskela, "Online RGB-D gesture recognition with extreme learning machines," in *Proceedings of the 15th ACM on International Conference on Multimodal Interaction (ICMI '13)*, pp. 467–474, ACM, Sydney, Australia, December 2013.

[23] G.-B. Huang, H. Zhou, X. Ding, and R. Zhang, "Extreme learning machine for regression and multiclass classification," *IEEE Transactions on Systems, Man, and Cybernetics, Part B: Cybernetics*, vol. 42, no. 2, pp. 513–529, 2012.

[24] B. Üstün, W. J. Melssen, and L. M. C. Buydens, "Facilitating the application of support vector regression by using a universal Pearson VII function based kernel," *Chemometrics and Intelligent Laboratory Systems*, vol. 81, no. 1, pp. 29–40, 2006.

[25] G. Zhang and H. Ge, "Support vector machine with a Pearson VII function kernel for discriminating halophilic and non-halophilic proteins," *Computational Biology and Chemistry*, vol. 46, pp. 16–22, 2013.

[26] A. Just, Y. Rodriguez, and S. Marcel, "Hand posture classification and recognition using the modified census transform," in *Proceedings of the 7th International Conference on Automatic Face and Gesture Recognition (FGR '06)*, pp. 351–356, IEEE, Southampton, UK, April 2006.

[27] D. Kelly, J. McDonald, and C. Markham, "A person independent system for recognition of hand postures used in sign language," *Pattern Recognition Letters*, vol. 31, no. 11, pp. 1359–1368, 2010.

[28] D. Dahmani and S. Larabi, "User-independent system for sign language finger spelling recognition," *Journal of Visual Communication and Image Representation*, vol. 25, no. 5, pp. 1240–1250, 2014.

[29] L. A. Shalabi, Z. Shaaban, and B. Kasasbeh, "Data mining: a preprocessing engine," *Journal of Computer Science*, vol. 2, no. 9, pp. 735–739, 2006.

[30] I. Dinç, M. Sigdel, S. Dinç, M. S. Sigdel, M. L. Pusey, and R. S. Aygün, "Evaluation of normalization and PCA on the performance of classifiers for protein crystallization images," in *Proceedings of the IEEE Southeastcon*, pp. 1–6, Lexington, KY, USA, March 2014.

11

Appraisals of Salient Visual Elements in Web Page Design

Johanna M. Silvennoinen and Jussi P. P. Jokinen

Department of Computer Science and Information Systems, University of Jyvaskyla, Mattilanniemi 2, 40100 Jyväskylä, Finland

Correspondence should be addressed to Johanna M. Silvennoinen; johanna.silvennoinen@jyu.fi

Academic Editor: Thomas Mandl

Visual elements in user interfaces elicit emotions in users and are, therefore, essential to users interacting with different software. Although there is research on the relationship between emotional experience and visual user interface design, the focus has been on the overall visual impression and not on visual elements. Additionally, often in a software development process, programming and general usability guidelines are considered as the most important parts of the process. Therefore, knowledge of programmers' appraisals of visual elements can be utilized to understand the web page designs we interact with. In this study, appraisal theory of emotion is utilized to elaborate the relationship of emotional experience and visual elements from programmers' perspective. Participants ($N = 50$) used 3E-templates to express their visual and emotional experiences of web page designs. Content analysis of textual data illustrates how emotional experiences are elicited by salient visual elements. Eight hierarchical visual element categories were found and connected to various emotions, such as frustration, boredom, and calmness, via relational emotion themes. The emotional emphasis was on centered, symmetrical, and balanced composition, which was experienced as pleasant and calming. The results benefit user-centered visual interface design and researchers of visual aesthetics in human-computer interaction.

1. Introduction

Visual design of user interfaces is significant to users interacting with different software. Through visual user interfaces, constructed of visual elements (i.e., color, size, and shape), interfaces communicate to the users and are expected to be both visually and emotionally appealing. However, visual user interface design is rather complex, because there is no universal formula of visual design to be applied in all user interface design contexts to elicit positive emotional experiences. Visual elements can be designed in countless different combinations and therefore, the same information content can be designed to appear in numerous visual forms which affect the users in different ways. For instance, different user interface genres, such as online banking web pages, are expected to visually represent the context in an appropriate way. If users' expectations and visual design solutions are not considered in the design process, interaction can lead to negative emotional outcomes, such as frustration. Thus, numerous perspectives are required to be considered when designing visual user interfaces. One approach is to empirically examine how visual elements are emotionally experienced and how

this knowledge informs user interface design decisions. This information is especially important when considering programmers' appraisals of visual elements. This is because often in a software development process programming and general usability guidelines are considered as the most important parts of the process, while neglecting experiential aspects of the interaction conveyed with visual user interfaces.

Therefore, in addition to the traditional efforts in human-computer interaction, current and future user interfaces need to be developed in a novel way to match the potentials offered by the newest computing technologies and the users' requirements based on their visual and emotional experiences. From a user-centered perspective, the rapid development of user interface technologies demands clarification of how visual elements should be utilized in user interface design to promote positive user experience. The improvement of visual aesthetics in user interface design enhances understandability of the product, by improving visual organization, clarity, and conciseness of user interfaces [1], and more profound understanding of how visual elements are experienced contributes to enhanced visual usability of user interfaces [2, 3], that is, how people represent visual elements and how the visual aspects of objects relate to the functions afforded by them. Moreover, in the current era of visual user interfaces, usable designs need to highlight aesthetic expression as meaningful presence for users instead of just providing designs as functional tools [4].

However, the snowballing research of user interface design has, until now, largely left aside the study of how visual elements in user interface design elicit emotional experiences. Current research of experiencing visual user interface designs, in the research area of visual aesthetics in human-computer interaction, has mainly focused on the overall impression of visual user interfaces (e.g., [5–7]), as a means of enhancing user experience with aesthetic pleasantness (e.g., [8]). In addition, more detailed approaches have focused, for example, on typography [9] and on high-level attributes (e.g., [10]). These high-level attributes include, for example, unity and prototypicality [11], novelty [12], and typicality and novelty [13]. Therefore, research of visual aesthetics in human-computer interaction lacks knowledge of emotional responses in experiencing low-level attributes, that is, visual elements (e.g., [14]), such as color, size, and balance [15]. In this paper, appraisal theory of emotion [16–18] is utilized to elaborate the relationship of emotional user experience and visual elements. Therefore, this study adopts an interactionist approach to human-technology experience; that is, it does not merely focus on either user interface design properties or users' impressions and preferences of visual user interface designs, but analyses screen-based visual elements and their appraised dimensions together. Screen-design based approach focuses on detecting the visual properties of design components and their spatial organization in user interfaces [19], which affect user experience. How these identified visual elements are appraised is the key to understanding their role in human-computer interaction and in web page design.

According to Tractinsky [10], usability experts and designers have come to the conclusion that these two aspects of design, visual aesthetics and usability, could and should coexist in the same context of use. Before this shift in the first decade of the 21st century, visual aesthetics and usability were often seen as having a contradictory relation in that when one was emphasized, the other one was automatically omitted. The shift has emerged mostly because recent research corroborates a positive correlation between aesthetic and usability principles (e.g., [5, 6, 19–22]). Due to this shift, aesthetic qualities are currently emphasized in designing software for human-computer interaction. In addition, advancements in computer graphics have opened a variety of new design possibilities, which have increased the importance of aesthetic design of user interfaces providing emotional experiences. Yet, often in software development process, only the implementation of software (e.g., programming) and the traditional, general usability design [23] are considered as the most important parts [24]. In reality, users' experiential needs are not taken into account in the software development process [25]. The essential deficit in user interface design lies in the absence of visual user interface design specialists in the process. Therefore, in this study, appraisals of salient visual elements are addressed from the

point of view of future programmers and engineers. Focusing on programmers' emotional experiences of visual elements in web page designs provides information on the visual elements that are considered essential and the way they are appraised. Understanding the appraisal process of the most salient visual elements among future programmers enriches the visual user interface design practice in software development and provides insights into visual design solutions applied in current user interface designs that we interact with.

The rest of the paper is organized as follows. First, the background concerning the visual elements and their capability in eliciting emotions in human-computer interaction is described with the appraisal theory of emotion. This is then concluded with presenting the research questions of the study. Second, the method is described including participant information, research procedure, stimuli, and data analysis. Third, the results are presented and discussed. Finally, the conclusions are presented with future research and limitations of the study.

2. Visual Elements and the Emotion Process

Establishing the connection between visual elements and the emotion response is one of the key elements in developing theory for describing visual elements in human-computer interaction. Visual elements in user interfaces are important factors in experiencing technological products due to their potential of eliciting attributed emotions and the ability to elicit actually felt emotions [26]. Additionally, visual elements are capable of evoking strong emotional responses in technology interaction and thus affect the overall experience [27]. While the psychological research on emotion has already posited the cognitive process, which connects an external event to emotional experience [16–18], this process has not yet received a satisfactorily discussion in user experience literature. However, research connecting the psychological theory of appraisal with emotional experience in human-technology interaction has started to produce promising examples concerning this [28–30].

Visual elements as the constructing units in user interfaces are the components through which the emotional process of experiencing visual user interfaces can be understood and approached in detail. By exploring users' emotional experiences of visual elements, an in-depth view on visual aesthetics in human-computer interaction can be approached. Emotional aspects of visual user interface design have been studied in relation to trust. For instance, beauty of simplicity [31], visual appeal [32], and color appeal [33] have been stated to affect feelings of trust in interacting with user interfaces. However, more profound and detailed knowledge is needed in order to understand how and which visual elements in user interfaces elicit emotions and in which contexts.

In this study, visual representations that draw on the theories of two-dimensional pictorial elements are utilized as theoretical vehicles to create novel insight into experiencing visual user interface design. The dispensation of visual theory is in that it provides knowledge of exact visual elements, such as size, value, hue, orientation, contrast, texture [34], shape, proportion, and position [1] and, for instance, form and expression [35], which are seen as visual elements inherent in contemporary user interfaces. Mullet and Sano [1] refer to visual language in designing visual user interfaces. Through visual language, based on visual elements, user interfaces communicate to the users. Visual language of user interface design is divided into visual design factors which are visual characteristics (shape, color, position, texture, size, orientation, etc.) in a specific set of design elements (point, line, volume, plane, etc.) and the factors by which they relate to each other, such as balance, structure, proportion, and rhythm. These elements facilitate exploring the salient visual elements that draw attention to website design, elicit emotions in users, and affect the interaction between users and user interfaces. Further, visual theory serves as a starting point in the study because aesthetic impressions conveyed by visual representations influence users' experiences of user interface qualities [6] that may promote positive feelings on user interfaces [36] due to the emotional nature of visual experience [37–39].

The cognitive process in which emotion episodes occur is called appraisal [16–18]. Appraisal is the evaluation of the personal significance of an event and its consequences and consists of multiple levels, such as motivational changes, physiological responses, and subjectively categorized emotions [18, 39]. There are various models of appraisal, which differ in the details of the emotion process, but most agree that the event is appraised at least from the following dimensions: implications to personal goals, pleasantness, causality, coping, and conformity [18, 28, 40]. Each is discussed here briefly, and their relation to visual user interface design is considered.

Events which satisfy one's personal goals are usually appraised as positive, while goal-incongruent events are appraised as negative [16]. The appraisal dimension of goal-relevance is understandably very salient in human-computer interaction research and design: usability problems, including visual usability problems, are usually taken to cause goal-incongruent events, which elicit negative emotions. Obstructions to efficient, goal-congruent use of systems result in frustration and anger, while successful mediation of the goal-oriented action results in feeling of competence [29, 30, 41]. However, pleasantness of an event is also appraised independently of the personal goals and current motivations, especially with the so-called aesthetic emotions, which can be contrasted with utilitarian emotions [39]. This notion is central in user experience research, where the focus is more on the noninstrumental side of interaction [42]. Positive experience of a user interface is not necessarily related to the immediate goals of the user.

The causality dimension of the appraisal process considers responsibility, that is, who caused the event and what was the motive behind these actions [18]. The agency can be attributed to oneself, such as when a user feels competent after being successful in demanding tasks [29, 41], or to other actors, for example, when evaluating visual user interface design choices made by designers. It is also possible to attribute the cause of the event to nonhuman agent. An example of this appraisal would be the aggression towards an inanimate object, such as a computer, when the goals of the actor are obstructed [43].

The coping dimension refers to the potential of the subject to manage the event or the emotion which results from the event. Coping is an individual's adaptation effort to events and as such is not associated only with negative events [44, 45]. Therefore, a response to a goal-incongruent computing event may result in either enthusiasm or anxiety, depending on how much the individual expects to be able to exert control over the event. There are two main coping strategies, problem-centered and emotion-centered. For example, in human-computer interaction, individual differences in how people are able to solve interaction problems and how well they are able to cope with their emotions play a significant role in the user experience process [29]. The conformity dimension of appraisal refers to the compatibility of the event in relation to self-concept and social norms and values [18]. Anger, for example, is the result of an event in which causality is attributed to someone who is appraised to act in a deliberate norm violation. In user interface design, violating the norms of established design practices may, therefore, cause negative emotions even if the norm-violating aspects do not cause goal-incongruent use events.

Of the all possible appraisal dimensions, perhaps the most frequently used scheme for describing emotion is the combination of valence and arousal [40]. Valence refers to the pleasantness of the experience and arousal to how much the emotion is associated with activation. For example, feeling calm is pleasant but not an active emotion, while feeling energetic is a pleasant and active emotion. Sadness is a negative and deactivating emotion, and anger is a negative and arousing emotion. While these two are not the only relevant dimensions of emotional experience, they are often the most salient and can be used for rich descriptions of emotion in human-computer interaction [41]. Regarding emotional experiences of pictorial representations, for instance, works of art can differ in their potential to cause arousal. Works of art which possess ability to evoke high arousal are most likely perceived as dramatic and dynamic, and works of art with low potential on eliciting arousal are generally perceived as static and harmonious [46].

This paper focuses on studying the most salient visual elements in user interfaces and their relation to emotions attributed and elicited by them from the perspective of future programmers, in order to provide usable insight for the evaluation and design of visual elements in user interfaces that promote user experience and thus to benefit user-centered visual user interface design. This study focuses on the following research questions: What are the most salient visual elements in web pages from programmers' point of view? What kind of emotions do the salient visual elements elicit? How are the salient visual elements evaluated in the appraisal process?

3. Method

3.1. Participants. Participants ($N = 50$) expressed their impressions and emotions regarding visual website designs with 3E-templates. Of the participants, 17.5% were female and 82.5% male. The average age of the participants was 25.4 years (SD = 5.4 and range 20–46). The participants were allowed to return the templates anonymously without information that could be used to identify them, because the data collection was organized as a part of a university course. Thus, the reported age and gender information is from 40 participants, while ten participants answered without identification information. However, the average age of the 40 participants did not differ much from the average age of the participants in the course: the average age of the participants in the course was 25.0 years (SD = 5.8 and range 19–50).

All the participants were university students, mainly from the Faculty of Information Technology. 67.5% of the participants who returned the templates with identification information were students of computer science, 27.5% were students of information systems, and 5% of the students were from other majors. From the students in the course, 66.7% had a major in computer science, 26% were students of information systems, and 7.3% were from other majors. The circumstances of the data collection were designed similarly for all the respondents. The stimuli of the study and the data collection template were presented to the participants at the same time with the same advice in an auditorium, and the participants were allotted the same amount of time for answering the template.

3.2. Research Procedure. The data collection was conducted as a part of a University course about user-centered design. The data was collected from the lecture dealing with layout design. The lecture introduced the participants with relevant terms to describe the user interfaces. From the beginning of the lecture, the participants were familiarized with the design process in general, the evaluation methods of visual user interfaces, and visual elements, such as visual rhythm, dynamics, balance, tension, symmetry, contrast, Gestalt laws, and other various different design principles. People who are experienced in creating visual representations are more capable of analyzing them and more aware of their responses to visual phenomena [47]. Therefore, the introduction of the visual design terminology was conducted to provide the participants a starting point for utilizing verbal vocabulary to express their visual experiences. The numerous terms were equally emphasized and the participants were not forbidden to use other terms to express their impressions. If the data would have been collected with questionnaires, with predetermined concepts of visual elements and emotion terms, the data would have been a result of a conception of the researchers' understanding of emotions attributed to visual elements.

Therefore, the data was collected with the 3E- (expressing emotions and experiences) template [48, 49]. The 3E-template was selected as a data collection method to allow respondents to express their thoughts both verbally and nonverbally: by writing and drawing (Figure 1).

After the introductory part of the lecture, participants were introduced to the 3E-template and asked to write and draw their thoughts and impressions of two still pictures of web pages, with a focus on the compositional elements of the web pages. The participants were not aware during the introductory part of the lecture that they would need to report their impressions of user interface designs with visual design

FIGURE 1: The 3E-tempalate.

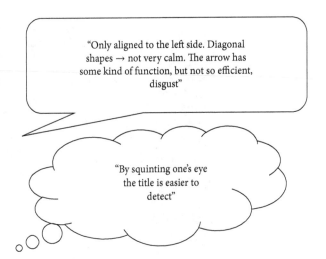

FIGURE 2: Examples of written expressions from one template.

terminology. In the templates, participants did not describe their impressions only with the concepts presented in the lecture, and they did not mention some of the presented concepts at all.

The participants took approximately 20 minutes in answering the two templates. The research data is comprised of the written and drawn reflections and interpretations on the compositional aspects of the example web pages. A total of 100 templates were returned, as each participant evaluated two web pages. One template was returned without any written or drawn reflections and was therefore excluded from the analysis. The templates that comprise the data were mainly used by the participants to express their impressions of the UIs in written form. Examples of written expressions in the speech and think bubbles are presented in Figure 2.

3.3. Stimuli. The objects for the compositional reflection were two web pages (Figures 3 and 4) from the CSS Zen Garden web page gallery, web pages created with CSS-based design [50]. All the gallery web pages have the exact same content but altering visual appearances. The web pages were

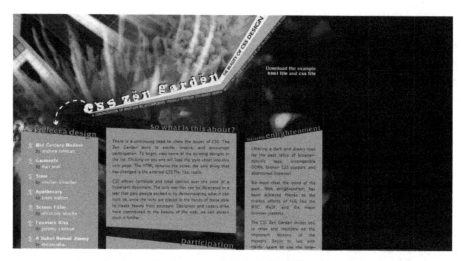

FIGURE 3: The first user interface used in data collection.

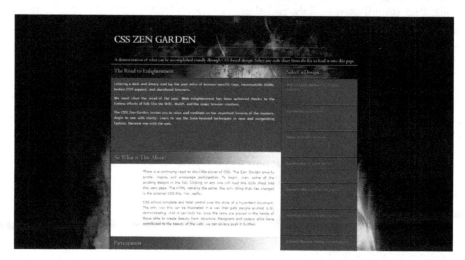

FIGURE 4: The second user interface used in data collection.

selected to serve as stimuli, because the altering visual designs with the same content enable reflecting on the visual elements of the designs without concentrating on the content. In addition, the CSS Zen Garden web pages were selected as the stimuli in order not to bias the respondents with product expectations [51], such as brand experience.

The CSS Zen Garden web pages were surveyed for two example layouts that would differ from each other, especially with regard to the amount of elements that divide the surface such as lines, shapes, and the overall use of space. The web pages were first divided into two categories and then compared step by step, finally resulting in two example web pages.

Emphasis on a choice of web pages according to their differentiating elements was made in order to provoke participants towards a comparative analysis between web page layouts. Bell [52] also emphasizes that evaluations with content analysis are often comparative. The web pages were, therefore, selected with a comparative setting, regarding the pages' differences in constructing visual elements. This was achieved in the study by using two different web pages

with similar content but differing visual appearances. In addition, these two web pages were asked to be reflected in detail. Therefore, the two selected web pages were considered sufficient for the present study with a comparative setting, since all pictorial representations are constructed with visual elements. A broader sample of stimuli could be studied in future research. But first, it is essential to understand in detail which elements are considered important and what kind of emotions is attributed to them.

3.4. Data Analysis. When people experience pictorial representations, such as visual user interfaces, numerous visual elements are encountered [53]. People may experience visual elements as both explicit and simple but also as elements involving interpretation. Therefore, the research method should facilitate the combination of the analysis of qualitative and quantified issues. As Collier [54] points out, a studied phenomenon must first be examined without premature analyses of the data, maintaining a focus on preexistent structures and points of interest. First, a data-driven content analysis was conducted to detect and describe the user interface elements depicted by the informants after having looked at the selected user interfaces. Second, the elements found and defined were quantified in order to identify the visual elements that are considered most salient in visual user interface design, particularly in layout design from the programmers' perspective. The aim was to find the visual elements that have drawn the most attention and can be seen to have importance due their frequent emergence and significance of the content. The quantification of the explicitly written words representing specific objects is important, but it also relates to the qualitative procedures. Krippendorf [55] emphasizes the meaning of context in content analysis. Texts and images are always produced in some specific cultural context and they also refer to wider cultural context. This aspect was considered by first deploying the interpretative viewpoint as an independent phase before quantifying the found elements.

The methodological decisions for the study are influenced by the nature of the visual viewpoint: instead of directly analyzing visual user interfaces, the data is comprised of participants' descriptions of the two example web pages. Therefore, many methods, for example, semiotics and iconography [56], as well as social semiotic visual analysis [57], are not applicable because they assume that the data along with the object of analysis are visual images. Furthermore, even though the data collected by other methods (such as eye tracking) could enable the extraction of specific points of attention, it would be impossible to analyze which particular element draws attention, color, form or, for instance, a visual tension between the elements. The analysis of the visual elements was conducted with these two procedures, which supported the analysis from two different viewpoints. The emotions elicited by salient visual elements were analyzed with same procedure.

The data analysis proceeded as follows. First, the data was observed as a whole by reading the templates. The purpose was to first focus on the visual elements in a neutral context in order to gain an understanding of the visual elements that are seen as important in visual user interface design despite the emotions they might evoke. The second phase was to create categories of relations and then to critically combine several different categories of relations between elements into main categories. For instance, from the example illustrated in Figure 2, the first observation about left side alignment is related to the spatial organization as is the second notion of diagonal lines. Stability refers to symmetry and the role of the arrow is related to perceived functionality. The human figure in the templates was only used in a few templates to illustrate emotions by drawing facial expressions. Almost none of the drawings emphasized the written content or the facial emotions of the figure but brought to attention something without a clear connection to the written content. Due to these characteristics of data, the focus of the analysis was on the written texts describing the visual elements and emotions attached to them. After the researchers had acquainted themselves with the data, an interpretation framework was developed and used to assist in the analysis. The interpretation framework included the items, which directed the focus on a conceptual level during the data analysis, in interpreting and comparing interesting insights within the data. The interpretation framework consisted of compositional interpretation [58] and visual elements in user interface design [1].

Compositional interpretation refers to describing the appearance of images with a detailed terminology. This form of visual analysis requires contextual knowledge of pictorial representations and a particular way of looking at images ("the good eye"), which is not methodologically explicit but functions as visual connoisseurship and is a specific way of describing images. Compositional interpretation focuses on the image itself by trying to comprehend its significance mostly by focusing on its compositionality. Interpretation does not focus on "external factors" such as the kind of messages the image sends and whether it has some functional meaning. The terminology of compositional interpretation includes several components. The first component is the content, that is, what the image actually shows. The second component is color, which is more specifically defined with concepts of hue, saturation value, and the harmony of color combinations. The third component is spatial organization, which includes volume, lines, static and dynamic rhythm, geometrical perspective, logic of figuration (how the elements of a picture offer particular viewing position outside the photo), and focalisers (the visual organization of looks and gazes inside the picture and in relation to the viewer's gaze). The fourth is light: the type of light that is represented and its sources. The last component is expressive content, which describes the "feel" of the image combining the effect of the subject matter and visual form. Compositional interpretation approach is established in Art History and is usually used in studying paintings [58]. Visual user interfaces can be comprehended as paintings or, in a more general viewpoint, as any two-dimensional pictorial representation that is constructed with visual elements, such as lines and shapes. Compositional interpretation can, therefore, also be extended to analyzing visual user interfaces.

Mullet and Sano [1] present visual user interface design factors, which are shape, color, position, texture, size, orientation, point, line, volume, balance, symmetry, scale, contrast, structure, proportion, rhythm, and position. The emphasis on visual factors in user interface design is to provide insight into designing good visual usability and effective visual communication. They also point out that negative space (i.e., empty or white space between visual elements and objects, opposite to active space) and grouping are important components in visual user interface design. The interpretation framework combined the discussed visual elements and guided the detection of the concepts related to visual elements in the coding phase of the analysis. The elements were derived from the two approaches described above and created the content of the interpretation framework. The interpretation framework included, but was not restricted to, the following components: color (hue, saturation, value, and harmony of color combinations), spatial organization, geometrical perspective, volume, lines, points, size, texture, shape, static and dynamic rhythm, orientation, balance, symmetry, scale, structure, proportion, negative space, grouping, position, figuration logic, focalisers, contrast, and light. From a compositional interpretation, the expressive content component was excluded from the interpretation framework in the analysis of salient visual elements, because of its emphasis on subject matter evoking emotionality which was not in focus in the first analysis phase of this study. The interpretation framework functioned as a "theoretical lens" in the analysis. The analysis required accuracy and concentration in detecting tiny nuances in finding the relations between the different visual elements, which required close attention in detecting how many altering ways there are, for instance, to describe the use of space in user interfaces. The goal was to create a model that illustrates the hierarchical order of visual elements. The structure of the model is data-driven but the logic is validated using theoretical framework of visual language.

The analysis of the emotions elicited by visual elements followed a procedure similar to the analysis of the salient visual elements. First, all templates were regarded as a whole with the focus on finding the emotions that had been expressed constantly and drawn most attention in relation to the salient visual elements. The construction of the interpretation framework for emotions was based on the appraisal theory of emotion, in which the appraisal of the subjective significance of an event results in subjective emotional experience. Overall, the participants used emotion words or categories clearly less often than visual elements: in total, 26 emotion words or categories in relation to visual elements were observed. Here, the interest was especially in the relationship between the visual elements of a user interface and the subjective emotional experience, that is, the feelings which arise as a response to visual elements. The interpretation framework for analyzing the emotion responses was derived from the appraisal dimensions described above. For the observed emotions, a relational theme which refers to the narrative explanation of the emotion was constructed [17]. The narrative can be constructed with the appraisal dimensions. For example, frustration is an unpleasant (valence) and activating (arousal) emotion, but this is not enough to understand frustration. Frustration results when there is an obstruction preventing the subject from reaching her goals, and the subject still feels some power over the situation [18, 29]. Therefore, in order to understand an emotional response, such as when a user is frustrated at a computer program, a thematic explanation relating the goals of the user to the events of the use, as well as a reference to the coping possibilities of the user, is required [29].

A template was included into the emotion analysis if it contained a common emotion word that is included in lists of emotions, (e.g., [18]) or was an appraisal dimension, for example, *pleasant* [40]. The following words relating to emotions were expressed: frustration, anxiety, calmness, apprehension, boredom, disgust, energetic, pleasant, disturbing, threatening, and confusing. From these, five thematic groups were created: frustration (including "frustration" and "disturbing" as the latter is part of the appraisal profile for frustration), calmness (which included "calmness," "apprehension," and "energetic" because they belong to the same appraisal dimension), "confusion," "boredom," and "pleasantness." Other words were discarded from the analysis,

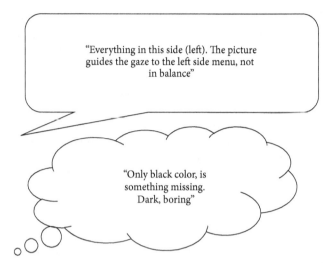

FIGURE 5: Examples of written emotional expressions from one template.

because they were mentioned in connection with the visual elements, which were not analyzed here due to their low frequency. Each thematic group was given a relational theme and was then connected to the visual elements in order to establish the explanatory logic between the user interface design and the emotional response. Examples of expressed emotions in relation to visual elements are presented in Figure 5.

4. Results

All the 100 templates were analyzed by writing down all the described elements in the templates and by counting the frequency of their occurrence. The number of times each visual element was mentioned in a template and the number of participants who at least once mentioned the visual element are presented in Table 1. The table illustrates the second level classification of visual elements. Different utterances were used to describe, for instance, guiding the gaze, such as *"the picture directs the gaze to the left side menu," "the gaze moves from up right to left down along with the title, and in addition, the gaze is guided with a separate arrow,"* and *"...directs the gaze outside of the user interface."* All these different notions were coded in the first phase of the analysis and were classified to the group of guiding the gaze in the second phase of the analysis. Visual elements that had been mentioned only three times or less were excluded from the analysis due to the low frequency.

The interpretation framework guided the detection of written reflections of the described elements. For instance, the interpretation framework did not include usability, which emerged from the data as a connective factor between relations of different elements, especially in terms of visual usability of the user interfaces. In many templates, think bubbles were used to express additional reflections, mostly about the supposed functionality of the user interface. The results of the study are data-driven; the most salient visual

TABLE 1: Notions of visual elements by participants.

Visual elements	Notions/participants
Guiding the gaze	21/17
Composition in general	15
Grouping	8/7
Grouping with similar contents & functions	10
Grouping with colors	1
Clarity	23/22
Symmetry	7
Asymmetry	8
Balance	14
Imbalance	20/19
Negative space	21/20
Active space	1
Impression of overall use of space	9
Alignment	13
Centering	12
Diagonal lines	15
Horizontal lines	9/8
Vertical lines	7
Lines in general	2
Understandability	5
Legibility	8
Font size & area	12
Font color	8
Background picture	9
Background color	9
Color contrast	22
Font contrast	3
Contrast in general	6
Layers	3
Colors in general	18
UI as a whole	8/7
Square	2
Golden ratio	1
Horizontal composition	2
Straight corners	1
Square	3
Visual tension	3
Color composition	1
Impression of 3-dimensionality	2

The salient visual elements are presented in Figure 6. The hierarchical structure of the results illustrates the different levels of visual elements from the lowest-level elements (e.g., diagonal lines) through the visual elements of organizing the lowest-level elements (e.g., alignment and asymmetry) to the main design dimensions (e.g., spatial organization), resulting as positioning of the viewer in appraising the most salient visual elements. Positioning of the viewer gathers all the results under one definition and functions as the main process outcome in experiencing visual user interfaces. Positioning of the viewer (including figuration logic and focalisers) was seen as a visual strategy that guides the viewer's gaze in the user interface, which functions through visual elements guiding the gaze. Overall, positioning of the viewer refers to the user interface's ability to communicate the whole content in a visual manner that is quick and easy to grasp.

Positioning the viewer was discussed in relation to visual elements contributing to spatial organization and color and contrast. Spatial organization and color and contrast were seen to apply both to communicability and to visual usability and interaction. Spatial organization and color and contrast are the main dimensions in visual user interface design language (e.g., [1]), which can be further described in detail with lower-level visual elements contributing to these higher level design dimensions. Spatial organization was emphasized by focusing on grouping and negative space. Imbalance, balance, asymmetry, and symmetry were seen as the primary visual elements affecting grouping and the use of negative space. In addition, grouping and the use of negative space through imbalance, balance, symmetry, and asymmetry were seen as contributing to the spatial organization of visual user interface elements in creating an impression of the user interface as a consistent totality, in which visual elements contribute to the impression of the user interface as a whole. Grouping of similar contents and functions were seen as substantive factors creating clarity. Spatial organization through balance and symmetry was seen as important regarding the overall use of space. Grouping and negative space were further discussed in terms of aligning or centering the content. In the data, spatial organization was reflected in detail and visual elements referring to this category were often mentioned.

Grouping with similar content and functions and negative space were seen in relation to the composition of the user interface in general and impression of overall use of space. Observations of balance and imbalance were seen in relation to symmetry and asymmetry. Alignment to the left or right and centering the content were seen to affect impressions of balance, imbalance, symmetry, and asymmetry. An important relation was often found between diagonal, horizontal, and vertical lines in creating impression of overall use of space and guiding the gaze. Diagonal, horizontal, and vertical lines were especially emphasized and seen as visual elements that guide the gaze forward. A strong emphasis was placed on describing how the visual elements function and how they support visual usability and interaction, especially the ways by which visual elements direct attention in the user interface towards the most important areas.

elements emerged from the data through content analysis, in which the theoretical framework was used to assist in detecting the utterances describing different elements. Therefore, the background theory of the visual language [1] and compositional interpretation [58] aided the analysis as a theoretical lens in detecting the visual elements as well as organizing the categories to hierarchical relations. For instance, the classification of the two main categories of visual elements, spatial organization and color and contrast, was conducted by reflecting on the background theory.

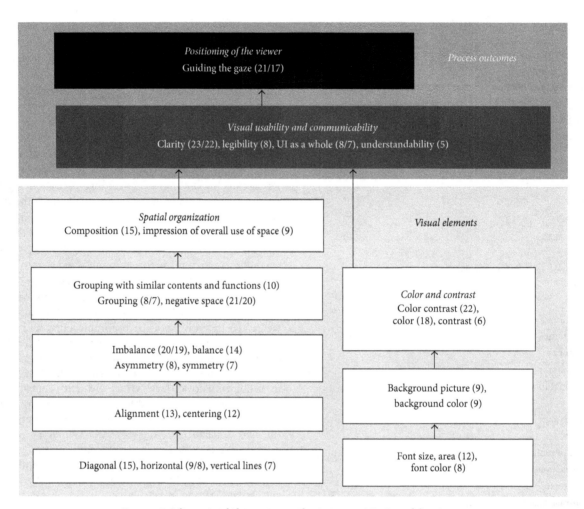

FIGURE 6: Salient visual elements contributing to positioning of the viewer.

Even though the participants were instructed to only use the template for reflecting the impressions of the compositional elements of the layout, attention was paid towards contrasting colors and their role in visual usability. In relation to contrast, most of the remarks were about color contrasts, especially between the colors of the texts and background colors, which were, moreover, attached to legibility. Size was only discussed in the context of the font size.

The relations of the five thematic groups to the salient visual elements are presented in Figure 7. The figure is based on the first phase of the analysis concerning salient visual elements. The structure of the figure has not been affected by the second part of the analysis due to the order of the analysis phases. The salient visual elements in all categories elicited and were attributed with emotion responses. However, emotions with negative valence were expressed more frequently than positive emotions, and emotions with higher activation, such as frustration, were more frequently expressed than emotions with lower activation, such as boredom.

Frustration was reflected regarding legibility, spatial organization, imbalance, asymmetry, diagonal lines, color and contrast, background picture, and font. Emotional utterances relating to calmness or unease were frequently expressed in reference to spatial organization, grouping, negative space, horizontal and diagonal lines, color, and user interface as a whole. Confusion was reported in relation to how colors in the user interface design were experienced. Boredom was connected to spatial organization, color, and background color. Pleasantness was reflected regarding the user interface as a whole, spatial organization, and centering the content.

5. Discussion

Positioning of the viewer functions as the main appraisal process outcome, in which the interactionist view combining the salient visual elements' ability to guide the interaction and the appraisals of these events is experienced. Positioning of the viewer functions through evaluations and experiences of communicability and visual usability. Visual usability includes the ways of how different visual elements guide the interaction and usability. User interfaces that fluently communicate the content in an understandable visual form are appreciated. Clarity, legibility, impression of the user interface as a whole, and understandability were considered as the most important factors in contributing to communicability and visual usability of the user interface. Thus, in designing visual

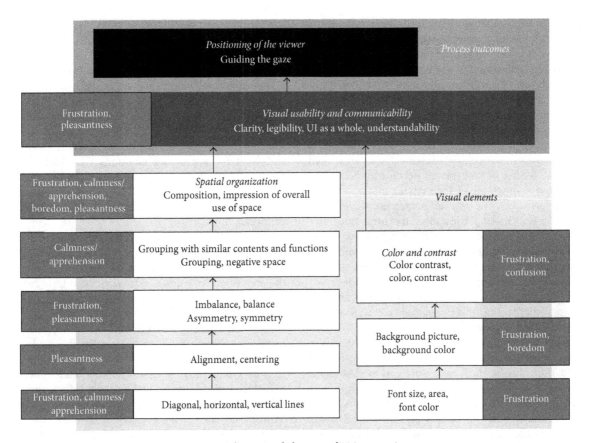

FIGURE 7: Salient visual elements eliciting emotions.

user interfaces, the power of the visual elements to guide users' attention needs to be taken into account. Besides visual usability, the communicative ability of the visual elements [1], in relation to the content suitability of the visual user interface design, affects positioning of the viewer. The overall visual impression of the user interface's appearance should be suitable for the context for which it is designed.

Alignment and centering the content were considered as constitutive factors influencing grouping, balance, and symmetry. Diagonal, horizontal, and vertical lines were highly emphasized as visual elements that strongly affect the positioning of the viewer and lead the interaction as the main low-level elements. In addition to spatial organization, color and contrast were seen as influential design dimensions. Functional and communicative impressions of the visual elements were implicated in terms of understandability and legibility of the content. Contrast between figures, fonts, and background picture and color was conveyed through different font sizes and color combinations. These ways of creating contrast between visual elements in user interfaces were often expressed, especially the contrast between background color and the size and the font colors. Designing contrast between these elements contributes to efficient visual usability, which promotes fluent user experience in interacting with visual user interfaces.

The visual elements are appraised with attributed potential for creating different emotions and eliciting emotional states. Frustration was expressed in connection with legibility, spatial organization, imbalance, asymmetry, diagonal lines, color and contrast, background picture, and font. Frustration is the response to a goal-incongruent event, that is, an event that frustrates, disturbs, or obstructs the subject [41, 43]. In particular, if the disturbing event is appraised as goal-incongruent and unfair and resulting from a deliberate norm violation, the feeling of frustration is strong and may result in anger or even aggression [18, 43]. When interacting with computers, the user may often appraise that an obstruction to her goals is the result of bad user interface design, which results in frustration response with an implicit causal attribution: *"It's disturbing that [the UI] is not fitted to the browser. This creates an impression of imbalance."* Likewise, poor readability of font obstructs grasping the user interface and frustrates the user, as expressed by one participant: *"The composition is frustrating, grey fonts disappear to the background."*

Emotion words relating to calmness or unease were common in the data and referred to spatial organization, grouping, negative space, horizontal/diagonal lines, color, and user interface as a whole. Being calm (or, on the opposite, apprehended) is dependent on the appraisal of the amount of control and power that the subject has over the event [18, 40]. The appraisal process evaluates certain visual elements in relation to the coping dimension, which results in feeling of control or loss of control. If the user of a user interface feels that she is not in control of the situation, she becomes uneasy, and if the situation is incongruent to the goals of the user and she would need to exert control to remedy this, the user may even feel anxious or threatened [41]. Participants emphasized calm, centered, and balanced composition: *"Only aligned to the left side. Diagonal shapes → not very calm."* Diagonal lines were considered apprehensive and horizontal calming: *"Diagonal lines cause apprehension."* and *"Text boxes […] are horizontal, reading them is calming."*

It is noteworthy that not all visual elements that are related to coping and feeling of control are necessarily related to the actual control functions of the system; that is, they do not signify affordances, but they are nevertheless associated with coping. This means that the appraisal process integrates low-level visual elements into a complete experience of the user interface, and some connections between the emotional experience and the details of the interface may not be explicitly clear. Further exploration of this issue could, for example, reveal that shapes and lines are associated with emotional coping, whereas the problem-focused coping would be connected to different visual elements.

Confusion was connected to colors in the participants' responses. Confusion is related to not being in control of the situation and is, therefore, closely related to both frustration and apprehension [41]. Avoiding confusion is critical in the context of human-computer interaction, where the user interface does not necessary reveal the inner logic of the software. Often, the user has norm-based expectations concerning the composition and functionality of the user interface, and deviations from this norm are confusing. However, conventional design is not necessarily good design. The explication of the connection between visual elements and emotional responses, such as confusion, should help the formulation of research-based design principles.

Boredom was expressed in relation to spatial organization, color, and background color. Boredom is an unpleasant feeling, which is associated with low effort and decreased attentional activity [40]. It is distinguished from other emotions in that a person feeling bored ignores what is happening; this often happens in a situation where the situation itself is uninteresting and there is nothing to occupy and stimulate the subject. If the composition of the user interface, for example, is not judged as interesting, the user may feel bored: *"The page is just a layer of things. Boring."*

Pleasantness was related to the user interface as a whole, spatial organization, and centering the content. As discussed above, pleasantness-related appraisals have two dimensions: satisfaction of goals and intrinsic pleasantness [18]. Pleasantness associated with the former dimension reflects the visual usability of the user interface, relating to goal-congruence in possible use cases, and the latter dimension is associated with subjective aesthetic preferences, relating to the intrinsic pleasantness appraisal dimension: *"[…] More pleasant to watch, and probably also to use. Everything is nicely centered."*

In general, negative emotions were used more frequently when evaluating the user interfaces. This observation is explainable by hedonic asymmetry, which means that adaptation to pleasant emotions happens more quickly than adaptation to unpleasant ones [16]. The participants were, therefore,

hastier to report negative than positive emotions. Although negative emotions were more salient in the participants' appraisals, there were also salient visual elements that elicited positive emotions. These were restricted to the spatial organization elements. Color and contrast did not provoke positive emotions. In addition to imbalance with valence, emotions with higher activation in the arousal dimension, such as frustration, were more frequently expressed than emotions with lower activation, such as boredom. It seems that the threshold for expressing emotions with higher activation is lower than expressing emotions with lower activation. However, unlike with valance, the arousal dimension was not observed to be distributed unevenly between different visual elements.

While all of the salient visual element categories were associated with some emotion words or dimensions, spatial organization clearly evoked emotions most frequently and the expressed emotions were also the most diverse. This is understandable as spatial organization is an umbrella term for lower-level elements constructing the user interface composition, and the visual elements belonging to spatial organization were the most frequently observed content in the analysis of salient visual elements.

Grouping with similar contents and functions was reflected to be calming and contributing to grasping the user interface as a whole and to understandability. Also, appropriate amount of negative space was experienced as calming. Both observations are in line with the narrative of calmness, especially, as understood with the help of the coping dimension of appraisal: the listed visual elements helped the participants maintain overall control over the user interfaces, which was reflected as calmness. Imbalance and asymmetry were experienced as frustrating. On the contrary, balance and symmetry were connected to pleasantness. In addition, centering the content was considered pleasant. As the lowest-level visual elements, diagonal lines were emphasized in general and in relation to emotions evoked by them. Diagonal lines were seen as important as constructing elements of the overall impression of the layout. However, the emotions attributed to diagonal lines were controversial. They were experienced as frustrating and apprehensive but also as contributing to elegant impression with dynamic tension.

Color and contrast were discussed frequently, but they were seldom connected to emotions. When color and contrast were discussed in relation to emotions, the connotation was negative (frustration, confusion, and boredom). This is explicable with color's essential role among visual elements. Color is considered as a primary visual element evoking aesthetic preferences [59] and strongly influencing legibility and content understandability.

6. Conclusion

The focus of the study was on future programmers and engineers appraisals of salient visual elements. The results of this study indicate which visual elements are considered as the most salient ones in web page design that contribute to communicability and visual usability and what kind of emotions they elicit or were attributed with. The appraisal process integrates the salient visual elements into an emotional experience. This results in positioning of the viewer, in which the user's experience of the user interface can be explained in terms of how the subjective relevance of the user interface is appraised. This connects salient visual elements with the pleasantness or unpleasantness of the experience, as well as to how well the user is able to cope during the interaction.

Spatial organization and color and contrast, with the lower-level elements which they are based on, such as diagonal lines and colors contrasts, are essential to users in web page designs that promote fluent interaction and visual usability. Characteristics of lines have an important role in emphasizing visual usability and interaction with user interfaces. Spatial organization through grouping with similar content and functions, appropriate use of negative space, and balance and symmetry contribute to the overall impression of the user interface as a clear and understandable totality. Contrast between figures, texts, and backgrounds enhances visual usability and interaction with the user interface. In addition, through contrast, user interfaces can be designed to communicate the content in an effortless manner by grasping the content with one glance. Communicability of the user interface also refers to the content's suitability in relation to the context. Without contrast between visual elements, user interfaces could not communicate the content to the users interacting with them. This notion emphasizes the essence of visual elements contributing to fluent human-computer interaction. User interfaces' ability to position the viewer through visual elements and emotions elicited by them is essential in interacting with different user interfaces.

The emotional responses to user interfaces were analyzed with relational themes created from appraisal dimensions [18, 40]. Connecting these themes to the salient visual elements created a coherent narrative of the process in which emotional experience occurs as a response to visual elements in web page design. Using this framework, future studies should focus on detailing the preliminary findings made here. For example, are all typical emotions encountered in human-computer interaction observed in a connection to all of the salient visual elements so that only the theme of the emotion is different between them? These findings are critical in design, which sets certain experiences as design goals and operationalizes concepts from the explanations which connect designable elements with the user's emotions.

Overall, the emotional emphasis was on centered, symmetrical, and balanced composition, which was experienced as pleasant and calming. Diagonal lines received controversial emotional expressions, as frustrating salient visual element, but also an element which creates a subtle dynamic tension. According to the results, it can be stated that if the goal of the design, from a programmers' perspective, is a pleasurable and controllable experience, the overall composition needs to provide an impression of static balance and symmetry by grouping, centering content, and appropriate use of negative space. This finding emphasizes how attaining feeling of control, another important design goal, is attained by focusing on these elements [28]. Designing with contrasting colors and diagonal lines needs to be considered in relation to the content the user interface is designed to communicate and to whom.

The salient visual elements experienced as pleasant and calming are appraisals of programming students. Visual elements in web page design might gain differing appraisals in different user groups. For example, coping with more various and dynamic combinations of visual elements can be influenced by the level of design expertise and visual literacy abilities [47]. Therefore, future research focuses on resolving differences between different user groups with varying design backgrounds. For more culturally varied results, future research should also be conducted with participants of different backgrounds: information on the cultural variation in the importance of different visual elements would be significant in today's user interface design.

Proceeding from specific contexts towards the discussion of a more general understanding of the studied phenomena is another suggested line for future research. For example, color's powerful position among other visual elements raises questions of its status in emotional interaction. Participants were asked to express their impressions regarding composition and layout design of the web pages, yet color design was frequently discussed in the templates. Therefore, future research should focus on studying the impact of color in user interface design and the emotions elicited by them in order to provide more profound insights into visual elements eliciting emotions in user interface design. Here, the color elements were mostly associated with frustration, which is connected to the goals of the user [41], but the relation of such appraisal dimensions as intrinsic pleasantness should also be investigated. In addition, the emotions triggered by visual elements could be approached in studying symbolist and abstract characteristics attached to the elements and how these meaning making processes influence emotional responses.

In addition, the validity of 3E-templates should be tested by triangulating data with various methods, such as emotion questionnaires, and with various stimuli. It is possible, for example, that with open-ended questions, not all emotions actually elicited by the user interfaces were recorded. Standardized emotion questionnaire would force the participants to rate their emotional experiences, and these results could then be correlated with similar ratings of the visual elements. Moreover, visual design of user interfaces is not universally understood and appreciated similarly in different cultures. Different meanings attached to, for instance, dimensions of visual space are highly influenced by the writing and reading direction [60]. Therefore, due to the context of this study, the results can be applied to Western culture. In addition, this study was conducted in relation to visual web site design and, therefore, might not be applicable to other visual user interface design contexts, such as mobile user interface design. Visual elements as the construction elements of visual mobile user interfaces might be appraised differently, for instance, due to the size and shape of the screen.

Competing Interests

The authors declare that they have no competing interests.

Acknowledgments

The research has been supported by COMAS (Doctoral School of the Faculty of Information Technology, University of Jyväskylä).

References

[1] K. Mullet and D. Sano, *Designing Visual Interfaces: Communication Oriented Techniques*, Prentice Hall, Upper Saddle River, NJ, USA, 1995.

[2] T. Schlatter and D. Levinson, *Visual Usability, Principles and Practices for Designing Digital Applications*, Morgan Kaufmann, Boston, Mass, USA, 2013.

[3] J. Silvennoinen, M. Vogel, and S. Kujala, "Experiencing visual usability and aesthetics in two mobile application contexts," *Journal of Usability Studies*, vol. 10, no. 1, pp. 46–62, 2014.

[4] L. Hallnäs and J. Redström, "From use to presence: on the expressions and aesthetics of everyday computational things," *ACM Transactions on Computer-Human Interaction*, vol. 9, no. 2, pp. 106–124, 2002.

[5] M. Hassenzahl and A. Monk, "The inference of perceived usability from beauty," *Human-Computer Interaction*, vol. 25, no. 3, pp. 235–260, 2010.

[6] N. Tractinsky, A. S. Katz, and D. Ikar, "What is beautiful is usable," *Interacting with Computers*, vol. 13, no. 2, pp. 127–145, 2000.

[7] P. van Schaik and J. Ling, "Modelling user experience with web sites: usability, hedonic value, beauty and goodness," *Interacting with Computers*, vol. 20, no. 3, pp. 419–432, 2008.

[8] M. Moshagen and M. T. Thielsch, "Facets of visual aesthetics," *International Journal of Human-Computer Studies*, vol. 68, no. 10, pp. 689–709, 2010.

[9] D. Tsonos and G. Kouroupetroglou, "Modeling reader's emotional state response on document's typographic elements," *Advances in Human-Computer Interaction*, vol. 2011, Article ID 206983, 18 pages, 2011.

[10] N. Tractinsky, "Visual aesthetics: in human-computer interaction and interaction design," in *Encyclopedia of Human-Computer Interaction*, M. Soegaard and D. Rikke Friis, Eds., The Interaction Design Foundation, Aarhus, Denmark, 2012, http://www.interaction-design.org/encyclopedia/visual_aesthetics.html.

[11] R. W. Veryzer Jr. and J. W. Hutchinson, "The influence of unity and prototypicality on aesthetic responses to new product designs," *Journal of Consumer Research*, vol. 24, no. 4, pp. 374–394, 1998.

[12] W.-K. Hung and L.-L. Chen, "Effects of novelty and its dimensions on aesthetic preference in product design," *International Journal of Design*, vol. 6, no. 2, pp. 81–90, 2012.

[13] P. Hekkert, D. Snelders, and P. C. W. Van Wieringen, "'Most advanced, yet acceptable': typicality and novelty as joint predictors of aesthetic preference in industrial design," *British Journal of Psychology*, vol. 94, no. 1, pp. 111–124, 2003.

[14] I. Reppa and S. McDougall, "When the going gets tough the beautiful get going: aesthetic appeal facilitates task performance," *Psychonomic Bulletin & Review*, vol. 22, no. 5, pp. 1243–1254, 2015.

[15] J. Silvennoinen, "Towards essential visual variables in user interface design," in *Proceedings of the 7th International Conference on Advances in Human-Computer Interactions*, pp. 229–234, Barcelona, Spain, March 2014.

[16] N. H. Frijda, "The laws of emotion," *American Psychologist*, vol. 43, no. 5, pp. 349–358, 1988.

[17] R. S. Lazarus, "Relational meaning and discrete emotions," in *Appraisal Processes in Emotion*, K. L. Scherer, A. Schorr, and T. Johnstone, Eds., pp. 37–67, Oxford University Press, New York, NY, USA, 2001.

[18] K. R. Scherer, "The dynamic architecture of emotion: evidence for the component process model," *Cognition & Emotion*, vol. 23, no. 7, pp. 1307–1351, 2009.

[19] N. Tractinsky, A. Cokhavi, M. Kirschenbaum, and T. Sharfi, "Evaluating the consistency of immediate aesthetic perceptions of web pages," *International Journal of Human Computer Studies*, vol. 64, no. 11, pp. 1071–1083, 2006.

[20] K.-C. Hamborg, J. Hülsmann, and K. Kaspar, "The interplay between usability and aesthetics: more evidence for the 'what is usable is beautiful' notion," *Advances in Human-Computer Interaction*, vol. 2014, Article ID 946239, 13 pages, 2014.

[21] A. Sonderegger, G. Zbinden, A. Uebelbacher, and J. Sauer, "The influence of product aesthetics and usability over the course of time: a longitudinal field experiment," *Ergonomics*, vol. 55, no. 7, pp. 713–730, 2012.

[22] M. Thüring and S. Mahlke, "Usability, aesthetics and emotions in human-technology interaction," *International Journal of Psychology*, vol. 42, no. 4, pp. 253–264, 2007.

[23] J. Nielsen, *Usability Engineering*, Morgan Kaufman, San Francisco, Calif, USA, 1993.

[24] J. Iivari, H. Isomäki, and S. Pekkola, "The user-the great unknown of systems development: reasons, forms, challenges, experiences and intellectual contributions of user involvement," *Information Systems Journal*, vol. 20, no. 2, pp. 109–117, 2010.

[25] B. Bygstad, G. Ghinea, and E. Brevik, "Software development methods and usability: perspectives from a survey in the software industry in Norway," *Interacting with Computers*, vol. 20, no. 3, pp. 375–385, 2008.

[26] D. Cyr, "Emotion and website design," in *Encyclopedia of Human-Computer Interaction*, M. Soegaard and D. Rikke Friis, Eds., The Interaction-Design Foundation, Aarhus, Denmark, 2013, http://www.interaction-design.org/encyclopedia/emotion_and_website_design.html.

[27] P. Desmet, K. Overbeeke, and S. Tax, "Designing products with added emotional value: development and application of an approach for research through design," *The Design Journal*, vol. 4, no. 1, pp. 32–47, 2001.

[28] E. Demir, P. M. A. Desmet, and P. Hekkert, "Appraisal patterns of emotions in human-product interaction," *International Journal of Design*, vol. 3, no. 2, pp. 41–51, 2009.

[29] J. P. P. Jokinen, "Emotional user experience: traits, events, and states," *International Journal of Human Computer Studies*, vol. 76, pp. 67–77, 2015.

[30] P. Saariluoma and J. P. P. Jokinen, "Appraisal and mental contents in human-technology interaction," *International Journal of Technology and Human Interaction*, vol. 11, no. 2, pp. 1–32, 2015.

[31] K. Karvonen, "The beauty of simplicity," in *Proceedings of the ACM Conference on Universal Usability (CUU '00)*, pp. 85–90, Washington, DC, USA, November 2000.

[32] G. Lindgaard, C. Dudek, D. Sen, L. Sumegi, and P. Noonan, "An exploration of relations between visual appeal, trustworthiness and perceived usability of homepages," *ACM Transactions on Computer-Human Interaction*, vol. 18, no. 1, article 1, 30 pages, 2011.

[33] D. Cyr, M. Head, and H. Larios, "Colour appeal in website design within and across cultures: a multi-method evaluation," *International Journal of Human Computer Studies*, vol. 68, no. 1-2, pp. 1–21, 2010.

[34] M. Wiberg and E. Robles, "Computational compositions: aesthetics, materials, and interaction design," *International Journal of Design*, vol. 4, no. 2, pp. 65–76, 2010.

[35] L. Hallnäs, "On the foundations of interaction design aesthetics: revisiting the notions of form and expression," *International Journal of Design*, vol. 5, no. 1, pp. 73–84, 2011.

[36] D. Norman, *Emotional Design*, Basic Books, New York, NY, USA, 2004.

[37] J. Dewey, *Art as Experience*, Capricorn Books, New York, NY, USA, 1958.

[38] P. Hekkert, "Design aesthetics: principles of pleasure in design," *Psychology Science*, vol. 48, no. 2, pp. 157–172, 2006.

[39] K. R. Scherer, "What are emotions? And how can they be measured?" *Social Science Information*, vol. 44, no. 4, pp. 695–729, 2005.

[40] C. A. Smith and P. C. Ellsworth, "Patterns of cognitive appraisal in emotion," *Journal of Personality and Social Psychology*, vol. 48, no. 4, pp. 813–838, 1985.

[41] P. Saariluomaand and J. P. P. Jokinen, "Emotional dimensions of user experience: a user psychological analysis," *International Journal of Human-Computer Interaction*, vol. 30, no. 4, pp. 303–320, 2014.

[42] M. Hassenzahl, "User experience (UX): towards an experiential perspective on product quality," in *Proceedings of the 20th Conference on l'Interaction Homme-Machine (IHM '08)*, pp. 11–15, ACM, Metz, France, September 2008.

[43] L. Berkowitz, "Frustration-aggression hypothesis: examination and reformulation," *Psychological Bulletin*, vol. 106, no. 1, pp. 59–73, 1989.

[44] S. Folkman and R. S. Lazarus, "If it changes it must be a process: study of emotion and coping during three stages of a college examination," *Journal of Personality and Social Psychology*, vol. 48, no. 1, pp. 150–170, 1985.

[45] R. S. Lazarus and B. N. Lazarus, *Passion and Reason*, Oxford University Press, New York, NY, USA, 1994.

[46] D. E. Berlyne, *Aesthetics and Psychobiology*, Appleton-Century-Crofts, New York, NY, USA, 1971.

[47] D. Curtiss, *Introduction to Visual Literacy: A Guide to the Visual Arts and Communication*, Prentice Hall, Englewood Cliffs, NJ, USA, 1987.

[48] M. Tähti and L. Arhippainen, "A proposal of collecting emotions and experiences," in *Interactive Experiences in HCI*, vol. 2, pp. 195–198, 2004.

[49] M. Tähti and M. Niemelä, "3E—expressing emotions and experiences," in *Proceedings of the WP9 Workshop on Innovative Approaches for Evaluating Affective Systems. HUMAINE (Human-Machine Interaction Network on Emotion)*, Stockholm, Sweden, February 2006.

[50] CSS Zen Garden Gallery, http://www.csszengarden.com.

[51] E. Raita and A. Oulasvirta, "Too good to be bad: favorable product expectations boost subjective usability ratings," *Interacting with Computers*, vol. 23, no. 4, pp. 363–371, 2011.

[52] P. Bell, "Content analysis of visual images," in *Handbook of Visual Analysis*, T. van Leeuwen and C. Jewitt, Eds., Sage, London, UK, 4th edition, 2004.

[53] H. Zettl, *Sight, Sound, Motion: Applied Media Aesthetics*, Wadsworth Publishing Company, Boston, Mass, USA, 1999.

[54] M. Collier, "Approaches to analysis in visual anthropology," in *Handbook of Visual Analysis*, T. van Leeuwen and C. Jewitt, Eds., Sage, London, UK, 4th edition, 2004.

[55] K. Krippendorf, *Content Analysis: An Introduction to Its Methodologies*, Sage, London, UK, 1980.

[56] T. van Leeuwen, "Semiotics and iconography," in *Handbook of Visual Analysis*, T. van Leeuwen and C. Jewitt, Eds., Sage, London, UK, 4th edition, 2004.

[57] C. Jewitt and R. Oyama, "Visual meaning: a social semiotic approach," in *Handbook of Visual Analysis*, T. van Leeuwen and C. Jewitt, Eds., Sage, London, UK, 4th edition, 2004.

[58] G. Rose, *Visual Methodologies: An Introduction to the Interpretation of Visual Materials*, Sage, London, UK, 2005.

[59] R. Poulin, *The Language of Graphic Design: An Illustrated Handbook of Understanding Fundamental Design Principles*, Rockport Publishers, Beverly, Mass, USA, 2011.

[60] T. van Leeuwen and G. Kress, *Reading Images. The Grammar of Visual Design*, Taylor & Francis, 2nd edition, 2006.

12

Cognitive Mimetics for Designing Intelligent Technologies

Tuomo Kujala ⓘ **and Pertti Saariluoma**

University of Jyväskylä, 40014 Jyväskylä, Finland

Correspondence should be addressed to Tuomo Kujala; tuomo.kujala@jyu.fi

Academic Editor: Marco Porta

Design mimetics is an important method of creation in technology design. Here, we review design mimetics as a plausible approach to address the problem of how to design generally intelligent technology. We argue that design mimetics can be conceptually divided into three levels based on the source of imitation. Biomimetics focuses on the structural similarities between systems in nature and technical solutions for solving design problems. In robotics, the sensory-motor systems of humans and animals are a source of design solutions. At the highest level, we introduce the concept of cognitive mimetics, in which the source for imitation is human information processing. We review and discuss some historical examples of cognitive mimetics, its potential uses, methods, levels, and current applications, and how to test its success. We conclude by a practical example showing how cognitive mimetics can be a highly valuable complimentary approach for pattern matching and machine learning based design of artificial intelligence (AI) for solving specific human-AI interaction design problems.

1. Introduction

Mimetic design is an important design methodology. It refers to technology design in which designers imitate some existing phenomenon or system to generate new technological solutions. The paragons can be anything, but often they are phenomena or systems of nature [1]. Yet, mimicking is not necessarily a simple concept. Design mimetics have often focused on structural and physical similarity between entities of nature and technical solutions. However, the structural and physical similarity between the source and idea may not be sufficient for getting the best out of mimicking. There are classes of design problems, which are not structural or physical but still could be of real use, if designers could find new ideas by studying possible solutions via mimicry. In this paper, our goal is to reanalyze design mimetics at a conceptual level in order to explicate the ways it can serve as an approach for addressing the problem of how to design technological solutions with artificial general intelligence [2].

Designing intelligent systems is becoming a core area in developing modern technologies [3]. Machine translation, image and speech recognition systems, self-driving cars, chatbots, and robot help desks are examples of current technological trends. All of these intelligent (or "smart") technologies

are enabled by artificial intelligence (AI) based on neural networks, pattern recognition, and machine learning. The consequence of these new developments is that computers are becoming more relevant in replacing or reallocating people in tasks, in which so far it has been necessary to use people in order to get the systems to work. Nevertheless, true progress in this area presupposes in-depth understanding of the human cognitive processes that should be replaced by machines. Therefore, it makes sense to rethink the conceptual foundations of design mimetics in this new technological era.

A naïve but intuitive example might help to clarify our position. Consider the way in which design mimetics could be used in designing a cyborg pianist. The first problem is to create the hands that play the piano. They must be like human hands with respect to size and elasticity of movement. They should have the right pressure, timing, and tempo to play like Lang Lang (a well-known Chinese concert pianist). Pianist robots' coordination should be able to mimic the sensory-motor processes of a human pianist. It should be able to hear the notes and respond accordingly.

A critical question here is whether the imitation of the human hands and eye-hand coordination processes are sufficient in expressing all human skills in piano playing. Skilled pianists often use their hands to play the keyboard in a routine manner but they also have to solve unique and complex problems. They have to rely on higher cortical processes such as categorization, inference, decision making, problem solving, and constructive thinking in order to be able to create new artistic visions and interpretations [4].

In building intelligent systems such as autonomous robots, it is thus not necessarily sufficient to mimic biological structures but it is also necessary to mimic sensory-motoric and even different levels of higher intellectual processes. To explain and to mimic a human expert's skills, one has to go beyond mere mechanical and sensory-motor levels towards even emotional modeling to be able to comprehend and model a creative and skilled pianist. Here, our common sense example could have been about any human expert at work. The key message is that, to replace activities of human experts with machine intelligence, it is necessary to model and mimic many levels of physical and intellectual work.

In this paper, we will argue for a three-level conceptual model of design mimetics and introduce a novel concept of cognitive mimetics to refer to the mimicry of higher cognitive processes for designing intelligent technology. The main goal of the paper is to review and argue for the need of cognitive mimetics in order to design artificial general intelligence [2] and intelligent human-AI interactions. In a world overrun with pattern recognition and machine learning approaches to AI, we suggest that mimicking actual cognitive processes in AI design is a matter for further consideration. Cognitive mimetics may prove to be an increasingly important design approach as it is expected that, in the near future, we will encounter novel interaction challenges in our confrontations with ubiquitous AI [3].

2. Three Levels of Mimetic Design

New design ideas often utilize existing solutions for problems of similar types. The main attribute of mimicry is that the solution for a design problem is found by imitating some existing object or system. The phenomenon that is the paragon for the design solution can be called the source and outcome idea. Mimicry has always been a component of engineering thinking [5, 6]. The Wright brothers as well as Leonardo da Vinci observed how birds flied and imitated these to design an airplane [7]. One can easily find numerous examples of respective design processes in which some aspect of nature has been mimicked to create new technological solutions. In the 1950s, this kind of design was attributed the label "design mimetics." As the source was often nature, the design approach was coined biomimetics by Otto Schmitt [8]. Ever since, it has had a solid role in engineering. We argue that there are three main levels of design mimetics that can be utilized when designing intelligent technology. In the following chapters, we will briefly discuss each level of mimetic design.

2.1. Mimicking Structural Similarities. An effective way of approaching the problems of replacing human capacities in work has been biomimetics (also biomimicry or bionics). It is an engineering paradigm, which is based on the imitation of the models, systems, and elements of nature for the purpose of solving complex technological problems [1, 6, 7]. A traditional part of biomimetics is based on imitating the processes of nature on the physical level. For example, bird wings were models and inspiration for designing airplane wings, which could enable airplanes to fly and thus enabling people to fly. The focus of biomimetics is thus more on designing a physical object than on replacing people with machines.

Biomimetics has been a very successful way to ideate new technological solutions from nanometric levels to large technical structures. The way evolution has "solved" construction problems can be applied to the technological sphere, though the solutions need not be identical. For example, the wings of any man-made flying technical artifact are not exactly bird wings, but still one can find many analogical properties. There are numerous examples of working technical solutions, of which design processes have been based on biomimetics. Robots may resemble ants or tortoises. Many fabrics have their origins in studies on biological organisms. Connectionist computational models of artificial intelligence have been inspired by neural networks [9]. Even recently, designers have learned more by studying the wings of the birds when designing airplanes and drones [10]. In photonics, engineers were inspired by the reflecting properties of butterfly wings, when they invented new display technologies [11].

Biomimetics illustrates some important properties of mimicry in design. Firstly, imitation is an important source of ideas in design thinking. Secondly, the source and idea are not identical. Rather, they exist in dialogue with one another. Consequently, much of the information required to generate the final solution is not directly related to the source. Thus, metals and rivets in airplane wings have little to do with bird wings. Furthermore, the solution does not need to be as equally efficient as the source. Instead, it may improve the original performance. Caterpillars are much more efficient in working with soil than human hands. The focus of mimicry is to advance forward in design thinking by finding key solutions.

In a closer look, it is problematic as to how well biomimetics suit the purposes of designing intelligent technologies. It rather concentrates on the structural and physical solutions for design problems such as the structures of robots, architectural solutions, or properties of materials and molecules. Structural similarities are not necessarily sufficient for innovating modern intelligent technologies.

2.2. Mimicking Sensory-Motor Processes. The story of industrial robotics is mostly very different from that of mimicking structural similarities. The goal of robots is to replace people in tasks, in situations where, for instance, people are not necessary, or in situations that are dangerous for humans. A substantial amount of industrial robotics, from a mimicry perspective, models the sensory-motor systems of human. Today, for instance, dexterity is one of the key problems in robotics as it would give robots new application areas [12].

A welding robot recognizes the metal body of a car, moves to the right welding spot, and finally welds the pieces together. Actually, the robot does everything that a welder would do and for this reason, it is possible to free people from many routine welding tasks. There are a large number of robots in similar tasks. They can pack things, they can take mail parcels, or they can operate in harbors, to take some examples. People have earlier carried out these tasks, as it was not possible to build sufficiently accurate robots. Computers have made it possible to reach sufficient accuracy in sensory-motor processing and get these kinds of robots to work.

The first robotic arms were created to replace human arms. Therefore, in this sense, they are imitating a human arm. However, there is more in them. They have sensors and programs, which control their behavior. Wiener's [13] theories of cybernetics and control were important in creating the first-generation automation robots in the sixties. They had sensors and some versions, such as Grey Walter's tortoises, could even wander around in one's apartment [14]. From the mimicking point of view, they had new kinds of properties. They could process information.

Early industrial robots carried out tasks, in which human operators relied on their sensory-motor information processing. In welding cars on conveyer belts, the robots are not supposed to think. They just carefully inspect the parts they need to join and then weld them together. Only in fault situations are more complex actions required, but these are typically rare and are often handled by people. Thus, one only needs to coordinate sensory information with movements to carry out these kinds of tasks. Nevertheless, in order to construct robots, one needs to additionally imitate human sensory-motor information processing in addition to biological structures. This kind of mimicry is qualitatively different in comparison to traditional biomimetics.

Imitation of sensory-motor processes only represents the lowest level of information processing mimetics. Machine vision is not only about enabling the machine to see things but also about actively recognizing objects. The recent developments in artificial intelligence and the rise of autonomous technologies call attention to yet another kind of information processing mimetics. This is based on imitating higher cognitive processes such as thinking.

2.3. Mimicking Higher Cognitive Processes. Human information processing is an interesting source for imitation. It is clearly different from structural biomimetics and also from sensory-motor mimetics, although the notion of embodied cognition [15] somewhat blurs the distinction between these levels of mimetics. There are many possibilities for naming this level of design mimetics. Perhaps the most logical term is *cognitive mimetics* as the source is human information processing. Human information processing has traditionally been called cognition [16]. Thus, all types of mimetics which are built on the idea of imitating human information processing can be called cognitive mimetics. This is in order to distinguish this form of mimetics from the lower levels of design mimetics.

As far as designers will improve physical and physiological properties of traditional human work such as sensory-motor processes on assembly lines by means of industrial robotics, they can rely on imitating and improving biological sensors and body movements. However, moving the scope of traditional biomimetics to the design of autonomous,

TABLE 1: A three-level conceptual model of design mimetics.

Level	Source of imitation in nature
Cognitive mimetics	Higher cognitive processes
Sensory-motor mimetics	Perception and motor functions
Biomimetics	Physical structure

intelligent technologies means an essential change of focus. This change of focus entails the shift from mimicking physical structures or sensory-motor processes to the higher cognitive processes. Instead of mimicking the physical movement of body limbs, which is common in assembly line robots, it has already become increasingly more important to mimic human intelligence and higher cognitive processes. Mental processes such as language comprehension and production, categorization, decision making, inference, problem solving, and constructive thinking will become more important in design mimetics.

Cognitive processes are important for human survival and they make it possible for people to behave in a flexible and creative manner. People can respond selectively and rationally to situations in which they have never been before (i.e., general intelligence). This means that people are different from many animals, as they are able to adapt more efficiently to new environmental conditions in an intentional manner and they can invent new ways of meeting the environmental demands. Thus, cognitive processes give people much more independence as regards variation in environment as compared to other animals.

When the goal of technology is to replace human intellectual performance, the understanding of cognitive processes and using this knowledge become important in design. In particular, artificial intelligence and robots can benefit from understanding human cognition and information processing as these will be cooperating more and more with people in novel sociotechnical systems. Generally, intelligent autonomous systems are technical devices that can flexibly and rationally respond to stimuli and environmental situations that they have not met before or which have not been programmed in advance. Thus, the stimulus-independence typical to the human mind should be one of the main criteria of (human-like) intelligence of autonomous systems (i.e., artificial general intelligence [2]). In contrast to biomimetics, cognitive mimetics concentrates on analyzing the human information processes and building intelligent systems on the grounds of modeling how people process information.

The three levels of design mimetics based on the source of imitation are presented in Table 1. Next, we will take a closer look on cognitive mimetics and argue more for its importance in designing intelligent technology.

3. Cognitive Mimetics

3.1. The Brief History of Mimicking Human Cognition. Cognitive mimetics is a unique design conception. However, it is based on the very core knowledge of modern cognitive science. The first example of mimicking human information processing is perhaps Turing's [17, 18] model of a mathematician, that is, the Turing machine. The idea led to the birth of computers and information technology. The core of Turing's idea was to construct a model or imitation of how mathematicians solve mathematical problems. Thus, his focus was not on structural aspects or sensory-motor processes of people but on how they process information. Turing's insights led to a number of important prototypical ways of thinking, which can be seen as the first examples of cognitive mimetics.

An excellent early example of cognitive mimetics can be found in game playing algorithms. Game playing became one of the first challenges for designing technical systems, which had some resemblance to the human mind [19]. The challenge was set in the early fifties by Turing [17] and Shannon [19]. De Groot [20] collected chess players' thinking-aloud protocols and noticed how they used pruned tree searches. Similarly, early AI researchers suggested that heuristic tree search might be a solution to be used by machines in solving search problems [21]. Consequently, through heuristic search, chess was used for forty years as a context for developing human-like artificial intelligence. In this example, the way human chess players processed information became the model of machine information processing. Thus, it was not any feature of a machine or any biological property of a human brain but the way people process information that became the model of this class of AI systems. Tree search was a suitably similar process between chess-playing computers and chess players, rendering it possible to use cognitive mimicry to develop machines capable of intellectual tasks possible only for people beforehand [22]. As is well known, a computer chess program could finally beat a chess world champion in 1997. More recently, examples can be seen in IBM Watson's [23] victory over two human experts in the Jeopardy game show in 2011 and also in Google's Deep Mind's victory over a grandmaster player in the Chinese game Go in 2016 [24].

A few years after Turing and Shannon's game-playing programs, in 1958, John McCarthy developed the term artificial intelligence (AI) to describe a new field of engineering [25]. At that time, one could find a number of important systems, which to some degree mimicked human information processing. Logic theories, Checkers, transformation grammar, and related computational linguistics can be taken as examples [26].

In early 1940s, another important line of cognitive mimicry began. McCullough and Pitts developed an AI system later known as Perceptron, which finally led to the fields of neurocomputing and connectionism [9, 27, 28]. These approaches to AI were developed on the ground of mimicking (at a highly reduced level) how human nerve cells and neural networks operate [27].

Later, symbolic production systems known as cognitive architectures, such as SOAR [29, 30] and ACT-R [31], were developed based on the General Problem Solver by Newell and Simon [22]. The cognitive models built on these systems tried to mimic the symbolic (representational) level of human information processing in the constraints given by the general cognitive architecture. In the 1970s, production systems were considered to be the key to modeling cognition, whereas in the 1980s and 1990s, connectionist approaches once again gained popularity in attempts to create AI and expert systems due to observed limitations in the production systems' capabilities to create AI. Since the 1990s, probabilistic models of human cognition based on Bayesian modeling have been replacing both the connectionist and production models among cognitive scientists due to their ability to significantly increase representational complexity [8]. Recently, the rapid successes of deep learning systems in several application domains (e.g., [2, 23, 24]) have brought neural networks that are capable of impressive pattern recognition capacity superior to humans back into the public spotlight. This is due to the advances in computing power, big data, and algorithms. However, these approaches are currently very different from the way human cognition operates [2, 32].

3.2. Goals. AI is a central concept in designing new intelligent technologies. However, cognitive mimetics and AI are not one and the same concept. Cognitive mimetics is one approach for designing and innovating intelligent technologies. AI can but it does not need to be based on cognitive mimetics. Analogously, all technology design does not rely on biomimetics, although it has been proven to be an important aid in design.

Cognitive mimetics presupposes the understanding of how both higher cognitive processes operate in human mind and how these processes can be imitated by computers. This problem belongs to the very core of cognitive science. The problem is the property of multiple realizability [33], which means that cognitive processes can be realized in human minds as well as in animals and technical systems.

However, the goal of cognitive mimetics is not to slavishly imitate human cognitive processes nor is it to construct devices that can perform tasks as effectively as people. The goal should rather be to produce technical systems that surpass human levels so that they can be of real help for improving human life. A pocket calculator that would make the same number of errors as people would not serve its purpose as well as they do today. Yet, a design is based on cognitive mimicry when the system has elements that can be identified and ideated on the grounds of human information processing.

Thus, a chess machine need not exactly search in the same way as people do. Indeed, these machines do not work in a similar manner to people. The machines consider hundreds of millions of moves, while people often do not generate more than fifty mental moves. Computer chess programs are similar to people in that they use very similar tree search process. Yet, they vary in their inability to distinguish between essential and inessential alternatives. The programs have to replace the selectivity by brute force. Their performance is as effective as that of any human being and if needed, they could replace people in chess competitions. Current mainstream approaches to the design of intelligent systems rely mostly on the enormous data crunching capacity of modern computers, machine learning, and pattern recognition in big data [2, 32, 34]. Cognitive mimetics can be a complementing approach to the design of generally intelligent autonomous systems that could better communicate, interact, and cooperate with humans. For instance, Strabala et al. [35] have shown that it is possible to model the way in which people hand over objects to each other (what, when, and where information) and to utilize the procedure in improving human-robot handovers. This is an example of a task that is trivial for humans, while it has been proven difficult to implement for robots.

3.3. Methods. Human capabilities exceed machine capabilities in certain tasks and vice versa. Thus, a critical target design task for cognitive mimetics is to find the optimal division of work between the AI and the human operator (see, e.g., [36]). One of the general tasks in which the human mind is (still) supreme over the machine is the finding of situationally relevant information and subgoals out of large amounts of available situational and dynamic data. Other critical tasks for cognitive mimetics include the modeling of optimal information sharing and control shifts in order to guarantee the highest level of situation awareness regarding the task-relevant information for both the human cooperator/supervisor and AI systems.

In addition, domain-specific expert behaviors can be modeled in order to find situation-specific goal prioritization and goal selection rules for each task of an AI system in the domain. For instance, Soh and Demiris [37] have developed an expert model that is capable of learning a human expert's tacit knowledge from demonstration. Their study indicates that it is both possible and useful to use algorithms to learn shared control policies by observing a human expert in the domain of smart wheelchair assistance for the disabled (i.e., how and when to assist).

The methods used in cognitive mimetics can also be based on computational modeling approaches such as ACT-R [31], which are capable of modeling the constraints of human information processing. However, the applicable methods are not limited to existing cognitive architectures. Recent computational design approaches for interaction design (e.g., [27]) try to optimize user interfaces by modeling users' behaviors with reinforcement learning and other machine learning algorithms. Compared to the modeling of average human behavior that has been of main focus since the 1980s with cognitive architectures (e.g., ACT-R [31]), the main goal in cognitive mimetics is to understand and model expert human behavior at such a level of detail that the behavior could be replicated by a computer. This is in line with the original idea behind cognitive modeling as introduced by Newell and Simon [22]. However, this approach necessitates understanding and modeling human error as well, as expertise is typically gained by significant experience on exposure to various kinds of even exceptional trial and error situations. The observation of only perfect task behavior and imitation of these by a machine would only lead to an unintelligent machine that would not be capable of adjusting its behaviors to unexpected, even minor, changes in situation parameters [32]. Reinforcement learning [38] is a machine learning method that has been found to be highly useful in teaching machines "bounded rationality" [39] similar (or superior) to expert humans in a given task, with given goals, constraints, and rewards, after a large number of task simulations [40].

The ultimate key to success in cognitive mimetics would be to create systems that are able to rapidly modify and learn to adjust their behaviors in a similar fashion to a human expert according to the recognition of a meaningful change in situation parameters [2, 32]. As plausible key solutions, Lake et al. [32] have suggested that generally intelligent artificial systems should have the same capacities as those of a human infant (innate or learned [34]) to

(1) build causal models of the world which support explanation and understanding (rather than mere pattern recognition),

(2) ground learning in intuitive theories of physics (e.g., persistence and continuity of objects) and psychology (e.g., human agents having intentions, beliefs, and goals),

(3) harness construction of new representations through the combination of primitive elements and learning-to-learn (i.e., learning a new task or concept can be accelerated through previous or parallel learning of other related tasks or other related concepts).

These capacities enable humans to rapidly acquire and generalize knowledge for novel tasks and situations.

The ideas of brains as an embodied prediction machine (e.g., [41]) may well offer cognitive science the grand unified theory of the mind. When these predictive processing models are coupled with Bayesian models of learning and inference [8], they may be the most promising current approach in this respect (1.-3. above). Other recent candidates for a grand unified theory of cognition (e.g., [42]) have considered analogical thinking as the core feature of human cognition (likewise it is the core of design mimetics). How to implement these kinds of innate capacities, structures, and mechanisms in AI remains an open question, but if it is solved, the consequences for the development of AI could be immense.

3.4. Levels. So far, utilization of cognitive mimetics in the design of AI has been fairly limited. As reviewed earlier, biological neural networks were the early inspiration for artificial neural networks. Tree search similar to human search has been used since 1950s in a number of AI solutions. These solutions range from different games to logic, fifth-generation computers, and, most recently, in Google's AlphaGo variants beating the best human experts in the game of Go [24, 40]. Reinforcement learning was a key to the superhuman performance of the AlphaGo Zero in the same game [40]. Reinforcement learning can be seen as highly similar to the behaviorist view of human learning, which was found to be significantly deficient for explaining human learning in the so-called cognitive revolution of the 1950s [38, 43].

There may well be many other examples of the success of cognitive mimetics in the design of intelligent technology. However, one can ask if cognitive mimetics has been utilized sufficiently in the design of AI for achieving artificial general intelligence [2, 34]. From this point of view, Marcus [2] has argued for the necessity of hybrid AI systems, which would more closely resemble the organization of human cognition. A hybrid AI system could have various parallel subsystems, maybe similar to deep learning networks, but that are orchestrated by higher-level mechanisms similar to reinforcement learning, as well as by central executive processes working at an even higher symbolic level. AlphaGo Zero [40] is a recent example of how a hybrid system (combining deep learning, reinforcement learning, and tree search) can be superior to pure deep learning systems. Yet, the symbolic level of processing is still absent from systems such as AlphaGo Zero, which may limit its intelligence to certain domains (e.g., gaming).

3.5. Tests of Success. There are a number of suggested means that could be applied to test the success of cognitive mimetics, of which the most famous is Turing's test [41]. It can be used to assess whether the performance of an intelligent program is as good as the performance of a human being. Turing's test does not evaluate if a system processes information like people but it evaluates whether it can perform as well as people in an intellectual task. This is important when the replacement or reallocation of human work by technical systems is considered [31].

The original goal of Turing's [17] test was to answer one question: Can machines think (i.e., are machines intelligent)? The Turing test is an imitation game. The decisive criterion in these experiments is the capacity of the human interrogator to say whether the answer to a question was given by human or machine. If the interrogator cannot do this, then the machine has passed the test. Turing argued that if machines can imitate human thinking perfectly, they are intelligent. Therefore, the outcome of the experiment is that machines can think if they can perform human tasks in such a way that it is impossible for a competent observer to see the difference between human and machine.

Turing's imitation game gives an explicit (behavioristic) form of how to compare human and machine behaviors in intelligent tasks. Since the discussion on the intelligence of machines underpins much of modern cognitive science, psychology, and philosophy of the mind and it is also essential in developing AI robots and autonomous systems, it makes sense to consider the true value of Turing's test for both theoretical and practical purposes [44, 45]. To pass this test can be argued to be the ultimate goal for optimal interaction and communication between humans and an AI system in several practical domains, even if the pass would not imply strong AI in the sense of Searle [46].

However, one could ask as to whether or not it is enough for a system to pass the Turing test in a particular task in order to be as (generally) intelligent as a human. Does it matter how the system has reached this level in performance and if it is able to pass the test also in other tasks (i.e., generalizability of the skills)? The question dates back to a long-standing, but unsolved, debate between machine learning researchers (including statisticians) and linguists (including psychologists) [47].

Lake et al. [32] have recently published an extensive literature review comparing the current high-end pattern recognition systems' (i.e., neural networks') performance to human performance. They have also discussed what may be lacking in these systems preventing them from reaching the level of human skills. They argue that, despite the biological inspiration and performance achievements, the deep learning pattern recognition systems differ from human intelligence in crucial ways. They put forward strong arguments for cognitive mimetics without using the concept explicitly. Nowadays, pattern recognition system may be taught to reach a comparable, or higher, level of performance than a human in a specific task (e.g., a video game). However, the difference in the required amount of training between a human child and the system to achieve a comparable level of performance can be calculated in hundreds or even thousands of hours. Furthermore, a child can learn and handle a small change in game dynamics easily. A pattern recognition system may require full reconfiguration and a significant amount of training before reaching again a high level of performance. These observations suggest (at least) three criteria for a system to be as intelligent as a human cooperator:

(1) Pass in Turing's test

(2) Comparable level of performance with a comparable amount of training

(3) Generalizability of the acquired skills and knowledge to other tasks

AlphaGo Zero, as described by Silver et al. [40], may be argued to be able to pass easily 1. and to an extent also 2. in the game of Go. AlphaGo Zero has demonstrated not only human-level performance but also "superhuman proficiency" in the game. In addition, Silver et al. [40] argue that it achieved human level of performance without human (move) data only by reinforcement learning from self-play over less than 40 hours of self-training. Inarguably, these amazing results indicate the efficiency of the reinforcement learning approach for achieving superior performance in one particularly challenging domain for human cognition. However, as Marcus [34] points out, it remains a question as to how well and easily AlphaGo Zero's intelligence in this particular board game generalizes beyond gaming and even to other types of games, such as video games. Marcus [34] further argues that, despite Silver et al. [40] claiming that AlphaGo Zero was able to achieve superhuman proficiency "tabula rasa" without any knowledge of human Go games and moves, a critical aspect of its success was the tree search and reward logic of the reinforcement learning, which were built-in by its human creators. These critical aspects are highly similar to the mechanisms human players utilize in the game of Go. For the generalizability of the AI produced by cognitive mimetics, it is not sufficient that the AI design is able to produce seemingly intelligent behavior (i.e., pass Turing's test), but the types of processes that produce this behavior and how generalizable the artificial intelligence is across different tasks are what matters.

4. Application Example: Interactions with Autonomous Vehicles

The utility of cognitive mimetics for the design of intelligent technology can be illustrated by a practical example.

Autonomous vehicles (i.e., self-driving cars) are expected to be one of the megatrends of autonomous AI technologies in the near future. However, according to an analysis by the University of Michigan Transportation Research Institute [48], unexpectedly an autonomous car may be statistically more likely to be involved in an accident than a car with a human driver per million miles traveled. The severity of the accidents seems to be lower, the cars were not considered to be at fault in any accident, and most of the accidents were rear-end crashes (the autonomous car was hit from the back by a human driver). However, the findings seem to suggest that there could be something unexpected in the behavior of an autonomous car which can lead human drivers to be misinterpreted by the car's behaviors.

At intersections and junctions in particular, a common rhythm by the vehicles in a queue is highly important for the flow and safety of the traffic. A major advantage of an autonomous vehicle over a human driver is its ability to detect potentially risky situations well ahead of the human and react to these at a much higher intensity. The downside can be unexpectedly hard braking behaviors in situations where there is a false positive detection. For instance, a bicyclist approaching a crossing but who gives a sign of eye contact and yielding that is efficiently recognizable by a human driver, but not by an autonomous vehicle, can lead to unexpected behaviors. As long as there are human pedestrians, cyclists, or drivers in the traffic among the autonomous vehicles, the problem is real. The issue is even more pronounced in highly unstructured traffic environments, such as crowded city centers. In these environments, the human driver is able to take the own space even by aggressive gestures and other ways of human communication with fellow road users. Meanwhile, an autonomous vehicle can simply cease to move because it detects continuous possibility of crossing objects.

A recent study by Brown and Laurier [49] demonstrates how current autopilot systems (Tesla autopilot and Google self-driving car) are highly inefficient in detecting the intentions of the fellow human drivers and signaling the intentions of the car to other road users. They stress the importance of social interactions on the road: how human drivers are capable of coping in traffic with the fellow drivers by communicating and interpreting the subtle gestures in the movements of cars. Traffic, while there are humans involved, is a sociotechnical system.

Full automation and replacement of the human operators at once would be the optimal, although impossible, lowest-risk option in this domain. Those sociotechnical systems where the autonomous systems will be introduced to cooperate with humans at a fast pace or in safety-critical tasks will be the high-risk environments as there are still imperfect human operators involved in the same tasks. In these types of contexts, turbulence in cooperation due to the introduction of autonomous systems in human-operated ecosystems can be expected partly because human operators tend to satisfice [39], whereas autonomous systems may be designed for optimal performance. Furthermore, autonomous systems are often unaware of the limitations and constraints of human behavior and human information processing [32, 50]. This

makes it impossible for them to take these into account in their own behavior and communications.

In the automotive context, the SAE-J3016 [51] levels of vehicle automation of two to four are the challenging ones as the responsibility of driving is not fully on the driver (Levels 0-1) and not fully on the vehicle (Level 5). The shared responsibility on the control of a vehicle can lead to greater problems than giving the whole responsibility for the human (or machine) driver, if the task-relevant information and handovers are not communicated properly within a few seconds' timeframe from the machine to the human and back again. The findings of Itoh et al. [52] in a study on an assistance system for emergency collision avoidance aptly illustrate that the human drivers' choice of direction for an avoidance maneuver can well be different from the one selected by the system. Problems can be expected if the natural human tendencies and decision making processes are not taken into account in the development of these types of assistance systems. This can happen, for instance, when a system makes the decision to steer the vehicle in an emergency situation on the behalf of the driver, while the driver can still override the system by steering to another direction.

Cognitive mimetics could be utilized to solve all of these particular problems, among many other similar interaction problems in different application domains. Lake et al. [32] suggest that perfect autonomous vehicles should have intuitive psychology similar to humans and use this psychological reasoning in order to enable fluent cooperation in traffic with human codrivers. They argue that this kind of reasoning would be especially valuable in unexpected, challenging, and novel driving circumstances for which there is little relevant training data available. These circumstances include, for instance, navigating through highly unstructured construction zones. Another great research question for the near future is how much intelligent technologies require mimicry and understanding of human emotions in order to interact fluently with humans.

In a similar fashion, yet on a more technical level, autonomous vehicles' machine vision systems' classification performance could be improved by incorporating a form of intuitive physics similar to human (as discussed briefly earlier), for improved object recognition in unexpected conditions. These conditions include, for instance, poor visibility or objects disappearing behind other objects and suddenly appearing again. These kinds of anticipation capacities could provide the vehicle with a human-like ability to "see beyond the lead car." Even if the autonomous vehicles already outperform human drivers in a great many ways, people are expecting the autonomous car to rapidly recognize, for example, a tractor-trailer that is pulling in front of the vehicle. This looming effect is something that is immediately recognizable even to a human infant. Even if autonomous vehicles may statistically decrease the overall accident risk, the autonomous vehicle should not perform worse than a human driver in any safety-critical subtask. The exact mechanisms of how AI could be given intuitive psychology and intuitive physics engines similar to humans are still unclear. Yet, as argued, these are important topics of study.

There is still a great need to understand and replicate how humans mentally model situations for solving various AI-interaction problems.

Trafton et al. [50] provide various examples on how ACT-R/E (ACT-R/Embodied) cognitive architecture can be utilized to provide robots with a better understanding of the constraints in human information processing and behavior and, thus, to enable more fluent interactions with their human cooperators. This is a two-way street; the human cooperators could also be made aware of the limitations of machine thinking [53] and maybe to prepare for unexpected behaviors of the robot cooperators. As it is probable that, at least during the early stages of development, an AI system is at most capable of animal-level communication with humans, Phillips et al. [54] have suggested human-animal interactions as an analogy for designing human-robot interactions. This is yet another example of mimicking cognitive behavior found in nature.

5. Conclusions

Design mimetics can be conceptually divided into three levels based on the source of imitation. Firstly, biomimetics focuses on the physical and structural similarity between the source of imitation and the technical solution. Secondly, sensory-motor mimetics pay attention to the sensory-motor processes that can be found in nature for enabling technical solutions for perceptual and motoric tasks. Thirdly, the highest level of design mimetics relates to mimicking the higher cognitive processes of human experts in a task, that is, cognitive mimetics. The three-level conceptual model of design mimetics was introduced in order to clarify the difference between designing, for instance, a neural network (structural mimetics), machine vision (sensory-motor mimetics), and higher decision making processes (cognitive mimetics). All of these can be design goals for an artificially intelligent system but to imitate the structure of human vision system is far from sufficient for reaching a human level of intelligence in recognizing visual objects.

Current AI systems try to mimic intelligent human behavior on limited application areas, but in order to produce AI systems that can adapt to changes and possess generic solutions to unexpected and untrained situations, the processes behind the seemingly intelligent behaviors should better mimic the higher cognitive processes of human experts. For instance, human-to-human communication is full of unexpected and untrained situations. AI systems should manage these at a similar level to humans in order to produce as fluent human-to-AI communications as human-to-human communications as possible. These points are well known in AI literature but our critical point is that we should not stop working towards solving these problems, if we want to achieve AI that is capable of similar general intelligence as human experts are. Instead, we have suggested that more research should be devoted to what we have labeled here as cognitive mimetics.

Here, cognitive mimetics has been introduced as a hypernym for different design approaches using higher (human) cognitive processes as a source of imitation in design. The explication is important in order to make this significant approach for designing intelligent systems visible and better known as a viable path to autonomous systems with artificial general intelligence. We have shown that the approach may enable and complement the development of AI solutions that can efficiently and pleasantly understand, communicate, cooperate, and interact with their fellow human cooperators.

Acknowledgments

The authors want to thank Rebekah Rousi for proofreading the article. The work was partly funded by DIMECC D4Value project.

References

[1] Y. Bar-Cohen, "Biomimetics: Using nature to inspire human innovation," *Bioinspiration & Biomimetics*, vol. 1, pp. 12-10, 2006.

[2] G. Marcus, *Deep Learning: A Critical Appraisal. arXiv preprint*, 2018, arXiv:1801.00631.

[3] L. E. Holmquist, "Intelligence on Tap: Artificial Intelligence as a New Design Material," *Interactions*, vol. 24, no. 4, pp. 28–33, 2017.

[4] J. A. Sloboda, "Musical expertise," in *Toward a General Theory of Expertise: Prospects and Limits*, K. A. Ericsson and J. Smith, Eds., pp. 153–171, Cambridge University Press, 1991.

[5] Y. Bar-Cohen, "Biomimetics, Using nature to inspire human innovation," *Bioinspiration & Biomimetics*, vol. 1, pp. 1–12, 2006.

[6] O. H. Schmitt, "Some interesting and useful biomimetic transforms," in *Proceedings of the 3rd International Biophysics Congress*, vol. 3, Boston, MA, 1969.

[7] J. F. V. Vincent, O. A. Bogatyreva, N. R. Bogatyrev, A. Bowyer, and A.-K. Pahl, "Biomimetics: its practice and theory," *Journal of the Royal Society Interface*, vol. 3, no. 9, pp. 471–482, 2006.

[8] R. A. Jacobs and J. K. Kruschke, "Bayesian learning theory applied to human cognition," *Wiley Interdisciplinary Reviews: Cognitive Science*, vol. 2, no. 1, pp. 8–21, 2011.

[9] W. S. McCulloch and W. Pitts, "A logical calculus of the ideas immanent in nervous activity," *Bulletin of Mathematical Biology*, vol. 5, no. 4, pp. 115–133, 1943.

[10] M. Di Luca, S. Mintchev, G. Heitz, F. Noca, and D. Floreano, "Bioinspired morphing wings for extended flight envelope and roll control of small drones," *Interface Focus*, vol. 7, no. 1, 2017.

[11] P. Ball, "Nature's color tricks.," *Scientific American*, vol. 306, no. 5, pp. 74–79, 2012.

[12] R. R. Ma and A. M. Dollar, "On dexterity and dexterous manipulation," in *Proceedings of the IEEE 15th International Conference on Advanced Robotics: New Boundaries for Robotics, ICAR 2011*, pp. 1–7, Estonia, June 2011.

[13] N. Wiener, *Cybernetics: Control and Communication in the Animal and the Machine*, Wiley, New York, NY, USA, 1948.

[14] Wikipedia, *William Grey Walter*, 2016, https://en.wikipedia.org/wiki/William_Grey_Walter.

[15] M. Wilson, "Six views of embodied cognition," *Psychonomic Bulletin & Review*, vol. 9, no. 4, pp. 625–636, 2002.

[16] U. Neisser, *Cognition and Reality: Principles and Implications of Cognitive Psychology*, WH Freeman/Times Books/Henry Holt & Co, 1976.

[17] A. M. Turing, "Computing machinery and intelligence," *Mind*, vol. 59, no. 49, pp. 433–460, 1950.

[18] A. M. Turing, "On computab le numbers, with an application to the entscheidungsproblem," *Proceedings of the London Mathematical Society*, vol. 42, no. 2, pp. 230–265, 1936.

[19] C. E. Shannon, "A chess-playing machine," *Scientific American*, vol. 182, no. 2, pp. 48–51, 1950.

[20] de Groot, *Thought and Choice in Chess*, The Hague: Mouton, 1965.

[21] A. Newell, J. C. Shaw, and H. A. Simon, "Elements of a theory of human problem solving," *Psychological Review*, vol. 65, no. 3, pp. 151–166, 1958.

[22] A. Newell and H. A. Simon, *Human Problem Solving*, Prentice-Hall, Englewood Cliffs, NJ, 1972.

[23] IBM Systems and Technology, *Watson – A System Designed for Answers: The Future of Workload Optimized Systems Design*, IBM Whitepaper, 2011, http://www-03.ibm.com/marketing/br/watson/what-is-watson/a-system-designed-for-answers.html.

[24] D. Silver, A. Huang, C. J. Maddison et al., "Mastering the game of Go with deep neural networks and tree search," *Nature*, vol. 529, no. 7587, pp. 484–489, 2016.

[25] J. McCarthy, *Programs with Common Sense*, National Physical Laboratory Teddington, UK, 1958.

[26] S. Russell and P. Norvig, *Artificial Intelligence: A Modern Approach*, Prentice-Hall, Englewood Cliffs, NJ, 1995.

[27] D. O. Hebb, *The Organization of Behavior: A Neuropsychological Theory*, New York: Pub, 1949.

[28] F. Rosenblatt, "The Perceptron: A probabilistic model for information storage and retrieval in the brain," *Psychological Review*, vol. 65, pp. 386–407, 1956.

[29] J. E. Laird, *The SOAR Cognitive Architecture*, MIT Press, 2012.

[30] J. E. Laird, A. Newell, and P. S. Rosenbloom, "SOAR: An architecture for general intelligence," *Artificial Intelligence*, vol. 33, no. 1, pp. 1–64, 1987.

[31] J. R. Anderson, D. Bothell, M. D. Byrne, S. Douglass, C. Lebiere, and Y. Qin, "An integrated theory of the mind," *Psychological Review*, vol. 111, no. 4, pp. 1036–1060, 2004.

[32] B. M. Lake, T. D. Ullman, J. B. Tenenbaum, and S. J. Gershman, "Building machines that learn and think like people," *Behavioral and Brain Sciences*, vol. 40, 2017.

[33] C. Gillett, "The metaphysics of realization, multiple realization and the special sciences," *Journal of Philosophy*, vol. 100, pp. 591–603, 2003, http://www.jstor.org/stable/3655746.

[34] G. Marcus, *Innateness, AlphaZero, and Artificial Intelligence*, 2018, arXiv:1801.05667.

[35] K. W. Strabala, M. K. Lee, A. D. Dragan et al., "Towards Seamless Human-Robot Handovers," *Journal of Human-Robot Interaction*, vol. 2, no. 1, pp. 112–132, 2013.

[36] M. C. Dorneich, E. Letsu-Dake, S. Singh, S. Scherer, L. Chamberlain, and M. Bergerman, "Mixed-Initiative Control of a Roadable Air Vehicle for Non-Pilots," *Journal of Human-Robot Interaction*, vol. 4, no. 3, p. 38, 2015.

[37] H. Soh and Y. Demiris, "Learning Assistance by Demonstration: Smart Mobility With Shared Control and Paired Haptic Controllers," *Journal of Human-Robot Interaction*, vol. 4, no. 3, p. 76, 2015.

[38] A. M. Andrew, " Reinforcement Learning:983Richard S. Sutton, Andrew G. Barto. ," *Kybernetes*, vol. 27, no. 9, pp. 1093–1096, 1998.

[39] H. A. Simon, "Theories of bounded rationality," in *Decision and Organization*, B. McGuire and R. Radner, Eds., vol. 12, pp. 161–176, North-Holland, Amsterdam, 1972.

[40] D. Silver, J. Schrittwieser, K. Simonyan et al., "Mastering the game of Go without human knowledge," *Nature*, vol. 550, no. 7676, pp. 354–359, 2017.

[41] A. Clark, "Whatever next? Predictive brains, situated agents, and the future of cognitive science," *Behavioral and Brain Sciences*, vol. 36, no. 3, pp. 181–204, 2013.

[42] D. Hofstadter and E. Sander, *Surfaces and Essences: Analogy as the Fuel and Fire of Thinking*, Basic Books, 2013.

[43] G. A. Miller, "The cognitive revolution: A historical perspective," *Trends in Cognitive Sciences*, vol. 7, no. 3, pp. 141–144, 2003.

[44] M. A. Boden, *Artificial Intelligence and Natural Man*, Basic Books, 1977.

[45] P. Saariluoma and M. Rauterberg, "Turing test does not work in theory but in practice," in *Proceedings of the International Conference on Artificial Intelligence (ICAI'15)*, pp. 433–437, WorldComp, 2015.

[46] J. R. Searle, "Minds, brains, and programs," *Behavioral and Brain Sciences*, vol. 3, no. 3, pp. 417–424, 1980.

[47] S. Cass, *Unthinking Machines*, 2011, https://www.technologyreview.com/s/423917/unthinking-machines/.

[48] M. Sivak and B. Schoettle, "Should We Require Licensing Tests and Graduated Licensing for Self-Driving Vehicles?" Report No. UMTRI-2015-33, UMTRI, 2015.

[49] B. Brown and E. Laurier, "The Trouble with Autopilots," in *Proceedings of the the 2017 CHI Conference*, pp. 416–429, Denver, Colorado, USA, May 2017.

[50] G. Trafton, L. Hiatt, A. Harrison, F. Tanborello, S. Khemlani, and A. Schultz, "ACT-R/E: an embodied cognitive architecture for human-robot interaction," *Journal of Human-Robot Interaction*, vol. 2, no. 1, pp. 30–55, 2013.

[51] Society of Automotive Engineers, *Taxonomy And Definitions For Terms Related To On-Road Motor Vehicle Automated Driving Systems (SAE J3016)*, SAE, 2014.

[52] M. Itoh, H. Tanaka, and T. Inagaki, "Toward Trustworthy Haptic Assistance System for Emergency Avoidance of Collision with Pedestrian," *Journal of Human-Robot Interaction*, vol. 4, no. 3, p. 4, 2015.

[53] D. Levin, C. Harriott, N. A. Paul, T. Zheng, and J. A. Adams, "Cognitive Dissonance as a Measure of Reactions to Human-Robot Interaction," *Journal of Human-Robot Interaction*, vol. 2, no. 3, 2013.

[54] E. K. Phillips, K. Schaefer, D. R. Billings, F. Jentsch, and P. A. Hancock, "Human-Animal Teams as an Analog for Future Human-Robot Teams: Influencing Design and Fostering Trust," *Journal of Human-Robot Interaction*, vol. 5, no. 1, p. 100, 2016.

13

Emergentist View on Generative Narrative Cognition: Considering Principles of the Self-Organization of Mental Stories

Taisuke Akimoto (iD)

Graduate School of Computer Science and Systems Engineering, Kyushu Institute of Technology, 680-4 Kawazu, Iizuka, Fukuoka 820-8502, Japan

Correspondence should be addressed to Taisuke Akimoto; akimoto@ai.kyutech.ac.jp

Guest Editor: Akinori Abe

We consider the essence of human intelligence to be the ability to mentally (internally) construct a world in the form of stories through interactions with external environments. Understanding the principles of this mechanism is vital for realizing a human-like and autonomous artificial intelligence, but there are extremely complex problems involved. From this perspective, we propose a conceptual-level theory for the computational modeling of generative narrative cognition. Our basic idea can be described as follows: stories are representational elements forming an agent's mental world and are also living objects that have the power of self-organization. In this study, we develop this idea by discussing the complexities of the internal structure of a story and the organizational structure of a mental world. In particular, we classify the principles of the self-organization of a mental world into five types of generative actions, i.e., connective, hierarchical, contextual, gathering, and adaptive. An integrative cognition is explained with these generative actions in the form of a distributed multiagent system of stories.

1. Introduction

The computational modeling of an autonomous intelligence that can adapt to external environments (physical and social situations including other humans) is an essential issue for realizing human-like artificial intelligences. In cognitive architecture studies, computational frameworks of autonomous intelligence have been explored with biological inspirations, including psychology and neuroscience [1, 2]. In the early years of artificial intelligence, Schank and his colleagues argued the importance of narrative ability and narrativity-based memory in higher-level cognition and learning. They proposed several significant theories, including script knowledge [3] and a dynamic memory framework [4]. His dynamic memory framework demonstrated a systematic cognitive mechanism of flexible reminding (remembering), reconstruction, generalization, and organization of story-form memories. Although a large part of his idea was not implemented, it provided an important insight into the autonomous development of intelligence.

Based on the above background, we assume that generative narrative cognition is an essential aspect of an autonomous intelligence, which develops through interactions with external environments. Here, generative narrative cognition refers to an agent's mental system of dynamically generating and organizing stories for interacting and adapting to environments. In this study, we use the term "story" to refer to a mental representation of a part of the world of an agent. It is used as a concept unifying episodic memories, autobiographical memories, the contextual structures of current situations, prospective memories, planned or imagined futures, and fictive or virtual stories. On the contrary, a narrative expressed through language or other media of expression is referred to as a "narrative" or a "discourse."

We can state several reasons for the importance of generative narrative cognition in cognitive architectures. First, a story is a universal information format that integrates various informational elements, including events, entities, relationships, abstract concepts, intents, goals, emotions, nonverbal information (e.g., memories of visual images), and hypothetical events. Second, a narrative is a universal way of communicating world information with others. Third, a story forms the contextual structure of an unfolding situation involving temporal reach into the past (i.e., experiences and results of one's actions) and future (i.e., expectations and plans). In this sense, a story is the basis of a higher-level perception-action system. Fourth, memories of past experiences become reusable knowledge when they are organized as stories. Moreover, the importance of narrative ability in cognitive architectures, artificial agents, and human-computer interaction has been discussed from various perspectives [5–8].

However, the computational modeling of generative narrative cognition is an extremely complex problem that has challenged researchers for many years in artificial intelligence studies [9, 10]. Although most previous narrative generation systems have focused on the production of narrative texts such as fairy tales and literary narratives, the basic problem is common: using generative narrative cognition as the foundation of an agent's mind. There exist several difficult problems in the computational modeling of generative narrative cognition. In particular, a story or a narrative has a complex structure, and human narrative cognition is based on a vast store of experiential knowledge, including informal, tacit, and cultural knowledge. Such a complex problem is difficult to model on the basis of classical symbolic processing. Although connectionist models including deep neural networks are applied to various domains including image-recognition systems and end-to-end natural language processing systems, this type of approach does not fit the essential part of generative narrative cognition. The critical issue of generative narrative cognition is to explore a computational framework and the underlying principles of the generation and organization of stories in the mental system of an agent. Therefore, we must seek an alternative method from a long-term perspective.

In this paper, we propose a conceptual-level theory for the computational modeling of generative narrative cognition based on a type of emergentist approach. Our basic idea can be described as follows: stories are living objects having the power of self-organization. This is similar to a multiagent system. Here, an agent is not a character, but a representational element in an agent's mental system. For example, in Minsky's *The Society of Mind* [11], the cognitive mechanism of a mind is explained as a type of distributed multiagent system based on the collaborative activities of diverse simple functional agents. However, we assume that the central agents forming a mind are stories.

The rest of this paper is organized as follows. Sections 2 and 3 describe the basic idea of how generative narrative cognition plays a crucial role in an autonomous intelligence. Section 4 discusses the necessity of an emergentist approach for the computational modeling of generative narrative cognition. Based on this idea, Section 5 provides a macroscopic classification of the principles of the self-organization of a story and a mental world formed by many stories. Section 6 contains concluding remarks with future research directions. Although this paper provides only conceptual descriptions, creating a vision for solving this complex problem (generative narrative cognition) is a significant step for the future of artificial intelligence.

2. Stories Forming an Agent's Mental World

The motivation behind this study is based on an assumption that generative narrative cognition is an essential aspect of an autonomous artificial intelligence. From this perspective, we have been addressing the conceptual systematization of a cognitive architecture. The initial concept is presented in [12]. The key concept of our architecture is an agent's mental world formed as an organization of many stories.

2.1. Story. In general terms, a story refers to the information of chronologically and semantically organized events recounted in a narrative. Here, an event refers to a character's action or a happening (e.g., "Taro eats an apple").

The notion of story is rooted in narratological terminologies (narratology is the discipline of theoretical studies on narrative, inspired by structuralism and semiology). In terms of narratology, a "narrative" basically refers to an expression of events in a real or fictional world based on a language or other sign system [13]. However, a narrative has a close relationship with the form of mental representation of knowledge and memory. To clearly distinguish the representational aspect from an expressed narrative, we introduce the notions of story and discourse based on a reinterpretation of narratological terminology [13, 14]. The terms "story" and "discourse" are generally used to distinguish between the content and expression planes of a narrative. More precisely, a discourse refers to the narrative text itself and a story corresponds to the content, i.e., information of events recounted in a discourse or a text. However, because a story is intangible, the notion of stories is slightly unclear. From a narrative-communication perspective, the relationship between the content and expression planes of a narrative can be reinterpreted as the relationship between a mental representation and the surface expression. A sender (author or teller) writes or tells a discourse based on a story that is remembered or generated inside the mind. A receiver (reader or hearer) mentally constructs a story by interpreting or comprehending the discourse. Stories between the sender and the receiver are not the same objects.

Based on the above conception, we use the term "story" as a uniform mental representation involving an episodic memory, an autobiographical memory, the contextual structure of a current situation, a prospective memory, a planned or imagined future, and a fictional or virtual story.

2.2. Mental World. An agent's mental world contains individual meaning and a rich temporal extent with numerous and diverse stories, as illustrated in Figure 1. A story corresponds to a piece of the world for an agent. Stories contained in a mental world can be classified from several perspectives. In the relationship with an external world, these stories include past, future, and fictive or hypothetical stories. With respect to the manner of generation, there are stories based on an agent's own experiences (experience-based stories),

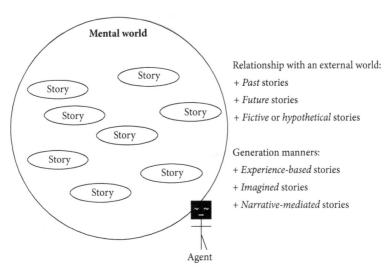

Relationship with an external world:

+ *Past* stories

+ *Future* stories

+ *Fictive* or *hypothetical* stories

Generation manners:

+ *Experience-based* stories

+ *Imagined* stories

+ *Narrative-mediated* stories

Agent

FIGURE 1: An agent's mental world formed by stories.

imaginative power (imagined stories), and interpretation or comprehension of others' narratives (narrative-mediated stories). A more systematic description of structural properties and functions of an agent's mental story are presented in our previous study [15].

From a perspective of computational knowledge representation, a story itself forms only a relational structure of concrete events and entities. However, we assume that the semantic aspect of a story is underpinned by associations with the following three types of mental elements:

(i) **Concept:** a concept corresponds to a primitive linguistic element corresponding to meanings of a word. Concepts include general concepts (i.e., nominal, verbal, adjectival, and adverbial concepts) and ontological (or proper) concepts for identical entities.

(ii) **Schema:** a schema refers to a generalized structure based on one or more concrete stories. A schema is a structured composition of two or more concepts or (sub)schemas. Schemas underpin topdown and abstract-level cognitions of stories. The idea of schemas is rooted in Minsky's frame theory [16]. Script knowledge [3] and memory organization packets (MOPs) [4] form the schematic knowledge relevant to narrative cognition.

(iii) **Mental image:** a mental image represents nonsymbolic information, including verbal, visual, auditory, and haptic images.

3. Dynamic Generation and Organization of Mental Stories

How generative narrative cognition plays an essential role in an agent's intelligence can be explained from its functional generality. In particular, generative narrative cognition forms the common basis of a higher-level perception-action system, linguistic communication about world information, and formation of a self or identity. We will describe the first

two aspects later in this section. The thoughts behind the third aspect (formation of a self or identity) can be found in philosophy, psychology, or other disciplines [17–19].

In an autonomous intelligence, dynamic generation and organization of stories includes two aspects, i.e., (1) interaction with an environment by generating a story and (2) adaptation to environments by developing the organizational structure of a mental world. Figure 2 illustrates these two aspects, and we will describe each aspect in the following two subsections. Here, assumed environments include various social and physical situations over the course of an agent's activities, e.g., shopping at a supermarket, climbing a mountain, linguistic communication with others, housework, and creation of literary work.

3.1. Interaction with an Environment by Generating a Story. An agent interacts with an environment based on a story. This idea is rooted in our previous consideration of the structure of an agent's subjective world while interacting with an environment [15]. A story for interacting with an environment can be explained through the following two perspectives:

(i) **Action and perception:** in an agent's mind, interaction with an environment is based on the continual (re)construction of a story (see Figure 3(a)). In particular, acting in an environment corresponds to performing mentally constructed events placed in the future. Perceiving the movement of an environment, including the results of one's actions, corresponds to the construction of past episodic events. Both actions and perceptions always occur in the context of a story, i.e., a chain of events across the past (experiences and results) and future (expectations and plans).

(ii) **Expression and interpretation (linguistic communication):** a narrative is the universal way of exchanging world information, and story generation is the core mental process in this activity (see Figure 3(b)).

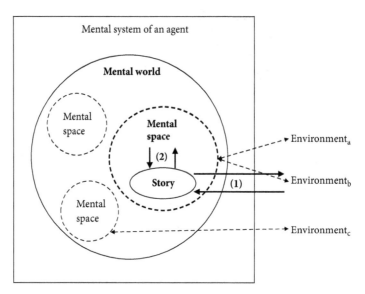

FIGURE 2: Two dynamic aspects of a mental world: (1) the generation of a story and (2) development of the organizational structure of a mental world.

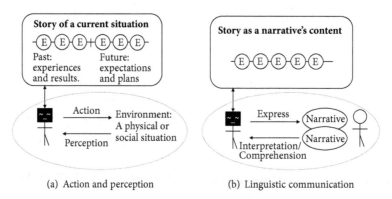

(a) Action and perception   (b) Linguistic communication

FIGURE 3: Action/perception and linguistic communication based on a story.

When an agent expresses a narrative to others, a story for the source of the narrative is remembered or imagined in the mind. The mental process of recalling includes not only memory retrieval but also flexible editing of memories (stories) according to the situation or goal of the narrative communication. On the contrary, the fundamental mental process of interpreting or comprehending another's narrative is to compose a mental story over the course of hearing/reading it.

It is also important that generative narrative cognition integrates the above two fundamental human activities. A human develops mental stories in various ways, e.g., the organization of one's own experiences, imagination, and the reception of various narratives. The acquisition of stories from narratives has great significance in constructing rich world knowledge beyond one's own experiences and imaginative power. In addition, humans cocreate world knowledge by communicating narratives, such as the histories and current states of societies and visions for the future.

3.2. Adaptation to Environments by Developing a Mental World. A mental world is a holistic memory system that provides knowledge resources for generating new stories. At the same time, a mental world organizes the pieces required to direct the dynamic generation of stories in various environments. The cognitive mechanism of the autonomous development of a mental world through the accumulation of experiences is the foundation of an environmental adaptability, i.e., the potential to build abilities to generate adequate stories in various environments.

The developmental process of a mental world is conceptualized as the formation of a "mental space," which is the basic organizational unit of a mental world. This concept is inspired by Schank's dynamic memory framework [4]. In general terms, a mental space corresponds to a generalized structure of similar stories. The basic role of a mental space is to provide a framework that directs and restricts story generation for smoothly interacting with similar type of environments, e.g., shopping in a supermarket and communication about a specific theme (politics, local events, etc.). In addition, a mental space organizes memories of experiences,

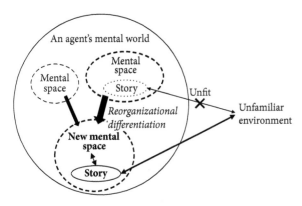

FIGURE 4: Reorganizational differentiation of a mental space.

i.e., previously generated stories in that space, as knowledge resources for generating a new story in a similar situation.

The framework of a mental space is formed by a schema, i.e., a general structure covering similar type of stories. In particular, the schema of a mental space provides a thematic and stylistic framework based on a compound of multiple subschemas. A schema adaptively forms or reforms by the generalization of stories and reorganization of existing schemas. When an agent is facing a relatively familiar environment, a story is generated in an existing mental space corresponding to that environment. The schema of this space may be adjusted or reformed according to a generated story (i.e., experience). Moreover, when an agent is facing an unfamiliar environment, the agent's mental system tries to adapt to that environment by reorganizing one or more existing schemas to create a story with a new mental space (see Figure 4). We call this specific mental process of adapting to a new environment "reorganizational differentiation." (This notion is similar to abduction in C. S. Perce's theory.)

4. Necessity of an Emergentist Approach to Generative Narrative Cognition

Computationally implementing a dynamic mental world described in the previous section is a hugely complex problem. For solving this problem, we argue the necessity of an emergentist approach.

4.1. Structural Complexity of a Story. The necessity of an emergentist approach can be described from the following two perspectives:

First, from a cognitive perspective, the developmental process of a mental world (or a memory system in general terms) is generally assumed as a type of self-organization phenomenon. The ability to build diverse mental spaces with new intellectual functions is a key aspect of a dynamic mental world. These functions should not be externally embedded but emerge through adaptive interactions with environments.

The second reason refers to the structural complexity of a story itself. A story as a world representation can be viewed as a complex structural object in which events (a character's action or a happening) and entities (an individual existence including a character, object, and place) are organically organized. Although the central elements of a story are events, these events are potentially accompanied by various types of informational elements, e.g., relationships, abstract concepts, intents, goals, emotions, nonverbal information, and hypothetical events. Because of this property, it is assumed that the cognitive process of story generation is based on a flexible collaboration of multiple cognitive modules. In addition, the structure of a story involves interdependencies in the whole-part and part-part relationships. In a well-organized story, for example, a small change in a story's part may cause incoherence in the story's whole structure or the lack of contextual coherence over the course of its events. Based on an extensional reinterpretation of our hierarchical graph model of multidimensional narrative structure [20] and a structural conception of an agent's subjective world [15], we arrange general structural properties of a story as follows (Figure 5 illustrates these notions):

(a) A story has a hierarchical whole-part structure. A higher-level part (e.g., a scene, a semantic or functional unit, and a larger section) of a story is formed from two or more lower-level parts (e.g., events and scenes).

(b) Parts of a story (including events) are mutually connected by temporal, causal, or other types of relationships.

(c) There are two types of interdependencies in a story's hierarchical structure: (1) vertical interdependencies, including top-down restriction (from a higher-level part to the lower-level parts) and bottom-up abstraction (from lower-level parts to the higher-level part) and (2) horizontal interdependencies based on the contextual coherence between parts.

(d) A story contains a story world, i.e., the organization of entities relevant to the story. It is similar to the setting of the world and there exists an interdependency between a story and the story world.

(e) A story is formed based on the reconstructive reuse of existing mental resources including relationships with other stories. In this sense, a story itself is not an independent mental object.

(f) There exists an interdependency between a story and an external environment. In particular, a story based on one's own experiences is formed based on perceived environmental information. At the same time, the expectational aspect of the agent's story directs or restricts the perception of environmental information.

In the above six items, (e) is derived from the discussion in Section 3.2 and (f) is an ordinary notion from a cognitive perspective. To explain notions (a)–(d), the next subsection uses an example story structure.

4.2. Example Story Structure. Box 1 shows an English expression of a simple story written by the author. An example

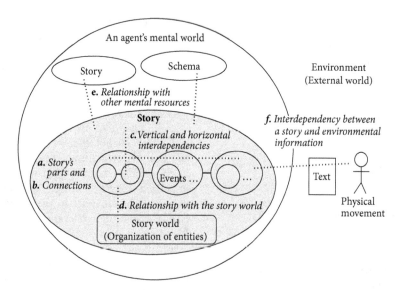

FIGURE 5: Structural complexity of a story. Dot-lines represent interdependencies or relationships among a story's parts and other mental objects.

(s1) Lisa and Sally are sisters that get along well. (s2) They play together every day. (s3) One day, Sally found a chocolate in Lisa's desk when Lisa was not in the room. (s4) Sally stole and ate the chocolate. (s5) The next day, Lisa saw that the chocolate was gone. (s6) Lisa assumed that the chocolate was eaten by Sally. (s7) Then, Lisa threw Sally's doll out a window. (s8) Sally cried.

Box 1: English expression of an example story.

of how the structure of this story text can be interpreted is shown in Figure 6. In this structural representation, each sentence in Box 1 is simply imagined as an event. From the perspectives of (a)–(d) in the above list, we can examine the cognitive processes of creating and manipulating this fictional story.

(i) **Hierarchical structure (a):** this story is divided into three scenes (intermediate parts): the setting (daily life), the stealing by Sally, and the revenging of the theft by Lisa.

(ii) **Relationship between parts (b):** there are anteroposterior and causal relationships between the different parts. The anteroposterior relationships are depicted as arrowed lines. The block arrow from the second scene to the third scene represents the causal relationship, i.e., Lisa's reason or motivation for taking revenge.

(iii) **Vertical interdependency (c):** a change in a part may cause a change in the higher- and/or lower-level parts. For example, when event s4 is changed to "Sally put a cookie beside the chocolate," it will propagate and influence the meaning of the second scene, e.g., "gift to Lisa."

(iv) **Horizontal interdependency (c):** a change in a part also propagates in horizontal directions. For example, when the second scene is changed to "gift to Lisa," the

third scene, "revenging of the theft by Lisa," becomes an unnatural reaction (at least from our common-sense perspective). This inconsistency causes a global reorganization of a story.

(v) **Relationship with the story world (d):** in the structural representation in Figure 6, the story world contains several entities, i.e., Lisa, Sally, a desk, a chocolate, and a doll, and their relationships such as "Lisa and Sally are sisters" and "Lisa and Sally like chocolate." A change in the setting of the world propagates to events or the story's parts. For example, if the setting is changed to a fantasy world (e.g., Lisa is a witch and all children like dried frogs), the chocolate element will become a dried frog and the way Lisa takes revenge will change to become a magical attack.

4.3. Emergentist Approach. In studies of computational narrative generation, an orthodox approach is to model the process of generating a story (or a narrative) based on a centrally controlled symbolic processing (see Figure 7(a)). For example, narrative generation using a story grammar is a traditional story-generation method [21, 22]. The simplest implementation is a pipelined procedure of composing a story using a story grammar in a top-down manner, from the abstract structure to the detailed contents. However, this type of inflexible framework will be limited when

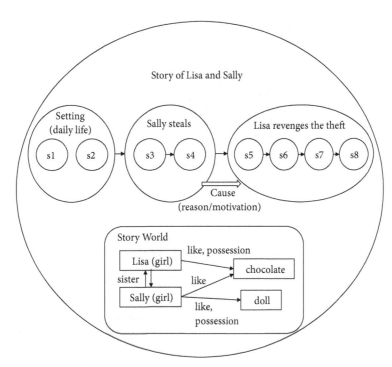

FIGURE 6: A structural representation of the example story in Box 1 (s1–8 in the small circles correspond to sentences in Box 1).

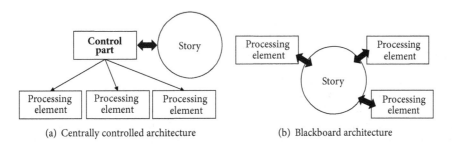

(a) Centrally controlled architecture   (b) Blackboard architecture

FIGURE 7: A centrally controlled architecture and a blackboard architecture.

modeling a complex and dynamic narrative cognition and does not lead to our objective. An advanced challenge is to model narrative generation as a more flexible procedure. For example, a blackboard architecture (see Figure 7(b)) that shares a processing object, i.e., a story, among various types of cognitive modules has the potential of flexible collaboration of cognitive modules in generating a story (e.g., [23]). However, a blackboard architecture requires knowledge of the principles of directing the collaborative cognitive activities, and how to model it remains a difficult problem.

Therefore, we propose an alternative approach as an extension of the blackboard architecture. Our basic idea is to build the power of self-organization into stories and mental spaces themselves. Figure 8 illustrates this concept. Each part at each level in a story structure has the power of generating one's own structure in the relationship with other mental objects. The story's whole structure emerges from distributed collaborative functioning of the parts (see Figure 8a). On the contrary, a mental space forms one's own schema through interactions with stories and other mental spaces (see Figure 8b). We introduce the term "generative actions" to refer to the basic principles of driving these self-organization activities. A mental world is developed by the distributed collaborative functioning of the generative actions of stories and mental spaces.

5. Classification of the Generative Actions of a Story and Mental Space

Based on the above concept, we can classify generative actions in a mental world. According to the structural properties of a story and the notion of a mental space, we can classify generative actions into five basic types: *connective*, *hierarchical*, *contextual*, *gathering*, and *adaptive*. The last type (adaptive) drives the self-organization of a mental space. The first four types, which drive the self-organization of a story, are derived from the structural complexity of a story; this is described in Sections 4.1 and 4.2. In particular, the connective action is relevant to (b) and (c), the hierarchical action is relevant to (a)

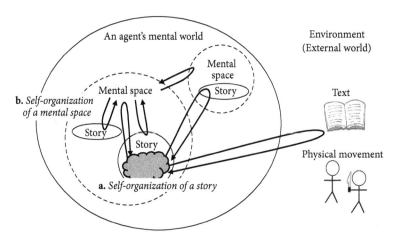

FIGURE 8: Powers of the self-organization in a mental world.

FIGURE 9: Connective actions.

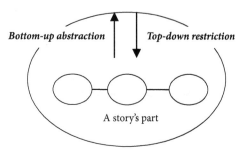

FIGURE 10: Hierarchical actions.

and (c), and the contextual and gathering actions are relevant to (c)–(f).

In the following subsections, the concept and principles of each basic type are presented. The presented principles are basically rooted in general notions of cognitive science and artificial intelligence studies such as abstraction, generalization, analogy, schema, and relationship. However, the main contribution of the following ideas is to provide a conceptual-level theory of an integrative cognition from an emergentist perspective.

5.1. Connective Actions: Relation. A connective action is the most fundamental action of organizing events. The basic principle of making a connection is a relationship between a story's parts. The major relationship types in a story structure are as follows (see also Figure 9):

  (i) **Temporal relationship:** this denotes a relative temporal relationship between two parts. Allen [24] classified temporal relationships between two events or actions into "before," "equal," "meets," "overlaps," "during," "starts," "finishes," and their inverses, on the basis of anteroposterior relationships and temporal intervals of events. This classification can be adopted to temporal relationships in a story.

 (ii) **Causal relationship:** this denotes a causal relationship between any two parts of a story.

(iii) **Other type of relationships:** because the computational modeling of relationships in a story structure or narrative is an essential but complex problem, further

consideration is required. For example, various types of relationships in a discourse structure are proposed in the area of natural language processing, e.g., Hobbs's coherence relations [25] and the rhetorical structure theory by Mann and Thompson [26].

5.2. Hierarchical Actions: Top-Down Restriction and Bottom-Up Abstraction. Hierarchical actions form or reform upper- and lower-level structures in a story. They are the basis of the vertical interdependency between upper- and lower-level parts. Hierarchical actions can be broadly classified into top-down restriction and bottom-up abstraction (see also Figure 10):

  (i) **Top-down restriction:** a higher-level part restricts the lower-level structure by creating the expectation of a blank based on a schema or similar story that is associated with the higher-level part. An expectation refers to the generation of subsequent information in a dynamic story-generation process during interactions with an environment. In particular, an expectation drives the perception of environmental information based on a schema or similar story. A blank denotes a lack of information in the lower-level structure, and it drives the filling of that part using a schema or similar story.

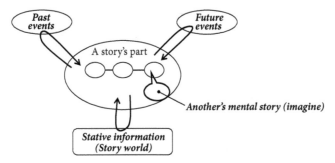

FIGURE 11: Contextual actions.

(ii) **Bottom-up abstraction:** in this action, a higher-level part is formed or reformed from an aggregation of lower-level parts. This type of cognition, which generates higher-level meaning from lower-level elements, is generally referred to as abstraction [27]. In a story, abstractions arise in various structural levels, i.e., temporal segmentation of events from sensory information and the formation of a higher-level meaning from two or more events or parts. Whereas an abstraction is a bottom-up action, it always functions under top-down restriction. In particular, a higher-level structure (the meaning and power of top-down restriction) is formed by matching and reorganizational diversion of associated mental resources, i.e., a schema or another story's part that is similar to the lower-level structure.

5.3. Contextual Actions: Associations of Events and States. Using contextual actions, a part draws contextual information relevant to the organization of one's own structure. These actions generate horizontal interdependency in a story. Contextual actions can be classified into the following subclasses, from the perspective of the position of source information (see also Figure 11):

(i) **Past:** a part draws relevant past events (e.g., the background or reason behind an action by the agent or another character).

(ii) **Future:** a part draws relevant future events (e.g., an intent, desire, objective, and goal for the agent's action).

(iii) **State:** a part draws relevant stative information from the story world (e.g., a character's emotion and whether conditions).

(iv) **Another's mental story:** a part associates another's imagined mental story. This is relevant to the ability to imagine others' mental states, known as the theory of mind. From a structural perspective, an imagined mental story about another person is represented as a nesting of stories ("a story within a story") [15].

5.4. Gathering Actions: Mental Space, Similarity/Analogy, and Perception. Gathering actions gather mental resources externally (memories including stories, schemas, mental images,

and concepts) or environmental information (perception) for generating their own structures of a part. These mental resources are used by other types of generative actions, as materials, general structures, or cases. Gathering actions include the following three subclasses (see also Figure 12):

(i) **Mental space:** a story's part gathers mental resources from the mental space in which the story is generated. As we described in Section 3.2, a mental space organizes relevant knowledge including (sub)schemas and stories for generating stories in similar environments.

(ii) **Similarity/analogy:** similarity or analogy is a key principle for the flexible reuse of existing mental resources across boundaries of mental spaces or problem domains. Particularly, analogy is an essential human cognition for reusing mental resources by making a structural correspondence between two different representational elements [28–30]. Case-based reasoning [31] is also rooted in analogical cognition.

(iii) **Perception:** perception is the action of gathering environmental information. It is basically driven by an expectation as a top-down restriction. When a part gets unexpected information from an environment, reformation of part of the story may be done to maintain coherence.

5.5. Adaptive Actions: Generalization and Differentiation. Adaptive actions form or reform the schema of a mental space to adapt environments. Whereas the above four types are a story's activities, adaptive actions are the activities of a mental space. Adaptive actions can be classified into the following three types (see also Figure 13):

(i) **Inductive generalization:** a mental space forms or reforms one's own schema based on structural commonality among stories in that space. Abstraction of a story (forming a higher-level structure of a story) and analogies between stories (creating structural correspondences between stories) provide the basis for this action.

(ii) **Failure-based generalization:** a mental space adjusts one's own schema according to a failure in interacting with an environment. A failure refers to a type of negative feedback from an environment. A similar concept is discussed in Schank's dynamic memory

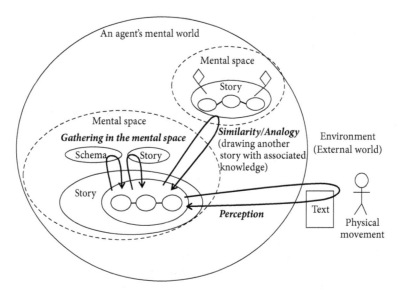

FIGURE 12: Gathering actions.

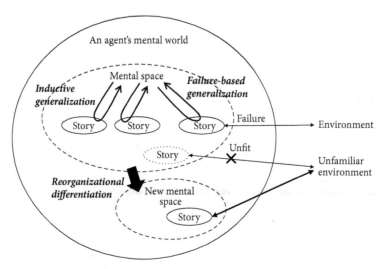

FIGURE 13: Adaptive actions.

framework [4]. It is also relevant to the general notion of reinforcement learning.

(iii) **Reorganizational differentiation:** when an agent faces an unfamiliar environment that existing mental spaces do not cover, a new mental space emerges in the agent's mental world to generate a story for interacting that environment. This new mental space is formed by the reorganization of existing mental spaces or mental resources. We call this mental action reorganizational differentiation. This is the essence of the ability to develop by adapting to environments. At the same time, this is the fundamental principle of creativity, which seeks to construct new ideas, styles, social environments, etc.

5.6. *Integrative View.* As we described previously, the key point of the proposed theory is to integrate various types of

cognition in the form of a distributed multiagent system of story generation. Because this idea reflects a complex system, it is difficult to show a concrete image of the system's holistic behavior until the idea is computationally implemented. However, a simplified image of the integrative operations of various cognitive processes can be seen from the example story presented in Section 4.2.

From an integrative perspective, the following two notions will be the key points for the computational implementation of this theory:

(i) The main agent of the system is an "event" (in a broad sense) formed at various levels of abstraction, e.g., a character's action (Lisa threw away Sally's doll), a scene or a semantic segment of actions (Lisa took revenge on Sally), and the story itself.

(ii) Because the connection between agents, i.e., events or stories, is a foundation of various generative actions—

connective, contextual, gathering, and adaptive—and the integrated operations of these generative actions, the agents must be associated with each other.

6. Concluding Remarks

We proposed a new approach for the computational modeling of an autonomous intelligence based on generative narrative cognition. Throughout this paper, we conceptualized the developmental and generative process of an agent's mind as a type of self-organization on both levels: the organizational structure of a mental world and the internal structure of a story. Under this concept, as the principles of the self-organization of a mental world, we presented five types of generative actions: connective, hierarchical, contextual, gathering, and adaptive actions. Although the mechanisms of these generative actions are still abstract and implementing the proposed concept remains a distant goal, we showed the total picture of a mental system using the above concept.

The basic direction of future work will be to develop a theory of integrating generative actions in the form of a multiagent system. Agents of generative actions (in the mental system of an artificial agent) are stories and mental spaces. Although we listed many generative actions in Section 5, there are several key issues relevant to a wide array of mental activities. For example, similarity or analogy of stories is a common principle of reusing existing mental resources in various types of generative actions such as gathering actions, top-down restriction, inductive generalization, and reorganizational differentiation. Moreover, in terms of knowledge representation, how a story represents the integrated world information in an agent's mind is still unclear. The structure of a story itself, including relationships with other mental elements, needs to be considered more closely.

Acknowledgments

This work was supported by JSPS KAKENHI Grant Number JP18K18344 and The Telecommunications Advancement Foundation.

References

[1] B. Goertzel, R. Lian, I. Arel, H. de Garis, and S. Chen, "A world survey of artificial brain projects, Part II: Biologically inspired cognitive architectures," *Neurocomputing*, vol. 74, no. 1-3, pp. 30–49, 2010.

[2] A. V. Samsonovich, "On a roadmap for the BICA challenge," *Biologically Inspired Cognitive Architectures*, vol. 1, pp. 100–107, 2012.

[3] R. C. Schank and R. P. Abelson, *Scripts, Plans, Goals, and Understanding: An Inquiry into Human Knowledge Structures*, Lawrence Erlbaum, 1977.

[4] R. C. Schank, *Dynamic Memory: A Theory of Reminding and Learning in Computers and People*, Cambridge University Press, 1982.

[5] P. Sengers, "Schizophrenia and narrative in artificial agents," in *Narrative Intelligence*, M. Mateas and P. Sengers, Eds., pp. 259–278, John Benjamins Publishing, 2003.

[6] N. Szilas, "Towards narrative-based knowledge representation in cognitive systems," in *Proceedings of 6th Workshop on Computational Models of Narrative*, pp. 133–141, 2015.

[7] C. León, "An architecture of narrative memory," *Biologically Inspired Cognitive Architectures*, vol. 16, pp. 19–33, 2016.

[8] J. de Greeff, B. Hayes, M. Gombolay et al., "Workshop on Longitudinal Human-Robot Teaming," in *Proceedings of the Companion of the 2018 ACM/IEEE International Conference*, pp. 389-390, Chicago, IL, USA, March 2018.

[9] P. Gervás, "Computational approaches to storytelling and creativity," *AI Magazine*, vol. 30, no. 3, pp. 49–62, 2009.

[10] B. Kybartas and R. Bidarra, "A survey on story generation techniques for authoring computational narratives," *IEEE Transactions on Computational Intelligence and AI in Games*, vol. 9, no. 3, pp. 239–253, 2017.

[11] M. Minsky, *The Society of Mind*, Simon & Schuster, 1986.

[12] T. Akimoto, "Narratives of an artificial agent," in *Content Generation Through Narrative Communication and Simulation*, Advances in Linguistics and Communication Studies, pp. 241–264, IGI Global, 2018.

[13] G. Prince, *A Dictionary of Narratology, Revised Edition*, University of Nebraska Press, 2003.

[14] G. Genette, *Narrative Discourse: An Essay in Method*, Cornell University Press, 1980, J. E. Lewin Trans.

[15] T. Akimoto, "Stories as mental representations of an agent's subjective world: A structural overview," *Biologically Inspired Cognitive Architectures*, vol. 25, pp. 107–112, 2018.

[16] M. Minsky, "A framework for representing knowledge," *The Psychology of Computer Vision*, pp. 211–277, 1975.

[17] P. Ricoeur, *Temps et Récit (Tome I–III)*, Seuil, 1983–1985.

[18] J. S. Bruner, *Acts of Meaning*, Harvard University Press, 1990.

[19] D. P. McAdams, *The Stories We Live by: Personal Myths and the Making of the Self*, The Guilford Press, 1993.

[20] T. Akimoto, "Computational modeling of narrative structure: A hierarchical graph model for multidimensional narrative structure," *International Journal of Computational Linguistics Research*, vol. 8, no. 3, pp. 92–108, 2017.

[21] R. R. Lang, "A declarative model for simple narratives," Narrative Intelligence: Papers from the 1999 AAAI Fall Symposium FS-99-01, 1999.

[22] S. Bringsjord and D. A. Ferrucci, *Artificial Intelligence and Literary Creativity: Inside the Mind of BRUTUS, a Storytelling Machine*, Lawrence Erlbaum, 1999.

[23] N. Montfort, R. Pérez y Pérez, D. F. Harrell, and A. Campana, "Slant: A blackboard system to generate plot, figuration, and narrative discourse aspects of stories," in *Proceedings of the Fourth International Conference on Computational Creativity*, pp. 168–175, 2013.

[24] J. F. Allen, "Towards a general theory of action and time," *Artificial Intelligence*, vol. 23, no. 2, pp. 123–154, 1984.

[25] J. R. Hobbs, "Literature and Cognition," *CSLI Lecture Notes*, no. 21, 1990.

[26] W. C. Mann and S. A. Thompson, "Rhetorical Structure Theory: Toward a functional theory of text organization," *Text*, vol. 8, no. 3, pp. 243–281, 1988.

[27] J.-D. Zucker, "A grounded theory of abstraction in artificial intelligence," *Philosophical Transactions of the Royal Society B: Biological Sciences*, vol. 358, no. 1435, pp. 1293–1309, 2003.

[28] D. Gentner, "Structure-mapping: A theoretical framework for analogy," *Cognitive Science*, vol. 7, no. 2, pp. 155–170, 1983.

[29] D. Gentner and K. D. Forbus, "Computational models of analogy," *Wiley Interdisciplinary Reviews: Cognitive Science*, vol. 2, no. 3, pp. 266–276, 2011.

[30] K. J. Holyoak and P. Thagard, *Mental Leaps: Analogy in Creative Thought*, MIT Press, 1995.

[31] C. K. Riesbeck and R. C. Schank, *Inside Case-Based Reasoning*, Lawrence Erlbaum, 1989.

14

Developers as Users: Exploring the Experiences of using a New Theoretical Method for Usability Assessment

Lars-Ola Bligård, Helena Strömberg, and MariAnne Karlsson

Chalmers University of Technology, 412 96 Gothenburg, Sweden

Correspondence should be addressed to Lars-Ola Bligård; lars-ola.bligard@chalmers.se

Academic Editor: Jean Vanderdonckt

There is a need for appropriate evaluation methods to efficiently identify and counteract usability issues early in the development process. The aim of this study was to investigate how product developers assessed a new theoretical method for identifying usability problems and use errors. Two cases where the method had been applied were selected and the users of the method in them were asked to fill in a questionnaire and were then interviewed about their experiences of using the method. Overall, the participants (students and professionals) found the methods useful and their outcome trustworthy. At the same time, the methods were assessed as difficult to learn and as cumbersome and tedious to use. Nevertheless, both students and professionals thought that the methods would be useful in future development work. Suggestions for further improvement included provision of further instructions, for example, on how to adapt the methods and development of an IT-support tool.

1. Introduction

For most products, from simple artefacts to complex technical systems, safe and easy handling is essential. Therefore products need to be designed with a high level of usability [1]. A step towards creating products that are safe and easy to use is to try to identify and counteract mismatches in the interaction between users and products as early as possible in the development process, long before the product is to be used in a real use situation. The earlier in the process that problems can be detected, the better the possibilities to adjust the design [2, 3].

To be able to identify and counteract possible usability issues, there is thus a need for usability evaluation methods that can be applied early in the development process. A number of methods have been developed for this specific purpose, including theoretical or expert-based methods such as heuristic evaluation, link analysis, cognitive task analysis, and cognitive walkthrough [4–8]. In addition to being applicable early in the development process, theoretical or expert-based methods hold additional benefits compared to user-based methods including that they may be performed without first-hand access to users and that they require less time and effort (e.g., [9]).

However, the benefits can only be experienced if developers in actual development work use the methods. Knowledge on the dissemination of theoretical and expert-based methods in industry appears scarce. Nielsen (as one exception) completed one investigation in 1992, in which the participants in a course on usability inspection methods were surveyed 7-8 months after the course to find whether they used the methods they had been taught, why or why not, as well as which methods they in fact used [10]. According to the survey results, methods such as cognitive walkthrough were considered less useful and were used less than usability testing. In a more recent study Jerome and Kazman [11] found that even though approximately one-fourth of the tools used were cognitive walkthroughs, *"... the application and adoption of methods and processes from SE [Software Engineering] and HCI [Human-Computer Interaction] research has not yet trickled down into industry"* and further that *"HCI methods are being used far too late in the life cycle to be truly cost and time efficient."* There thus appears to be a need to further investigate how to increase the dissemination of such methods.

One way to facilitate the dissemination and adoption of these methods is to consider the methods as a "product" and apply user-centred design principles to the method development. One basic principle of user-centred design is to involve the end-users of a product in the development process. To consider the product developers as the end-users of a particular method and to elicit how these users perceive the method are consequently important in method development but this is most often not the case [12, 13]. One important keystone for a successful method development is therefore to evaluate the new method with the intended end-users. The efficiency of a usability method is obviously important, but the effectiveness and satisfaction are as important. If the developers cannot use the method or if they do not, for some reason or other, like the method, the likelihood that the new method will be used decreases. To investigate how users experience the use of a method is hence a significant activity in method development.

2. Aim and Scope

This paper presents a study comprising two cases where product developers (students and professionals) evaluated a combination of two recently developed theoretical methods: Enhanced Cognitive Walkthrough (ECW, [14]) and Predictive Use Error Analysis (PUEA, [15]). Both methods have primarily been used by their developers in development projects in order to identify usability problems and use errors [16–20] and in some documented cases the methods have been used by other people than the developers, for instance, by Moradi and Pour [21] and by Westerlund et al. [22]. In these cases, the methods have performed well and have provided useful knowledge for the improvement of, for example, medical equipment. However, there is further need to study whether the methods are able to perform equally well for other users than its developers.

The specific aim of the study presented here was to investigate how product developers assess the methods from a usability point of view, what strengths and weaknesses they see, how inclined they are to use the methods in future development work, and what their suggestions for improvements are.

3. Description of the Evaluated Method

The method evaluated in the two cases was a combination of Enhanced Cognitive Walkthrough (ECW) and Predictive Use Error Analysis (PUEA). ECW and PUEA are two submethods designed to be applied together in the methodological framework of CCPE (Combined Cognitive and Physical Evaluation). The CCPE framework consists of four phases: (1) definition of evaluation, (2) description of the human-machine system, (3) interaction analysis (with usability problem analysis and use error analysis), and (4) presentation. ECW and PUEA are used in the interaction analysis phase: ECW for the usability problem analysis and PUEA for the use error analysis. A more detailed description of the procedures is given in the following subsections.

The rationale for the development of the respective methods was to improve existing human factors engineering methods to create a methodology that integrates evaluation of use error and usability problems. Both ECW and PUEA have an analytical approach as they are performed by one or more analysts with support from theoretical models, such as explorative learning [23], the Skill, Rule and Knowledge-model [24], and Generic Error Modelling System [25]. The method is applied early in the development process, for instance, on a low fidelity prototype, with the intention that this should allow for the method to be used proactively and for the developers to detect and counteract usability problems and use errors before they are realized in the design of the product.

The method can be used by a single analyst or by a group of analysts. The group may consist of designers, engineers, human factors experts, and users. The most important factor when putting together the group is that the participating individuals have knowledge of who the users are, as well as the product(s) and its intended use.

The innovative features of the method are considered to be (1) the integrated analysis of usability problems and use error, describing the causes of identified mismatches in the interaction and the effects of the mismatch in the interaction, respectively, (2) the analysis on both a functional and an operational level, (3) the grading and categorisation in the analysis, and (4) the presentation of the result in the form of a matrix. The argued benefits are that the analysis becomes more comprehensive and coherent compared to the former methods.

The validity of the ECW/PUEA has been evaluated in a study by Bligård and Osvalder [26]. The study investigated how well the results from ECW and PUEA matched the results from usability tests on a vacuum cleaner and an office chair, respectively. The conclusions from the study were that ECW/PUEA worked well in finding usability problems (91%) and use errors (59%) compared to problems and errors identified with usability testing. The method also delivered the intended result (presumptive usability problems and use errors) to be a valuable tool for use in a product development process, especially in the early stages, before more extensive empirical evaluations are performed.

3.1. The Definition of Evaluation and Description of the Human-Machine System Phases. The first phase, *definition of evaluation*, establishes the boundaries for the analysis by stating the product, the intended user, use and use context. In the *description phase*, the human-machine system to be evaluated is specified. This includes a specification and a detailed description of the task, the user, the use situation, and the user interface of the product (i.e., "the machine"). The tasks are described using Hierarchical Task Analyses (HTA) [27]. The description phase is considered to have large impact on the quality of the result since the next step, the *analysis phase*, depends upon a correct and exhaustive description of the user, the situation, and the task.

3.2. Interaction Analysis. In the analysis phase, the interaction between the user and the product is evaluated by applying a detailed question process. The evaluation takes place both on a functional level (level 1) and on an operational level (level 2) where the operation level involves the actual actions and the function level concerns overlying objectives for a set of operations.

3.2.1. Usability Problem Analysis through the ECW Method.
The first part of the interaction analysis is to analyse usability problems in the human-machine system. The usability problem analysis is performed by the Enhanced Cognitive Walkthrough (ECW) method ([14]). ECW is a usability inspection method based on the third version of cognitive walkthrough (CW) [8, 23].

ECW is an analytical method which looks into potential usability problems by investigating what prevents the user from performing correct actions and why that happens. A usability problem is, according to Nielsen (1993), any aspect of the design that is expected, or observed, to cause user problems with respect to some relevant usability measure (e.g., learnability, performance, error rate, and subjective satisfaction) and that can be attributed to the design of the product. ECW employs a detailed procedure for simulating the interaction between user and product and the user's problem-solving process in each step of the interaction. Throughout, it is investigated whether the supposed user's goals and previous experience will lead to that the correct action is performed.

To predict usability problems, the analyst works through the question process in ECW for all the selected tasks. The interaction analysis is based on the described correct handling sequences in the HTA. The question process then generates conceivable usage problems. The question process is divided into two levels of questions as follows.

Analysis Questions for ECW

Level 1: Analysis of Tasks/Functions

(1) Will the user know that the evaluated function is available?

   Does the user expect, on the basis of previously given indications, that the function exists in the machine?

(2) Will the user be able to notice that the function is available?

   Does the machine give clues that show that the function exists?

(3) Will the user associate the clues with the function?

   Can the user's expectations and the machine's indications coincide?

(4) Will the user get sufficient feedback when using the function?

   Does the machine give information that the function has been chosen and the position the user is at in the interaction?

(5) Will the user get sufficient feedback to understand that the function has been fully performed?

   Does the user understand, after the performed sequence of actions, that the right function has been performed?

Level 2: Analysis of Operations

(1) Will the user try to achieve the right goals of the operation?

   Does the user expect, on the basis of previously given indications, what is to be performed?

(2) Will the user be able to notice that the action of the operation is available?

   Does the machine give clues that show that the action is available and how to perform it?

(3) Will the user associate the action of the operation with the right goal of the operation?

   Can the user's assumed operation and the machine's indications coincide?

(4) Will the user be able to perform the correct action?

   Do the abilities of the user match the demands by the machine?

(5) Will the user get sufficient feedback to understand that the action has been performed and the goal has been achieved?

   Does the user understand, after the performed operation, that he/she has done it correctly?

The first (level 1) is employed for the functions (the nodes in the HTA), and the second (level 2) for the operations (the lowest level in the HTA). In level 1, the machine's ability to "capture" the user is studied, and in level 2 its ability to lead the user to perform the function correctly is studied.

The analyst asks the questions for each node and operation, respectively, in the HTA diagram, following one branch all the way down before proceeding to the adjacent node. Each question is answered with a grade (a number between 1, a very small chance of success, and 5, a very good chance of success) and a justification for the grade. These justifications, called *failure/success stories,* are the assumptions underlying the choice of grades, such as that the user cannot interpret a displayed symbol. The grading, called *problem seriousness,* makes it easier to determine what it is most important to rectify in the subsequent reworking of the machine.

The next step is to identify the predicted problems. If the problem seriousness is between 1 and 4, that is, not with "a very good chance of success," it points to the existence of a potential usability problem. Based on the failure story, the usability problem is then described. The problem is the cause which prevents the user from performing the correct action. Each problem is further categorised by a problem type. The categorisation stems from the failure stories and the description of the problem. Depending on the machine and the task that the user is to solve with it, different problem types can be used. For more detailed information, see [14].

3.2.2. Use Error Analysis through the PUEA Method.
The second part of the interaction analysis is the use of error analysis. Here, the aim is to predict and identify presumptive use errors in the interaction. PUEA is a human reliability assessment method based on three methods: Action Error Analysis (AEA) [28], Systematic Human Error Reduction and

Prediction Approach (SHERPA) [29], and Predictive Human Error Analysis (PHEA) [30]. Also PUEA utilizes a detailed process to break down the user's tasks when interacting with the product into steps and, for each step, predicts and identifies potential use errors. A user error is an *"act or omission of an act that has a different result than intended by the manufacturer or expected by the operator"* to IEC [31, p 17].

To predict use errors, the analyst works through all the selected tasks. The interaction analysis is based on the correct handling sequences described with an HTA. To predict potential incorrect actions, a question process is employed. The question process is divided into two levels of questions as follows.

Analysis Questions for PUEA

Level 1: Analysis of Tasks/Functions

> What happens if the user performs an incomplete operation or omits an operation?

> What happens if the user performs an error in the sequence of operations?

> What happens if the user performs functions/tasks correctly but at the wrong time?

Level 2: Analysis of Operations

> What can the user do wrongly in this operation?

> What happens if the user performs the operation at the wrong time?

The first (level 1) is employed for the nodes in the HTA, and the second (level 2) for the operations in the HTA. On level 1, use errors are identified that may arise when actions are performed at the wrong time or in the wrong order. On level 2, use errors are identified that may occur in the individual action.

Guided by the questions, the analysts try to predict as many use errors as possible that can arise in the human-machine interaction. Each predicted use error is noted in a list. During this process, they also eliminate errors that are considered too unlikely to occur. This elimination is done in relation to how the simulated user is expected to make decisions and perform, in view of the machine and the social, organisational, and physical contexts. However, it is important to be careful about dismissing without further investigation improbable errors that would have serious consequences, as these can also constitute a hazard. If there are no use errors corresponding to the answers to the questions, this also should be noted.

The analysis proceeds in the same manner as the ECW, starting on a higher level node and moving down to the operations, before moving along the HTA. For each predicted use error, an investigation is made of eight items: (1) error type; (2) error cause; (3) primary consequence of the error; (4) secondary consequence of the error; (5) error detection; (6) error recovery; (7) protection from consequences of use error; and (8) prevention of use error. The first two concern the error itself, the next two concern its potential consequences, and the last four items concern mitigations of

the errors and consequences. Four of the items also contain a categorisation (1 and 2), a judgment of probability (5), or a judgment of severity (4). This is done to facilitate the compilation and assessment of the investigation. For more detailed information, see [15].

3.3. Presentation. The last phase is the presentation phase in which the results in the form of grades and categories are presented in matrices. The matrices are compiled and, by varying the issues from the results of the analysis in rows and columns, different aspects can be emphasized and make the result easier to overview.

3.4. Application. ECW and PUEA are designed to be applied together and they use a common template (Figures 1 and 2). In this way, the prediction and investigation of usability problems and use errors are conducted in parallel; that is, both the ECW question set and the PUEA items are posed at the same time for each node or operation in the HTA diagram. This simultaneous application is why the paper refers to the methods as one, ECW/PUEA; they are perceived as one method when used.

4. Study Procedure

This study is based on two cases where product developers used the ECW/PUEA method. In the first case (A), nine students used the method during a course in order to evaluate a range of user interfaces. In the second case (B), five professional developers used the method to evaluate a prototype in a medical device development project. Both cases were chosen as they represented instances where the method had been applied under circumstances known to the authors. In addition, the two different cases provided the opportunity to get input from individuals under training to become developers and well as from individuals with experience from actual, industrial product development. In order to collect information on the assessment of the method, a combination of questionnaires and interviews was used.

4.1. Participants and Procedure. In case A, nine students were involved in the evaluation. The students attended the second year of their master degree program in industrial design engineering or interaction design, and they were familiar with usability and some other usability methods. Working in pairs, they used the new method as one part of a university course with the aim to perform an extensive cognitive ergonomics evaluation of a human-machine system, including ultrasound machine, disk jockey mixing table, and system camera. The training the students received was limited to a short introduction to the method during a lecture by the first author. They then performed the method by themselves guided by a detailed description of the method. As a part of the examination, students wrote a short reflection on the methods they had used during the course. A month after the end of the course, the students were invited to complete the questionnaire and be interviewed by the second author (first author not present).

Function:	PS	Fail/Success Story		Usability Problem	PT	Notes
1. Will the user know that the evaluated function is available?						
2. Will the user be able to notice that the function is available?		ECW-part of template				
3. Will the user associate the clues with the function?						
4. Will the user get sufficient feedback when using the function?						
5. Will the user get sufficient feedback to understand that the function has been fully performed?						

- What happens if the user performs an incomplete operation or omits an operation?
- What happens if the user performs an error in the sequence of operations?
- What happens if the user performs this function at the wrong time?

Error & Type	Error Cause	Prim. Consequence	Sec. Consequence	Detection	Prevention	Recovery	Protection
	PUEA-part of template						

FIGURE 1: Template for function level analysis for the conjoint use of ECW and PUEA.

Operation:	PS	Fail/Success Story		Usability Problem	PT	Notes
1. Will the user try to achieve the right goals of the operation?						
2. Will the user be able to notice that the action of the operation is available?		ECW-part of template				
3. Will the user associate the action of the operation with the right goal of the operation?						
4. Will the user be able to perform the correct action?						
5. Will the user get sufficient feedback to understand that the action has been performed and the goal has been achieved?						

- What can the user do wrongly in this operation?
- What happens if the user performs this operation at wrong time?

Error & Type	Error Cause	Prim. Consequence	Sec. Consequence	Detection	Prevention	Recovery	Protection
	PUEA-part of template						

FIGURE 2: Template for operation level analysis for the conjoint use of ECW and PUEA.

In case B, five professional developers were involved in the evaluation. The professional developers had slightly different backgrounds, more specifically:

(i) One system architect with 15 years of work experience and 5 with medical technology

(ii) One clinical and quality expert, physician with 20-year work experience

(iii) One quality engineer with 16 years of work experience and 6 years with medical technology

(iv) Two human factors specialist: one with 7 years of work experience (all in medical technology) and one with 13 years of total work experience and 9 on them with medical technology

They applied the method as part of a risk analysis on an advanced medical device (ventilator), a prototype in real product development project. The professionals received more extensive training than the students. They were taught the method by the first author during half a day. The first author also return on a later occasion to lead the first method application session. The professionals all worked together when performing the analysis. After completing the risk analysis of the medical device they were handed the questionnaire and were then interviewed by the second author (first author not present). The last part of the case B was a focus group with the professional product developers, which was moderated by the first author with the second author present.

4.2. Data Collection and Analysis. The overall topics for the data collection were usability, acceptance, and cost-benefit

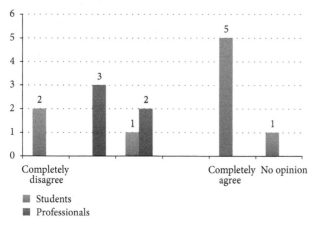

FIGURE 3: ECW/PUEA is very easy to learn.

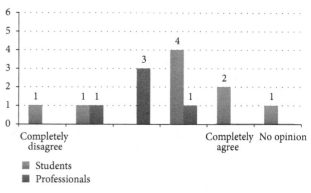

FIGURE 4: Once learnt, ECW/PUEA is very workable.

evaluation. Questions posed concerned learning the method; performing the method; output from the method; general opinions of the method; and possible improvements of the method.

The same questionnaire was used in both cases and it contained altogether 24 items. The items were formulated as statements and the respondents were asked to indicate on a 5-level scale their level of agreement or disagreement (so called Likert items). The option "I have no opinion" was also available. The questionnaire was collected before the interviews were conducted and thus formed the basis for the themes addressed in the interviews. The second author then ran the interviews with one respondent at a time, at the company for the professional and at the university for the students. The interviews were audio-recorded for later analysis.

The results from the questionnaires were compiled and presented in charts. The audio-recordings of the interviews were listened through by the second author, notes were taken, and relevant statements and comments were written down in full. In order to create an overview of the themes that emerged and their interrelations, mind maps of the content were created. All of the authors then together compared the results from the questionnaires and the thematically analysed material from the interviews in order to interpret the meaning and identify strengths, weaknesses, and potential improvements of the methods.

5. Result

The result from the questionnaires and the interviews are presented under the following headings: learning the method, performing the method, output from the method, general opinions of the method, and suggestions for improvement.

5.1. Learning the Method. According to the questionnaires, a majority of the students found the method easy to learn, while the professionals were less positive (Figure 3). There was also a wider distribution among the answers from the students. The same pattern was found regarding both participant groups' opinion on if the method is easy to carry out once learnt (Figure 4).

There was a noticeable deviation between the responses within the student group and also between the students and the professionals. In the interviews, many of the professional product developers commented on how hard it was to get started. They considered the method difficult to use for beginners. The students made similar comments about the learnability of the method.

All of the participants in the study agreed that the part of the method that is easiest to learn is the procedure, that is, learning how to follow the logical sequence of questions. One of the professional participants commented that one "... *got a structured help on how to think; one: think like this, two: think like this. Pretty much guiding exactly how you should think, very good guidelines for how to think. It is a problem I generally have in risk analyses that it is hard to think right, it is easy to get lost."*

The aspect that a major part of the participants considered the most difficult was to remember and differentiate between the different terms and rankings, especially when conducting the PUEA-part. The terminology was difficult to pick up, given the sheer amount of terms and the fact that they were similar sounding, for example, primary and secondary consequence. Since there are many categories and rankings to keep track of, the interviewees said that it was easy to just choose a number or category that you remembered without checking if there was a more appropriate one for the case at hand. Another aspect that was considered difficult was to understand which "*user's mind to enter,*" that is, which type of user to imagine. If you as an analyst act as a user with very good knowledge of the product and how it is used, the method may not yield so many problems and errors. On the other hand, if you act a novice user, many of the identified potential problems and errors may never occur in actual use.

5.2. Performing the Method. Most students and professionals agreed that the method was very good at creating consensus within the group (Figure 5). In the interviews, four out of the 14 participants stated "increased consensus in the group" as an important result. They here referred both to consensus on the problems and benefits of the product and consensus on what constitute a usability problem and high usability. The method was also considered to be a very good basis for group discussions by the professionals, whereas the

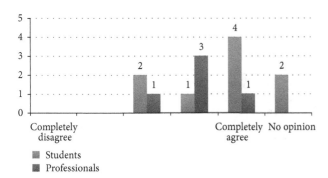

FIGURE 5: ECW/PUEA is a very good at creating consensus within the group performing it.

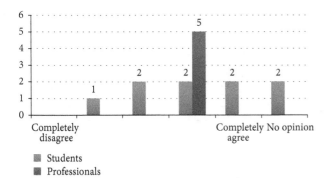

FIGURE 6: ECW/PUEA is a very good basis for group discussions.

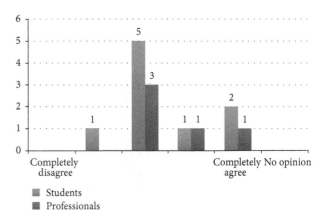

FIGURE 7: Statement: ECW/PUEA gives rise to a lot of new knowledge regarding possible use errors and usability problems.

students' opinions were more distributed (Figure 6). This might be explained by that the professionals used ECW/PUEA together as one group, while students worked in different groups.

When questioned on the drawbacks of performing the method, the most common answer was the amount of time required: "(It) *takes a very long time because it is so extensive*" *(professional)*. According to the participants, the reason for the time consumed was that the method was comprehensive and repetitive: "*(It is) tedious, the same thing over and over*" *(student)*. This was especially the case when the evaluation was performed on a product with an already satisfactory usability level since not so many problems and errors were detected. In particular, the students found it discouraging to not discover any problems and tedious to find the same type of problems repeatedly.

A few of the interviewees said that keeping up one's concentration level was the most difficult when performing the method. The tediousness of the method and the difficulties to keep alert were pointed out as something that negatively affected the quality of the result. The interviewees explained that after a while you cannot be bothered to find the correct term, judgement, or estimation and just pick one that you have used before. This was especially the case for the PUEA-part.

5.3. Output from Method. In the questionnaires, the participants neither totally disagreed nor agreed completely with the statement that the method results in a great deal of

new knowledge regarding possible use errors and usability problems (Figure 7). Somewhat contradictory, most of them (11 out of 14) commented in the interviews that the primary result from using the method was the discovered problem areas and suggestions for solutions to these problems. To get previously suspected problems confirmed, specified, and written down was found to be an important result.

When asked about their confidence, or trust, in the output from the method, the opinions of the participants differed (Figure 8); some agreed and others disagreed with the statement (with a wider distribution for the students). In the interviews, they explained that it was difficult to make the assessments during the analysis. In addition, it was hard to know if the results were reasonable and viable. Furthermore, they found it difficult to assess whether the method had been performed correctly and to know whether something had been missed. There were also concerns that the method produced results that were subjective, if subjective, one cannot trust the results. However, some participants, who initially considered the method to result in a subjective assessment, changed their mind after having gained experience of applying it: "*I first thought that it would be easily affected and subjective, but I realised that it is objective*" (student).

The inclination to use a method can be assumed to depend upon an assessment of the output compared to the effort required, that is, a kind of cost-benefit analysis [32]. According to the questionnaires, the opinions of the professionals and the students differed slightly when assessing if the method resulted in a large amount of information compared to the effort required. The professionals agreed more than the students with the statement that the method resulted in information of high quality in relation to the effort required (Figure 9).

Both groups disagreed with the statement that the result of the method was independent of the prior knowledge of the participants (Figure 10). They also disagreed with the statement that if different groups complete the method on the same product, they will reach the same result (Figure 11).

When asked about the reasons behind these assessments, a number of aspects were mentioned. One of the reasons was that the method was dependent on the knowledge of the

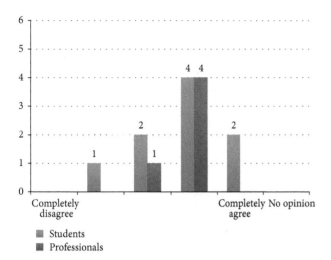

FIGURE 8: Statement: I have great confidence in the result of ECW/PUEA.

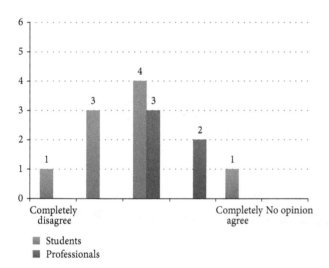

FIGURE 9: ECW/PUEA result in high quality information in relation to the effort it requires.

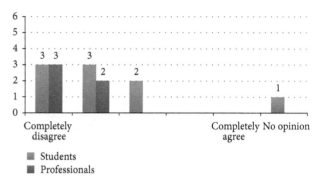

FIGURE 10: Statement: the result of ECW/PUEA is independent of the prior knowledge of the analysts.

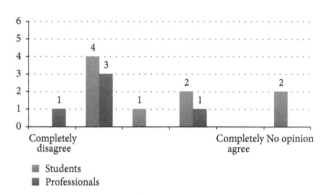

FIGURE 11: Statement: different groups performing ECW/PUEA on the same product will come to the same result.

analysts. If they lacked knowledge of the product, task, and/or user, this was believed to influence the result considerably. One of the students said "*[the result] is very much affected by the person performing the method, everybody plays the part of the user differently*". Another explained "*you can get false results if the practitioner does not have correct knowledge of the product.*" In addition to knowledge, the participants mentioned creativity and imagination, as well as energy to keep concentrated, as important characteristics. Another reason for differences in outcomes was believed to be the analyst's attitude towards the use of the method and the domain.

Many participants believed that the method required several participants in the group of analysts in order to get valuable output. According mainly to the professionals, the optimum would be that these analysts represented different areas of competence so that different perspectives could be applied. A couple of interviewees from both groups also mentioned that it would be useful to include a representative

user in the group, since it could be difficult to judge the reasonableness of which errors could occur and what really is a usability issue on your own.

5.4. Assessment of the Method. A main concern in the evaluation was, evidently, if the participants considered the method useful in product development and if they could consider using it in the future.

A majority of the participants (both students and professionals) agreed with the statement that the method is well worth using (Figure 12). They also agreed with the statement that the method felt like a serious method (Figure 13).

The professionals agreed slightly more so than did the students with the statement that the method felt like a very purposeful method. Most of the participants agreed that the method was a useful method during product development (Figure 14).

In addition, according the questionnaire, most participants could imagine using ECW/PUEA in future projects (Figure 15).

Overall, the method was considered systematic; it provided an easy overview of the issues, and offered clarity and awareness of the problems. There was consensus in the comments that a main strength is that the structured method encourages the developer to consider the usage of the product step by step: "*You have to analyse all steps in the task, steps which have become evident to you*" (student). The systematic approach makes it easier to think critically of a product: "*It

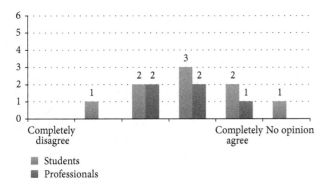

FIGURE 12: Statement: ECW/PUEA is a method well worth using.

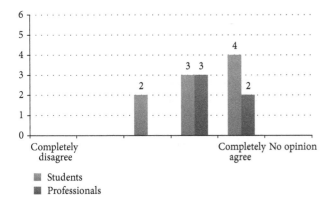

FIGURE 13: Statement: ECW/PUEA feels like a very serious method.

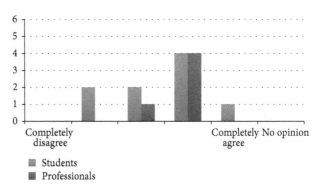

FIGURE 14: Statement: ECW/PUEA is a very useful method during product development.

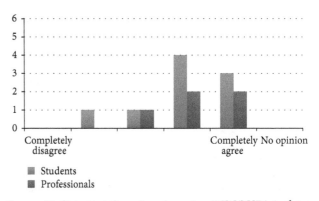

FIGURE 15: Statement: I can imagine using ECW/PUEA in future projects.

helps you become more critical of something that you have developed yourself" (professional). However, the systematic approach also resulted in the method being perceived as time-consuming, tedious, and unnecessarily complex for application on certain products. The method was by some participants considered to be too "engineery" as it "quantifies everything" (professional) and therefore it was perceived as boring and lengthy. Other participants interpreted this as though the method provides "an objective perspective" and one professional participant argued that the quantification facilitates communicating the concept of usability, which may appear as something "fuzzy" for those unfamiliar with the domain. The result of the method, in terms of a list with individual usability problems and use errors, contributes with a clear picture of the usability of the product. It is "... good way to prove to other people that there are problems and what their problems are" (student). A summary of main strengths and weaknesses of the method according the participants is provided as follows.

Strengths

(i) It provides a structure for findings potential problems and errors.

(ii) It helps structure your thoughts.

(iii) It facilitates reaching consensus within a group of developers.

(iv) It forces you to think through the usage of the product.

(v) It provides convincing arguments.

(vi) It quantifies results

(vii) It helps explain the fuzzy concept of "usability."

Weaknesses

(i) Time-consuming process

(ii) Tedious procedure

(iii) Difficult to grasp the terminology

(iv) Difficult to assess the quality and reliability of the results

(v) Results dependent on the competence and experience of the analyst

(vi) Quantifies results (the need to transform opinions into numbers)

The students and the professionals highlighted the same main strengths and weaknesses.

Three of the problems associated with executing the method were the difficulty to select tasks, prioritize between tasks, and create a good description of the user. The participants believed that the method would work better if the specified product user was a novice rather than an expert, since they found it more difficult to imagine what an expert might do.

5.5. Suggestions for Improvements. Some suggestions for improvements of the method emerged from the interviews. One concerned instructions. Some of the interviewees desired more instructions on how to select and prioritize between the tasks and how to choose user character. One suggestion from a student was "*either adapt [the method] to experienced users or clearly state which use situation and type of user that is suitable.*"

Another suggestion from a student concerned further information on how to adapt the method to the specific product under development: "[*The questions] must be adapted to the specific case.*" Another student indicated that you have to "*modify [the method] according to complexity of product, more like a checklist.*"

Less specific recommendations concerned simplifying the procedure. The method should "*be rendered more efficient, to reduce the time and effort needed*" according to one professional. One idea from a student was to develop an IT-based tool: "*… a programme or advanced Excel-tool,*" so that the analyst can focus on the results and less on the "*administrative task.*"

6. Discussion and Conclusion

The aim of the study was to investigate how two groups of product developers, professional developers and students, assess a new, theoretical method for identifying usability problems and use errors. Two main "conflicts" have been identified: time versus results and structure versus tediousness. These two conflicts are discussed below, followed by further discussion on learning the method, the value of a null result, and some comparison of the students' and professionals' experiences. The discussion ends with suggestions for further development of ECW/PUEA and a concluding remark on the paper.

6.1. Time versus Results. The first conflict could be considered an inherent contraposition. Time is generally considered a key issue in product development projects why any methods used in the process must be efficient and provide value for the resources allocated. According to the results from the study, most participants found the new method useful in product development and they trusted the results. At the same time, they found the method tedious and time-consuming. Even so, they indicated that they would consider using the method again in a product development context. This type of "cost-benefit" conflict has earlier been identified regarding structured walkthrough procedures (e.g., by Rowley and Rhoades [33]) and modifications in order to simplify and speed up the process have been suggested. For instance, Rowley and Rhoades [33] proposed a slightly modified "JogThrough" procedure and Spencer [34] proposed the "streamlined cognitive walkthrough." Little is however mentioned on the relative efficiency of these simplified versions. The input from the potential users of the developed method cannot be neglected, but the fundamental question is if the cost-benefit conflict can be resolved and if simplifications can be made to the ECW/PUEA method without a loss of quality. In fact, the rationale for developing the ECW/PUEA method identified

weaknesses of the existing methods: CW, AEA, SHERPA. and PHEA. The method was not intended to be an optimisation of resources versus detected conceivable use errors, but the aim was that it should detect as *many* problems as possible. In addition, it can be argued that a main part of the participants' difficulties was related to the preparatory work required. The ECW/PUEA was never designed to be a "standalone" method and much of the information needed for the analysis in ECW/PUEA should be readily available in the project. Knowledge on the users, the tasks, and the context of use is the basis for usability and the foundation for human factors work [35, 36] and should be present in every project. This is a clear indication for a need to make collection and presentation of that knowledge more effective and efficient.

6.2. Structure versus Tediousness. The second conflict could be considered a problem that arise in-between the participants in an ECW/PUEA session. Some participants in the study thought that a particular strength of the method was its structured approach and that the output was presented in a structured way and in numbers, which all contributed to them trusting the outcome. Other participants thought that these same characteristics made the method complex and tedious. Product development is believed to benefit from team members with different backgrounds and different personalities. However, these differences could also cause problems, for instance, when using a method and trusting its result. Members with an engineering background may be more inclined to accept and adopt a method that provides a clear logic and results in "objective" numbers whereas members with, for instance, a traditional design background may be more disposed to trust in intuition and the ability to put oneself in the position of the end-user [37]. If there is such a conflict within the development team, it is not easily solved. Other results from the evaluation points, however, in a more positive direction, such as that the members complemented each other when performing the method.

It is not certain that the result of a user interface evaluation is acknowledged by the designers of the same interface; that is, they may not believe that the result is correct. The result from an ECW/PUEA session can enhance this issue since ECW/PUEA is analytical to its character and lacks the conclusiveness of empirical usability tests. The identified problems of the design may result, as pointed out by, for instance Spencer [34], in more work for a development team already under time pressure. Some team members may try to defend their designs, be argumentative, and may "… reject seemingly obvious observations as being opinions that lack data to support them" (Spencer, 2000). An important comment made by the professional participants in the study was that the ECW/PUEA was believed to be a tool for improving the dialogue between the development team members and contributed to creating consensus within the team. A plausible measure to counteract this issue is therefore to include the designers in the ECW/PUEA session, so they can be part of the dialogue and develop an understanding for the results.

6.3. Learning the Method. Another and related result of the study was that, overall, the method was assessed as complicated and difficult to learn, in particular the terminology and the rankings. The responses were collected from first time users of the method and the efficiency in performing the method will probably increase over time. It must be acknowledged though that the method is not a "plug-in-and-play" method, that is, the method that can be employed without any initial training. The issue here is evidently how much training is required. It seems as though part of the problem when learning the method is "unfamiliarity" with the structured way of approaching the problem. However, the problem could also be at least partly explained by the participants' different responsibilities, background, and personalities and hence related to the second identified conflict regarding that the users experience ECW/PUEA in different ways.

6.4. The Value of a Null Result. Another issue worth considering, in particular when teaching the method, is that many of the participating students did not think that the method produced a good result since they did not detect a large number of errors and problems. In a real product development context, this would be a positive outcome. If you do not discover plenty of possible usability problems and use errors, it means that the probability for the product being a safe and useable is high. However, in cases where the method did not detect and problems or errors for the participants, this lack of findings instead resulted in an uncertainty regarding whether or not the method was performed correctly, or a disbelief that you have not discovered the possible problems and errors that are, indeed, there. Thus, when training in the methods, the understanding of the underlying principles of the methods should be emphasised. Even though most participants trusted the outcome of the method, the study revealed that there were those who felt uncertain about how to "approach" the method. Several participants meant that the method was only usable for finding the errors that a first-time user would encounter, not realizing the possibility of assuming a different type of user. This has to be clarified in the future dissemination of the ECW/PUEA method. Other participants found it difficult to know how a more experienced user would think and act because they lacked sufficient knowledge and understanding of end-users, their preunderstanding, the situation in which the product is used, and what effect these factors could possibly have on the behaviour of the user. Some of these issues that have been identified earlier in relation to structured walkthroughs (e.g. by [38]). The issues mentioned reflect the dependency on the participating analyst(s), a dependency which was mentioned by the participants in the study and which has previously been shown in several studies. For instance, Desurvire et al. [39] concluded that usability experts found more problems than nonexperts. Furthermore, Nielsen (1992) stated that usability experts identified more usability problems than nonexperts when conducting a heuristic evaluation, and further that usability experts who also had expertise with the type of interface (or the domain) being evaluated identified the most. It is therefore reasonable and appropriate to have evaluation methods, like ECW/PUEA, that aim to strengthen the skill of the experts.

6.5. Comparing Students and Professionals. Even though the study did not aim to compare the two cases, there are some discernible differences between the experiences of the students in case A and the professional developers in case B. These differences relate to the last two sections: learning the method and the value of a null result.

A majority of the students experience that the ECW/PUEA was easy to learn, while the professionals found it more difficult to learn. This is probably due to that the students were more accustomed to this type of usability methods, as they that had been taught similar methods earlier (e.g., CW). In addition, they were in a context where they were constantly expected to learn, the university, as well as taking a course focused on learning many different types of methods. The students were thus much more prepared and used to learning new things than the professionals, something that might have affected their appraisal of the method's learnability.

The professionals experienced more benefit from the method and saw no problem with a null result, in contrast to the students. The professional used method in a real development project where they relied on the results to demonstrate that they had carried out a risk analysis of use, in order to get certain certifications. Furthermore, to them, a null result meant that the evaluated product probably did not contain any flaws, a confirmation of a development work well done. In contrast, the students applied the method in a project aimed at finding design errors to correct, something which may have affected their view of a null result, in addition to the insecurity of having performed the method correctly as discussed above.

6.6. Further Development. The study has contributed to validating the new method with a focus on the users', that is, the product developers' experiences. Based on the input from the participants in the study, further development and simplification of the procedure are deemed desirable. A suggestion from the participants in the study was to provide computer support. The creation of an IT-supported version of the tool, where a template could be filled in on the computer screen and then used when creating the different tables and matrices, would most probably reduce the time that has to be allocated the presentation of results. In addition, complementary studies are needed. For instance, in order to assess the effectiveness as well as the efficiency of the new method, comparisons have to be made between the already existing theoretical and expert-based methods and the new, modified one. Such evaluations are important in order to argue the relative benefit of the method, something which is considered a key factor in the dissemination of the method (cf. [40]). Furthermore, the number of participants in the study reported here was limited, why only tentative conclusions can be drawn. The evaluations were carried out after a session where the participants learnt how to use the method and therefore it can be argued that the learnability of the method rather than the usefulness of the method has been addressed in this study. The usefulness of the ECW/PUEA should also be evaluated in actual product development work, without the participation of its developers, and with teams consisting of individuals with different backgrounds, to explore how this effects the procedure and the results.

6.7. Concluding Remarks. The study presented in this paper has shown that a user study of a usability method can be performed in the same manner as a usability study on a product. The study provided good insight into how the developers experienced the method and resulted in useful information about how to improve the method. Thus, showing that user studies with developers is a valuable asset in method development. It is important for developers of usability methods to consider the intended users, that is, the product developers, and not only focus on how well the methods evaluate, for instance, the usability of products. To increase the potential for dissemination of usability methods, the usability of usability methods is an important piece of the puzzle to reach applicability and credibility of methods.

Competing Interests

The authors declare that there are no competing interests regarding the publication of this paper.

References

[1] J. Nielsen, *Usability Engineering*, Academic Press, Boston, Mass, USA, 1993.

[2] H. Johannesson, J.-G. Persson, and D. Pettersson, *Produktutveckling: Effektiva Metoder för Konstruktion och Design*, Liber Läromedel, Stockholm, Sweden, 2004.

[3] B. L. Miles and K. Swift, "Design for manufacture and assembly," *Manufacturing Engineer*, vol. 77, no. 5, pp. 221–224, 1998.

[4] N. A. Stanton, A. Hedge, K. Brookhuis, E. Salas, and H. W. Hendrick, Eds., *Handbook of Human Factors and Ergonomics Methods*, CRC Press, New York, NY, USA, 2005.

[5] N. Stanton, *Human Factors Methods: A Practical Guide for Engineering and Design*, Ashgate, Aldershot, UK, 2005.

[6] G. Salvendy, *Handbook of Human Factors and Ergonomics*, Wiley, Hoboken, NJ, USA, 2006.

[7] J. Wilson and N. Corlett, Eds., *Evaluation of Human Work: Practical Ergonomics Methodology*, Taylor & Francis, London, UK, 1995.

[8] C. Lewis and C. Wharton, "Cognitive walkthrough," in *Handbook of Human-Computer Interaction*, M. Helander, T. K. Landauer, and P. Prabhu, Eds., pp. 717–732, Elsevier Science BV, New York, NY, USA, 1997.

[9] L. Kantner and S. Rosenbaum, "Usability studies of WWW sites: heuristic evaluation vs. laboratory testing," in *Proceedings of the 15th Annual International Conference on Computer Documentation (SIGDOC '97)*, pp. 153–160, ACM, Salt Lake City, Utah, USA, October 1997.

[10] J. Nielsen, "Finding usability problems through heuristuc evaluation," in *Proceedings of the SIGCHI Conference on Human Factors in Computing Systems (CHI '92)*, pp. 373–380, Monterey, Calif, USA, 1992.

[11] B. Jerome and R. Kazman, "Surveying the solitudes: an investigation into the relationships between human computer interaction and software engineering in practice," in *Human-Centered Software Engineering—Integrating Usability in the Software Development Lifecycle*, vol. 8 of *Human-Computer Interaction*, pp. 59–70, Springer, 2005.

[12] J. Andersson, L.-O. Bligård, A.-L. Osvalder, M. J. Rissanen, and S. Tripathi, "To develop viable human factors engineering methods for improved industrial use," in *Design, User Experience, and Usability. Theory, Methods, Tools and Practice*, vol. 6769 of *Lecture Notes in Computer Science*, pp. 355–362, Springer, Berlin, Germany, 2011.

[13] K. J. Vicente, C. M. Burns, and W. S. Pawlak, "Better handbooks, better design," *Ergonomics in Design*, vol. 6, no. 4, pp. 21–27, 1998.

[14] L.-O. Bligård and A.-L. Osvalder, "Enhanced cognitive walkthrough: development of the cognitive walkthrough method to better predict, identify, and present usability problems," *Advances in Human-Computer Interaction*, vol. 2013, Article ID 931698, 17 pages, 2013.

[15] L.-O. Bligård and A.-L. Osvalder, "Predictive use error analysis—development of AEA, SHERPA and PHEA to better predict, identify and present use errors," *International Journal of Industrial Ergonomics*, vol. 44, no. 1, pp. 153–170, 2014.

[16] L. Lundgren, L.-O. Bligård, S. Brorsson, and A.-L. Osvalder, "Implementation of usability analysis to detect problems in the management of kitesurfing equipment," in *Proceedings of the 5th Asia-Pacific Congress on Sports Technology*, Melbourne, Australia, 2011.

[17] L.-O. Bligård and J. Andersson, "Use errors and usability problems in relation to automation levels of medical devices," *VTT Symposium (Valtion Teknillinen Tutkimuskeskus)*, no. 258, pp. 111–114, 2009.

[18] L.-O. Bligård, S. Wass, E. Liljegren, and A. L. Osvalder, "Using a human factors engineering process to develop new user interfaces for home car air-flow generators," in *Proceedings of the 35th Annual Congress of the Nordic Ergonomics Society Conference*, Reykjavik, Iceland, 2003.

[19] L.-O. Bligård and A.-L. Osvalder, "Using enhanced cognitive walkthrough as a usability evaluation method for medical equipment," in *Proceedings of the International Ergonomics Association Conference (IEA '06)*, Maastricht, The Netherlands, 2006.

[20] L.-O. Bligård, *Predicting Mismatches in User-Artefact Interaction—Development of an Analytical Methodology to Support Design Work*, Department of Product and Production Development, Chalmers University of Technology, Gothenburg, Sweden, 2012.

[21] S. Moradi and N. A. Pour, "Usability problems and use errors appraisal in public transport website," in *Human Centred Automation*, D. De Waard, N. Gerard, and L. Onnasch, Eds., pp. 213–225, Shaker Pulishing, Maastricht, the Netherlands, 2011.

[22] A. Westerlund, W. Tancredi, M. Ransjö, A. Bresin, S. Psonis, and O. Torgersson, "Digital casts in orthodontics: a comparison of 4 software systems," *American Journal of Orthodontics and Dentofacial Orthopedics*, vol. 147, no. 4, pp. 509–516, 2015.

[23] P. G. Poison and C. H. Lewis, "Theory-based design for easily learned interfaces," *Human-Computer Interaction*, vol. 5, no. 2-3, pp. 191–220, 1990.

[24] J. Rasmussen, "Skills, rules, and knowledge; signals, signs, and symbols, and other distinctions in human performance models," *IEEE Transactions on Systems, Man and Cybernetics*, vol. 13, no. 3, pp. 257–266, 1983.

[25] J. Reason, *Human Error*, Cambridge University Press, Cambridge, UK, 1990.

[26] L.-O. Bligård and A.-L. Osvalder, "Evaluating usability problems and use errors—comparing analytical methods and usability test," *International Journal of Ergonomics and Human Factors*, In press.

[27] N. A. Stanton, "Hierarchical task analysis: developments, applications, and extensions," *Applied Ergonomics*, vol. 37, no. 1, pp. 55–79, 2006.

[28] L. Harms-Ringdahl, *Safety Analysiss—principles and Parctice in Occupational Safety*, Taylor & Francis, London, England, 2nd edition, 2001.

[29] D. Embrey, "SHERPA: a systematic human error reduction and prediction approach," in *Proceedings of the International Topical Meeting on Advances in Human Factors in Nuclear Power System*, pp. 184–193, American Nuclear Society, Knoxville, Tenn, USA, 1986.

[30] D. Embrey, "Qualitative and quantitative evaluation of human error in risk assessment," in *Human Factors for Engineers*, C. Sandom and R. Harvey, Eds., p. 361, Institution of Electrical Engineers, London, UK, 2004.

[31] IEC, *IEC 60601-1-6:2004 Medical Electrical Equipment—Part 1-6: General Requirements for Safety—Collateral standard: Usability*, IEC, Geneva, Switzerland, 2004.

[32] R. G. Bias and D. J. Mayhew, *Cost-Justifying Usability*, 2nd edition, 2005.

[33] D. E. Rowley and D. G. Rhoades, "Cognitive jogthrough: a fast-paced user interface evaluation procedure," in *Proceedings of the ACM Conference on Human Factors in Computing Systems (CHI '92)*, pp. 389–395, May 1992.

[34] R. Spencer, "Streamlined cognitive walkthrough method, working around social constraints encountered in a software development company," in *Proceedings of the Conference on Human Factors in Computing Systems "The Future is Here" (CHI '00)*, pp. 353–359, The Hague, Netherlands, April 2000.

[35] D. A. Norman and S. W. Draper, *User Centered System Design: New Perspectives on Human-Computer Interaction*, Erlbaum, Hillsdale, NJ, USA, 1986.

[36] A. Chapanis, "Some reflections on progress," in *Proceedings of the 20th Meeting on Human Factors Society*, pp. 1–8, Santa Monica, Calif, USA, 1985.

[37] S. Persson, *Toward Enhanced Interaction between Engineering Design and Industrial Design*, Department of Product and Production Development, Chalmers University of Technology, Göteborg, Sweden, 2005.

[38] R. Jeffries, J. R. Miller, C. Wharton, and K. M. Uyeda, "User interface evaluation in the real world: A comparison of four techniques," in *Proceedings of the SIGCHI Conference on Human Factors in Computing Systems (CHI '91)*, pp. 119–124, ACM, New Orleans, La, USA, May 1991.

[39] H. W. Desurvire, J. M. Kondziela, and M. E. Atwood, "Whats is gained and what is lost when using evaluation methods other than empirical testing," in *People and Computers VII*, A. Monk and D. Harrison, Eds., pp. 89–102, Cambrdge University Press, Cambrige, UK, 1992.

[40] E. M. Rogers, *Diffusion of Innovations*, Free Press, New York, NY, USA, 1983.

15

Kinect-Based Sliding Mode Control for Lynxmotion Robotic Arm

Ismail Ben Abdallah,[1,2] **Yassine Bouteraa,**[1,2] **and Chokri Rekik**[1]

[1]*Control and Energy Management Laboratory (CEM-Lab), National School of Engineers of Sfax, Sfax, Tunisia*
[2]*Digital Research Center of Sfax, Technopark of Sfax, BP 275, Sakiet Ezzit, 3021 Sfax, Tunisia*

Correspondence should be addressed to Yassine Bouteraa; yassinebouteraa@gmail.com

Academic Editor: Alessandra Agostini

Recently, the technological development of manipulator robot increases very quickly and provides a positive impact to human life. The implementation of the manipulator robot technology offers more efficiency and high performance for several human's tasks. In reality, efforts published in this context are focused on implementing control algorithms with already preprogrammed desired trajectories (passive robots case) or trajectory generation based on feedback sensors (active robots case). However, gesture based control robot can be considered as another channel of system control which is not widely discussed. This paper focuses on a Kinect-based real-time interactive control system implementation. Based on LabVIEW integrated development environment (IDE), a developed human-machine-interface (HMI) allows user to control in real time a Lynxmotion robotic arm. The Kinect software development kit (SDK) provides a tool to keep track of human body skeleton and abstract it into 3-dimensional coordinates. Therefore, the Kinect sensor is integrated into our control system to detect the different user joints coordinates. The Lynxmotion dynamic has been implemented in a real-time sliding mode control algorithm. The experimental results are carried out to test the effectiveness of the system, and the results verify the tracking ability, stability, and robustness.

1. Introduction

The use of manipulator robot controlled by a natural human-computer interaction offers new possibilities in the execution of complex tasks in dynamic workspaces. Human-robot interaction (HRI) is a key feature which differentiates the new generation of robots from conventional robots [1, 2].

Many manipulator robots have similar behavior with human arm. Thanks to the gesture recognition using Kinect sensor, the motion planning is easier when the robotic arm has the same degree of freedom of the human arm. Gesture recognition using Kinect sensor is based on the skeleton detection, although current development packages and toolkits provide base to identify the joints position of the detected skeleton.

Kinect is a motion detection and recognition smart sensor which allows human/computer interaction without the need of any physical controllers [3]. Indeed, Kinect sensor is a motion sensor that provides a natural user interface available for several applications in different fields including game-based learning systems [4, 5], stroke rehabilitation [6, 7], helping visually impaired people [8, 9], navigation systems [10–12], and other fields [13, 14]. Based on its internal processor, Kinect sensor can recognize human movement patterns to generate a corresponding skeleton coordinates that can be provided in a computer environment such as Matlab [15, 16] and LabVIEW [17, 18]. Therefore, the dynamic gesture recognition technology has gained increased attention.

Several approaches have been developed, in order to improve recognition or take advantage of the existing algorithms. Reference [19] proposes easy gesture recognition approach in order to reduce the effort involved in implementing gesture recognizers with Kinect; the practical results with these developed packages are acceptable. Furthermore, an eigenspace-based method was developed in [20] for identifying and recognizing human gestures by using Kinect

3D data. A user adaptation scheme for this method was added to enhance Eigen3Dgesture and the performance of the constructed eigenspace of Kinect 3D data. Based on Microsoft's "Kinect for Windows SDK," [21] uses the API for measuring movement of people with Parkinson's disease.

Gesture control is mainly used for telemanipulation in several modes. In [22], a client/server structured robot teleoperation application system is developed in networked robot mode. Reference [23] describes gesture based telemanipulation of an industrial robotic arm in master-slave mode for unstructured and hazardous environments, a maximum velocity drift control approach is applied allowing the amateur user to control the robot by simple gestures, and force control was combined with the gesture based control to perform safe manipulation. However, this solution is costly and depends on reliability of the force-torque sensor. In addition, a method of human-robot interaction using markerless Kinect-based tracking of the human hand for teleoperation of a dual robot manipulator is presented in [24]. Based on hand motion, the user can control the robot manipulators to perform tasks of picking up and placing; the work was applied in virtual environment.

For robot teleoperation, many researches have been done providing the possibility of controlling the robotic systems dedicated for complex tasks [25]. Several techniques are used to control robot motion; a human-robot interface based on hand-gesture recognition is developed in [26–30]. Others have based on hand-arm tracking; [31] presents a method of real-time robot manipulator teleoperation using markerless image-based hand-arm tracking.

Many problems occurred during the human-robot interaction when using the Kinect sensor. After the acquisition of 3D data Kinect, these data will be processed to control the robot. Several approaches have been used to check the control. A Cartesian impedance control is used to control the dual robot arm [32]; this approach allows the robot to follow the human arm motion without solving inverse kinematic problems and avoiding self-collision problems. Likewise, a proportional derivative control is implemented with inverse kinematic algorithm in [33]. In [34], a PID controller is also used to control a 2-degree of freedom Lego Mind storm NXT robotic arm.

Based on online HIL (Hardware-in-the-Loop) experimental data, the acquired input data from the Kinect sensor are processed in a closed loop PID controller with feedback from motors encoders. Although these results are satisfactory side position control, they remain imperfect from velocity control stand point due to the use of simple controller used. Moreover, compared to the conventional computed torque control used in [35], the Lynxmotion dynamic has been implemented in a real-time sliding mode control algorithm.

To combine the real and virtual objects and the implemented algorithms, we need to design a user interface that manages the overall system. Indeed, the human-machine interface (HMI) is highly recommended in robotics fields and many human-machine interfaces have been developed to control the robotic systems [36, 37]. In [38], a human-machine interface is designed to control the SCARA robot using Kinect sensor. This interface is implemented in C# using Kinect library OpenNI.

In this paper, we have used the package provided by Virtual Instrument Package Manager for LabVIEW. The recognition algorithm calculates the angle of each human arm joint dedicated for control. This algorithm is detailed in Section 1.

Compared to Shirwalkar et al. [23], firstly, the proposed control strategy takes into account the dynamics system. Also our algorithm detects all user joints and not only the hand, while for the security side we propose an algorithm security which avoids any type of parasite that may occur in the Kinect sensing field. Moreover, the proposed algorithm avoids any singularity position.

Likewise, a proportional derivative control is implemented with inverse kinematic algorithm [33]. However, on the one hand, this classic controller ignores the robot dynamics. On the other hand, this controller is limited to position control and does not consider the motion control.

Regarding the work in [38], we develop a generic interface that encompasses the different components of the global system: virtual 3D manipulator, Kinect sensor feedback values, skeleton image, implemented dynamic model, implemented sliding mode control, implemented recognition algorithm for calculating the joints position, and implemented security algorithm. This LabVIEW-based user interface is described in Section 5.

The present paper is organized as follows: in Section 2, we presents the recognition method. The dynamic model of the Lynxmotion robotic arm is detailed in Section 3. In Section 4, the control design based on the sliding mode control approach is described. Human-machine interface is presented as well as experiment results in Section 5. Finally, we conclude with a work summary.

2. Recognition Method

Several methods are used to detect the human arm movements. Kinect sensor is the most popular thanks to skeleton detect and depth computing. The Kinect is a motion sensor that can measure three-dimensional motion of a person. In fact, Kinect sensor generates a depth and image (x, y, and z) of human body. In addition, the Kinect sensor can provide space coordinates for each joint.

To enjoy these benefits, we need an Application Programmer's Interface (API) to the Kinect hardware and its skeletal tracking software. Microsoft's "Kinect for Windows SDK" was used to provide an API to the Kinect hardware. This API provides an estimate for the position of 20 anatomical landmarks in 3D at a frequency of 30 Hz and spatial and depth resolution of 640×480 pixels as shown in Figure 1. The default smoothing parameters are as follows:

(i) Correction factor = 0.5.

(ii) Smoothing factor = 0.5.

(iii) Jitter radius = 0.05 m.

(iv) Maximum deviation radius = 0.04 m.

(v) Future prediction = 0 frames.

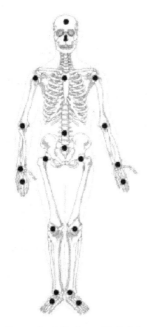

FIGURE 1: Kinect for Windows SDK detected joints.

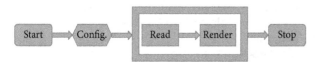

FIGURE 2: Operational Layout for the Kinect LabVIEW toolkit.

FIGURE 3: Skeleton and user display screen.

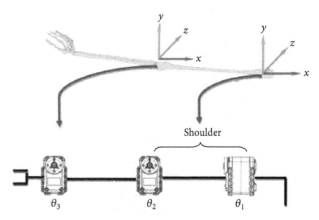

FIGURE 4: Human arm and manipulator robot model.

Based on Microsoft Kinect SDK, the Kinesthesia Toolkit for Microsoft Kinect is developed at University of Leeds initially for the medical rehabilitation and surgical tools. In addition, the toolkit helps the NI LabVIEW programmers to access and use the popular functions of the Microsoft Kinect camera such as RGB video, depth camera, and skeletal tracking. The toolkit comes fully packaged using JKI's VI Package Manager.

In addition, the toolkit allows the user to initialize and close the Kinect's different components through polymorphic VIs (RGB camera, depth camera, and skeletal tracking) dependent on the functionalities they require. The Operational Layout for the Kinect LabVIEW toolkit is described in Figure 2.

The first step is to initialize the Kinect; this act opens the device and returns a reference. The second step is to configure the Kinect. In this step, we can choose the RGB stream format, enable the skeleton smoothing, and select the appropriate event (video feedback from the RGB camera, 3D skeleton information, or depth information). In the next step, we can get skeleton, depth, and video information from the Kinect in the main loop such as while loop. The additional implementations can be put in the same loop. Finally, we stop the Kinect and close the communication.

In this paper, a user interface containing a skeleton display screen has been developed as shown in Figure 3. The screen

has been reserved to the skeleton display and the user video recording.

In this work, we focus on the human arm portion of the skeleton data. In fact, the human arm can be considered as being a 4DOF manipulator arm similar to Lynxmotion robotic arm. In our case, a robot manipulator model has been developed with a 3DOF. Therefore, we assume that the user has the opportunity to control the robot based on his right arm gestures. The three considered movements are as follows:

(i) Flexion-extension for the right shoulder joint.

(ii) Abduction-adduction for the right shoulder joint.

(iii) Flexion-extension for the right elbow joint.

The similarity of the human arm and the robot manipulator model is shown in Figure 4.

After the acquisition of each elementary joint position, an additional calculation is performed to determine the desired speed and acceleration. All these parameters will be considered as the desired trajectories for the manipulator robot control algorithm.

3. Dynamic Model of Lynxmotion Robotic Arm

The dynamic model deals with the torque and force causing the motion of the mechanical structure. In this section, robotic arm dynamic model has been computed based on

Euler-Lagrange formulation. The potential and kinetic energies of each link have been computed by the two following equations:

$$u_i = -m_i g^T\,{}_i^i P,$$

$$K_i = \frac{1}{2} m_i v_{c_i}^T v_{c_i} + \frac{1}{2}\,{}_i^i w^T\,{}_i^i I\,{}_i^i w, \tag{1}$$

where m_i is the ith link mass, v_{c_i} is the ith link linear velocity, ${}_i^i w$ is the ith link angular velocity, ${}_i^i I$ is the ith inertia tensor, and ${}_i^i P$ is the ith link position.

Further calculation, the dynamic model of a full actuated robot manipulator is expressed as follows:

$$M(q)\,\ddot{q} + N(q,\dot{q}) = \tau, \tag{2}$$

where τ is $n \times 1$ vector consisting on applied generalized torque, $M(q)$ is $n \times n$ symmetric and positive definite inertia matrix, $N(q,\dot{q})$ is the vector of nonlinearity term, and $q \in R^{n \times n}$.

The vector of nonlinearity term hails from centrifugal, Coriolis, and gravity terms described in the following equations:

$$N(q,\dot{q}) = V(q,\dot{q}) + G(q),$$

$$V(q,\dot{q}) = B(q)\,[\dot{q},\dot{q}] + C(q)\,[\dot{q}]^2. \tag{3}$$

Here, robot manipulator dynamic equation can be written as

$$\tau = M(q)\,\ddot{q} + B(q)\,[\dot{q},\dot{q}] + C(q)\,[\dot{q}]^2 + G(q), \tag{4}$$

where $B(q)$ is matrix of Coriolis torque, $C(q)$ is matrix of centrifugal torque, $[\dot{q},\dot{q}]$ is vector of joint velocity obtainable by $[\dot{q}_1 \cdot \dot{q}_2, \dot{q}_1 \cdot \dot{q}_3, \dots, \dot{q}_1 \cdot \dot{q}_n, \dot{q}_2 \cdot \dot{q}_3, \dots]^T$, and $[\dot{q}]^2$ is vector witch can be obtained by $[\dot{q}_1{}^2, \dot{q}_2{}^2, \dot{q}_3{}^2, \dots]^T$.

In our work, a 3 DOF manipulator model has been developed using the Lagrange formulation. The goal was to determine the Coriolis, centrifugal, and gravitational matrices for real implementation reasons.

4. Control Design

Robot manipulator has highly nonlinear dynamic parameters. For this reason, the design of a robust controller is required. In this section, we study the motion controller "sliding-mode control."

The dynamic model of the robot manipulator is described as follows:

$$M(q)\,\ddot{q} + C(q,\dot{q})\,\dot{q} + g(q) = \tau, \tag{5}$$

where $q = [q_1, q_2, q_3]^T$ and $\tau = [\tau_1, \tau_2, \tau_3]^T$.

Let $q_d(t)$ denote the desired trajectory. The tracking error is defined as

$$e = q_d(t) - q(t). \tag{6}$$

Define $\dot{q}_r = \dot{q}_d + s(q_d - q)$, where s is a definite positive matrix.

According to the linear characteristic of robotic, we obtain

$$\widehat{M}(q)\,\ddot{q}_r + \widehat{C}(q,\dot{q})\,\dot{q}_r + \widehat{g}(q) = \gamma(q,\dot{q},\dot{q}_r,\ddot{q}_r)\,\widehat{P}, \tag{7}$$

where $\widehat{P}$ is the robot estimated parameters vector and $\gamma(q,\dot{q},q_r,\dot{q}_r)$ is a repressor matrix.

Define

$$\widetilde{H}(q) = H(q) - \widehat{H}(q),$$

$$\widetilde{C}(q) = C(q,\dot{q}) - \widehat{C}(q,\dot{q}), \tag{8}$$

$$\widetilde{g}(q) = g(q) - \widehat{g}(q).$$

The sliding vector is selected as

$$s = \dot{e} + \mu * e. \tag{9}$$

We propose the sliding mode control law as follows:

$$\tau = \widehat{M}(q)\,\ddot{q}_r + \widehat{C}(q,\dot{q})\,\dot{q}_r + \widehat{g}(q) + s + k * \mathrm{sgn}(s), \tag{10}$$

where $k_i = \sum_j \bar{\gamma}_{ij} \overline{\widetilde{P}}_j$.

Define

$$\begin{aligned} \widetilde{P}_i \quad \text{Such} \quad &\forall i \ |\widetilde{P}_i| \le \overline{\overline{q}}_i, \\ \bar{\gamma}_{ij} \quad \text{Such} \quad &\forall i \ |\gamma_{ij}| \le \overline{\gamma}_{ij}. \end{aligned} \tag{11}$$

Theorem 1. *The proposed controller guarantees the asymptotic stability of the system.*

Proof. Select the LEC as

$$V(t) = \frac{1}{2} s^T M(q)\, s \Longrightarrow$$

$$\begin{aligned} \dot{V}(t) &= s^T M(q)\,\dot{s} + \frac{1}{2} s^T \dot{M}(q)\, s \\ &= s^T M(q)\,\dot{s} + s^T C(q)\, s \\ &= s^T \left[M(q)\,\ddot{q}_r + C(q,\dot{q})\,\dot{q}_r + g(q) - \tau \right]. \end{aligned} \tag{12}$$

Replacing τ by its expression (10) yields

$$\dot{V}(t)$$

$$= s^T \left[\widetilde{M}(q)\,\ddot{q}_r + \widetilde{C}(q,\dot{q})\,\dot{q}_r + \widetilde{g}(q) - k * \mathrm{sgn}(s) - s \right] \tag{13}$$

$$= s^T \left[\gamma(q,\dot{q},\dot{q}_r,\ddot{q}_r)\,\widetilde{P} - k \cdot \mathrm{sgn}(s) - s \right],$$

where $\gamma(q,\dot{q},\dot{q}_r,\ddot{q}_r) = [\gamma_{ij}]$ such as $|\gamma_{ij}| \le \overline{\gamma}_{ij}$.

And $\widetilde{P} = [\widetilde{P}_i]$ such as $|\widetilde{P}_i| \le \overline{\widetilde{P}}_{ij}$.

Yield

$$\dot{V}(t) = \sum_i \sum_j s_i \gamma_{ij} \widetilde{P}_j - \sum_i s_i K_i\,\mathrm{sgn}(s_i) - \sum_i s_i^2$$

$$= \sum_i \sum_j s_i \gamma_{ij} \widetilde{P}_j - \sum_i \sum_j |s_i|\,\overline{\gamma}_i \overline{\widetilde{P}}_j - \sum_i s_i^2 \le -\sum_i s_i^2 \tag{14}$$

$$\le 0.$$

This proves the stability. $\qquad\square$

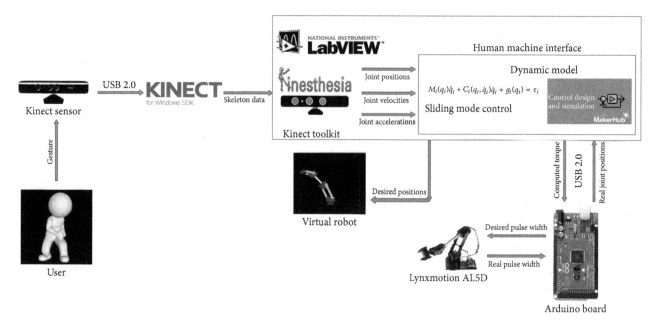

FIGURE 5: System overview.

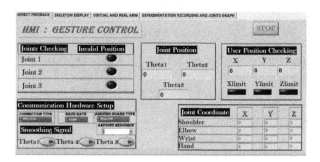

FIGURE 6: First screen of the user interface.

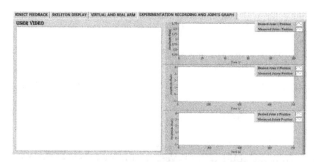

FIGURE 8: Fourth screen of the user interface.

FIGURE 7: Third screen of the user interface.

5. Experiment Results

In the beginning, we had some packages to install. Indeed, the JKI's VI Package Manager such as Kinesthesia Toolkit for Microsoft Kinect, LabVIEW Interface for Arduino (LIFA), and control design and simulation module are strictly required for the implementation and then for the proper system functioning.

In this section, we present a LabVIEW-based human-machine interface. The virtual robot has been designed in 3D LabVIEW virtual environment. The virtual robot has the same kinematics parameters of the real robot such as joints axes and links distances. A user interface screen has been reserved to display the virtual robot movement versus the real robot.

The control law based on the sliding mode control has been successfully implemented with the parameters discussed in the previous section.

Going from gesture applied by the human arm, Kinect sensor captures the human arm motion and abstracts it in 3D coordinates. Using Kinect for Windows SDK, the skeleton data are provided and transmitted to the recognition algorithm. Based on Kinesthesia Toolkit for Microsoft Kinect, the human arm joint positions, velocities, and accelerations are computed and considered as desired trajectories of the robotic arm. By helping of LabVIEW control design and simulation, the developed dynamic model of 3DOF Lynxmotion robotic arm is implemented. Also, a sliding mode control algorithm is implemented ensuring the high performance in the trajectories tracking. Furthermore, the computed torque

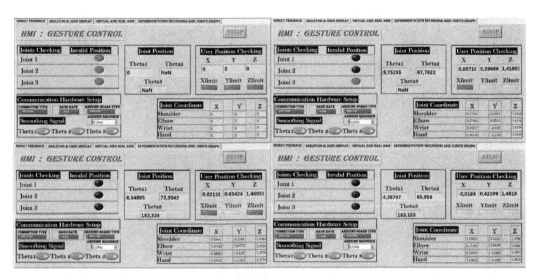

FIGURE 9: User position checking process.

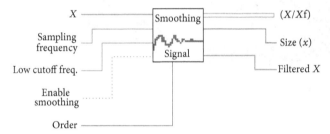

FIGURE 10: Butterworth-based designed filter.

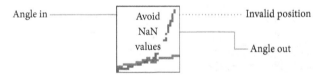

FIGURE 11: Avoid invalid position sub-VI.

is transmitted to the servomotors moving the mechanical structure of the robotic arm. Moreover, the desired joint positions are applied in the virtual environment to move the virtual robot in order to prove the compatibility of the desired motion in both real and virtual environment. Hence, an augmented reality approach is proposed to validate the control system.

The system overview can be presented by Figure 5.

In our experiment, we only use the first three joints and the remaining joints are not considered. Note that the user interface contains four screens.

The first screen is designed to the setting and hardware configuration. The screen displays the tracking process state such us invalid positions, joint positions, and 3D coordinates and user position checking. A security algorithm has been developed to secure the tracking process. Note that where the security program indicates a skeleton detection error, for one reason or another, the last calculated angle (already

validated) of each joint will be sent to the robot until the operator solves the problem. Based on the feedback node which returns the last valid result with a nonnumeric input, the security algorithm is developed and abstracted in sub-VI for importing in the user interface. Figure 11 illustrates the imported sub-VI. In addition, the user can also set the Arduino board communication such us connection type and baud rate and Arduino board type and select the Arduino resource.

In the tracking process, the operator's arm can twitch, leading to unwanted random movement. In order to avoid this undesired movement, we propose a Butterworth low pass filter-based smoothing signal algorithm. In the same screen, the user can enable the smoothing signal algorithm by pressing on the bouton control. The designed filter is abstracted in a sub-VI as shown in Figure 10. The filtered trajectories, presented as the desired trajectories in Figures 15, 16, and 17, demonstrate the effectiveness of the filtering algorithm.

Finally, the stop button is set in the developed interface to stop the tracking process and close all connected hardware. This screen is developed as shown in Figure 6.

The second screen, presented in Figure 3, is designed to record the user's video and skeleton display. Figure 7 shows the third screen to prove the augmented reality. In this page, we show the virtual and real environment. The user and the virtual robot will be displayed in the user video portion whereas the virtual robot will be presented in the virtual environment software.

The remaining screen describes the joints graphs and operator's video recording during the experimentation as shown in Figure 8.

After running, the operator must select the first screen, called Kinect Feedback, to adjust its position. A user position checking is triggered to secure the operator's position in the Kinect sensing field. A green color of the signaling LED indicates the good state of the recognition process. Otherwise, the LED color changes to red to indicate the

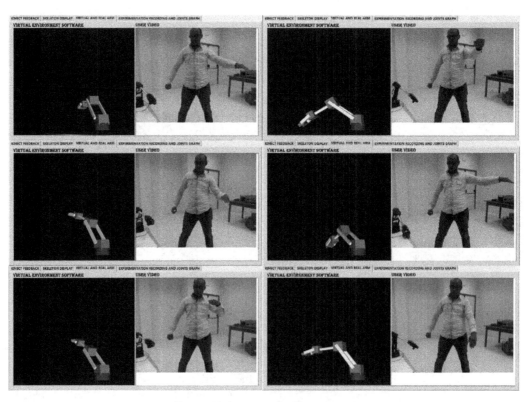

FIGURE 12: Augmented reality process.

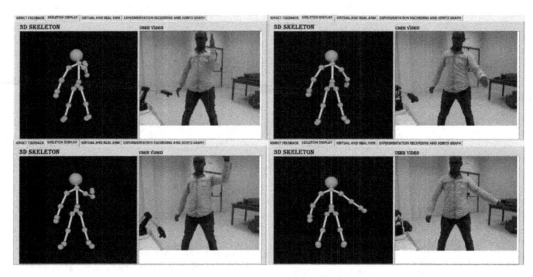

FIGURE 13: User and skeleton display.

problem of tracking. Figure 9 describes the executed screen in the user position checking process.

Based on Kinect toolkit for LabVIEW, the operator's skeleton data will be read by the LabVIEW interface. Then a gesture recognition method is executed to determine each joint angle. The calculated joint positions are considered as desired trajectories for the sliding mode control implemented in the developed software. Ultimately, the computed torque will be sent to the Atmel-based Arduino card via USB protocol. Therefore, the servomotors of the three first joints

will be actuated to move the mechanical structure of the Lynxmotion robot.

A three-degree of freedom virtual robot is used to perform this experiment. Essentially, the augmented reality evaluated both the ability of the robot manipulator to copy human hand, arm motions, and the ability of the user to use the human-robot manipulator interface. The proposed controller is validated by the augmented reality. In fact, by building a virtual robot by using LabVIEW other than the real robot, as shown in Figure 12, virtual robot movements

Figure 14: Gesture control process and real-time graphs.

are similar to the real robot. Therefore, the proposed control method is validated.

Figure 13 proves how the user can control the manipulator robot based in his detected skeleton.

Photographs series depicting gesture control process execution, each five seconds, with real-time graphs have been presented in Figure 14.

In the teleoperation process, the tracking error convergence is very important and the performance of our system is based on the tracking error optimization. Indeed, in the case that the elementary joint cannot track his similar human arm joint, the robotic arm will not be able to perform the desired task because of the accumulation of each joint position error. In this case, the end-effector localization is different regarding the desired placement. Therefore, the user must adapt the gesture with the current end-effector position to reduce the end-effector placement error. Hence, the adaptive gestures estimated by the user require a particular intelligence and such expertise. In another case, when the user applies the desired gesture with a variable velocity, in this situation, the control algorithm must respect the applied velocities and accelerations to conserve the convergence of the tracking

error. In order to overcome this constraint, the use of high performance sliding mode controller is highly required.

Figures 15, 16, and 17 show trajectories of each joint and the desired trajectory for each. Both trajectories are as a function of time. The illustrated results show the effectiveness of the proposed control approach. The illustrations have only one second as response time. In experimental condition, this time can be regarded as excellent. This control strategy should be improved if we hope to exploit this system in telemedicine applications. Moreover, the developed teleoperation approach can be used for industrial applications, in particular, for pic and place tasks in hazardous or unstructured environments. The real-time teleoperation system offers a benefit platform to manage the unexpected scenarios.

6. Conclusion

This paper applies the gesture control to the robot manipulators. Indeed, in this work we use the Kinect technology to establish a human-machine interaction (HMI). The developed control approach can be used in all applications,

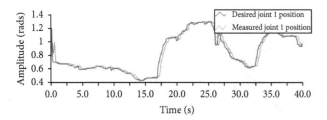

FIGURE 15: Desired and measured joint 1 position.

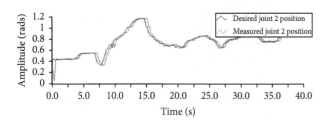

FIGURE 16: Desired and measured joint 2 position.

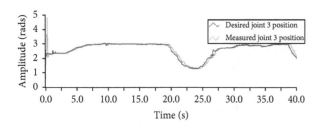

FIGURE 17: Desired and measured joint 3 position.

which require real-time human-robot cooperation. Trajectory tracking and system stability have been ensured by sliding mode control (SMC). Control and supervision both have been provided by a high-friendly human-machine interface developed in LabVIEW. Experiments have shown the high efficiency of the proposed approach. Furthermore, the Kinect-based teleoperation system is validated by augmented reality. In conclusion, the proposed control scheme provides a feasible teleoperation system for many applications such as manipulating in hazardous and unstructured environment. However, there are some constraints when applying the proposed method, such as the sensibility of the desired trajectory generated by the human arm even in case of random and unwanted movements. Indeed, the work space and the regional constraints must be respected in the control schemes by filtering the unaccepted trajectories. Moreover, for pic and place applications, grasping task is not considered in the proposed telemanipulation system. In perspective, this drawback can be overcome by using the electromyography biosignal for grasping task control.

Competing Interests

The authors declare that they have no competing interests.

References

[1] Y. Bouteraa, J. Ghommam, N. Derbel, and G. Poisson, "Nonlinear control and synchronization with time delays of multiagent robotic systems," *Journal of Control Science and Engineering*, vol. 2011, Article ID 632374, 9 pages, 2011.

[2] Y. Bouteraa, J. Ghommam, G. Poisson, and N. Derbel, "Distributed synchronization control to trajectory tracking of multiple robot manipulators," *Journal of Robotics*, vol. 2011, Article ID 652785, 10 pages, 2011.

[3] G. A. M. Vasiljevic, L. C. de Miranda, and E. E. C. de Miranda, "A case study of mastermind chess: comparing mouse/keyboard interaction with kinect-based gestural interface," *Advances in Human-Computer Interaction*, vol. 2016, Article ID 4602471, 10 pages, 2016.

[4] C.-H. Tsai, Y.-H. Kuo, K.-C. Chu, and J.-C. Yen, "Development and evaluation of game-based learning system using the microsoft kinect sensor," *International Journal of Distributed Sensor Networks*, vol. 2015, Article ID 498560, 10 pages, 2015.

[5] C.-H. Chuang, Y.-N. Chen, L.-W. Tsai, C.-C. Lee, and H.-C. Tsai, "Improving learning performance with happiness by interactive scenarios," *The Scientific World Journal*, vol. 2014, Article ID 807347, 12 pages, 2014.

[6] K. J. Bower, J. Louie, Y. Landesrocha, P. Seedy, A. Gorelik, and J. Bernhardt, "Clinical feasibility of interactive motion-controlled games for stroke rehabilitation," *Journal of NeuroEngineering and Rehabilitation*, vol. 12, no. 1, article 63, 2015.

[7] M. Štrbac, S. Kočović, M. Marković, and D. B. Popović, "Microsoft kinect-based artificial perception system for control of functional electrical stimulation assisted grasping," *BioMed Research International*, vol. 2014, Article ID 740469, 12 pages, 2014.

[8] N. Kanwal, E. Bostanci, K. Currie, and A. F. Clark, "A navigation system for the visually impaired: a fusion of vision and depth sensor," *Applied Bionics and Biomechanics*, vol. 2015, Article ID 479857, 16 pages, 2015.

[9] H.-H. Pham, T.-L. Le, and N. Vuillerme, "Real-time obstacle detection system in indoor environment for the visually impaired using microsoft kinect sensor," *Journal of Sensors*, vol. 2016, Article ID 3754918, 13 pages, 2016.

[10] D. Tuvshinjargal, B. Dorj, and D. J. Lee, "Hybrid motion planning method for autonomous robots using kinect based sensor fusion and virtual plane approach in dynamic environments," *Journal of Sensors*, vol. 2015, Article ID 471052, 13 pages, 2015.

[11] T. Xu, S. Jia, Z. Dong, and X. Li, "Obstacles regions 3D-perception method for mobile robots based on visual saliency," *Journal of Robotics*, vol. 2015, Article ID 720174, 10 pages, 2015.

[12] W. Shang, X. Cao, H. Ma, H. Zang, and P. Wei, "Kinect-based vision system of mine rescue robot for low illuminous environment," *Journal of Sensors*, vol. 2016, Article ID 8252015, 9 pages, 2016.

[13] H. Kim and I. Kim, "Dynamic arm gesture recognition using spherical angle features and hidden markov models," *Advances in Human-Computer Interaction*, vol. 2015, Article ID 785349, 7 pages, 2015.

[14] A. Chávez-Aragón, R. Macknojia, P. Payeur, and R. Laganière, "Rapid 3D modeling and parts recognition on automotive vehicles using a network of RGB-D sensors for robot guidance," *Journal of Sensors*, vol. 2013, Article ID 832963, 16 pages, 2013.

[15] A. Procházka, O. Vyšata, M. Valis, and R. Yadollahi, "The MS kinect use for 3d modelling and gait analysis in the Matlab

environment," in *Proceedings of the 21th Annual Conference: Technical Computing 2013*, Prague, Czech Republic, 2013.

[16] B. Y. L. Li, A. S. Mian, W. Liu, and A. Krishna, "Using Kinect for face recognition under varying poses, expressions, illumination and disguise," in *Proceedings of the IEEE Workshop on Applications of Computer Vision (WACV '13)*, pp. 186–192, Tampa, Fla, USA, January 2013.

[17] C. Muhiddin, D. B. Phillips, M. J. Miles, L. Picco, and D. M. Carberry, "Kinect 4 ... holographic optical tweezers," *Journal of Optics*, vol. 15, no. 7, Article ID 075302, 2013.

[18] P. Qiu, C. Ni, J. Zhang, and H. Cao, "Research of virtual simulation of traditional Chinese bone setting techniques based on kinect skeletal information," *Journal of Shandong University of Traditional Chinese Medicine*, no. 3, pp. 202–204, 2014.

[19] R. Ibañez, Á. Soria, A. Teyseyre, and M. Campo, "Easy gesture recognition for Kinect," *Advances in Engineering Software*, vol. 76, pp. 171–180, 2014.

[20] I.-J. Ding and C.-W. Chang, "An eigenspace-based method with a user adaptation scheme for human gesture recognition by using Kinect 3D data," *Applied Mathematical Modelling*, vol. 39, no. 19, pp. 5769–5777, 2015.

[21] B. Galna, G. Barry, D. Jackson, D. Mhiripiri, P. Olivier, and L. Rochester, "Accuracy of the Microsoft Kinect sensor for measuring movement in people with Parkinson's disease," *Gait & Posture*, vol. 39, no. 4, pp. 1062–1068, 2014.

[22] K. Qian, H. Yang, and J. Niu, "Developing a gesture based remote human-robot interaction system using kinect," *International Journal of Smart Home*, vol. 7, no. 4, pp. 203–208, 2013.

[23] S. Shirwalkar, A. Singh, K. Sharma, and N. Singh, "Telemanipulation of an industrial robotic arm using gesture recognition with Kinect," in *Proceedings of the IEEE International Conference on Control, Automation, Robotics and Embedded Systems (CARE '13)*, Jabalpur, India, December 2013.

[24] G. Du and P. Zhang, "Markerless human–robot interface for dual robot manipulators using Kinect sensor," *Robotics and Computer-Integrated Manufacturing*, vol. 30, no. 2, pp. 150–159, 2014.

[25] A. Hernansanz, A. Casals, and J. Amat, "A multi-robot cooperation strategy for dexterous task oriented teleoperation," *Robotics and Autonomous Systems*, vol. 68, pp. 156–172, 2015.

[26] F. Terrence, F. Conti, G. Sébastien, and B. Charles, "novel interfaces for remote driving: gesture, haptic and PDA," in *SPIE Telemanipulator and Telepresence Technologies VII*, vol. 4195, pp. 300–311, 2000.

[27] E. Ueda, Y. Matsumoto, M. Imai, and T. Ogasawara, "A hand-pose estimation for vision-based human interfaces," *IEEE Transactions on Industrial Electronics*, vol. 50, no. 4, pp. 676–684, 2003.

[28] J. Zhang and A. Knoll, "A two-arm situated artificial communicator for human–robot cooperative assembly," *IEEE Transactions on Industrial Electronics*, vol. 50, no. 4, pp. 651–658, 2003.

[29] B. Ionescu, D. Coquin, P. Lambert, and V. Buzuloiu, "Dynamic hand gesture recognition using the skeleton of the hand," *EURASIP Journal on Applied Signal Processing*, vol. 13, pp. 2101–2109, 2005.

[30] Y. Kim, S. Leonard, A. Shademan, A. Krieger, and P. C. W. Kim, "Kinect technology for hand tracking control of surgical robots: technical and surgical skill comparison to current robotic masters," *Surgical Endoscopy*, vol. 28, no. 6, pp. 1993–2000, 2014.

[31] J. Kofman, S. Verma, and X. Wu, "Robot-manipulator teleoperation by markerless vision-based hand-arm tracking," *International Journal of Optomechatronics*, vol. 1, no. 3, pp. 331–357, 2007.

[32] R. C. Luo, B.-H. Shih, and T.-W. Lin, "Real time human motion imitation of anthropomorphic dual arm robot based on Cartesian impedance control," in *Proceedings of the 11th IEEE International Symposium on Robotic and Sensors Environments (ROSE '13)*, pp. 25–30, Washington, DC, USA, October 2013.

[33] R. Afthoni, A. Rizal, and E. Susanto, "Proportional derivative control based robot arm system using microsoft kinect," in *Proceedings of the International Conference on Robotics, Biomimetics, Intelligent Computational Systems (ROBIONETICS '13)*, pp. 24–29, IEEE, Jogjakarta, Indonesia, November 2013.

[34] M. Al-Shabi, "Simulation and implementation of real-time vision-based control system for 2-DoF robotic arm using PID with hardware-in-the-loop," *Intelligent Control and Automation*, vol. 6, no. 2, pp. 147–157, 2015.

[35] I. Benabdallah, Y. Bouteraa, R. Boucetta, and C. Rekik, "Kinect-based Computed Torque Control for lynxmotion robotic arm," in *Proceedings of the 7th International Conference on Modelling, Identification and Control (ICMIC '15)*, pp. 1–6, Sousse, Tunisia, December 2015.

[36] H. Mehdi and O. Boubaker, "Robot-assisted therapy: design, control and optimization," *International Journal on Smart Sensing and Intelligent Systems*, vol. 5, no. 4, pp. 1044–1062, 2012.

[37] I. Ben Aabdallah, Y. Bouteraa, and C. Rekik, "Design of smart robot for wrist rehabilitation," *International journal of smart sensing and intelligent systems*, vol. 9, no. 2, 2016.

[38] C. Pillajo and J. E. Sierra, "Human machine interface HMI using Kinect sensor to control a SCARA robot," in *Proceedings of the IEEE Colombian Conference on Communications and Computing (COLCOM '13)*, pp. 1–5, Medellin, Colo, USA, May 2013.

16

The Quantified Athlete: Associations of Wearables for High School Athletes

Kwok Ng (ID)[1] **and Tatiana Ryba** (ID)[2]

[1]Department of Physical Education and Sport Sciences, University of Limerick, Limerick, Ireland
[2]Department of Psychology, University of Jyvaskyla, Jyväskylä, Finland

Correspondence should be addressed to Kwok Ng; kwok.ng@hbsc.org

Guest Editor: Filipe M. Clemente

The adoption of wearable technology in competitive sports can be an advantage to performance and training. Athletes who use personalised data to quantify their performances with the possibilities of sharing with others may use wearables to reinforce the athletic identity. Despite these changes, few studies have actually examined the associations between wearables and developing athletes in their quest for professional sports. Student athletes (n = 437, age = 17y) still in high schools completed a web-based survey about their professional aspirations, athletic identity, and the association with wearables. Wearables were measured by ownership and usage of apps, fitness trackers, or sports watches. Odds ratio (OR) and 95% confidence intervals (CI) were reported. Most high school athletes had apps (64.3%) or fitness trackers (65.2%) and over half of the athletes (58%) had aspirations for professional sport. Athletic identity was positively associated with ownership and usage of apps and fitness trackers. The OR was greater for professional sport aspiration with fitness trackers owners (OR = 2.60, CI = 1.44-4.73) and users (OR = 4.04, CI = 2.09-7.81) than athletes without fitness trackers. Wearables were common among high school athletes and it was part of their athletic identity. For professional aspiring athletes, wearables have the potential to help provide data to support suitable training and competition schedules at a time when students may be overloaded with academic pressures.

1. Introduction

The technological advances, lowered costs, and public interest have allowed wearables to be widely available. Although the majority of users have been targeted for adult use, there has been recent interest among high school students' use [1]. As high school athletes attempt to strive for excellence in their sports, they are also expected to complete their education at the same time [2]. High school athletes may find it difficult to cope with the pressures and expectations of them [3]. Some may feel they are considered as athletes first and then student, and others may feel they are high school student first and then athlete. High school athletes need to manage time so that they can complete their academic achievements as well as sporting ones. With the advent of technological tools in the last 10 years, such as wearables, mobile apps, and online programs, there is good potential that high school athletes can find the right balance with their schedules. As such, it

is surprising how few studies have investigated the mediating effect of wearables among high school athletes [1].

Wearables consist of sensors that athletes wear on them [4]. The majority are designed whereby there is a graphical user interface that provides information about the sensor. For the majority of commercially available wearables, the graphical user interface is designed in a way to provide personalised data. More advanced interfaces allows the users to share their data to others, and for athletes, this could be for their coach, team mates, rivals, and the public. In professional arenas, data from wearables are used to supplement sport commentary [5]. For example, the NBA set up six cameras above the court and take detailed information about all the athlete's movements at a rate of 25 times per second, resulting in approximately 72,000 unique movements per game [6]. Although data from professional sport may be public, in the form of match statistics and individual performances, another aspect that has increasing interest is the quantified self (hereafter, QS) movement [7]. Examples of this in sport are often seen among endurance athletes who have reported the use of QS tools to tailor their training programmes [8] as well as in team sports for training loads [9].

The appeal of QS for tools that lead to optimisation is present among top athletes who use rational choice theories and actions related to calculated optimal choices [10]. Early experiments that provided real-time emotion tracking in the 1980s by Mihaly Czikszehtmihalyi suggested that the tracking tools had the capability to provide physiological data as well as logging psychological states, moods, and emotions [11]. The QS is "focused on the individual self, improving the self, and developing self-knowledge" [12] and hence presents a bridge between sports performance data and self-awareness of individuals who aspire towards professional sports. These advances make use of wearables a common place for athletes. However, less is known about the effect of wearables on the athletes' identity, which may be important for understanding the way high school athletes may balance their academic and sporting activities.

The formation of the athletic identity during adolescence is crucial. High school athletes reported five key demands; (1) to achieve a work-life balance between sport and other life goals, (2) to find one's individual path in sport, (3) to handle the pressures of selections, (4) to acquire prestige from peers, judges, and others involved in the sport, and (5) to cope with potential relationship problems [13]. Management of these demands can lead to anxiety and worry because there is a high level of uncertainty in the future of the athlete's career. Earlier research has indicated that coping strategies used by athletes were effective through 'choice of coping strategy' and 'automaticity' [14]. Self-quantifiers can select the information they have available to them, thus making the appropriate choice of coping strategies more effective based on the information available.

When athletes associate their roles as athletes, they may be more committed to training and focus more on sport goals. However, too strong athletic identity can also lead to dependency on performance outcomes [15], which may lead to sport termination. QS influences adolescent's understanding of values that sport can offer and extend to the way individuals define themselves, that is, the individuals' concept of self. The theory of self-construal [16] could help explain how the athletic identity goes beyond the themes previously hypothesized by Brewer, Van Raalte, and Linder [15], which included 'exclusivity', 'negative affectivity', and 'social identity'. The self-construal can help in distinct ways people understand themselves in their social context [17]. Self-construalism takes place among athletes where they organise their behaviour based on their own thoughts, feelings, and actions, rather than on others [18], and at the same time identify themselves within a group, as athletes.

1.1. Human Computer Interfaces and Athletes. Mobile application usage in relation to sport allows the athletes to quantify their own training and monitor their performance as well

as the possibility of sharing them with others. Applications like Google Fit, Apple Health app, and other downloadable apps may ease the experience to start tracking individual activity. Adolescents can capture the time of activity through self-input, automated registered through phone components, or both, and the results can be shared to their closed or wider social networks. These latter features are linked with athletic identity concepts, specifically the domains of socialisation and feedback. Specific athlete centred programs can be designed to meet specific personalised goals. One such example is the growth in professional personal analysts hired to improve performance outcomes [4]. As the data becomes specific to sport and performances, there could be a tendency for the athletes to instil such knowledge into their identity as an athlete.

In Finland, over half of the adolescents own apps on their phones that track physical activity; however, only one in six actually reported to use them. Moreover, in terms of sports watches and heart rate monitors, a quarter of adolescents aged between 11 and 15 own them, and only ten percent reported to actually use them [19]. In the United Kingdom, few adolescents value the use of wearables for promotion of physical activity as the primary market has been intended for adults [20]. However, there is a place for wearables, because in Finland, the ownership and usage of wearables were more strongly associated with individuals who reported to meet physical activity recommendations [19]. These preliminary investigations were limited to young adolescents, and information about sport specialisation was missing in the analysis by Ng and colleagues.

Heart rate monitors or sports watches are able to capture data when the phone is not close enough to pick up the physical activity measurements. Studies have described the importance of comfort over reliability among adolescents [1]. It is not known if high school athletes question the reliability as much as it is done in scientific research. For example, there are criticisms of such tools to measure physical activity because there are uncertainties in the degree of accuracy that can really improve lifestyles [21]. Despite its scientific flaws, athletes who choose to rely upon devices for self-quantifying can strengthen their identity with the data they have. The data from the wearables can be shared with the coach and family members to assist with training and competition schedules to balance the critical moments of development in sport and academic achievements.

1.2. Purpose of the Study. Given the paucity of literature on the athletic digital natives' use of quantified self, we intend to use this paper as an exploratory study into the associations between athletic identity and professional sport aspiration, with wearables mediating this relationship. More specifically, we examine whether wearables would enhance the athletic identity of high school athletes, particularly in athletes with aspirations for professional sport (Figure 1). It is very likely that certain athletic characteristics may be confounders to these associations, more specifically, the predominant sport type, current sport level, biological sex and,

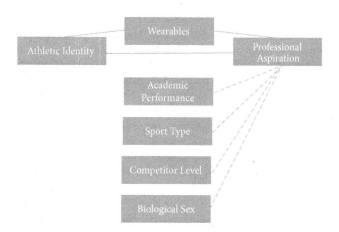

FIGURE 1: Mediation model of wearables in the relationship between athletic identity and professional aspiration, with athletic performance, sport type, and competitor level as covariates.

because these athletes are still in high school, their academic performance.

2. Materials and Methods

2.1. Participants. The study was approved by the University of Jyvaskyla's Ethical committee. Second-year adolescents of elite sport upper secondary school (age = 17y) were recruited to take part in this study. Seven of the possible 13 upper secondary schools with sports specialisations (in Finnish, urheilulukio) from the South, North, and Central Finland were randomly selected. A total of 490 adolescents took part in the study. A web-based questionnaire was completed during school hours in a classroom in March 2017, with the purpose of collecting data on adolescents' development [22]. Survey completion was conducted voluntarily, whereby students could miss certain questions or end the questionnaire when they desired. For the purposes of this study, 102 adolescents had missing data (total cases; physical activity wearables questionnaire; n = 50, gender; n = 3, professional aspirations; n = 74) with the largest sample size of n = 437. To maximise population statistics, cases were only removed for specific analyses.

2.2. Measures

2.2.1. Athletic Identity. The athletic identity measure scale (AIMS) is a 10-item scale encompassing social, cognitive, and affective elements of athletic identity [15]. Each item has a seven-point Likert scale with extremities of 'strongly disagree' and 'strongly agree'. A global sum score of all items has been demonstrated to have adequate internal consistency (Cronbach's alpha = 0.93) for a unidimensional construct and suitable test-retest reliability (r = 0.89) [15]. In this study, the reliability of the scale was slightly lower, but acceptable [23] with Cronbach's alpha = 0.79. The scores were summed when used as a measure of overall athletic identity.

2.2.2. Physical Activity Wearables. Physical activity wearables (PAW) included one item about heart rate monitors or sport watches (HRM) and one item about mobile phone applications (apps) for physical activity tracking. Both items had response options of (1) "do not have", (2) "do have but do not use", and (3) "do have and use". Volunteers from the survey took part in focus groups to test the face validity of this item. Following the focus group, there was 100% agreement that responses would not have changed, therefore confirming its face validity. Therefore, the groups classification were (1) nonowner, (2) owner, and (3) user.

2.2.3. Professional Aspirations. A single item was used to measure developing athletes' aspirations. The question wording was "Are you aiming to become a professional athlete?" with response options of "yes" and "no". Coding of this variables was dichotomised, with 'no' as the reference category.

2.2.4. Other Possible Confounders. Potential confounders to the associations included gender, sport type, competition level, and academic performance. Gender, a background variable, was used to determine the sex of the athlete. Athletes provided information about their main sport and this was grouped into individual sports or team sports. Individuals reported their competition level and were grouped into national level athlete, European level, or world level. The reference category was 'national level'. Academic performance was measured by athletes' reporting their previous school year grade point average (GPA). Low GPA (lower than 7), between 7 and 8 and between 8 and 9, and high GPA (above 9 out of 10) groups were formed. The reference category was 'low GPA'.

2.3. Statistical Methods. Descriptive statistics were performed to report the ownership and usage of PAWS among the athletes. Chi-square tests test proportion differences in the background variables of gender and sport type. Separate analysis of variance (ANOVA) tests with post hoc tests was conducted to test the differences in means between nonowner, owner, and user of (1) phone apps and (2) fitness trackers.

Multiple binary logistic regressions were performed with professional sport aspiration as the dependent variable. The basic model was tested with athletic identity as a continuous variable, gender (with females as the reference category), GPA (with less than 7 as reference category), competition level (with national as the reference category), and type of sport (with individual sports as the reference category). Three mediated models were used, one for apps, one for fitness trackers, and one for both apps and fitness trackers. Nagelkerke R^2 was used to determine the approximate goodness of fit models, and 95% confidence intervals (CI) of the adjusted odds ratio (OR) were used to determine the level of significance and the effect of the associations.

3. Results

There were the same number of females (n = 218) and males (n = 219), and a few more team sport (n = 230)

TABLE 1: Sample characteristics (%) and chi-square test of independence.

	Apps				Fitness Tracker			
	None	Own	Use	p	None	Own	Use	p
	N = 157	N = 220	N = 63		N = 153	N = 150	N = 137	
Sex				.685				.036
Female	48.4	49.5	54.8		41.4	54.7	54.1	
Male	51.6	50.5	45.2		58.6	45.3	45.9	
Sport				.036				<.001
Individual	55.5	42.3	44.3		37.5	41.3	64.9	
Team	44.5	57.7	55.7		62.5	58.7	35.1	
Level				.829				.301
National	48.2	43.4	46.2		43.5	43.2	50.0	
European	38.1	38.9	40.4		43.5	36.4	36.5	
World	13.7	17.7	13.5		13.0	20.5	13.5	
Academic				.026				.050
GPA mean	8.17	7.93	7.89		7.87	8.07	8.11	
GPA SD	.88	.90	1.06		.86	.92	.98	
Aspiration				.014				<.001
Professional	48.3	62.0	66.1		41.7	59.3	72.4	
Non-professional	51.7	38.0	33.9		58.3	40.7	27.6	
	35.7%	50.0%	14.3%		34.7%	34.1%	31.1%	

than individual sport (n = 206) athletes (Table 1). However, there were significantly more females who own and use fitness trackers than males (p = .036). In addition, there were significantly more athletes in team sports who have and use apps for tracking fitness than athletes from individual sports (p = .036). However, fitness trackers were significantly more common among individual sport athletes than in team sports to the extent that twice as many fitness trackers users were from individual sports athletes compared with athletes in team sports. Just over a third of the athletes did not have either apps (35.7%) or fitness trackers (34.7%); however the distribution between ownership and usage differed between apps and fitness trackers. Almost half of the athletes with fitness trackers (47.7%) reported to use them, whereas fewer owners (22.2%) reported to use apps. Almost half of the athletes (44.7%) reported to own or use both apps or fitness trackers, with over half of athletes (57.3%) who do not own apps reported to use fitness trackers and similar proportions of athletes (56.2%) who reported they did not have a fitness tracker, but owned or used apps.

3.1. Professional Sport Aspirations. In Table 2 there are column percentages of athletes who aspire for professional and nonprofessional career in sport. Almost two-thirds of adolescents who have aspirations for professional sports were males (61.1%), whereas the majority of female athletes were without this aspiration (63.8%). Furthermore, a greater proportion of professional aspiring athletes had academic grades of 8 and less (46.3%), when compared with athletes without this aspiration (30.7%). For both athletes who aspired for professional and nonprofessional sport, the proportions remained the same for competition level and whether they

were involved in individual or team based sports. For both apps and fitness trackers, the proportions of professional aspiring athletes were greater for owning and usage when compared with nonowners.

There were strong associations (Table 3) between professional sport aspiration and athletic identity (OR = 3.28, CI = 2.37-4.55) as well as gender (OR = 3.14, CI = 1.93-5.09). When compared with the lowest grade (less than 7), athletes with the highest grades (over 9) were less likely to have professional sport aspirations (OR = 0.31, CI = 0.11-0.88). Neither competition level nor sport type was significantly associated with professional sport aspiration.

3.2. Phone Apps. Athletes who reported ownership (M = 5.17, SD = .81) had significantly greater athletic identity (p = .015) than nonowners (M = 4.92, SD = .89) of apps (Table 4). This result was particularly pronounced in the AIMS negative affectivity subscale and was not evident in either the exclusivity or the social identity subscales.

Ownership and usage of phone apps were not associated with professional aspirations, although the regression model improved from Nagelkerke R^2 = 0.30 in the null model to R^2 = 0.31 in the model with the apps included. After controlling for apps, the estimate for athletic identity was slightly lower, yet for gender it was greater than in the null model.

3.3. Fitness Trackers. The differences in athletic identity were more noticeable between users (M = 5.31, SD = 0.76), owners (M = 5.09, SD = .075), and nonowners (M = 4.81, SD = 0.93) of fitness trackers (p < .001). In the social identity (p < .001), exclusivity (p = .008), and negative affectivity (p = .033),

TABLE 2: Proportions (in %) of professional aspiring athletes by demographics.

	Not Professional (n = 175)	Professional (n = 238)	Total (n = 413)	χ^2	p
Sex				24.94	<.001
Female	63.8	38.9	49.4		
Male	36.2	61.1	50.6		
GPA				14.85	.002
-7	5.1	11.8	9.0		
7-8	24.6	34.5	30.3		
8-9	46.3	39.9	42.6		
9+	24.0	13.9	18.2		
Level				1.75	.418
National	41.7	48.3	45.6		
European	42.3	36.6	39.0		
World	16.0	15.1	15.4		
Sport				3.51	0.061
Individual	52.9	43.6	47.5		
Team	47.1	56.4	52.5		
Apps				8.56	0.014
None	44.0	30.3	36.1		
Own	45.1	54.2	50.4		
Use	10.9	15.5	13.6		
Trackers				26.51	<.001
None	46.3	24.4	33.7		
Own	32.6	34.9	33.9		
Use	21.1	40.8	32.4		

TABLE 3: Binary logistic regressions of sport aspiration with phone apps and fitness trackers.

		OR	LCI	UCI	OR	LCI	UCI	OR	LCI	UCI	OR	LCI	UCI
AIMS		3.28	2.37	4.55	3.18	2.30	4.40	2.90	2.07	4.05	2.85	2.03	3.99
Sex													
	Female	REF			REF			REF			REF		
	Male	3.14	1.93	5.09	3.23	1.99	5.28	3.69	2.22	6.14	3.77	2.26	6.30
GPA													
	-7	REF			REF			REF			REF		
	7-8	0.78	0.29	2.08	0.83	0.31	2.25	0.68	0.25	1.89	0.72	0.26	2.03
	8-9	0.49	0.19	1.29	0.54	0.20	1.43	0.43	0.16	1.16	0.46	0.17	1.26
	9+	0.31	0.11	0.88	0.33	0.12	0.95	0.23	0.08	0.68	0.25	0.08	0.73
Levels													
	National	REF			REF			REF			REF		
	European	0.71	0.42	1.21	0.71	0.42	1.20	0.83	0.48	1.43	0.82	0.47	1.43
	Worlds	1.08	0.54	2.17	1.04	0.52	2.10	1.13	0.55	2.31	1.10	0.53	2.27
Sport													
	Individual	REF			REF			REF			REF		
	Team	1.29	0.80	2.07	1.21	0.75	1.96	1.68	1.01	2.81	1.60	0.95	2.68
Apps													
	None				REF						REF		
	Own				1.50	0.90	2.50				1.31	0.77	2.23
	Use				2.12	0.99	4.53				1.63	0.73	3.65
Trackers													
	None							REF			REF		
	Own							2.69	1.49	4.85	2.61	1.44	4.73
	Use							4.36	2.28	8.33	4.04	2.09	7.81
Nagelkerke R^2		0.301			0.313			0.360			0.365		

OR: Adjusted Odds Ratio, LCI: lower 95% confidence interval, UCI: upper 95% confidence interval, and REF: reference category.

TABLE 4: Mean scores of athletic identity of apps and fitness tracker users.

	Apps				Fitness Tracker			
	None	Own	Use	ANOVA	None	Own	Use	ANOVA
	N = 157	N = 220	N = 63	p	N = 153	N = 150	N = 137	p
AIMS	4.91	5.17†	5.10	.020	4.81	5.09†	5.31‡	<.001
Social	5.77	5.88	5.90	.461	5.61	5.90†	6.04‡	<.001
Exclusivity	3.25	3.57	3.56	.062	3.24	3.40	3.73‡	<.009
Negative Affectivity	4.62	5.00†	4.48	.005	4.58	4.83	4.99‡	.041

†Post hoc test between unused and none <.05. ‡Post hoc test between use and none <.05.

users of fitness trackers had significantly higher scores than nonowners.

The association between fitness trackers ownership and professional aspirations was positive (OR = 2.69, CI = 1.49-4.85) when compared with athletes who did not have fitness trackers. A stronger association was between fitness tracker users (OR = 4.36, CI=2.28-8.33) and professional sport aspiration compared to athletes without fitness trackers. The effect of athletic identity was reduced from the null model, although there is a stronger association with gender. In addition, athletes in team sports were positively associated with professional aspirations (OR = 1.68, CI = 1.01-2.81) when compared with individual sport athletes. Nagelkerke R^2 = .360 was stronger than the null model.

The final model included both apps and fitness trackers, and the model was slightly improved (Nagelkerke R^2 = 0.365). The strength of the associations for professional sport aspiration with fitness trackers was still positive for owners (OR = 2.6, CI = 1.44-4.73) and users (OR = 4.04, CI = 2.09-7.81) when compared with athletes without fitness trackers, but slightly less. The adjusted odds were also lower for athletic identity but increased for gender, and sport type was no longer significantly associated with professional sport aspiration.

4. Discussion

According to the results of this study, the majority of high school athletes have apps, fitness trackers, or both and over half had aspirations for professional sport. Ownership and use of fitness trackers were also associated with increased athletic identity and each of its subdomains. Finally, fitness trackers, athletic identity, gender, academic performance, and type of sports were predictors for professional sport aspirations, whereas the associations with apps were not significant.

4.1. PAWS Prevalence. The proportions of apps and fitness trackers ownership were much higher than previously indicated from studies of the general population [19]. This was expected for a number of reasons. The first concerns the sample from this study, whereby in this study, developing athletes were only included, whereas previous studies have been designed to include the general population [1]. Another possible reason is that the data were collected in more recent times. With increasing types of apps, there are more opportunities for adolescents to express themselves through social media and thus reinforce the identity. The number of followers in a social media account can turn an individual into a minicelebrity and the identity that is associated with that [24]. Technology in sports is a fast growing field, which enables more products to be more affordable and provides more purposeful human computer interactions. In addition, a third consideration is the average age of athletes being in the late teens. Ng and colleagues [19] noticed stronger associations in use of apps and fitness trackers with age, and as adolescents get older, they become more competent with existing products that have been designed for adults, thus increasing the appeal to use apps and fitness trackers.

4.2. Trackers and Athletic Identity. There was a positive association between owning a fitness tracker and athletic identity. This was most pronounced in the athletic identity social domain and unclear in the exclusivity and negative affectivity subdomains. However, fitness trackers users had the highest level of athletic identity and this was significant in subdomains too, when compared with athletes without fitness trackers. This was also expected, because the use of fitness trackers are associated with being fit among adolescents [25]. Data ownership from the quantified self allows the athletes to change their own behaviours and could then be shared with others [26]. It is suggested that trackers are a product which can be associated with sports equipment and is used to help improve sport performance. Since trackers provide real time as well as postperformance data, the information forms a source of feedback and has the potential to change training practices, competition performances, and improved performance, if used in the right way [8]. The potential to share quantifiable data to provide reasons for the poor performances needs further investigations as such social activities may become a protective factor against burnout.

Owning apps were also associated with athletic identity, but not for users of apps. More specifically, there was a higher negative affectivity score among owners when compared with athletes without apps. In the face validity focus groups, some athletes felt that apps were not appropriate for the serious athletes. Although the purpose of the study was not to analyse the details from the focus group data, interpretation of this response suggests that there are divides among users of technology. Within smartphones, there are many sensors which the apps can convert into information used by the athlete, yet making it coherent and purposeful for the user can be challenging [27]. Data presented by the majority of free apps were used to provide health promotion goals and do not seem to be valued by youth [20], suggesting that more tailored user experiences for young people in physical activity and competitive sport apps are needed. Moreover, it has been pointed out that adults who traditionally provide support for adolescents such as parents and coaches need better awareness for how apps can be useful for athletes [28].

4.3. Professional Sport Aspirations. Athletic identity and gender were two strong predictors for professional sport aspirations. According to the binary logistic models, as athletic identity increased, the stronger are the odds of selecting an athlete with professional aspirations. In addition, more males had professional aspirations than females, and as the variables from PAWS were entered into the model, the odds increased when compared with females. This may have been due to the fact that the females in this study had higher athletic identity than males, but fewer females had professional sport aspirations. In addition, athletes with the highest academic grades (above 9) were less likely to have professional aspirations than athletes with the lowest academic (below 7) grades. These findings may be explained through a number of studies that have examined athletic identity.

From previous research, the identity of student athletes impacted their career decision-making and future plans; that is, a high level of athlete identity was associated with a tendency to choose careers in sport [29], lower academic aspirations and efficacy [30], and difficulties balancing other life roles [31]. Moreover, female athletes showed higher levels of identification with the student role when compared with male athletes [30] and higher academic motivation [32] that might be explained with the limited professional sport opportunities for women. On the contrary, male athletes with a higher athletic identity, especially in high revenue sports, tend to have lower GPAs [33].

Fitness trackers variable was strongly associated with professional sport aspirations. In addition, the fit of the model improved from the null model. Athletes who want to use an advantage over their rivals can use fitness trackers to give personalised training and planning knowledge [9]. Moreover, to improve performance in professional sports, technology is constantly used [11]. The commonality of trackers has recently reached the information sharing with spectators in some professional sports [6]. Sensors have become a part of the competition. For example, in the 2017 Beach Volleyball World Tour, athletes used a sensor that the media used to report calories burnt during a phase in the game with the number of jumps they had performed. These additions have made trackers use as part of the equipment and also the identity of the athlete. This cause issues not only surrounding ownership of data [12], but also the need for athletes to practice and compete in their sports with technology as an extra peripheral.

4.4. Limitations and Strengths. There are some important study limitations to consider by the reader. First and foremost, this study is an exploratory study; therefore there would be many things that could be done better once more studies can help drive study hypotheses. In this study, we have not been able to go into detail about how trackers and apps were used, and it would be important to gather this information, perhaps through qualitative inquiry. Particular details about how coach and athletes may communicate with each other based on the objective and subjective feedback from training and competition are other potential areas for future research. Another limitation to the study was its cross-sectional nature, thus an infeasibility to discuss cause and effect. The study was lacking some of the specificity, such as current use, commonly used features, history of the use of PAWS, the social environment, social economic status, human computer interaction, and how that may benefit or hinder athleticism. Other variables to describe some lifestyle management and psychological variables that influence athletic identity were not included due to space in the questionnaire. It has been an important decision to balance the holistic perspective of high school athletes and the amount of questions that can be answered in a survey. The strength of the study was that the data collection was from sport schools around the country and represents a national overview of high school athletes; however generalisability may be extended only to the Finnish context. Similar studies in different countries would be important when extending the constructs presented in this paper. In addition, the measures were limited to professional sport aspirations, and it would be important to know how these aspirations turn out in reality by follow up data.

5. Conclusions

High school athletes in Finland do use apps and trackers and this is associated with their athletic identity. Fitness trackers may be more useful for professional sports as it can provide live and postperformance data that can give an added advantage over people without this type of data. Coaches may need to take this data into consideration when planning short, medium, and long term training schedules and training plans. For professional aspiring athletes, wearables have the potential to help provide data to support suitable training and competition schedules, which is important as the students may be overloaded with academic pressures.

Acknowledgments

The project was funded by the Finnish Ministry of Education and Culture (Opetus- ja kulttuuriministeriö), Grant no. OKM/13/626/2015.

References

[1] N. D. Ridgers, M. A. McNarry, and K. A. Mackintosh, "Feasibility and effectiveness of using wearable activity trackers in youth: a systematic review," *JMIR mHealth and uHealth*, vol. 4, no. 4, Article ID e129, 2016.

[2] Directorate-General for Education and Culture, *EU Guidelines on Dual Careers of Athletes; Recommended Policy Actions in Support of Dual Careers in High-Performance Sport*, European Commission, Brussels, Belgium, 2012.

[3] M. Sorkkila, K. Aunola, and T. V. Ryba, "A person-oriented approach to sport and school burnout in adolescent student-athletes: The role of individual and parental expectations," *Psychology of Sport and Exercise*, vol. 28, pp. 58–67, 2017.

[4] D. Lupton, *The Quantified Self: A Sociology of Self-Tracking*, Polity Press, Cambridge, UK, 2016.

[5] L. Zach, *From BMI to TMI: The NBA is Leaning Toward Wearable Tech*, 2016, http://grantland.com/the-triangle/from-bmi-to-tmi-the-nba-is-leaning-toward-wearable-tech/.

[6] P. S. Torre and T. Haberstoh, *New Biometric Tests Invade the NBA*, http://www.espn.com/nba/story/_/id/11629773/new-nba-biometric-testing-less-michael-lewis-more-george-orwelll.

[7] D. Nafus and J. Sherman, "This one does not go up to 11: The quantified self movement as an alternative big data practice," *International Journal of Communication*, vol. 8, no. 1, pp. 1784–1794, 2014.

[8] V. Ville, *Predicting and Monitoring Individual Endurance Training Adaptation and Individualizing Training Prescription: With Endurance Performance, Cardiac Autonomic Regulation and Neuromuscular Performance [Ph.D. thesis]*, 2016.

[9] L. Pekka, A. Nummela, and K. Lipponen, "Physical Loading, Stress and Recovery in a Youth Soccer Tournament," *Journal of Sports Science and Medicine*, vol. 6, supplement 10, pp. 76-77, 2007.

[10] M. Ruckenstein and M. Pantzar, "Beyond the Quantified Self: Thematic exploration of a dataistic paradigm," *New Media & Society*, vol. 19, no. 3, pp. 401–418, 2017.

[11] W. Gary, *Know Thyself: Tracking Every Facet of Life, from Sleep to Mood to Pain, 24/7/365*, 2016, https://www.wired.com/2009/06/lbnp-knowthyself/.

[12] A. Baerg, "Big Data, Sport, and the Digital Divide: Theorizing How Athletes Might Respond to Big Data Monitoring," *Journal of Sport and Social Issues*, vol. 41, no. 1, pp. 3–20, 2017.

[13] B. Stambulova Natalia, "Talent Development in Sport: The Perspective of Career Transitions," in *Psychology of Sport Excellence*, E. Tsung-Min Hung, R. Lidor, and D. Hackfort, Eds., pp. 63–74, Fitness Information Technology, Morgantown, Va, USA, 2009.

[14] A. R. Nicholls and R. C. J. Polman, "Coping in sport: A systematic review," *Journal of Sports Sciences*, vol. 25, no. 1, pp. 11–31, 2007.

[15] B. W. Brewer, L. Judy, Van. Raalte, and D. E. Linder, "Athletic Identity: Hercules' Muscles Or Achilles Heel?" *International Journal of Sport Psychology*, vol. 24, pp. 237–254, 1993.

[16] H. R. Markus and S. Kitayama, "Culture and the self: implications for cognition, emotion, and motivation," *Psychological Review*, vol. 98, no. 2, pp. 224–253, 1991.

[17] S. E. Cross, E. E. Hardin, and B. Gercek-Swing, "The what, how, why, and where of self-construal," *Personality and Social Psychology Review*, vol. 15, no. 2, pp. 142–179, 2011.

[18] H. Y. Li and M. B. Andersen, "Athletic identity in China: Examining the AIMS in a Hong Kong sample," *International Journal of Sport and Exercise Psychology*, vol. 6, no. 2, pp. 176–188, 2008.

[19] K. Ng, J. Tynjälä, and S. Kokko, "Ownership and Use of Commercial Physical Activity Trackers Among Finnish Adolescents: Cross-Sectional Study," *JMIR mHealth and uHealth*, vol. 5, no. 5, p. e61, 2017.

[20] V. A. Goodyear, C. Kerner, and M. Quennerstedt, "Young people's uses of wearable healthy lifestyle technologies; surveillance, self-surveillance and resistance," *Sport, Education and Society*, pp. 1–14, 2017.

[21] G. J. Welk, C. B. Corbin, and D. Dale, "Measurement issues in the assessment of physical activity in children," *Research Quarterly for Exercise and Sport*, vol. 71, no. 2, pp. S59–S73, 2000.

[22] T. V. Ryba, K. Aunola, S. Kalaja, H. Selänne, N. J. Ronkainen, and J.-E. Nurmi, "A new perspective on adolescent athletes' transition into upper secondary school: A longitudinal mixed methods study protocol," *Cogent Psychology*, vol. 3, no. 1, 2016.

[23] J. Cohen, "A power primer," *Psychological Bulletin*, vol. 112, no. 1, pp. 155–159, 1992.

[24] S. MacIsaac, J. Kelly, and S. Gray, "'She has Like 4000 Followers!': The Celebrification of Self within School Social Networks," *Journal of Youth Studies*, vol. 21, no. 6, pp. 816–835, 2017.

[25] A. Depper and P. D. Howe, "Are we fit yet? English adolescent girls' experiences of health and fitness apps," *Health Sociology Review*, vol. 26, no. 1, pp. 98–112, 2017.

[26] C. S. Carver and M. F. Scheier, "Control theory: a useful conceptual framework for personality-social, clinical, and health psychology," *Psychological Bulletin*, vol. 92, no. 1, pp. 111–135, 1982.

[27] H. op den Akker, V. M. Jones, and H. J. Hermens, "Tailoring real-time physical activity coaching systems: a literature survey and model," *User Modeling and User-Adapted Interaction*, vol. 24, no. 5, pp. 351–392, 2014.

[28] V. A. Goodyear and K. M. Armour, "Young People's Perspectives on and Experiences of Health-Related Social Media, Apps, and Wearable Health Devices," *The Social Science Journal*, vol. 7, no. 8, pp. 1–15, 2018.

[29] T. M. Cabrita, A. B. Rosado, T. O. Leite, S. O. Serpa, and P. M. Sousa, "The Relationship Between Athletic Identity and Career Decisions in Athletes," *Journal of Applied Sport Psychology*, vol. 26, no. 4, pp. 471–481, 2014.

[30] E. Sturm Jennifer, L. Deborah, and A. Todd, "A Comparison of Athlete and Student Identity for Division I and Division III Athletes," *Journal of Sport Behavior*, vol. 34, pp. 295–306, 2011.

[31] P. S. Lally and G. A. Kerr, "The career planning, athletic identity, and student role identity of intercollegiate student athletes," *Research Quarterly for Exercise and Sport*, vol. 76, no. 3, pp. 275–285, 2005.

[32] J. L. Gaston-Gayles, "The factor structure and reliability of the Student Athletes' Motivation toward Sports and Academics Questionnaire (SAMSAQ)," *Journal of College Student Development*, vol. 46, no. 3, pp. 317–327, 2005.

[33] A. Y. Bimper, "Game changers: The role athletic identity and racial identity play on academic performance," *Journal of College Student Development*, vol. 55, no. 8, pp. 795–807, 2014.

17

Effects of Human Connection through Social Drones and Perceived Safety

Hwayeon Kong [ID],[1] Frank Biocca,[1] Taeyang Lee,[2] Kihyuk Park,[2] and Jeonghoon Rhee[2]

[1]*Department of Interaction Science, Sungkyunkwan University, Seoul, Republic of Korea*
[2]*Human ICT Convergence, Sungkyunkwan University, Seoul, Republic of Korea*

Correspondence should be addressed to Hwayeon Kong; flohello@gmail.com

Academic Editor: Marco Porta

This study investigates whether people perceive social drones differently depending on pilot type and perceived safety. A "drone campus tour guide" social drone service was examined to explore these values. This study involves a between-subjects experiment using two drone control types (human-driven and algorithm-driven) and two levels of perceived safety (low and high). The results demonstrate that the drone pilot type changes the service experience when the drone is flying in an unsafe manner. In the group where the drones were flown in an unsafe manner, participants exhibited higher levels of satisfaction with the algorithm-driven drone guide, while both types of drones received the same level of satisfaction when they were flown safely. The results have implications for understanding how expectations influence service evaluations in relation to human connection.

1. Introduction

Following the recent growth in the drone industry, there has been an increase in drone services that assist or collaborate with humans. In particular, advances in drone technology have made it possible for drones to autonomously perform given tasks by moving to a specified location and along a specified path based on a global positioning system (GPS) [1]. In fact, more sophisticated drones can be developed by applying conventional human-robot interaction (HRI) technology. For example, in the near future, we will be able to use drones to lead exercise groups while moving together with people [2], to guide people visiting cultural areas for the first time (e.g., Skycall, MIT), to guide the blind [3], or to act as bodyguards to ensure safe journeys home [4].

As the use of drones becomes increasingly prevalent, research on effective communication with humans and HRI for social robots is necessary in order to facilitate the acceptance of drones in everyday environments. We refer to these drones as social drones. Gongora and Gonzalez-Jimenez [5] examined the technology for surveying drone maneuvers using GPS, and Cho et al. [6] examined the aspect of usability, considering the approachability of drone control to the general public. However, there has been a lack of research on service evaluations based on the perceptions of the humans (users) that interact with drones. Therefore, we consider what variables must be considered in human-drone interactions and what effects these variables have on service evaluations.

As defined by Clarke [7], control over drone-flight may be exercised by a human pilot or an autopilot. A review of remote control and autopilot functions for small drones can be found in the work of Chao et al. [8]. As such, regarding the control of a drone, one cannot help but consider these two particular types. Meanwhile, remotely controlled drones and drones that operate autonomously based on a fixed algorithm are related to the concepts of avatars and agents as discussed under the topic of human-computer interaction (HCI). According to the claims of several studies on HCI, the perceptions and evaluations of users vary between the use of avatars and agents [9–12].

Furthermore, as social robots, drones face a robot-ontological issue, namely, safety. Dautenhahn and his colleagues [13] studied human comfort while interacting with a social robot. They thought that feelings of safety with a robot would be impossible to study and instead user comfort should be the focus. In this paper, perceived safety includes both of these meanings and we constructed a variable that could influence the level of satisfaction in social drone services. Little by little, academic focus has shifted to human perceptions of social drones. Cauchard and her colleagues [14] studied drones as a type of social computing that features an affective factor. However, this is merely a starting point in the study of social drones. In this paper, we will explore the relationship between user satisfaction and two fundamental issues: drone control conditions and perceived safety. Thus, in order to empirically investigate this relationship, the present study examines the following research question.

Research Question. What is the relationship between tourist satisfaction and drone control type or perceived safety?

2. Literature Review and Hypotheses

2.1. Human-Driven versus Algorithm-Driven. Bailenson and Blascovich [15] define an avatar or an agent as follows: "a perceptible digital representation whose behaviors reflect those executed, typically in real time, by a specific human being." These terms are often encountered when using a computer application or playing a game. Examples include the clipper in MS office, Siri on an iPhone, and various avatars featured in the game Second Life. Depending on who controls these characters (a human versus the system), there can be different perceptions or service evaluations. Lim and Reeves [9] studied the engagement of avatars and agents, part of the game experience, and found that playing a game with avatars showed improved engagement over the use of agents. Concerning general interactions, Cauchard and her colleagues [14] studied the social evaluations during interactions with digital human representations and observed that there is a difference in social evaluations of avatar and agent environments when digital human representations were made to smile, one of the social cues of interaction. Namely, there was a tendency toward a negative evaluation of the smile of a digital human, which is an agent.

(H1) The group using an algorithm-driven tour guide will have a higher level of satisfaction than the group using a human-driven drone tour guide.

2.2. Perceived Safety. Duncan and Murphy [16] examined the maneuver position of a drone that minimizes danger or stress when a drone interacts with people in public places. It was found that drones that interact with people are considered social robots (beings) and, hence, are required to remain at an appropriate distance or position, similar to humans interacting with humans in daily life. Whether human or not, social beings that interact with people can either be stable to interact with or, on the contrary, be unstable to interact with, which can indeed affect the service evaluation. Dautenhahn and his colleagues [13] also studied focusing on human comfort, which can be interpreted as perceived safety. Young and his colleagues [17] pointed to safety as a factor affecting acceptance because robots have the potential to injure humans. Researchers in social robotics continue to reconfirm that perceived safety, a psychological comfort with

human-robot interaction, is a major factor to be considered [18–20].

(H2) A drone tour guide flying stably will receive a higher level of satisfaction from participants than a drone tour guide flying in an unstable manner.

3. Materials and Methods

3.1. Participants. We recruited 60 undergraduate or graduate students from Sungkyunkwan University in South Korea. Subjects took part in the experiment voluntarily by responding to an online announcement on the university's main website. Females made up 47% of the sample and the age range of subjects was 19–29 (M = 23.72, SD = 2.36).

For ethical reasons, the guidelines proposed by Brownhill [21] (informed consent, privacy, incentives, the right to withdraw, and protection of the researcher) were followed, and our researchers distributed a detailed information sheet prior to the experiment and spent approximately five minutes obtaining consent. The information sheet explained the experimental procedure and the required time commitment. The participants were asked if they felt comfortable participating in the experiment, as it was presented in an open space; they were also asked to inform the accompanying researchers of any discomfort during the experience. It was explained that the survey following the experiment would be anonymous and that approximately 5,000 KRW would be provided as an incentive. Following the explanations, it was confirmed that the participants understood all the details.

3.2. Experimental Design. A between-participants, 2×2 full factorial experiment was designed to extrapolate how human connection cues for levels of perceived safety regarding social drone services influence user satisfaction.

3.3. Procedure. To study social drones, we operated a trial drone service where people could tour a college campus while communicating with a drone guide. The drone, as a social robot, could provide humans with information on a specific location or building during the four-minute tour.

The participants were instructed to be in front of a designated structure at a predetermined time. Researchers introduced how the drone would work: either controlled by a remote guide or moving along a preprogrammed route. They were provided receivers through which they could hear the guidance of the drone. Once three to five participants were ready, the tour began. The drone used weighed approximately 420 g and had a smooth external cover. The drones were controlled in the same manner, by a well-trained guide in a "Wizard of Oz" setup.

The drone's interpretation was transmitted through the earphones of the receivers that were provided to participants, who followed the movement of the drone and received information on buildings and structures as they approached them. The recorded voice was that of a well-trained female student announcer. An excerpt of the guidance script is shown below:

Now, let us begin with the campus guide. Our university traces its origins to ... the 7th year of the rule of the first king of the Chosun dynasty in 1398. This campus is a natural science campus, which is devoted to the research and development of natural science and contains the departments of natural science, engineering, pharmacy, and medical science. The building on your left looks like it is a single building, but it is composed of four zigzagging buildings. When viewed from the sky, it looks like a honeycomb. The designer of the building admitted that he got the inspiration for the architecture from a honeycomb [to be continued].

Researchers provided participants with a manual about their respective drone guide and took the time to explain how the drone worked. There were manuals for both drone types: human-driven drone and algorithm-driven drone.

> Group 1 (Drone Tour Guide Service Manual for a Human-Driven Drone): a flying drone guide provides guide service to the campus. You can listen to the voice of the drone guide through the supplied receiver. The drone is being remotely controlled by someone who guides you around the campus while viewing the route through the camera on the front of the drone. Experience the campus guide service led by the drone's guide.

> Group 2 (Drone Tour Guide Service Manual for an Algorithm-Driven Drone): a flying drone guide provides guide service to the campus. You can listen to the voice of the drone guide through the supplied receiver. This drone is a guide service robot that flies according to a predefined algorithm and stops and give explanations about buildings or structures. Experience the campus guide service led by the drone's guide.

The values of perceived safety were divided into two groups, high and low, around the median value. Each group contains a balanced number of males and females. Perceived safety of the high-level group includes 15 males and 15 females, and the low-level group includes 17 males and 13 females.

3.4. Measures. All measurements were adopted from previous studies and revised for this exhibition guidance service context. All items were 7-point scaled items: strongly disagree (1) to strongly agree (7).

3.4.1. Satisfaction. Satisfaction with the guidance service experience was measured (mean = 16.26, standard deviation = 2.55, and Cronbach Alpha = .76) by rating 7-point scaled items [22, 23]. The scale ranged from strongly disagree (1) to strongly agree (7) for each of the following statements: "I do not have a positive attitude or evaluation about the service" (inversed), "I think the system is very helpful," and "Overall, I am satisfied with the system."

3.4.2. Perceived Safety. Perceived safety of the guidance service was measured (mean = 13.18, standard deviation = 3.51, and Cronbach Alpha = .72) by rating the following bipolar, 7-point scaled items [18]: "Anxious to Relaxed," "Agitated to Calm," and "Quiescent to Surprised" (inversed).

4. Results

A factorial 2 (human-driven versus algorithm-driven) $\times$ 2 (perceived safety: low versus high) analysis of variance (ANOVA) was conducted with the two drone control type variables (human-driven and algorithm-driven) as the between-participants factor and the two-category level of perceived safety variable (low, high) as the between-participants factor.

When the ANOVA was performed with satisfaction as the dependent variable, there is no significant difference between the two groups: human-driven drone (M = 5.30) and algorithm-driven drone (M = 5.54). Therefore, our data did not support (H1). However, when the ANOVA was performed with satisfaction as the dependent variable, a significant effect for perceived safety was found. Study participants showed lower satisfaction levels with the human-driven drone (M = 5.12) than with the algorithm-driven drone (M = 5.72), $F(1, 45) = 8.44$, and $p = .005$. Therefore, our data supported (H2).

Additionally, in the ANOVA with the human connection index, there was a significant two-way interaction, $F(1, 59) = 4.20$, $p < .05$, and $\eta^2 = .07$, indicating that participants felt a higher level of satisfaction (M = 5.35, SD = 0.59) with the algorithm-driven drone than the human-driven drone (M = 3.43, SD = 0.73) when they felt less safe with the drone.

5. Discussion

Firstly, the results confirmed that the control type of a social drone does not influence users' evaluation levels, which highlights that human connection cues would do not impact satisfaction in a social drone context. According to the Computers Are Social Actors (CASA) paradigm proposed by Nass and his colleagues [24, 25], HCI follows the social rules of human-human interactions. In particular, it was suggested that humans mindlessly confuse the computing medium in question as a social being and exhibit reactions based on social rules owing to the anthropomorphic cues that apply to computing media, for instance, gender, personality, and voice, as well as the elements of the social rules [26, 27]. Such a paradigm also applies to our test drone, which corresponds to HRI, and one can therefore evaluate that when a drone interacts through a voice, the drone itself is regarded as a social being during the service experience regardless of who controls the drone, leading to the same level of satisfaction.

However, we found that perceived safety significantly affects levels of satisfaction; thus, we reiterate that perceived safety is still a critical factor in the social drone service environment.

We also found an interaction effect between type of drone control and level of perceived safety. Both groups of participants with high perceived safety had similar levels of satisfaction regardless of whether or not the drone was human controlled. On the contrary, the level of satisfaction becomes significantly lower for participants when the drone is controlled by a human, and the participants feel that the drone guide is not flying the drone safely. This could indicate that participants expect the human-controlled drone to exhibit a higher quality flight; however, when they experienced a lower quality flight, they became critically disappointed. This can be understood from a perspective similar to Oliver [28], whose work showed that disconfirmation of expectation affects the attitude or satisfaction of a customer. Furthermore, Oliver and DeSarbo [29] showed that disconfirmation of expectation is the most important factor in customer satisfaction.

6. Conclusions

The implications of this study are as follows. We showed that human connection affects user perceptions of a drone service. The research on user service evaluations with human-driven drones has been mostly conducted in the field of HCI, and it has been assumed that social robots are independently controlled using a fully autonomous algorithm. However, considering the appearance of telepresence robots or the necessity of human supervision due to the limitations on perfect automatic robot control [30, 31], it was highly valuable finding that human supervision of social robots is a major factor affecting service evaluation.

Moreover, we verified that perceived safety, a continuing issue in social robotics, still acts as a service quality improvement factor in social drones. Furthermore, the observation that human connection has an interaction effect supports the interpretation that the imperfectness of the automated robotic service is recognized and there are high expectations for human-driven robots. We believe that this is in line with the findings of Zimmerman and his colleagues [32], who studied embodied agents. In their work, user perceptions of agents with humanoid and non-humanoid exterior designs were examined, and it was found that agents with humanoid designs are perceived to be more intelligent.

Another interpretation is as follows. The group with low perceived safety exhibited lower service satisfaction with human-controlled drones than with algorithm-driven drones. This may indicate that when a robot is unstable, the control capability of artificial intelligence (AI) is trusted more than that of a human [10, 11]. Based on numerous works on consumer perception where trust is in a defining relationship with satisfaction [33, 34], it may be possible to infer that low confidence in the human control of drones led to low satisfaction in our study. Regardless, we wish to claim that the second implication of this study is that the control method of a robot can act as a major factor in user service evaluation when designing a service robot that assists or collaborates with humans.

We aimed to examine our hypotheses based on a laboratory experiment, which is an unusual situation [35]. One limitation of this method is that participants in their natural context may not pay full attention to the guide and often do other things while walking, whereas the subjects of the experiment were asked to specifically focus on the service. Additionally, they experienced the service for only five minutes. Participants may have felt that the time allotted for the experience was insufficient.

The findings of the study should be carefully generalized. The sample size was insufficient to represent the population of drone guidance service. The participants not only were of a younger generation but also were university students familiar with new media technology. It is natural for them to experience new technologies [36], such as drones. It is necessary to verify the results in another setting to generalize the findings to a drone guidance service population.

In addition, the experiment was conducted in South Korea. The network infrastructure in South Korea is suitable to communicate with others synchronously without delay. The experience of a drone guidance system would be affected by these factors. Thus, it is also necessary to compare this study with studies in different cultures to generalize the current findings.

Acknowledgments

Partial support for this research was provided by the Department of Human ICT Convergence in Sungkyunkwan University.

References

[1] D. Scaramuzza, M. C. Achtelik, L. Doitsidis et al., "Vision-controlled micro flying robots: From system design to autonomous navigation and mapping in GPS-denied environments," *IEEE Robotics and Automation Magazine*, vol. 21, no. 3, pp. 26–40, 2014.

[2] F. F. Mueller and M. Muirhead, "Understanding the design of a flying jogging companion," in *Proceedings of the 27th Annual ACM Symposium on User Interface Software and Technology, UIST 2014*, pp. 81-82, New York, NY, USA, October 2014.

[3] M. Avila, M. Funk, and N. Henze, "DroneNavigator: Using drones for navigating visually impaired persons," in *Proceedings of the 17th International ACM SIGACCESS Conference on Computers and Accessibility, ASSETS 2015*, pp. 327-328, Portugal, October 2015.

[4] M. Delmont, "Drone encounters: Noor Behram, Omer Fast, and visual critiques of drone warfare," *American Quarterly*, vol. 65, no. 1, pp. 193–202, 2013.

[5] A. Gongora and J. Gonzalez-Jimenez, "Enhancement of a commercial multicopter for research in autonomous navigation," in *Proceedings of the 23rd Mediterranean Conference on Control and Automation, MED 2015*, pp. 1204–1209, Torremolinos, Spain, June 2015.

[6] K. Cho, M. Cho, and J. Jeon, "Fly a Drone Safely: Evaluation of an Embodied Egocentric Drone Controller Interface," *Interacting with Computers*, vol. 29, no. 3, pp. 345–354, 2017.

[7] R. Clarke, "Understanding the drone epidemic," *Computer Law and Security Review*, vol. 30, no. 3, pp. 230–246, 2014.

[8] H. Chao, Y. Cao, and Y. Chen, "Autopilots for small unmanned aerial vehicles: A survey," *International Journal of Control, Automation, and Systems*, vol. 8, no. 1, pp. 36–44, 2010.

[9] S. Lim and B. Reeves, "Computer agents versus avatars: Responses to interactive game characters controlled by a computer or other player," *International Journal of Human-Computer Studies*, vol. 68, no. 1-2, pp. 57–68, 2010.

[10] C. Clerwall, "Enter the Robot Journalist," *Journalism Practice*, vol. 8, no. 5, pp. 519–531, 2014.

[11] H. A. J. Van der Kaa and E. J. Krahmer, "Journalist versus news consumer: The perceived credibility of machine written news , Paper presented at the Computation + Journalism Symposium," in *Proceedings of the the Computation + Journalism Symposium*, New York, NY, USA, 2014.

[12] R. E. Guadagno, K. R. Swinth, and J. Blascovich, "Social evaluations of embodied agents and avatars," *Computers in Human Behavior*, vol. 27, no. 6, pp. 2380–2385, 2011.

[13] K. Dautenhahn, M. Walters, S. Woods et al., "How may I serve you?" in *Proceedings of the 1st ACM SIGCHI/SIGART Conference*, pp. 172–179, Salt Lake City, Utah, USA, March 2006.

[14] J. R. Cauchard, K. Y. Zhai, M. Spadafora, and J. A. Landay, "Emotion encoding in human-drone interaction," in *Proceedings of the 11th Annual ACM/IEEE International Conference on Human-Robot Interaction, HRI 2016*, pp. 263–270, March 2016.

[15] J. N. Bailenson and J. Blascovich, "Avatars," in *Encyclopedia of Human-Computer Interaction*, W. S. Bainbridge, Ed., pp. 64–68, Berkshire Publishing Group, Great Barrington, Mass, USA, 2004.

[16] B. A. Duncan and R. R. Murphy, "Comfortable approach distance with small Unmanned Aerial Vehicles," in *Proceedings of the 22nd IEEE International Symposium on Robot and Human Interactive Communication: "Living Together, Enjoying Together, and Working Together with Robots!", IEEE RO-MAN 2013*, pp. 786–792, Kyeongju, Republic of Korea, August 2013.

[17] J. E. Young, R. Hawkins, E. Sharlin, and T. Igarashi, "Toward acceptable domestic robots: Applying insights from social psychology," *International Journal of Social Robotics*, vol. 1, no. 1, pp. 95–108, 2009.

[18] C. Bartneck, D. Kulić, E. Croft, and S. Zoghbi, "Measurement instruments for the anthropomorphism, animacy, likeability, perceived intelligence, and perceived safety of robots," *International Journal of Social Robotics*, vol. 1, no. 1, pp. 71–81, 2009.

[19] C. W. Lee, Z. Bien, G. Giralt, P. I. Corke, and M. Kim, "Report on the First IART/IEEE-RAS Joint Workshop: Technical Challenge for Dependable Robots in Human Environments," IART/IEEE-RAS Robotics and Automation Society Magazine Report, Seoul, Korea, 2001.

[20] I. R. Nourbakhsh, C. Kunz, and T. Willeke, "The Mobot Museum Robot Installations: A Five Year Experiment," in *Proceedings of the 2003 IEEE/RSJ International Conference on Intelligent Robots and Systems*, pp. 3636–3641, usa, October 2003.

[21] S. Brownhill, "The Researcher and the researched: Ethical research in children's and young people's services," in *Empowering the children's and young people's services: Practice based knowledge, skills and understanding*, S. Brownhill, Ed., pp. 45–61, Routledge, Abingdon, UK, 2014.

[22] T. McGill, V. Hobbs, and J. Klobas, "User-developed applications and information systems success: A test of DeLone and McLean's model," *Information Resources Management Journal*, vol. 16, no. 1, pp. 24–45, 2003.

[23] A. Rai, S. S. Lang, and R. B. Welker, "Assessing the validity of IS success models: An empirical test and theoretical analysis," *Information Systems Research*, vol. 13, no. 1, pp. 50–69, 2002.

[24] C. Nass, Y. Moon, B. J. Fogg, B. Reeves, and D. C. Dryer, "Can computer personalities be human personalities?" *International Journal of Human - Computer Studies*, vol. 43, no. 2, pp. 223–239, 1995.

[25] B. Reeves and C. Nass, *The media equation: How people treat computers, television, and new media like real people and places*, Cambridge University Press, New York, NY, USA, 1996.

[26] C. Nass, J. Steuer, and E. R. Tauber, "Computers are social actors," in *Proceedings of the the SIGCHI Conference*, pp. 72–78, Boston, Mass, USA, April 1994.

[27] K. M. Lee and C. Nass, "The multiple source effect and synthesized speech: Doubly-disembodied language as a conceptual framework," *Human Communication Research*, vol. 30, no. 2, pp. 182–207, 2004.

[28] R. L. Oliver, "What is customer satisfaction?" *Wharton Magazine*, vol. 5, no. 3, pp. 36–41, 1981.

[29] R. L. Oliver and W. S. DeSarbo, "Response determinants in satisfaction judgments," *Journal of Consumer Research*, vol. 14, no. 4, pp. 495–507, 1988.

[30] K. Misawa and J. Rekimoto, "Wearing another's personality: A human-surrogate system with a telepresence face," in *Proceedings of the 19th ACM International Symposium on Wearable Computers, ISWC 2015*, pp. 125–132, Japan, September 2015.

[31] K. Kraft and W. D. Smart, "Seeing is comforting: Effects of teleoperator visibility in robot-mediated health care," in *Proceedings of the 11th Annual ACM/IEEE International Conference on Human-Robot Interaction, HRI 2016*, pp. 11–18, Christchurch, New Zealand, March 2016.

[32] J. Zimmerman, E. Ayoob, J. Forlizzi, and M. McQuaid, "Putting a face on embodied interface agents," in *Proceedings of Designing Pleasurable Products and Interfaces Conference*, S. Wensveen, Ed., pp. 233–248, Technical University Press, Eindhoven, Netherlands, 2005.

[33] C. Moorman, R. Deshpande, and G. Zaltman, "Factors affecting trust in market research relationships," *Journal of Marketing*, vol. 57, no. 1, pp. 81–101, 1993.

[34] R. C. Caceres and N. G. Paparoidamis, "Service quality, relationship satisfaction, trust, commitment and business-to-business loyalty," *European Journal of Marketing*, vol. 41, no. 7-8, pp. 836–867, 2007.

[35] J. M. McLeod and B. Reeves, "On the nature of mass media effects," in *Television and social behavior: Beyond violence*, S. B. Withey and R. P. Abeles, Eds., pp. 17–54, Lawrence Erlbaum Associates, Hillsdale, NJ, USA, 1980.

[36] T. Syvertsen, G. Enli, O. J. Mjøs, and H. Moe, *The Media Welfare State: Nordic Media in the Digital Era*, University of Michigan Press, Ann Arbor, Mich, USA, 2014.

18

Designing a Human Machine Interface for Quality Assurance in Car Manufacturing: An Attempt to Address the "Functionality versus User Experience Contradiction" in Professional Production Environments

Nikolaj Borisov ⓘ,¹ Benjamin Weyers ⓘ,² and Annette Kluge ⓘ³

¹*University of Duisburg-Essen, 47057 Duisburg, Germany*
²*Computer Science Department, RWTH Aachen University, 52074 Aachen, Germany*
³*Department of Psychology, Ruhr-University Bochum, 44801 Bochum, Germany*

Correspondence should be addressed to Benjamin Weyers; weyers@vr.rwth-aachen.de

Guest Editor: Tareq Ziad Ahram

The complexity of nowadays car manufacturing processes increases constantly due to the increasing number of electronic and digital features in cars as well as the shorter life cycle of car designs, which raises the need for faster adaption to new car models. However, the ongoing digitalization of production and working contexts offers the chance to support the worker in production using digital information as well as innovative, interactive, and digital devices. Therefore, in this work we investigate a representative production step in a long-term project together with a German car manufacturer, which is structured into three phases. In the first phase, we investigated the working process empirically and developed a comprehensive and innovative user interface design, which addresses various types of interactive devices. Building up on this, we developed the device score model, which is designed to investigate interactive system and user interface in production context due to ergonomics, UI design, performance, technology acceptance, and user experience. This work was conducted in the second phase of the project, in which we used this model to investigate the subjective suitability of six innovative device setups that implement the user interface design developed in phase one in an experimental setup with 67 participants at two locations in south Germany. The major result showed that the new user interface design run on a smart phone is the most suitable setup for future interactive systems in car manufacturing. In the third and final phase, we investigated the suitability of the two best rated devices for long term use by two workers using the system during a full shift. These two systems were compared with the standard system used. The major conclusion is that smartphones as well as AR glasses show very high potential to increase performance in production if used in a well-designed fashion.

1. Introduction

In the last decades, the rapid development of information technology fosters growing digitization in various contexts, such as in context of home automation [1] or in context of the Internet of Things [2] and Industry 4.0 [3]. In automotive production, the increase of digitization on the one hand offers an increase in productivity but on the other increases the complexity of automotive production environments for the worker [4]. The latter implies new requirements for their working methods and tools. Additionally, workers are confronted with a continuously growing amount of information

necessary for vehicle assembling, testing, and diagnosis emerging from increasing complexity of nowadays cars [4].

For a long time, the main criteria for the design of devices in manufacturing and production including car manufacturing were *functionality* and *reliability* [5]. Meeting industry standards was the relevant criteria neglecting aesthetical aspects such as *design* and *appearance*. But since more than a decade of private smart phone use, the expectations regarding the design and appearance of manufacturing devices have been changed as discussed by Kluge et al. [6, 7]. Even if not formally allowed, many maintenance workers, for instance, in fault diagnosis and repair, use their private phone to search for solutions and hints and use text messages to chat with colleagues to ask for support and ideas. They perceive this practice to be easier, more intuitive, and faster than using the equipment provided by the manufacturer or the suppliers [7]. In the past years, decision-makers became more open to the idea that an appealing design, user experience, hedonic qualities, intuitive use, and industry standards are not a contradiction but can be united as discussed by Vogel-Heuser [8].

Thus, the purpose of the present study was to design and comparatively evaluate six devices as "Human Machine Interfaces of the Future," which meet the criteria of *functionality*, *ergonomics*, *user acceptance*, and *user experience* in parallel. Therefore, we investigated the suitability of existing mobile devices of various sorts for testing and diagnosis of built-in electronic parts after final vehicle assembly. We identified this diagnosis as a representative digitized process in production and conducted this investigation in close collaboration with a renowned German car manufacturer between 2012 and 2016. In this three-phase project, we conducted three field studies in real production environment. In study 1, we conducted a field observation and interviews as part of Phase 1. In study 2, we conducted a field experiment with 67 workers who tested six devices conducted as part of Phase 2. In Phase 3, we conducted a third user study to investigate two devices with two workers under real working conditions for a longer duration (one full shift).

Our primary focus was to determine which different interaction techniques performed best for this part in car manufacturing and by which interaction devices workers were most satisfied. Based on these empirical results, we designed a software architecture and introduced a new user interface design that supports workers for this task.

The paper is structured as follows: First the production environment and the worker's task are introduced by presenting the status quo of the inspection process, potential errors, and the lack to flexibility in the process as well as the diagnosis system itself including the presentation of the status quo of the user interface designs and devices used. Second, in Section 3, we describe the conceptual development (Phase 1) and practical implementation of the device score model (DSM, Phase 2) which is the basis for the evaluation and selection of the devices for the final test (Phase 3).

2. Background: The Production Environment

In the outlined production environment, after final assembly, the primary goal is to verify the functionality of built-in electronic parts of a produced vehicle. One challenge is that a vehicle manufacturer may offer different vehicle models. In addition, all models may also vary in their individual configuration, which results in a large variety of component combinations. This makes tracking and testing of the present configuration challenging [4]. To manage this complexity, *diagnostic programs* are used to support workers by semi-automating the test procedure, where each component combination of a vehicle model is mapped to an individual test program. Before testing and execution of this program, a worker must connect a mobile device representing the front end of the diagnostic system to the vehicle and start the

test program. Via a unique vehicle number, the test program knows which electronic parts must be tested. Depending on the type of the test as part of the whole procedure, the test program either runs the test fully automatic with no intervention by the worker or prompts the worker with instructions describing the necessary manual intervention. Thus, there are two distinct intervention types.

Intervention Type I: workers apply certain actions to the car's electronic by, e.g., pressing a button. If the car does not react as expected, the worker records the function as not working.

Intervention Type II: workers check functions via visual inspection (e.g., the worker checks whether a lamp is enlightened). Only in case of type II interventions, the worker can make incorrect input by recording a certain function not working if it is or vice versa. Thus, in worst case the vehicle is delivered to the customer with a malfunction.

Both manual interventions include awareness of special noises, status displays, and lights which have been installed in doors, foot rooms, consoles, roofs, etc. Some electronic parts can only be tested on dedicated events. For example, the door entry lighting can only be checked when the respective door is open, which has been done by the worker on request by the test program.

2.1. Status Quo: Worker Errors during the Testing Procedure Routine. As mentioned above, during the testing procedure and the manual intervention, errors can occur. As the task requires accurate and fast responses to approximately 150 tests in 7-10 minutes (as observed in our study), and due to its repetitive character, errors tend to occur in particular in that case if many elements have to be inspected and confirmed in quick succession and if recurring in similar order. In terms of Hollnagels CREAM classification of errors [9], this represents a *decision error*. Decision errors may occur in this particular setting, as each worker inspects more than 50 vehicles per day on the production line and can therefore remember inspection steps after a short training phase. This results in workers knowledge and anticipation at which point in the test sequence the test of certain electronic parts is requested by the test program and where these parts are located in the car. This anticipation leads to a fast response in addition to the highly repetitive work at the production line, so that errors can happen without the worker realizing it. In addition to the problem of marking parts falsely functional or nonfunctional, parts may be marked as being functional although they have not been tested at all.

2.2. Status Quo: Lack of Flexibility. In addition to the problem of routine task execution and potentially resulting (decision) errors, we identified another critical problem in the system design: the test program does not provide any flexibility:

(1) If a worker has noticed an incorrect input, in most cases, the test program does not allow changing the wrong input because of technical reasons.

(2) During automatic test execution without worker intervention, the worker has to wait until the automatic test process is completed. During this time,

Inspection of electronic parts

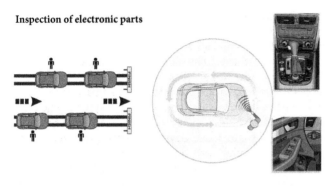

FIGURE 1: Inspection of electronic parts in automotive production environments. From left to right: production line, vehicle inspection from outside, vehicle inspection inside.

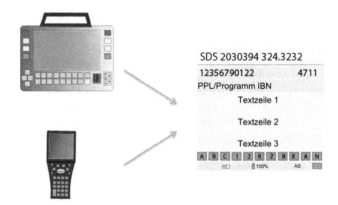

FIGURE 2: Diagnostic devices present in 2012, text and line based display.

vehicles continue to move on the production line, which results in less time for type I and II interventions.

For instance, as introduced above, an inspection of a fully equipped limousine may take up to 7-10 minutes and may have over 150 type I and II interventions the worker needs to execute. To compensate for these delays, experienced workers go through untested electronic parts and remember the respective states by heart. Thus, they try to bypass the test order at some point. When these electronic components are requested for testing, workers quickly confirm results from their mind. At this point, further incorrect inputs can occur, e.g., if test steps are confirmed without waiting until the instruction is fully displayed, which may result in missing or wrong feedback if a different component is requested.

2.3. Status Quo: The Testing Device. On production line, workers use handheld devices to receive instructions from the test program and to input the outcome of type I and II interventions as feedback to the test system running the test program (see Figure 1). Currently, these systems are provided by the manufacturer that also provides the diagnosis back-end system that executes the test program and implements the communication with the car's electronic. Existing industry standards make these devices heavy and bulky where they are very versatile and have far more functions and buttons than workers need.

In the term of this project, we analyzed two diagnostic devices as seen in Figure 2. The main diagnostic device MFT (multifunction terminal), which runs the diagnostic program, gets attached by the worker to the steering wheel of the inspected car and is connected to the vehicle via cable before starting the testing procedure. Another mobile diagnostic device HT (handheld terminal) is used by the worker and is held in the hand for the whole testing procedure. HT is used to confirm instructions wireless outside of the vehicle. Both diagnostic devices provide a screen for displaying instructions as well as status messages and a keyboard for input. Instructions appear identically in text form on both diagnostic devices and independent of the differing screen sizes. The devices offer the following operations to the worker: OK, NOK (to notify function or nonfunction), go-back (if

technically possible and permitted), abort test, reprint error page, and scan vehicle barcode.

In summary, based on the described current status, high potential to increase usability and user experience can be identified, which may lead to better devices and user interfaces to increase productivity (by decreasing number of errors) as well as to increase the level of ergonomics if, e.g., considering weight and size of the used devices.

3. Materials, Methods, and Results

To address the previously identified potential of redesigning the interaction concepts and devices, we conducted a research project subdivided into three phases: In Phase 1, we investigated the previously outlined status quo in more detail using empirical methods, on which basis we developed a novel device and interaction design. To consider various different potential solutions, we developed different types of interaction concepts and used various devices. In Phase 2, we developed a rating concept that enables us to rate the developed interfaces under realistic conditions, which were investigated in a user study involving 67 workers in a realistic environment. In the third and final phase, we tested the two best rated devices and design with two workers over a longer period. The next section will present each phase in more detail after presenting the ethical statement for all phases in detail. Each phase will be discussed by first introducing the used and/or developed method followed by the gathered empirical results.

3.1. Ethical Statement. Field studies in an organizational context do not need the approval of the ethical committee of the conducting department at the university. For applied research and for the present study, an approval by the car manufacturers work council was necessary for Phases 2 and 3, which is a special characteristic of the German Industrial Constitution Law that includes the right of codetermination of the companies' work council with respect to field experiments, as well as online and offline surveys or interviews.

Phase 1 was carried out with employees receiving payment over and above standard salary who do not require the approval of the works council. In addition, the participants of the first phase were employees of the client's department. Additionally, for workers who participated in Phase 1, and for those participating in Phases 2 and 3, the approval of both the works council committee "employee surveys" and the committee "data protection" was required. Both committees approved the investigation. The participants volunteered for participation. All participants in Phases 1, 2, and 3 were informed prior to the investigation about the purpose of the investigation and their right to cancel their participation at any time without giving reasons. Participants additionally signed an informed consent. After the examination, the participants were again informed regarding the purpose of the study and we thanked them for their participation. At the end of the project, results were fed back to the workers, the work council, and the client, and recommendations were concluded for the worker-centered design of the Human Machine Interface of the future.

3.2. Phase 1—Analyzing the Status Quo, Workers' Expectations, and Selecting the User Interface Design and Evaluation Criteria, Methods. In this section we describe phase 1, which is separated into two steps (detailed below). In the first step, we observed and interviewed workers followed by the second step, which focuses on discussions with representatives of the manufacturer.

Step 1 (worker observation and interviews). In order to select the most appropriate interaction techniques for the testing procedure (and especially considering type I and II interventions), we first had to understand which activities are part of a vehicle inspection and which tools are used for each task. For this purpose, we conducted a field study, published in more detail in [10–12], in which we observed and interviewed workers in their activities. The survey method contained 23 questions addressing the following topics:

(i) Evaluation of the equipment in terms of usefulness and performance

(ii) Evaluation of the interface design with a focus on functionality, security, and usability

(iii) Evaluation of multimodality, help, support, adaptability, customization, and usability of the current user interface

(iv) The use of innovative user interfaces (data glasses, smartphone, hand gestures, etc.)

(v) Evaluation of the diagnostic process flow

36 production workers participated in the field observations. We conducted the study in two production sites where the working experience (tenure) of the workers varied from a few days up to 40 years [10–12]. As introduced above, the study was approved by the local work council committees "employee surveys" and "data protection" and the volunteering participants signed an informed consent.

In regard of usability standards, such as ISO 9241-11, we were able observe that the used mobile devices were effective in terms of addressing requirements in production but failed in terms of perceived ease of use if subjectively rated by the worker. The worker mentioned that the diagnosis

devices provide various features to be applied in various contexts, which resulted in keyboards with many buttons structured in a standard layout. On the one hand, workers reported that this potentially results in higher error rates forced by wrong button presses. On the other hand, they also show a high degree of adaption to this circumstance that enables them to use the diagnosis system efficiently and properly. An additional outcome was that the potential acceptance of alternative devices that we presented to the workers was rather low. In the interviews, we observed that most workers had problems with imagining the use of these alternative devices in their working environment. One concern mentioned was the wearing of devices on the own body, such as data glasses or headsets, due to hygienic issues. Finally, it turned out that workers are not willing to use new interaction devices and methods despite the fact that there is a convincing increase of ergonomics and usability.

Step 2 (workshop with the representatives from the engineering department of the car manufacturer). For the selection of the relevant criteria that should drive the design and development of a new user interface, we conducted a survey using the Kano model [13] together with the responsible executives of the car manufacturer. The goal of this survey was to work out a common mental model of evaluation criteria on which basis the alternative interaction techniques can be evaluated in our field studies in Phases 2 and 3. From the knowledge gained in the preliminary study conducted in step 1 (see above, as discussed by Borisov et al. [10–12]), 55 relevant evaluation criteria (functional and nonfunctional) were selected, which address 10 topic groups. The subject groups address ISO 9241-110 (principles of dialogue design), ISO 9241-210 (process for designing usable interactive systems), user-centered interface reconfiguration [14], and aspects of emotional design. We also considered the design guidelines of Google Android (2013) and Apple iOS (2013) to be compatible with global design standards.

Results Phase 1: Specification of User Interface Design. Based on the outcome of steps 1 and 2, we created a user interface design detailed below. During the examination of the devices in use (step 1), we saw no homogeneous design for hardware and software. As already described in Section 2, we noticed that the handheld terminal had too many unnecessary keys and the keyboard layout was not designed for diagnostics and was also rather arbitrary, like the MFT device attached to the steering wheel. Important keys were not marked with distinct colour or text. Thus, wrong keys could be pressed during usage. In the worst case, the complete vehicle test could already be aborted when the handheld device was put away. The ABORT key is located very close to the OK key and could be accidentally pressed. The used software user interface was also not designed following usability requirements. If the ABORT key is pressed, the vehicle diagnosis will immediately abort the testing procedure without the possibility to cancel this action by the worker. We found also many screens with cryptic abbreviations in the instruction texts, no helpful pictures, and no feedback about the progress. As a novice, we also needed a lot of training time to understand the various

FIGURE 3: Our prototypes/interaction techniques used in the field experiment (study 2).

abbreviations and to learn the right position of each element to be checked inside and outside of the vehicle. If there are user errors, no hints are shown by the device. In stressful situations, it may happen that workers do not understand why the vehicle testing program does not continue or does not even start. The latter may happen because of connection loss to the diagnostic system or vehicle controls have to be set differently for corresponding transmissions. Beside usability, we also wanted to empirically find out what interaction techniques are most effective for this particular task.

3.3. HMI Mobile Devices Concept. For testing and implementation of the new device and user interface design, we developed a software system that enabled us to freely change devices without the need to adapt or change the existing diagnosis backend. Our client software (named HMI mobile client in the following), which we used for all the peripheral devices, offers a minimal feature set for a vehicle inspection. The HMI mobile client can simulate the diagnostic of any vehicle model and also communicate with a real diagnostic interface used by the car manufacturer. For simulation, we were able to record an entire diagnostic test of any vehicle and use the so-generated log data. Additionally, we use the log data to filter all instructions of each vehicle. The connection to the diagnostic interface was established over WLAN via TCP and the proprietary exchange protocol of the manufacturer used for the proprietary diagnosis systems (MFT and handheld device). The challenge for using our software additionally to the existing testing system was to integrate our client into the existing domain without any modifications to the actual diagnostic system. To achieve this, we had to develop our own interpreter for the proprietary protocol, which filters important data frames of the diagnostic steps from TCP communication in right order and transforms them to our HMI client. Furthermore, interactions from the HMI mobile clients needed to be communicated back into the proprietary diagnostic system.

We used the following mobile devices such that we were able to investigate various interaction techniques identified during our work in steps 1 and 2 (see Figure 3):

(a) *Tablet* and *smartphone* with touch technology and different display sizes (7", 4,8", and 4" inches) to find out how size influences handling. For input, we developed a new user interface and interaction design tailored to the use of touch screens in the addressed diagnosis process. The most used actions during diagnostic are OK and NOK confirmations. Our approach was not to use fixed buttons on the display or physical buttons of the device. Instead, we used swipe gestures that can be adapted as needed and are more ergonomic (see *HMI UI Design* for detailed description). Our design also aimed at enabling the work to perform these swipe gestures regardless of where the worker touches the display.

(b) Using a *Bluetooth headset*, our HMI client sent appropriate test instructions to workers for the respective test step. For type I and II interventions, workers had to confirm instructions via the built-in microphone using special voice commands to confirm an instruction with OK, NOK, or ABORT. To prevent voice input from becoming too monotonous and boring, we have allowed several voice commands for each command. For example, to positively confirm an instruction, worker could use either the word "OK" or the word " Continue." If a worker did not understand an instruction for the first time or he was interrupted, he could also let the HMI client repeat the instruction by using a special voice command: REPEAT. Experienced workers had the possibility to confirm instructions already during the playback without hearing it to the end. At the end of an inspection, the worker received the diagnostic result via voice including further instructions. For speech recognition, we used the Microsoft Speech Recognition Framework (msdn.microsoft.com/en-us/library/office/hh361633(v=office.14).aspx).

(c) The combination of *hand gestures* for inputting the various confirmations and the previously presented Bluetooth *headset* for communicating the instructions to the work offered free hands during diagnosis. This supports safety, free movement, and ergonomics, similar to the headset only scenario described above. We placed one hand and gesture detection sensor inside and one outside of the vehicle. Inside the vehicle we used the Leap Motion Controller (leap-motion.com) and outside the Kinect controller of the Xbox (xbox.com/en-US/Kinect). A white projection panel for instructions has been installed in front of the vehicle so that it can be read from almost any position. A pocket projector, which was also mounted at the front, projected the instructions onto this white panel. To have a comparison to the display medium, we also tested headphones as output device.

(d) *Data glasses* were used as an alternative interaction device. We used data glasses from the company Optinvent (optinvent.com). These data glasses were

Figure 4: Smart watch Pebble 301RD used as input device for data glasses.

Figure 5: Example of a real photograph and the finished image of instruction.

still a prototype at the used time, but in comparison to other devices available on the market (2013/2014) it was the only one with the required projection size and a clear view for both eyes, as the projection has to be always in view. For input, we used hand gestures, a microphone, and a *smartwatch* (Pebble 301RD, see Figure 4). While the instructions were confirmed on the headset via microphone, on the smartwatch we used the built-in buttons. The display on the smartwatch was not yet relevant for our purpose but used to additionally show the type of confirmation mapped to the buttons (see Figure 4).

In summary, we investigated the following device combinations:

(i) Smartphone

(ii) Tablet

(iii) Headset

(iv) Data glasses with microphone as input device

(v) Data glasses with hand gestures as input device

(vi) Projector projection (visual output) with microphone as input device

(vii) Projector projection (visual output) with hand gestures as input device

For the study conducted in Phase 3, we used

(i) Smartphone

(ii) Data glasses with smart watch as input device

(iii) PDA device introduced by diagnostic system manufacturer (developed in parallel by the car manufacturer)

3.4. HMI Content. In our HMI mobile client, we designed and implemented a completely new dialog design, which is separated into visible (display) and speech/voice (headset) output. The challenge here was to find a compromise between the needs of an experienced and less experienced worker. To address this, we introduced two levels of experience, which we made selectable by the worker during the start of a vehicle diagnosis. Thus, we mapped each individual instruction emerging from the log data to a short text without

abbreviations and with an assisting image when using a visual display. For more experienced workers, we used abbreviations and left out the assisting image. For our experimental setup and for the audio-based output, we let students record all instructions by reading them out. In the future, this might be replaced by nowadays technologies such as those used in navigation systems.

We identified the following requirements for instruction content in our previous investigations conducted in steps 1 and 2:

(i) Information needs to be presented in a very compact and consistent way (at maximum 2-3 lines on the display)

(ii) No abbreviations should be shown for novice or user with a low level of experience

(iii) Important words and abbreviations should be highlighted (e.g., bold typeface) for display output

(iv) The content should be prepared to be internationalized and adaptable to the location

(v) The content should be adapted to the HMI device

All used assisting images should fit the inspected vehicle model and therefore need to be created for each vehicle model. In our experiment, we used only one vehicle model and created 118 images. Therefore, we used photographs taken of the vehicle and the components the worker has to inspect (see Figure 5, left) such that a worker is able to recognize quickly where this component is located. Therefore, the images created need to fulfil the following requirements:

(i) The test object must be immediately recognizable for workers in the image.

(ii) As for the text, the images should be internationalizable and adaptable to the location.

(iii) In the image, the current position of the worker has to be clearly visible forced by the perspective from which the photograph was taken.

(iv) Assisting images for display output should be used that are optimized to be rendered together with text to support the understanding of the instruction and to reduce workload

To visualize the instruction, we enriched the images with pictograms (see Table 1), which represent the needed test step (see Figure 5, right). For the instruction pictograms, we

TABLE 1: Pictograms for the representation of various interventions.

touch/press	release	move/direction	push by foot	illumination	air conditioning
type I	type I	type I/type II	type I	type II	type II

used selective focus, orientation arrows, symbols, colours, and annotations to highlight the relevant components to be tested in the image and to represent the test instruction. Therefore, the pictograms are designed in a way that they can be combined.

Based on these requirements, the raw photographs were processed in three steps:

(1) *Image processing*: In this step, essential elements are extracted from the photograph using Adobe Photoshop (adobe.com/products/photoshop.html) and the images are transferred to grayscale. The result is stored in PNG/PSD format to prevent compression artefacts, which negatively influence vectorization (see next step).

(2) *Vectorization stage 1*: The PNG/PSD images are vectorized using Adobe Illustrator (adobe.com/products/illustrator.html) and the corresponding instruction pictogram is integrated.

(3) The final vector graphic gets *exported* for all HMI mobile devices considering their specific requirements such as screen size, resolution, and supported file format.

3.5. HMI UI Design. Our dialogue design for display-based systems, e.g., smartphone devices, consists of two different views as shown in Figure 6. The first view offers various operations to configure the upcoming test process where the second view is used for the vehicle diagnostic.

In the configuration view, we use clear, simple, and unambiguous pictograms as well as widgets, e.g., to select the level of expertise. Workers can perform the following actions in the configuration view:

(i) Enter his/her personal number in a text field

(ii) Scan a barcode by using the device's camera

(iii) Choose a role (Standard or Expert, see below)

(iv) Change the display language

(v) Display additional information about this screen

(vi) Go to additional settings (e.g., device settings, score-display)

(vii) Go to the next screen

During vehicle diagnostic, we use for type II intervention only simple slide inputs for OK and NOK, but also additional menu settings for advanced functions like abort vehicle diagnostic, call help, etc. (as shown in Figure 6, right). To ensure that workers perceive the readiness for input for type

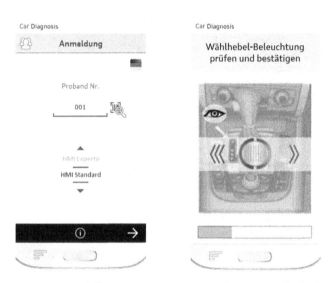

FIGURE 6: Two different interaction views: configuration and vehicle diagnostic.

II interventions, an interaction element is displayed on the screen, which uses animations to indicate the slide gesture. This interaction element disappears automatically after a few seconds to avoid overlapping the displayed elements. Once the interaction element appears, an animation is played. First the animation shows the OK direction and afterwards the animation shows the NOK direction. As soon as the animation completes, or no interaction has taken place, the interaction element disappears. On touching the display, the interaction element will be displayed again at the touched position. This allows workers to use the mobile device independently of how they hold it in their hands from any hand position. We have chosen the slide control also to avoid accidental inputs. Thus, to confirm a type II instruction, a specified distance (depending on the display size) must be reached with the finger on the display without taking it off.

For data glasses, we used only the built-in camera to scan barcodes and smart watch with built-in buttons or microphone to confirm selections.

3.6. HMI UI Assistance. Beside the new organization of the information representation of the diagnostic steps, we developed various assistive elements integrated into our user interface design, which are presented in detail in the next paragraph.

Novice vs. Expert Assistant: The developed HMI design provides two different experience roles for affecting the displayed information in the used mobile devices (see Figure 7). The major difference between the *HMI-Standard* or

HMI - Standard

HMI - Expert

Visual inspection with image
and instruction text

Help text for
current instruction

Visual feedback
after interaction:
▪ OK green
▪ NOK red

Visual inspection without picture
and with original instruction text

Progress bar is displayed independently of the user role

Awareness signals:
(color, eye, arrow, highlighting, context)

FIGURE 7: Two different roles of experience.

novice role and the *HMI-Expert* role is the type of content that is presented to the worker. For experienced workers (HMI-Expert), the instruction text is most important because they know it for a very long time. For unexperienced or less experienced workers (HMI-Standard), image and text are presented where the image takes up the most space of the display. For experts, the only image-based information (shown in Table 2) shown is to distinguish the intervention type of the instruction.

Memory Assistant: Many built-in electronics are already automatically tested in the background by the testing system. During the automatic test time, no inspections of vehicle components are allowed and requested. During this time, the worker has to wait for the automated process to be completed. Nevertheless, in step "Worker Observation and Interviews," we observed that experienced workers would like to perform the visual inspections while the automated tests are running. This makes it necessary to remember all inspection steps and their result in mind to confirm them later on request. With the memory assistant integrated into the UI design (see Figure 8) it is now possible to access a view that lists all known next visual inspection steps (type II interventions). In this list, workers have the possibility to confirm future visual inspections before requested by the diagnostic system. If a saved instruction is requested by the diagnostic system, the HMI client confirms this instruction with the stored result automatically without the need for further action by the worker.

Gamification: Gamification can be defined as "…applying game design elements to non-game contexts. The integration of gamification into the workplace adds a stimulating

TABLE 2: Visual signals of interaction types for expert role.

touch/press	release
type I	type II

and captivating game-like layer to the working experience of employees" [15]. Therefore, we integrated gamification artefacts into the HMI design, which should support the motivation of the worker and thereby increase attention and improve performance during the inspection. We implemented a statistic that shows the worker's own performance by the current number of vehicles inspected (during the current day), the average time of all inspections, and the inspection time of the current inspection. This gives workers an overview about their own performance. After finishing a vehicle inspection, a new dialog appears with the test result as well as a presentation of the statistic (see Figure 9). Furthermore, if the car was recorded NOK, the screen is highlighted red and green otherwise. The red colour is supposed to raise worker's attention.

Awareness Assistant: By pressing buttons inside a vehicle or open and close doors (type I intervention), the worker always perceives this haptic and aural feedback. However, if an instruction is to be confirmed via the mobile device, we also wanted to transmit a recognizable signal to the worker after interaction. Therefore, we added the following feedback implementations to the devices:

FIGURE 8: Memory assistant for visual inspections.

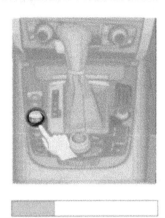

FIGURE 10: Progress indicator during vehicle inspection.

FIGURE 9: Statistic shown after vehicle inspection.

(i) For the audio headset, we used two different short noises depending on the instruction result (OK/NOK).

(ii) For smartphones or mobile devices with display support like data glasses, we overlapped the screen for a short time with a transparent colour: green for OK and red for NOK. In addition, depending on the device, we also used different vibration types for a haptic feedback: one short vibration for OK and two short vibrations for NOK.

Help Assistant: Especially for workers with little experience, but also for experienced workers in stressful situations, sometimes the diagnosis process is system-side interrupted. A hint for the current instruction can be requested immediately or after a time out it will be displayed on a display or transmitted via voice message over headset. This is done either automatically by the HMI client by a timeout or manually either via a voice command with headset or via menu command on smartphone.

Battery Assistant: Before starting a vehicle diagnosis, the battery status of the current HMI mobile device is checked.

If the battery is too low for an inspection, a warning dialog appears and the worker has the option to start the diagnosis and risk that the device will switch off during inspection or take another available device.

Progress Indicator: During diagnosis, the worker always sees the current inspection progress (as shown in Figure 10). For this purpose, the HMI system must first learn dialog sequences of all instructions for the respective vehicle model as has been described above.

3.7. UI Design for Data Glasses. The UI design for the used data glasses needed to be adapted from the mobile device version. While making experiments by using data glasses, we discovered that bright colours limit the worker's view. Furthermore, dark colours mix up the projection with the field of view and the displayed elements became very difficult to separate from their background. Since the projection in the data glasses is horizontally aligned, we have experienced that the use of the entire projection area makes spatial orientation in the close production environment very difficult. In addition, the risk of accidents increases because workers can collide or injure themselves with equipment or other vehicles standing around while moving. To minimize the risk of injury, we decided to use the horizontal projection only partially. The result is shown in Figure 11. The small boxes mark the area in the projection that is transparent for the user. Additionally, the visible projection is provided with a white frame to separate it clearly from the environment. The only difference when using the data glasses is that we found it much more pleasant for the eyes if the text instruction is displayed at the bottom line of the projection and the instruction image is displayed above. The other HMI design elements were identical to other display devices and vary only according to screen resolution.

3.8. Phase 2—Development of the Device Score Model. Based on the workshop results in Phase 1 step 2, we developed the

TABLE 3: Description of sample.

Age group (in years)				
< 20	20-30	31-40	41-50	> 50
-	27	15	11	14
General Work experience at car manufacturer (in years)				
< 1 year	1-5	6-15	> 15	
7	8	19	33	
Education (nominal)				
Vocational training	Technician	supervisor	Engineer	Other
46	1	1	6	13
Experience with devices for test procedure in general (in years)				
< 1	1-5	6-15	> 15	
14	27	19	7	

FIGURE 11: Dialogue design for data glasses.

so-called *device score model* (DSM), which aims at quantifying the subjective quality and suitability of an interactive device in the outlined production context. Therefore, the DSM includes evaluation criteria measuring ergonomics, software design, performance, technology acceptance, and user experience of the newly designed HMI and devices.

Ergonomics and *software design* were rated in terms of the German school grades system as the workers are familiar with that scheme (from 1 = *very good* to 5 = *very bad*); thus, the smaller the grade, the better the result. Criteria for measuring the *ergonomic* aspects were as follows: How many hands are free when working with this device? How heavy is the device? How large is the device (compared to the old one or other future HMIs)? Does the device need to be put away during the testing procedure? Does the device require eye movements? According *to the UI design,* questions were as follows: Is the interaction flexible? How fast is the interaction speed? How accurate is the interaction understood and received?

Performance was measured by analyzing gathered eye tracking data and log files. We calculated the mean of actions and visual tests, the number of errors made (either a wrong OK confirmation or no visual test before OK confirmation), and motivation that we measured as the subjectively rated motivation a worker experienced while working with the device.

A questionnaire was developed to measure *usability and attractiveness* based on the questionnaire measuring user experience (based on [16]). Items addressed hedonic quality (identification, attractive features), hedonic stimulation, pragmatic quality, and attractiveness (altogether 28 item poles). Sample poles of the polarity profile are (7-point profile) good-bad, convenient-inconvenient, easy-difficult, ugly-beautiful, stylish-bad style, predictable- unpredictable, uninspired-creative; confusing-giving overview, repellent-attractive, fractious-manageable, human-technical, and motivating- discouraging.

Additionally, a questionnaire was developed to measure *technology acceptance* based on the Technology Acceptance Model 3 (TAM 3, [17]). Items addressed perceived usefulness (e.g., "The device supports the execution of my task"; "The device enhances my productivity"), user friendliness (e.g., "The device is easy to use"; "The devices does exactly what I want it to do"), level of being self-explaining (e.g., "An introduction how to use the device is not needed"), appeal of the test instructions (e.g., "I had no difficulties understanding the instruction given by the device"), health and hygiene aspects (e.g., "I do not mind wearing the device close to my body"; "I think the device is not problematic concerning hygiene aspects"), input quality (e.g., "Inputs are easy to learn"; "The device can be used intuitively"), first impression (e.g., " I think I will talk to other workers and share my experiences about the device"; "I would like to use this device"), and general use of technology (e.g., "electronic devices make my life easier"; " I know most of the functions of the technical device I own").

We measured *sociodemographic data* (age, working experience; see Table 3. Sample description) and individual motivation while participating in the study (e.g., "While I was executing the testing procedure I forgot that I participate in a study"; "I was concentrated as if I am in a real car testing situation").

With this model, any changes to the UI design or the introduction of new prototypes and devices can be reevaluated and compared with other prototypes or existing devices in use or developed before. Additionally, the model allows each individual requirement to be weighted and evaluated even during the planning or introduction of new diagnostic devices. The DSM evaluation system is dynamic and changes with new adaptations and requirements. Further evaluation factors can be defined in the model. This allowed us to continuously reevaluate the entire HMI concept. As a result, a test device that has been rated very well in the past may no longer be suitable for practical use or may no longer be state of the art due to new requirements. Thus, the DSM not only enables the evaluation of individual systems but also documents changing requirements over time.

The weightings for individual categories and criteria according to the model are determined by the responsible authority. Since each production line can have different specifications and requirements, it is recommended to duplicate the model for different work areas and define an individual scaling.

For the application of the DSM, we entered all technical, determined, and collected values for each device into a MS Excel data sheet, which implements the calculation schema as outlined below. In this sheet, each column represents a sub-evaluation-criteria of the DSM. Furthermore, each column is also divided into two subcolumns: value and school grade. The school grade is calculated based on corresponding values of compared devices by a specific formula given as formula (1)-(4), below. Considering the possible best and the possible worst case of each criteria ΔC_{φ} and each evaluated value of a device D depicted as ΔV_D, we consider 2 different cases:

Case 1 (local value comparison between evaluated devices). (a) Higher value (max) is better (e.g., for scale rating) (see (1))

(b) Lower value (min) is better (e.g., for time performance rating) (see (2))

$$C_{\varphi_1}(D_\delta) = 1 + \frac{5 * \left(\max \left(\{ V_{D_1}(\varphi_1), \ldots, V_{D_n}(\varphi_1) \} \right) - V_{D_\delta}(\varphi_1) \right)}{\max \left(\{ V_{D_1}(\varphi_1), \ldots, V_{D_n}(\varphi_1) \} \right) - \min \left(\{ V_{D_1}(\varphi_1), \ldots, V_{D_n}(\varphi_1) \} \right)} \tag{1}$$

$$C_{\varphi_2}(D_\delta) = 1 + \frac{5 * \left(V_{D_\delta}(\varphi_2) - \min \left(\{ V_{D_1}(\varphi_2), \ldots, V_{D_n}(\varphi_2) \} \right) \right)}{\max \left(\{ V_{D_1}(\varphi_2), \ldots, V_{D_n}(\varphi_2) \} \right) - \min \left(\{ V_{D_1}(\varphi_2), \ldots, V_{D_n}(\varphi_2) \} \right)} \tag{2}$$

Case 2 (global vs. local value comparison between evaluated devices based on custom defined possible best value V_B and possible worst value V_W ror each devive D_δ). (a) Higher value (max) is better (e.g., for scale rating) (see (3))

(b) Lower value (min) is better (e.g., for time performance rating) (see (4))

$$C_{\varphi_1}(D_\delta) = 1 + \frac{5 * \left(\max \left(\{ V_{D_1}(\varphi_1), \ldots, V_{D_n}(\varphi_1), V_B(\varphi_1), V_W(\varphi_1) \} \right) - V_{D_\delta}(\varphi_1) \right)}{\max \left(\{ V_{D_1}(\varphi_1), \ldots, V_{D_n}(\varphi_1), V_B(\varphi_1), V_W(\varphi_1) \} \right) - \min \left(\{ V_{D_1}(\varphi_1), \ldots, V_{D_n}(\varphi_1), V_B(\varphi_1), V_W(\varphi_1) \} \right)} \tag{3}$$

$$C_{\varphi_2}(D_\delta) = 1 + \frac{5 * \left(V_{D_\delta}(\varphi_2) - \min \left(\{ V_{D_1}(\varphi_2), \ldots, V_{D_n}(\varphi_2), V_B(\varphi_1), V_W(\varphi_1) \} \right) \right)}{\max \left(\{ V_{D_1}(\varphi_2), \ldots, V_{D_n}(\varphi_2), V_B(\varphi_1), V_W(\varphi_1) \} \right) - \min \left(\{ V_{D_1}(\varphi_1), \ldots, V_{D_n}(\varphi_2), V_B(\varphi_2), V_W(\varphi_2) \} \right)} \tag{4}$$

For all these formulas, the result in DSM will always be a decimal scale of German school grade (1–6): 1, very good (best case), up to 6, insufficient (worst case). Custom defined values for the best and worst case need to be adjusted manually in case of changing requirements. For example, a customer can define by himself a best value of x-milliseconds and a worst value of y-milliseconds to be used as the basis for the grade calculation for the performance criteria for all instructions.

In certain cases, grades must be entered manually in the current model, as these depend on other underlying factors. For example, if the weight of a device (e.g., Smartphone ca. 135g) is very light to hold in the hand, it can be too heavy for data glasses worn on head or nose. The model cannot currently take such classifications into account. However, this can be corrected by further improvements to the model in future work. For each superset criteria (ergonomics, performance, technical acceptance, and user experience), the developed Excel sheet provides a separate table containing the calculated grades.

3.9. Field Experiment. In order to collect data to be used for the DSM, a field experiment was conducted with 67 workers that worked with the newly designed devices.

3.10. Description of the Sample. To compare and evaluate the six devices as outlined above, 67 workers (47 males) from the car manufacturing partner located in the south of Germany participated in a field experiment. Per day, 5-6 workers were tested individually. The complete field experiment lasted 2.5 weeks and 12 working days.

As presented in Table 3, the sample has several years of work experience and is experienced with several devices used for the testing procedure. We can therefore assume that the sample is able to execute the testing procedure proficiently and to compare the various devices and device combination using the new UI design with the current devices.

TABLE 4: Device score model: results overview (the lower the better).

DEVICE SCORE MODEL		Smartphone	Tablet	Headset	AR-Mic.	AR-Gest.	Proj.-Mic.	Proj.-Gest.
Overall grade		2,1	2,2	3,0	2,6	3,5	3,6	4,2
Criterion	Weight.	Grade	Grade	Grade	Grade	Grade	Grade	Grade
Ergonomics	25%	2,4	3,4	3,2	3,2	3,1	2,9	3,0
Performance	40%	1,7	1,9	1,7	2,9	4,4	5,8	2,8
Technology acceptance	15%	1,7	1,1	3,3	2,0	5,1	4,4	5,0
User Experience	20%	2,7	2,3	3,2	6,0	1,7	2,6	1,8

AR-Mic = augmented reality: data glasses with microphone as input device.
AR-Gest. = augmented reality: data glasses with hand gesture as input device.
Proj.-Mic. = display instructions over projection with microphone as input device.
Proj.-Gest. = display instructions over projection with hand gesture as input.

3.11. Procedure. Each worker used two devices (out of 6) one after the other. For each worker, the field experiment took approx. 90 min. After workers were welcome in the test center of the car manufacturer, each worker was introduced to how to operate device 1 (approx. 10 min) and then the eye tracker was calibrated (5 min). The worker used device 1 for three different testing scenarios consecutively (approx. 10 min) and rated the device according to the criteria in a questionnaire described below and was also interviewed to learn about his/her impressions which were eventually not captured by the questionnaire (10 min). Subsequently, he/she was introduced to device 2 (10 min), the eye tracker was calibrated again (5 min), and after three additional test scenarios (10 min) the worker filled in the questionnaire, this time referring to device 2 (10 min).

3.12. Results of Field Experiment. All results are shown in Table 4 (overview) and Table 5 (all criteria). They are based on weightings as defined by the automobile manufacturer's managers. The greatest attention is paid to performance at 40%, followed by ergonomics at 25%, user experience at 20%, and technical acceptance at 15%.

In terms of ergonomics, smartphones were rated higher. The weightings were given to us as follows: safety of operation with 35%, hand-free work with 30%, weight and size each of the device with 15%, and interaction distance, which can be defined as number of single user actions needed to generate a specific input to the system (e.g., confirm OK or NOK), with only 5%. Workers had only one hand free when wearing a mobile device, but the ergonomic size and weight, interaction safety, and short latency times for instructions made them preferable in comparison to the other devices and device combination. Interaction distance, on the other hand, was negatively affected. For example, the device always had to be taken off when the seatbelt was put on and always requires eye contact for every instruction. Both potentially cost more time compared to the other solutions.

The tablet received the worst marks in ergonomics for size and weight compared to the other devices. For devices with gestures and voice input, the biggest problem was the reliability. Both interaction techniques work based on recognition algorithms that do not work fully accurately. For example, gestures and speech input had to be repeated several times in case of background noise to confirm an instruction. Another

disadvantage of both interaction techniques is if overlapping communication between worker-device and worker-operator occurs, gesture or talking can be interpreted as input and thus causes unwanted actions.

Additionally, we measured user errors and the worker's motivation as performance indicators for both intervention types I and II. User errors were counted if the worker did not look correctly or not at all in the right direction during an instruction. Another error was counted if the worker confirmed an instruction incorrectly. We measured both with using an eye tracking system. In this device category (including data glasses with voice input), the smartphone also received the best marking. Additionally, we observed shortest interaction distance if the data glasses were used. This resulted in efficient tests of intervention type I. However, in the case of type II instructions, time was lost due to lower reliability of speech input.

In terms of technical acceptance, the tablet scored best in the technical acceptance survey. The smartphone came in second place. The result may vary, since the workers who worked with the smartphone were less technically sophisticated (technology skills: grade 2.5) than the workers who worked with the tablet (technology skills: grade 1.2). This would at least explain the differences in the subcriteria *self-explaining* and *representation*. We found very little acceptance with the headset as well as with the projection devices using the two interaction techniques of speech input and hand gestures. All criteria were equally weighted by those responsible for technical acceptance. Only the single criterion *technology skills* was weighted at 0%, as it is not important to the responsible persons for this activity.

Like technical acceptance, user experience was evaluated as a subjective opinion of each device via a questionnaire. All criteria were equally weighted by those responsible persons. Except for the data glasses with hand gestures, almost all workers had a positive experience with the alternative interaction techniques.

In Table 6, we present examples of workers qualitative responses and reaction to the six devices, which reflects the personal experience and confirms the quantitative ratings.

3.13. Phase 3—Comparison between the Two Prototypes and the Diagnostic Device in Use. In Phase 2, we applied the innovative HMI standard mode for the new mobile devices

TABLE 5: Device score model: for all criteria (lower is better).

Ergonomics		Smartphone	Tablet	Headset	AR-Mic.	AR-Gest.	Proj.-Mic.	Proj.-Gest.
Overall grade		2,4	3,4	3,0	3,2	3,2	3,1	2,9
Criterion	Weight.	Grade	Grade	Grade	Grade	Grade	Grade	Grade
hands-free	30%	3,5	3,5	1,0	1,0	1,0	1,0	1,0
weight	15%	2,2	6,0	1,2	1,8	1,6	1,2	1,0
size	15%	3,0	6,0	2,0	3,0	3,0	2,0	1,0
interaction distance	5%	3,5	3,5	2,3	2,3	2,3	3,5	3,5
interaction safety	35%	1,0	1,0	6,0	6,0	6,0	6,0	6,0
Performance		Smartphone	Tablet	Headset	AR-Mic.	AR-Gest.	Proj.-Mic.	Proj.-Gest.
Overall grade		1,7	1,9	2,8	1,7	3,5	4,4	5,8
Criterion	Weight.	Grade	Grade	Grade	Grade	Grade	Grade	Grade
Type I	20%	2,1	2,6	3,2	1,0	3,8	3,5	6,0
Type II	30%	1,3	1,4	1,0	2,6	5,2	4,4	6,0
User error rate	40%	1,5	1,9	3,7	1,6	1,0	4,5	6,0
Motivation	10%	3,4	1,9	3,5	1,0	2,2	6,0	4,0
Technical acceptance		Smartphone	Tablet	Headset	AR-Mic.	AR-Gest.	Proj.-Mic.	Proj.-Gest.
Overall grade		1,7	1,1	5,0	3,3	2,0	5,1	4,4
Criterion	Weight.	Grade	Grade	Grade	Grade	Grade	Grade	Grade
Useful	14%	1,0	1,1	3,1	2,4	2,2	4,2	6,0
User friendly	14%	1,1	1,0	4,4	1,8	2,0	6,0	5,0
Self-explaining	14%	2,6	1,0	4,7	3,1	3,1	4,0	6,0
Representation	14%	2,9	1,0	6,0	3,2	1,8	5,0	3,8
Health care	14%	1,0	1,1	5,6	5,0	2,1	6,0	2,2
Input quality	14%	2,0	1,0	5,3	2,2	2,0	6,0	5,7
First impression	14%	1,4	1,6	6,0	5,3	1,0	4,4	2,4
Technology skills	0%	2,5	1,2	4,8	3,3	4,8	6,0	1,0
User Experience		Smartphone	Tablet	Headset	AR-Mic.	AR-Gest.	Proj.-Mic.	Proj.-Gest.
Overall grade		2,7	2,3	1,8	3,2	6,0	1,7	2,6
Criterion	Weight.	Grade	Grade	Grade	Grade	Grade	Grade	Grade
HQ identity	25%	1,6	1,5	1,0	5,0	6,0	1,2	3,4
HQ stimulation	25%	3,7	3,2	2,7	1,0	6,0	3,4	2,5
Pragmatic quality	25%	3,5	3,5	2,7	4,2	6,0	1,0	2,6
Attractivity	25%	2,0	1,1	1,0	2,4	6,0	1,4	1,9

and evaluated their performance in the study considering the DSM. Until now, workers have not been able to choose between HMI standard and HMI expert mode. Everyone had to use the HMI standard mode with image preview. Our primary objective in the study was to identify the two best vehicle diagnostic devices in cooperation with workers. After evaluation, the two mobile devices were selected via DSM: smartphone and data glasses with microphone as input source.

In Phase 3, the goal of a final study was to evaluate a direct comparison with the new diagnostic device (PDA) already in use on the production line. The new diagnostic device was developed in parallel to our project directly by the diagnostic system manufacturer starting in 2012 and introduced to us in 2016. It was much smaller than the devices used before (see discussion above) and instead of a keyboard it also had a touch screen and only 5 fixed keys for vehicle diagnostics.

However, the instructions were also displayed as pure texts and with abbreviations on 3-4 lines.

Beside the new *reference device*, the HMI clients were upgraded for the final study with the following functionality: choice between HMI standard and HMI expert mode, visual feedback (OK: green, NOK: red), user statistics, instruction notice, battery notification, and memory assistant from the HMI dialog design as described above. The DSM has also been upgraded by these new criteria. In Phase 2 study, we observed that microphone input had very low reliability, which had a negative effect on efficiency. Cross-talk and noise on the production line led to many misinterpretations of speech input and commands were either misinterpreted by the speech system or not recognized at all. Thus, we decided to use a smartwatch as input device with the data glasses instead of a microphone. After the review of available devices on the market in 2014, we selected a smartwatch manufactured by

TABLE 6: The worker's statements about the devices.

Device	Pro	Contra
Smartphone	The best Super, easy-to-handle Much more comfortable than the existing device	The put away has disturbed Strap is missing for fixation
Tablet	Tablet was cool Handling very good Touch is super	Too bulky Handicapped at work
Headset	Favourable, because both hands are free Perfect, great, pleasantly light	Annoying instructions Can't talk to people
AR – Mic.	Very good Easy to understand Hands-free	Too heavy Partially restricted view
AR – Gest.	Good idea Must be improved Hands-free	Safety of interaction must be provided
Proj. – Gest.	Gesture control is ok Satisfied	Not practical Difficulty in handling
Proj. – Mic.	OK Better because of the visualization	Better be confirmed by yourself No personal dialogues

Pebble because it had a very long battery life (more than 3 days) and four physical keys for input. The use of these physical keys solved the problem of a too small touch area offered by other smartwatches.

Field Experiments. In order to collect data to be used for the DSM, a small field experiment was conducted with only two workers, who did not know the HMI mobile devices.

Description of the Sample. To compare and evaluate the three devices as outlined above, two workers (male) from the vehicle manufacturing partner located in the south of Germany participated in this field experiment. Per day, the two workers were tested individually. Both workers already have very good knowledge about vehicle diagnostics. The complete field experiment lasted 3 days and about 100 minutes per person and per device.

Procedure. Each worker used all three devices. For each worker, the field experiment took approx. 300 min. On the first day, workers were welcome in the test center of the vehicle manufacturer and got an introduction to the test procedure (approx. 10 min). We presented the smartphone to the worker, which gave him a first impression of this device. Subsequently, we gave the worker time to get used to the reference device PDA (approx. 15 min) and asked him to rate it according to the criteria in the questionnaire described above. Additionally, we interviewed him to learn about his impressions of the device (10 min). Subsequently, he was introduced to the smartphone (10 min) and conducted three test runs with it (each 15 min), the first in HMI Expert-Mode, the second in HMI Standard mode, and the third in HMI

Standard mode in combination with the memory assistant. After the last run, the worker filled out the questionnaire again (10 min).

On the second day, we conducted a performance test using the smartphone and the reference device PDA. First, the worker tested a vehicle with the PDA (15 min) and rated this device with a performance questionnaire (5 min). After a break of one hour, the worker did the same test with the smartphone, but this time in three runs (30 min). For the performance test, the worker was able to choose the HMI mode (Standard/Expert) and the use of memory assistant as he wished. After the last run, the worker filled out the performance questionnaire (5 min). Finally, the worker was introduced to the data glasses such that he was able to gain a first impression of the device (10 min). Then he ran the same vehicle diagnostic (35 min). This was followed by an interview (10 min).

On the third day, we conducted a performance test for the data glasses (15 min), which again was followed by filling out a questionnaire (10 min).

Results of Field Experiment. All results are shown in Table 7 (overview) and Table 8 (all criteria). For the evaluation of the results, only the first performance measurement of the vehicle test was evaluated for each person, because only in this case the persons tested all test steps correctly (repetition error). Due to health concerns, data glasses could only be used once a day.

The results show that the smartphone is the better diagnostic device. The smartphone met all criteria regarding ergonomics, acceptance, and performance and stands out significantly from the two other devices. The used data glasses

TABLE 7: Device score model: results overview (the lower the better).

DEVICE SCORE MODEL		Smartphone	Data glasses	Current PDA
Overall grade		1,7	3,9	2,8
Criterion	Weight.	Grade	Grade	Grade
Ergonomics	13%	1,7	3,6	2,3
Software-Design	13%	1,3	1,3	4,4
Performance	40%	1,7	5,5	2,2
Technology acceptance	15%	1,7	3,2	2,8
User Experience	20%	1,8	3,1	3,5

had the worst performance in this field study and were not well accepted by the workers. Regarding ergonomics, smartphone performs better and with a special wristband the rating can be increased even further. Data glasses fail due to health grade, weight, and size. Due to the introduced software design, the new HMI design concept offers a lot of potential for improvement in usability. The wiping on the smartphone still needs some adaptation. Using the data glasses, a complete test took about 1 minute longer compared to the other devices. The workers accepted the smartphone immediately; also they were able to use the reference device after the first briefing. Overall, the smartphone was very positively rated due to user experience.

The workers had filled out the questionnaire twice for each device. We wanted to know if there is any change of opinion about the device after the performance test. After the second run, the workers found the smartphone and PDA even more interesting and stimulating in terms of increased HQ stimulation. However, there were no visible changes for the data glasses.

In Table 9, we present examples of workers qualitative responses and reaction to the three devices which reflects the personal experience and confirms the quantitative ratings.

4. Discussion

The purpose of the present study was to design and comparatively evaluate 7+2 devices as "Human Machine Interfaces of the Future," which meet the criteria of *functionality*, *ergonomics*, *user acceptance*, and *user experience* in parallel, which represents an attempt to address the "Functionality versus User Experience Contradiction" visible in various professional production environments. Taking all results together, we can draw the following conclusions.

All workers saw the *smartphone* as generally suitable and as a nice new approach for vehicle diagnostics. The new graphical representation of the instructions was experienced positively and the touch gestures including vibration are at least as good as tactile buttons. The workers perceived the smartphone as intuitive and all were able to work with it without extensive training. The introduced memory assistant increased productivity and led to higher satisfaction compared to the new reference device investigated in the final study.

In the Phase 2 study with 67 workers, the *tablet* performed as good as the smartphone. The workers perceived it as very intuitive to use and as a useful tool in contrast to

currently used devices (MFT and handheld). Only the groups of older and very experienced workers did not see any positive improvement for their work using the tablet.

The use of the *Bluetooth audio headset* was mainly supported by the workers. We noticed that workers' concentration was even higher by using the headset compared to other mobile devices. Due to the higher motivation and concentration of the headset, the number of errors was significantly lower. However, listening to an instruction via headset may reduce the working speed but, simultaneously, the use of natural language was perceived as self-explaining and the learning effort was reduced. The first impression of the headset differs between men and women and is more positive among men. One potential reason for this effect might be that women were more concerned about health issues raised by using these devices than men.

Data glasses (AR) combined with a microphone require a longer learning period for the workers. This device has been perceived as attractive and useful, and workers were more motivated by using this device during the field study. Workers who had experience with it had fewer problems with the visualization of the instructions through the data glasses and saw no health or hygiene issues. We noticed that the younger group of workers reported a more positive experience. The performance and error rate were independent of gender, age, and work experience. However, well experienced workers were rather less convinced by the combination of data glasses with audio input.

For data glasses (AR) combined with hand gesture, we made similar experiences compared to data glasses with audio input. Workers who could handle gestures better also saw more potential in this device for their work. The results showed us that portable equipment must be designed very ergonomically in terms of hardware, software, and hygiene to satisfy workers in a production context. Overall, data glasses and gesture control are very new concepts to use in this environment and require an additional adaptation phase. This device was rated equally positive and/or negative by both genders and regardless of the device experience. Particularly, younger workers were more comfortable with gesture handling than older workers.

The Phase 3 study confirmed the results from the Phase 2 study regarding doubts on health issues if it comes to the use of data glasses (AR). The continuous use of data glasses was experienced as stressful and very dependent on the ambient light situation. Due to change of eye focus between

TABLE 8: Device score model: for all criteria (lower is better).

Software design		Smartphone	Data glasses	Current PDA
Overall grade		1,3	1,3	4,4
Criterion	Weight.	Grade	Grade	Grade
Corporate design	20%	1,0	1,0	2,7
User-adaption	20%	1,0	1,0	4,8
HMI assistant	20%	1,4	1,4	4,5
Dialog design	20%	2,3	2,3	4,8
Multimedia content	20%	1,0	1,0	5,4
Ergonomics		Smartphone	Data glasses	Current PDA
Overall grade		1,7	3,6	2,3
Criterion	Weight.	Grade	Grade	Grade
hands-free	20%	3,5	1,0	3,5
weight	10%	1,3	6,0	3,1
size	15%	1,0	6,0	3,5
interaction distance	5%	3,5	3,5	4,8
interaction safety	25%	1,0	1,0	1,0
Health	25%	1,0	6,0	1,0
Performance		Smartphone	Data glasses	Current PDA
Overall grade		1,7	5,5	2,2
Criterion	Weight.	Grade	Grade	Grade
Type I	33%	1,0	6,0	3,9
Type II	50%	1,9	6,0	1,0
User error rate	0%	-	-	-
Motivation	17%	2,3	3,0	2,5
Technical acceptance		Smartphone	Data glasses	Current PDA
Overall grade		1,7	3,2	2,8
Criterion	Weight.	Grade	Grade	Grade
Useful	14%	1,0	3,3	3,1
User friendly	14%	1,6	2,5	3,1
Self-explaining	14%	2,9	3,3	3,5
Representation	14%	1,6	3,1	2,5
Health care	14%	2,0	4,3	2,7
Input quality	14%	1,6	2,7	2,0
First impression	14%	1,2	3,5	2,5
Technology skills	0%	1,6	1,0	1,2
User Experience		Smartphone	Data glasses	Current PDA
Overall grade		1,8	3,1	3,5
Criterion	Weight.	Grade	Grade	Grade
HQ identity	17%	1,6	2,9	2,9
HQ stimulation	17%	2,6	2,6	4,4
Pragmatic quality	17%	1,3	3,0	3,0
Attractivity	17%	1,3	3,5	3,8
Ergonomics	17%	2,0	3,0	3,6
Worker grade	17%	1,8	3,8	3,3

the projection surface and the test element, eye pain and headache occurred. However, workers who had experienced the data glasses positively tend to see no health or hygiene issues.

The projector device with the projection panel for visual output and microphone as input device required a longer training period similar to the use of data glasses. Workers felt unreliable with this interaction device as communication with colleagues becomes more difficult. The more motivated the workers were, the more efficiently they completed visual inspections. Workers who rated projection and microphone as user-friendly and useful also saw the health benefits. There

TABLE 9: The worker's statements about the devices.

Device	Pro	Contra
Smartphone	Wiping is great The idea with the list assistant is great (++) Wiping is state of the art Statistics are very good Device feels faster than current device	Hand strap missing. Gives an additional feeling of safety at work Statistics do not increase motivation You have to adapt to the wiping first
Data glasses		Very stressful due to poor projection quality Burning eyes Uncomfortable and heavy to wear it The noseband is very pressing Problematic projection with white-coloured vehicles Hardware is not ready-made to use Not suitable for people with glasses
Current PDA		Sideways keys are difficult to operate The device could be a little lighter Slow screen refresh, hangs and is bulky

was no impact rating negative and/or positive by both sexes or age group.

With projection device and with hand gesture as input investigated in the Phase 2 study, we noticed that workers who had experienced the device positively were more skilled in technology and much more motivated to use this device. Workers who rated this device as easy-to-use also saw the health benefits of this immaterial interaction. Similar to projection with microphone, age and gender had no negative or positive influence. However, the novel immaterial interaction concept initially causes confusion among participants. In general, the performance was negatively affected by hand gesture interaction.

In summary, the project has shown that, for future use, smartphones and data glasses seem to be the better diagnostic devices for the presented production step in the automotive industry. The devices using projection with interaction by hand gestures performed most poorly. We assume that the result is strongly influenced by the use and habit of the old technology. Above all, the workers were highly enthusiastic concerning the combination of hand gestures and projection from a distance. This has something to do with the closeness and distance of interaction with the diagnostic system, operating accuracy, and the feedback when an instruction is confirmed. We noticed that some workers tried to confirm the instructions to the direction of the projection panel by hand gesture and not in needed field area of the installed hand gesture device inside and outside of the vehicle. This caused the problem that instructions were not confirmed at all and we had to remind the workers to perform the hand gestures inside the sensor area. The new technique must first be understood and learned. In our experiment, the workers only got 15 minutes to become familiar with the new interaction technology before the start of experiment. The results are all based on a very short usage time to confirm that the established diagnostic devices in this project are absolutely applicable for the production line. For a recommendation,

we would first have to make a long-term study in which the workers at least complete one complete using the new equipment, best several days in a row.

5. Conclusions

This paper summarizes a project of 3.5 years during which we performed various field studies to develop and evaluate the application of an innovative Human Machine Interface (HMI) in automotive manufacturing together with a German car manufacturer. In this work, we focused on a representative production step in which the electronic system of a produced vehicle gets inspected by the worker. The project was conducted in three phases. In the first phase, we investigated the working process empirically and developed a comprehensive and innovative user interface design, which addresses various types of interactive devices. Building up on this, we developed the device score model (DSM), which is designed to investigate interactive system and user interfaces in production context due to ergonomics, UI design, performance, technology acceptance, and user experience. This work was conducted in the second phase of the project. We used this model to investigate the subjective suitability of six innovative device setups that implement the user interface design developed in Phase 1. The experimental setup was executed with 67 participants at two locations in south Germany. The major result showed that the new user interface design run on a smart phone is the most suitable setup for future interactive systems in car manufacturing for the selected production step. In the third and final phase, we investigated the suitability of the two best rated devices resulting from the Phase 2 study over a longer term. These two systems were compared with the standard system used at this time. The outcome showed that light and ergonomic smartphones have a very high potential to be used in the future of production. Nevertheless, if considering addressing health and hygienic issues of data glasses, also AR technology showed high potential to be used in future production environments. The study has clearly shown that functionality already provided by current devices is sufficient for quality testing, but does not take the user into account at all. Instead, the Human Machine Interfaces for quality assurance in car production environments presented here have noticeably increased the satisfaction among workers.

References

[1] M. Friedewald, O. Da Costa, Y. Punie, P. Alahuhta, and S. Heinonen, "Perspectives of ambient intelligence in the home environment," *Telematics and Informatics*, vol. 22, no. 3, pp. 221–238, 2005.

[2] l. Kong, Z. Gu, and T. Li, "Biomechanical optimization of implant diameter and length for imeddiate loading: a nonlinear finite element analysis," *The International Journal of Prosthodontics*, vol. 22, no. 6, pp. 607–615, 2009.

[3] H. Lasi, P. Fettke, H.-G. Kemper, T. Feld, and M. Hoffmann, "Industry 4.0," *Business & Information Systems Engineering*, vol. 6, no. 4, pp. 239–242, 2014.

[4] H. Schleich, J. Schaffer, and L. F. Scavarda, "Managing complexity in automotive production," in *Proceedings of the International Conference on Production Research*, vol. 100, Valparaiso Chile, 2007.

[5] J. Backman and H. Helaakoski, "Mobile technology to support maintenance efficiency Mobile maintenance in heavy industry," in *Proceedings of the 2011 9th IEEE International Conference on Industrial Informatics*, pp. 328–333, 2011.

[6] A. Kluge and V. Hagemann, "Neue und Soziale Medien in der Fertigung und der Personalentwicklung – am Beispiel von Industrie 4.0 und E-Coaching aus Sicht der AOW Psychologie," *Zeitschrift Wirtschaftspsychologie*, pp. 5–21, 2016, https://www.wiso-net.de/document/BLIS_7922D1C7D809CEAE5E73179D2927D839.

[7] A. Kluge and A. Termer, "Human-centered design (HCD) of a fault-finding application for mobile devices and its impact on the reduction of time in fault diagnosis in the manufacturing industry," *Applied Ergonomics*, vol. 59, pp. 170–181, 2017.

[8] B. Vogel-Heuser, "Herausforderungen aus Sicht der IT und der Automatisierungstechnik," in *Industrie 4.0 in der Produktion, Automatisierung und Logistik. Anwendung. Technologie. Migration*, T. Bauernhansl, M. ten Hompel, and B. Vogel-Heuser, Eds., pp. 37–48, Springer, Wiesbaden, Germany, 2014.

[9] E. Hollnagel, *Cognitive Reliability and Error Analysis Method (CREAM)*, Elsevier, Oxford, UK, 1998.

[10] N. Borisov, A. Kluge, W. Luther, and B. Weyers, *Integrating Production Workers into User Interface Design for Diagnosis Devices in Automotive Production Environments: Field Experiences and Lessons Learned*, C. Stephanidis, Ed., Springer, Berlin, Heidelberg, Germany, 2013.

[11] N. Borisov, B. Weyers, A. Kluge, and W. Luther, *Kontextabhängige Modellierung der Mensch-Maschine-Interaktion in Mehrbenutzersystemen - eine explorative Untersuchung*, Kognitive Systeme 1, 2013.

[12] N. Borisov, A. Kluge, W. Luther, and B. Weyers, "User interface design for test and diagnosis software in automotive production environments," in *Ubiquitous Computing and Ambient Intelligence. Personalisation and User Adapted Services, LNCS XX*, pp. 372–375, 2014.

[13] N. Kano, "Attractive quality and must-be quality," *The Journal of the Japanese Society for Quality Control*, pp. 39–48, 1984.

[14] B. Weyers, D. Burkolter, A. Kluge, and W. Luther, "User-centered Interface Reconfiguration for Error Reduction in Human-Computer Interaction," in *Proceedings of The Third International Conference on Advances in Human-Oriented and Personalized Mechanisms, Technologies, and Services (CENTRIC)*, R. Hariprakash, E. Egyed-Zsigmond, and M. Hoffmann, Eds., pp. 50–55, IEEE Verlag, 2010.

[15] M. Liu, Y. Huang, and D. Zhang, "Gamification's impact on manufacturing: Enhancing job motivation, satisfaction and operational performance with smartphone-based gamified job design," *Human Factors and Ergonomics in Manufacturing & Service Industries*, vol. 28, no. 1, pp. 38–51, 2018.

[16] M. Hassenzahl, M. Burmester, and F. Koller, "AttrakDiff: Ein Fragebogen zur Messung wahrgenommener hedonischer und pragmatischer Qualität," in *Mensch & Computer*, pp. 187–196, Vieweg+ Teubner Verlag, 2003.

[17] V. Venkatesh and H. Bala, "Technology acceptance model 3 and a research agenda on interventions," *Decision Sciences*, vol. 39, no. 2, pp. 273–315, 2008.

Permissions

List of Contributors

Mohd Kamal Othman, Muhd Nur Shaful Sulaiman and Shaziti Aman
Faculty of Cognitive Sciences and Human Development, Universiti Malaysia Sarawak, Kota Samarahan, Sarawak, 94300, Malaysia

Regina Jucks, Gesa A. Linnemann and Benjamin Brummernhenrich
University of Muenster, Institute of Psychology for Education, Germany

Pierre Taner Kirisci and Klaus-Dieter Thoben
University of Bremen, Faculty of Production Engineering, Bagdasteiner Str. 1, 28359 Bremen, Germany
Bremer Institut für Produktion und Logistik GmbH (BIBA), University of Bremen, Hochschulring 20, 28359 Bremen, Germany

Annamaria Goy, Diego Magro, Giovanna Petrone, Claudia Picardi, Marco Rovera and Marino Segnan
Dipartimento di Informatica, Universit`a di Torino, C. Svizzera 185, 10149 Torino, Italy

Maria Uther
Department of Psychology, University of Winchester, Sparkford Rd, Winchester SO22 4NR, UK
Department of Psychology, University of Wolverhampton, Faculty of Education, Health and Wellbeing, MC Building (Room MC305), University ofWolverhampton, Wolverhampton WV1 1LY, UK

Anna-Riikka Smolander and Katja Junttila
Cognitive Brain Research Unit, Department of Psychology and Logopedics, Faculty of Medicine, University of Helsinki, 00014 Helsinki, Finland

Sari Ylinen
Cognitive Brain Research Unit, Department of Psychology and Logopedics, Faculty of Medicine, University of Helsinki, 00014 Helsinki, Finland
Cicero Learning, Faculty of Educational Sciences, 00014 Helsinki, Finland

Mikko Kurimo, Reima Karhila and Seppo Enarvi
Department of Signal Processing and Acoustics, School of Electrical Engineering, Aalto University, 00076 AALTO Espoo, Finland

Mohd Kamal Othman, Khairul Izham Idris, Shaziti Aman and Prashanth Talwar
Faculty of Cognitive Sciences and Human Development, Universiti Malaysia Sarawak, Kota Samarahan, 94300 Sarawak, Malaysia

Antonio P. Volpentesta, Alberto M. Felicetti and Nicola Frega
Department of Mechanical Energy and Management Engineering, University of Calabria, Arcavacata di Rende (CS), 87036, Italy

Way Kiat Bong, Weiqin Chen and Astrid Bergland
Department of Computer Science, Faculty of Technology, Art and Design, OsloMet-Oslo Metropolitan University, Pilestredet 35, 0166 Oslo, Norway

Lamia Alam and Mohammed Moshiul Hoque
Department of Computer Science & Engineering, Chittagong University of Engineering & Technology, Chittagong 4349, Bangladesh

Bineet Kaur and Garima Joshi
Department of Electronics and Communication Engineering, University Institute of Engineering and Technology, Panjab University, Sector 25, Chandigarh 160036, India

Johanna M. Silvennoinen and Jussi P. P. Jokinen
Department of Computer Science and Information Systems, University of Jyvaskyla, Mattilanniemi 2, 40100 Jyväskylä, Finland

Tuomo Kujala and Pertti Saariluoma
University of Jyväskylä, 40014 Jyväskylä, Finland

Taisuke Akimoto
Graduate School of Computer Science and Systems Engineering, Kyushu Institute of Technology, 680-4 Kawazu, Iizuka, Fukuoka 820-8502, Japan

Lars-Ola Bligård, Helena Strömberg and MariAnne Karlsson
Chalmers University of Technology, 412 96 Gothenburg, Sweden

Chokri Rekik
Control and Energy Management Laboratory (CEM-Lab), National School of Engineers of Sfax, Sfax, Tunisia

Ismail Ben Abdallah and Yassine Bouteraa
Control and Energy Management Laboratory (CEM-Lab), National School of Engineers of Sfax, Sfax, Tunisia
Digital Research Center of Sfax, Technopark of Sfax, BP 275, Sakiet Ezzit, 3021 Sfax, Tunisia

Kwok Ng
Department of Physical Education and Sport Sciences, University of Limerick, Limerick, Ireland

Tatiana Ryba
Department of Psychology, University of Jyvaskyla, Jyväskylä, Finland

Hwayeon Kong and Frank Biocca
Department of Interaction Science, Sungkyunkwan University, Seoul, Republic of Korea

Taeyang Lee, Kihyuk Park and Jeonghoon Rhee
Human ICT Convergence, Sungkyunkwan University, Seoul, Republic of Korea

Nikolaj Borisov
University of Duisburg-Essen, 47057 Duisburg, Germany

Benjamin Weyers
Computer Science Department, RWTH Aachen University, 52074 Aachen, Germany

Annette Kluge
Department of Psychology, Ruhr-University Bochum, 44801 Bochum, Germany

Index

9 781682 857601